Praise for [PassPorter]

S0-BZA-854

"A nifty travel guide that works overtime as a planner, organizer, and journal..."

— Jacky Runice
Daily Herald–Chicago

"[PassPorter] is a brilliant travel aid... the most practical, sanity-saving guide you could take along to Disney World."

— Stephanie Gold,
Amazon.com

"[PassPorter] has become the Bible for those of us who want to experience Walt Disney World to the max."

— Kim Cool,
Venice Gondolier Sun

"Vacationers who want to enjoy all that Disney World has to offer should make sure they take along this PassPorter guide."

— ForeWord Reviews

I love this book. It's my Disney Bible!!! Thank you to ALL for this incredible book! For first timers like ourselves this book is AMAZING!

— Ann Petersoli
in Massachusetts

PassPorter is wonderful. I call it the best and most complete Disney World guide. You are AWESOME! Thank you so much.

— Joey Morehead
in Tennessee

You guys are the best. You make an unorganized person feel like they have it all under control. This will be my first vacation that isn't utter chaos. Thank you.

— Sarah Rhue
in Pennsylvania

We love the full color, glossy pages and the number of pockets for holding receipts and other details. This is our only vacation guide that we buy -- others pale badly in comparison.

— Byron Etzel in N. Carolina

What's Unique in PassPorter

- **Coverage of the most recent changes** throughout Walt Disney World—thanks to our later production schedule, this is the most up-to-date 2013 guidebook available! We have the recent pass price changes, resort price increases, and the Disney Dining Plan additions and changes.

- **Special glossy photo supplement** at the back of the book

- **Comprehensive yet concise information** is packed into our pages—PassPorter is information-rich and padding-free!

- **Full color** brings life and clarity to our maps and photos.

- **Blending of personal experience** and photographs from your authors and the collective wisdom of tens of thousands of readers means a guidebook that's full of heart and soul.

- **Well-organized chapters and pages** make it easy to find what you need. We edit our information carefully so that sections always begin at the top of a page.

- **Worksheets** to jot notes and make travel arrangements.

- **Our famous organizer PassPockets** to plan your trip, store your maps and papers, and record your vacation memories.

- **Floorplans of Disney resort hotel rooms** to give you a better sense of the layout.

- **Fold-out maps** of the four major Disney theme parks, printed in full color on heavy paper to stand up to rugged use.

- **Custom-designed attraction charts** provide all the information you need at a glance.

- **ToddlerTips, KidTips, TweenTips, and TeenTips** offer advice for kids by kids.

- **Color, self-stick tabs** to mark your chapters.

- **Original color photos** to see the *real* Walt Disney World!

- **Personalization labels and stickers** to customize your book.

- **Magical memories** from fellow travelers convey the spirit and wonder of Walt Disney World.

- **Disney changes highlighted** with a light green background to mark significant changes since our last edition.

- **Expert peer reviewers** to ensure accuracy and thoroughness.

...and much more! Visit us at http://www.passporter.com *for a complete list of what's new and unique in PassPorter's Walt Disney World 2013!*

PassPorter's®
Walt Disney World® 2013
15th Edition

The unique travel guide, planner, organizer, journal, and keepsake

Jennifer Marx,
Dave Marx,
Allison Cerel Marx,
and Alexander Marx

PassPorter Travel Press

An imprint of MediaMarx, Inc.
P.O. Box 3880, Ann Arbor, Michigan 48106
877-WAYFARER

PassPorter's® Walt Disney World®–2013 Edition

by Jennifer Marx, Dave Marx, Allison Cerel Marx, and Alexander Marx

© 2012 by PassPorter Travel Press, an imprint of MediaMarx, Inc.

P.O. Box 3880, Ann Arbor, Michigan 48106
877-WAYFARER or 877-929-3273 (toll-free)
Visit us online at http://www.passporter.com

About the Authors

Name: Jennifer Marx
Date of birth: 10/09/68
Residence: Ann Arbor, MI
Signature: *Jennifer Marx*

Jennifer Marx fell in love with Walt Disney World on her first visit as a teenager in 1983. She has since returned more times than she can count on her fingers and toes many times over, visiting every park, attraction, resort, and restaurant at least once. As author of more than a dozen popular books, she yearned to write one about Walt Disney World but felt no interest in churning out yet another travel guide when there were so many excellent books already available. When she hit upon the idea of the PassPorter, she knew she could offer her fellow vacationers something unique and valuable. With the help of the PassPorter, Jennifer has organized gatherings at Walt Disney World for individuals, groups, and families of all ages and stages. Jennifer lives in Ann Arbor, Michigan and is a loving mother to her young son Alexander.

Dave Marx may be considered a Renaissance Man, a jack-of-all-trades, or a dilettante, depending on how you look at things. He took a 20-year hiatus between his early journalism training and the commencement of his full-time writing career. Beyond co-authoring numerous books with Jennifer, he's been a radio writer/producer; recording engineer; motion picture music editor; broadcast engineering supervisor; tax preparer; cab driver; whitewater safety and rescue instructor; developer and instructor of online publishing courses; and board member for the Independent Book Publishers Association. He has also co-authored and contributed to numerous books about America Online and the Internet. He discovered the "World" (Walt Disney World, that is) in 1997 and spent more than six months there over the following five years. Dave is from New Jersey and now makes his home in Ann Arbor, Michigan.

Name: Dave Marx
Date of birth: 04/07/55
Residence: Ann Arbor, MI
Signature: *Dave Marx*

Allison Cerel Marx ("Allie") is a veteran visitor to Walt Disney World (and Dave's 20-year-old daughter). She has a maniacal grin, especially when spinning one of Mad Hatter's teacups at top speed. She's camped at Fort Wilderness, celebrated New Year's Eve in the Magic Kingdom, and photographed animals at Animal Kingdom Lodge Resort. She shares her "A-OK!" ratings and her popular tips for kids, "tweens" (pre-teens), and teens on the attractions in the Touring the 'World' chapter. Allie also offers her thoughts on the childcare clubs on property. Allie is pictured here with her little brother, Alexander, who "contributes" his own ToddlerTips and KidTips in this edition.

PassPorter Team

Our 18 Expert Peer Reviewers painstakingly checked our text, photos, and maps, and helped us ensure PassPorter's accuracy, readability, and thoroughness. Thank you for helping to make PassPorter the best it can be!

Sandy Bostwick is an Occupational Therapist and professor. She helps kids and young adults overcome challenges in classrooms and online. She loves writing helpful books and articles. Sandy travels from North Jersey to Walt Disney World yearly to share in the evolution of Walt's dream. She is a PassPorter guide for the Special Needs Forum and Disney Online Trivia Chat.

Dianne Cook and her husband Tom had a Walt Disney World honeymoon and now "do Disney" twice a year with their sons Andrew and Matthew. A Disney Vacation Club member since 1996, Dianne is also a PassPorter Guide for the "Getting There (and Back)," "Touring the 'World,'" "Owning the Magic ", "Trip Reports," and "The Office" forums on the PassPorter message boards.

Bernie Edwards is currently on the Walt Disney World Moms Panel, having also served on the panel in 2010, 2011, and 2012. He, his wife Laura, and their two sons, Christopher and Thomas, all love visiting Walt Disney World as often as possible. Bernie travels worldwide for work, but the Wilderness Lodge is his favorite hotel in the whole world and his favorite place to be is in the Magic Kingdom.

Marisa Garber-Brown is a Destination Specialist with MouseEarVacations.com. Her parents started taking her to Disney in 1979 and she has visited multiple times every year since. She enjoys spending time with her husband Tim. She is also a PassPorter message board Guide for the "Planning Your Disney Cruise Voyage" and "Sharing Your Adventure: Disney Cruise Reports Forums" forums.

LauraBelle Hime enjoys helping others through her experiences as a frequent Disney traveler. She has traveled to Disney destinations with all of her family, her PassPorter family, but expecially enjoys trips with her grandchildren Alexis, Olivia, Caleb, Jacob, Samantha, and Lucianno. LauraBelle is a PassPorter Guide for "The Porch," "The Family Room," "Disneyland Feasting & Snacking," and "Disneyland Staying in Style."

Kelly Hughes loves Walt Disney World, especially the Carousel of Progress and all things Cheshire Cat! But she also adores her family of four-legged kids and her awesome husband, Brian. Ever since their 2005 Disney honeymoon, they've been back every year and even joined the Disney Vacation Club in 2008. With 50 more years of going "home," it's no wonder she's a Guide in the "Planning Your Adventure" forum!

Ann Johnson is a PassPorter message board Guide in "The Sunroom" and "Going Behind the Scenes" forums, as well as a huge Walt Disney World fan! Ann and her husband, Allen, are Disney Vacation Club members and have enjoyed the magic of Walt Disney World more than 20 times with their three sons, their daughter-in-law, and many friends! Ann is also a peer reviewer for PassPorter's Disney Cruise Line and Its Ports of Call.

Deb Kendall is a PassPorter message board Guide and a Disney Vacation Club member. She has been married to husband Mike for 36 years and they are both are long time Disney lovers. Deb grew up in Southern California and her parents introduced her to Disneyland as a child. Deb and Mike love taking yearly trips to Florida to visit Walt Disney World.

Sue Kulick is a PassPorter Guide and a Disney Vacation Club Member. She has traveled to Walt Disney World more than 15 times with friends and family, and has been on four Disney cruises, including a DVC Member Cruise. Sue enjoys helping fellow vacationers with planning their Disney memories as a Guide in the "Owning The Magic," "The Family Room," "The Space Coast and Other Florida" forums.

Cam Matthews has been a Disney Vacation Club member since 2004 and has made 15 trips home. Knowing how much their daughter Stefanie loved trips to Disney World, Cam and husband Luke planned carefully to make every trip magical for her because, if anyone understood magic, it was Stefanie. Cam is a Guide for "Sharing the Adventure," "The Darkroom," and "The Library" forums on the PassPorter message boards.

PassPorter Team

Bruce Metcalf has loved and studied Disney parks since 1958. He works at a major Central Florida resort where he frightens the natives with his impressive knowledge of Disney trivia and history. Bruce has been an expert peer reviewer for nearly every PassPorter guidebook since 2000, and our guidebooks are all the better for his eagle eye and attention to detail.

Allison Palmer-Gleicher lives so close that she has visited Walt Disney World over 60 times since 1973. In the past, Allison worked for the Disney Store and has been a Guide on the PassPorter Boards since 2000. Twelve years ago Allison and her family became members in the Disney Vacation Club and she is an annual passholder. In her free time she plans vacations for herself, her family, and her Disney group called LOWD.

Cheryl Pendry and her husband Mark usually visit Walt Disney World every year, despite the fact they live in England. They became Disney Vacation Club members in 2002 and Cheryl is the author of *PassPorter's Disney Vacation Club Guide*. She is also the author of *PassPorter's Walt Disney World for British Holidaymakers* and is a PassPorter Message Board Guide.

Terri Sellers is a Disney Vacation Club member, PassPorter message board Guide, and avid Disney vacation fan. She often helps family and friends plan their Disney adventures. She has made more than 50 trips to Disney World since 2001 and introduced her husband Chris to magic of Disney vacations while planning their 2010 wedding! Terri is also a peer reviewer for *PassPorter's Disney Cruise Line and Its Ports of Call*.

Ann Smith, a PassPorter Message Board Guide, has been to Disney World over 20 times. She's experienced many magical memories with her family—her husband, Jim, and children, Jamie, Brendan, and Shelby. One of her fondest Disney World memories was watching both of her sons perform on Main Street with their High School marching band several times over the past six years.

Marnie Urmaza, her husband Matt, and kids Alexa and Colin, have made seven trips to Walt Disney World, taken two Disney cruises, and have visited Disneyland in California. They are looking forward to heading back to Walt Disney World to enjoy the Fantasyland renovations in the near future. Marnie also enjoys being a PassPorter message board Guide in the "Family Room", "Disney World Trip Reports", and "Globetrotting Trip Reports."

Sara Varney is the Co-Host of the PassPorter Moms Podcast and the Editor of PassPorter News. Sara is also a Travel Planner affiliated with Mouse Fan Travel. Sara has traveled to Walt Disney World more than 20 times, been to Disneyland three times, and cruised on the Disney Cruise Line six times. She lives in New England with her husband Shawn and their 8-year-old son Ryan.

Don Willis is a retired government appraiser living in Northern California. He has enjoyed three Disney Cruises and tries to visit Walt Disney World and Disneyland annually. He is a Message Board Community Guide for several forums on the PassPorter message boards and is also a peer reviewer for *PassPorter's Disney Cruise Line and Its Ports of Call*.

A special thank you to the Guides (moderators) of our own message boards: Tiffany Bendes, Tanya Blissman, Sandra Bostwick, Dyan Chaplin, Michelle Clark, Dianne Cook, Pam Dorr, Lesley Duncan, Dawn Erickson, Marisa Garber-Brown, Rob Gatto, Kristin Grey, Debbie Hendrickson, LauraBelle Hime, Linda Holland, Christina Holland-Radvon, Kelly Hughes, Claudine Jamba, Ann Johnson, Deb Kendall, Robin Krening-Capra, Susan Kulick, Marcie LaCava, Denise Lang, Jodi Leeper, Eileen Lloyd, Keri Madeira, Heather Macdonald, Janine Marshall, Cam Matthews, Yvonne Mitchell, Sarah Mudd, Bill Myers, Rebecca Oberg, Allison Palmer-Gleicher, Cheryl Pendry, Sheana Perry, Susan Rannestad, Sabine Rautenberg, Carol Ray, Terri Sellers, Ann Smith, Donna Sonmor, Marie St. Martin, Mindy Stanton, Marnie Urmaza, Sara Varney, Susan Wagner, Suzi Waters, Don Willis, Debbie Wright, and the 60,000+ readers in our amazing community at http://www.passporterboards.com/forums.

Special recognition goes to **Cheryl Pendry**, who not only peer reviewed this edition, but also contributed many of the photos that appear here!

Our gratitude to these very important folks "behind the scenes" at PassPorter:
  Printer: Oceanic Graphic Printing (Thanks, Dean and Becky!)
  Online Coordinator and Newsletter Editor: Sara Varney
  Assorted Pixies: Dave Hunter, Kim and Chad Larner, Greg Reese, and Bob Sehlinger

Acknowledgments

A "world" of thanks to our readers, who've contributed loads of tips, stories, and photos since PassPorter's debut. A special thanks to those who generously allowed us to include their **contributions and photographs** in this edition:

Kimberley Abt, Maggie Akers, Sharon Allen, Jennifer Arnold, Matt Asplen, Heather Baker, Diana Barthelemy-Rodriguez, Jennifer Berry, Jennifer Blain, Charity Boughner, Beth Borja, Wendy Braddick, Carolyn Brooke, Lissette Brito, Alicia Bruce, Chloe C., Megan Caceres, Michelle Clark, Nicole Clayton, Vicki Collins, Chris Cook-Leitz, Dawn Chugg, Tricia Davids, Laura Dawson, Michael Dawson, Jyl Deshler, Heather DiFulvio, Lois Ann Dolley, Brigett Duncan, Lesley Duncan, Sean Dunham, Sharon Ellis, Dawn Erickson, Debbie Ernest, Byron Etzel, Eileen Farnsworth, Elizabeth Ferris, Stephanie Fieldstad, Danielle Fortin, Brenda G., Cyndi Gai, Jennifer Gallion, Monica Gauvin, Victoria Goeler, Holli Goetz, Marianne Goode, Jennifer Griggs, Susan H., Misty Hailey, Denise Hand, Gayle Hartleroad, Melissa Hasbrouck, David Hilton, Catie Hiltz, Alison Hinsley, Lura Honeycutt, Elizabeth Hudock, Amanda Hulse, Patricia Hunt, Andrea Johnson, Kay Jojola, Lindsay Jones, Brad K., Patti Kalal, Joyce Kelly, Brent Key, Elizabeth Key, Janet Kovacs, Angie Lambert, Denise Lang, David Latoundji, Jodi Leeper, Michelle Lisanti, Melissa Loflin, Mayra Lopez, Priscilla Lopez, Marc Lorenzo, Heather Mahon, Karen Majeau, Christine Mak, Joseph Marchewka, Sheila Masters, Cam Matthews, Bonnie McCarty, Leanna Metteer, Lisa Miller, Rae Mills, Lynn Mirante, Joey Morehead, Darren Mosher, Bill Myers, Nicole Myers, Amanda Nash, Kelly Michelle Narvaez, Erin Newman, Alisa Niethammer, Amy Novak, Lisa O'Meara, Debra Ortiz, Carrie Owens, Melissa Lynn Page, Tom Panzella, Cheryl Pendry, Gina Pesca, Ann Petersoli, Penny J. Pettigrew, Jean Philo, Pamela Pollaro, Andrea Popovits, Melissa Potter, Michelle Price, Denise Preskitt, Kori Radloff, Sarah Rhue, Paula Rogers, Amy Rupp, Ben Rupp, Hope Rupp, Marianne Swan, Scott Theus, Kurt Ulrich, Jamie S., Amy Sellars, Suzanne Sevier, Janet Simonsen, Lisa Siverns-LeClair, Melissa Sorrells Galley, Rebecca Smith, Nancy Stansbury, Keith Stanton, Mindy Stanton, Hiromi Stone, Wendy Suchomel, Francis T. Tewey, Regina Thomas, Tina Thornton, Kurt Ulrich, Marnie Urmaza, Pam VanAustin, Joy Vodnik, Rick Wagner, Shannon Wellnitz, Katey Westcott, Donald Willis, Lisa Wilson, Teresa Wilson, Gina Winnette, Tammy Wright, Mark Zielberg, Nicole Zoncki, Ann, Disney Event Group, imadisneygirl, JustLorri, Nalagh, and SuperNemo. May each of you receive a new magical memory for every reader your words touch.

PassPorter would not be where it is today without the support of the **Internet Disney fan community**. Our thanks to the friendly folks below and to all whom we didn't have room to include!

- AllEars.net (http://www.allears.net). Thanks, Deb W., Deb K., and Mike S.!
- DIS—Unofficial Disney Information Station (http://www.wdwinfo.com). Thanks, Pete!
- Disney Food Blog (http://www.disneyfoodblog.com). Thanks, AJ!
- MouseEarVacations.com (http://www.mouseearvacations.com). Thanks, Jami!
- Mouse Fan Travel (http://www.mousefantravel.com). Thanks, Beci, Annette, and Sara!
- MousePlanet.com (http://www.mouseplanet.com). Thanks Mike D., Mark, Adrienne, & Tony!
- MouseSavers.com (http://www.mousesavers.com). Thanks, Mary!
- Planning Strategy Calculator (http://pscalculator.net). Thanks, Scott!
- Sorcerer Radio (http://www.srsounds.com). Thanks, Wayne and Kirsten!

A heartfelt thank you to our **family and friends** for their patience while we were away on trips or cloistered at our computers, and for their support of our dream: Alexander Marx; Carolyn Tody; Fred and Adele Marx; Kim, Chad, Megan, and Natalie Larner; Dan, Jeannie, Kayleigh, Melanie, and Nina Marx; Jeanne and David Beroza; Greg Reese; Tracy DeGarmo; Ben Foxworth; and Bruce and Marta Metcalf. A special thank you to Jennifer's father, Tom Anderson, who passed away in 2012 and always supported our work with PassPorter!

Last but not least, we thank Walter Elias Disney for his dream.

About Our Cover Photo

The smiling faces on our front cover belong to Cam Matthews and her daughter Stefanie, who were photographed as they rode on one of the floats in Mickey's Jammin' Jungle Parade at Disney's Animal Kingdom last summer. This edition is dedicated to the memory of Stefanie, who passed away in 2012. Please read the wonderful magical memory from her mother, Cam, at the end of chapter 6 on page 292. We love you, Stefanie!

Contents

Contents
(continued)

Contents
(continued)

Bonus Features...

Disney Dreaming photo section
....pages 319–350

Florida Map ....front cover flap

2013/2014 Planning Calendars
.........................under front cover flap

Bookplate for personalization
.........................under front cover flap

Labels and tabs to customize your
PassPorter .... in front of pockets

Disney Map .... back cover flap

Important Phone Numbers, Reminders,
and Addresses
.... under back cover flap

An elastic band to keep your book
securely closed (spiral ed. only)
.... under back cover flap

The PassPorter Way

PassPorter guidebooks are **independently published** by a family-owned and family-run small business. As journalists, we strive to present accurate information with a fair and balanced viewpoint. Our books are "unofficial," meaning we can call it as we see it.

We travel as our readers do. Although we enlist the help of local experts who live and breathe our destinations, we fly or drive long distances from our home base in Michigan, and stay in the hotels, giving us a perspective that no "local" can possess. We make all our own reservations and arrangements, sometimes with the help of a travel agent, but mostly we "shop direct." We pay our own way, so we're always looking for the best deal. We buy our own admission, pay for all our excursions, tours, and add-ons. We make our reservations through normal channels—no VIP treatment, no media discounts or freebies. We need to know that our experience will be like yours and hasn't been enhanced for the sake of a better review. While we may be invited to visit a hotel, restaurant, or attraction as members of the media, we do not use those visits to evaluate matters like quality of service or level of amenities offered, as regular guests may not receive quite the same treatment.

PassPorter guidebooks are truly a community effort. Through our PassPorter.com web site, message board community, PassPorter News weekly e-newsletter, and many face-to-face encounters, we interact with you, our readers, year-round. Whether or not we join a particular discussion, we're always watching the message boards to see what's important to you, and we're thinking of how we can better address those issues in our books. You contribute in so many ways! These pages are filled with your tips and photos, and your suggestions and questions over the years have led to improvements large and small. Your reports on our message board make you our field researchers, witnessing and experiencing far more than we could ever manage on our own. Dozens of you, as Peer Reviewers, pore over each manuscript, and each manages to uncover items to be updated, clarified, or fixed that nobody else has managed to find. Few publishers, in any field, subject their manuscripts to this level of scrutiny. Unlike many travel books, which, once printed, are set aside until it's time to produce the next edition, we're immersed in our topic 365 days a year, following the news and rumors, and keeping in constant touch with you.

All of this makes PassPorter a uniquely interactive guidebook. Together, we've created what we like to think of as "book 2.0" and we're proud to be innovators of a new generation of guidebooks that encourage collaboration. Here are some of the special interactive features in this edition:

PassPorter Photos: We truly believe that a picture tells a thousand words, so this edition is enhanced with more than 500 full-color photos! The majority of these photos were contributed by our amazing readers, as we feel a wider range of perspective makes a better guidebook. The photos that appear at the top of pages are "Photo Slices," because they give you just a slice of Disney—they are intended to convey a general look, a feeling, or an idea. All of the photos were hand-picked from our vast personal collection and the online PassPorter Photo Archive. Want a closer look? If the ⓘ symbol and 4- to 5-digit code appears with the photo, go to http://www.passporter.com/i and look it up!

PassPorter Articles: You just can't fit everything in a guidebook, so when we have more to tell you, we lead you to one of our feature articles and/or photo collections on our web site. Just look in the lower right margin for the ⓘ icon accompanied by a keyword, visit http://www.passporter.com/i and enter the keyword (type it exactly as it appears). Note that multiple article keywords are separated by the | symbol. Here's an example ☛

More at ⓘ passporter-way | making-of-passporter

Congratulations!

First, congratulations are in order—you're going to Walt Disney World! You are about to embark on an experience that will amaze and, hopefully, delight you. This isn't an ordinary, run-of-the-mill trip—after all, you're going to spend your vacation in the heart of Mickey Mouse land!

The Walt Disney World Resort is a world unto itself, full of heralded amusements and hidden gems. Yet the very fact that it is so vast can make a visit to Walt Disney World seem more like a race in a maze than a relaxed vacation. And worse yet, pleasant memories of a great vacation may disappear beneath the stress and worries that accompanied it.

Happily, after fifty-plus trips to Walt Disney World, we've learned to dispel our stress with one simple and enjoyable task: **planning ahead**. In fact, it is no task at all—planning is as much fun as the vacation itself. Planning gave birth to the PassPorter concept. Originally, Jennifer made itineraries on her computer and placed them in a binder. During the trip she kept the binder handy, using it to store passes, brochures, and receipts. After the vacation, these organizers had turned into scrapbooks, full of pixie-dusted memories and goofy smiles. When Jennifer's writing career took off, she didn't have the time to create binders for every trip. She wished for a simpler version that she could use each trip without a lot of fuss. It was on a Disney bus that the idea came to her. She could make an easy-to-use, book-based version and offer it as a resource to fellow vacationers!

Now, after much work, you hold PassPorter in your hands. The first edition of PassPorter debuted in 1999, creating a sensation in the Disney fan community, winning 13 national awards, and helping hundreds of thousands plan great vacations. This edition is our fifteenth, which features large color photos on beautiful glossy paper for your viewing pleasure!

It is our greatest hope that PassPorter helps you "discover the magic" through your own eyes, as it did for us. To get you in the spirit, read "Disney Dreaming" on the next page and prepare for your adventure!

Smiles and laughter,

Jennifer, Dave, Allison, and *Alexander*

We'd love to hear from you! Visit us on the Internet (http://www.passporter.com) or drop us a postcard from Walt Disney World!

P.S. We finished this edition's updates in November 2012. For the latest changes, updates, and news, be sure to consult our page of free book updates at http://www.passporter.com/customs/bookupdates.htm.

Top Photo Slice: Wishes fireworks at the Magic Kingdom (①11580) © Jamie S.

Disney Dreaming

A good part of the fun of going to the Walt Disney World Resort is the anticipation before your trip! To really get you into "Disney Dreaming," we present some of our favorite tips to feed your excitement and prepare you for the adventure that lies ahead. This is magical stuff—don't blame us if you get the urge to hop on the next plane to Orlando.

Watch a Movie
Disney movies—animations and live action alike—capture the Disney spirit wonderfully. Rent your favorite from the local video store and settle in for a cozy evening. You can also request a free vacation planning video of the Walt Disney World Resort— call Disney at 407-934-7639 to order your free video. (To get a free Disney Cruise Line video, call 888-325-2500.)

Listen to Music
Load up your CD player with Disney music or listen to a Disney-themed Internet radio station. We recommend Sorcerer Radio, which features both Disney tunes and shows! Listen at http://www.srsounds.com.

Go Shopping
You may enjoy a visit to The Disney Store for its delightful theming and foot-tapping music. You can buy park admission at a discount, and special offers may be had with the Disney Rewards Visa (see page 10).

Reminisce
If you've visited the "World" before, think back to your vacation and the things you enjoyed most about it. Dig out your souvenirs, photos, and home movies and view them with fresh eyes. If you used a PassPorter last time, go through your PassPockets carefully to refresh your memory and find the notes you made "for next time." If you haven't gone to Walt Disney World before, talk to all the friends and family members who have gone and get their impressions, tips, and stories.

Network With Others
Disney fans tend to gravitate toward online services and the Internet. If you've got an Internet connection, you'll find many Disney sites—even one for PassPorter planners! (See page 7 for more information.) No access to the Internet? Try your workplace and school.

Plan, Plan, Plan
Few things are better than planning your own trip to the Walt Disney World Resort. Cuddle up with your PassPorter, read it through, and use it to the fullest—it makes planning fun and easy. PassPorter really is the ultimate in Disney Dreaming!

More at ⓘ getting-your-disney-fix

Planning Your Adventure

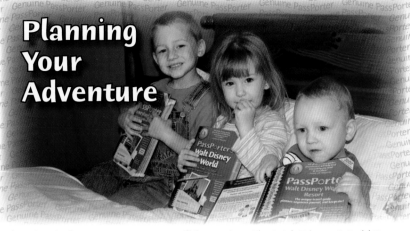

Planning

Getting There

Staying in Style

Touring

Feasting

Making Magic

Index

Notes & More

Planning is the secret to a successful vacation. The Walt Disney World Resort is vast and overwhelming without a game plan. Good planning is rewarded by a far more magical Disney experience. Planning is also wonderful fun. It increases the anticipation and starts the excitement months before the vacation begins.

PREPARE the best possible vacation

Planning begins with learning about the Walt Disney World Resort. Your PassPorter has all the information you need for a great vacation, and then some! Written to be complete yet compact, PassPorter can be your only guidebook or act as a companion to another. You can use it in a variety of ways: as a travel guide, a vacation planner, an organizer, a trip journal, and a keepsake. We designed it for heavy use—you can take it with you and revisit it after your trip is just a fond memory. You can personalize it with your plans, notes, souvenirs, and memories. We even crafted it with extra room in the binding to hold the things you'll squeeze and jam into the pockets along the way. PassPorter is the ultimate Walt Disney World Resort guide—before, during, and after your vacation.

MAKE the most of your PassPorter

This first chapter helps you with the initial planning stage: gathering information and budgeting. Your PassPorter then continues through the planning stages in order of priority. Sprinkled throughout are ways to personalize your trip, little-known tips, and magical Disney memories.

BUDGET your time, money, and resources $$$$$

Above all else, have fun with your plans, both now and when you reach the Walt Disney World Resort. Leave room for flexibility, and include time to relax and refresh. You might be tempted to see and do it all, but an overly ambitious plan will be more exhausting (and frustrating) than fun. Don't get so bogged down with planning and recording that you miss the spontaneous magic of a Disney vacation. To paraphrase Robert Burns, "The best laid plans of mice and men go oft astray." Use your PassPorter to plan ahead and be aware of your options so you can relax and enjoy your vacation, no matter what it brings.

LEARN where to find information on Disney

Top Photo Slice: It's never too early to plan your trip! (①14621) © Alisa Niethammer

Planning

Getting There

Staying in Style

Touring

Feasting

Making Magic

Index

Notes & More

Planning With Your PassPorter

Each important aspect of your vacation—budgeting, traveling, packing, lodging, touring, and eating—has a **special, dedicated worksheet** in your PassPorter. Don't be shy; we designed these worksheets to be scribbled upon at will. Not only do they take the place of easy-to-lose scraps of paper, they are structured specifically for your vacation.

We recommend you **use a standard ball point pen or soft-lead pencil** on the worksheets in your PassPorter, as it will work best on our glossy paper. You can **keep your pen handy, too!** Slip the pen inside the book's spiral binding and secure the pen's pocket clip to one of the spirals.

Additions and significant changes at Disney World since our last edition are highlighted in green, just like this paragraph. This is not to be confused with general changes and tweaks to PassPorter, which are plentiful.

Your PassPorter is most useful when you keep it handy before and during your vacation. It fits compactly into backpacks and shoulder bags. Or tuck your PassPorter into a **waist pack** (at least 6.5" x 9" or 17 x 23 cm).

Your PassPorter loves to go on rides with you, but try to **keep it dry** on Splash Mountain and Kali River Rapids. The heavy cover offers good protection, but a simple resealable plastic bag (gallon size) is a big help.

Personalize your PassPorter! **Write your name** under the front cover flap, along with other information you feel comfortable listing (we recommend that you do not list your room number for safety reasons). Your hotel name, trip dates, and cell phone number help if you misplace your PassPorter. Under the back cover flap are places for your important **phone numbers**, **reminders**, and **addresses**. Use the checkboxes to mark items when done. The **label page** at the end of the text is a fun feature—use the labels to personalize your PassPockets and attach the tabs to mark your chapters!

Two tools you may find helpful for planning are a **highlighter** (to mark "must-sees") and those sticky **page flags** (to mark favorite pages).

It's normal for the **handy spiral binding** in your PassPorter to rotate as you flip pages. If this causes your binding to creep up, you can easily rotate it back—just twist the binding while holding the pages securely.

Your PassPorter's **sturdy cover** wraps around your book for protection, and you can fold it back and leave the book open. The binding is a bit bigger than necessary to fit your stuff. We crafted a pocket for each day of your trip (up to 10 days), plus special ones for your journey, lodging, and memories. Read more about these "PassPockets" on the next page.

Note: Most of the tips on these two pages apply to the regular edition (spiral-bound); if you have a deluxe edition (ring-bound), visit http://www.passporter.com/wdw/deluxe.htm.

Planning

Getting There

Staying in Style

Touring

Feasting

Making Magic

Index

Notes & More

Keep everything you need for your journey together here in one place, such as maps, tickets, coupons, reservation numbers... even passports!

Using Your PassPockets

In the back of your PassPorter are 14 unique "PassPockets" to help you plan before you go, keep items handy while you're there, and save memories for your return. Just pencil in your trip information and itinerary on the front; store brochures, maps, receipts, and such inside; and jot down impressions, memories, expenses, and notes on the back. Use the PassPockets in any way that suits you, filling in as much or as little as you like. You can even personalize your PassPockets with the included labels!

Read the advice or tip.

Use the pockets as printed, or personalize with a label.

Write your itinerary here, including times, names, and confirmation numbers. Or just record what you did.

Jot down things you want to remember, do, or visit.

Make notes before you go or add notes during your trip.

Store items you want to have on hand during your trip, or things you collect along the way, in this roomy pocket. Guidemaps, brochures, and envelopes all fit inside.

Slip small items in this smaller slot, such as receipts, claim tags, and ticket stubs.

Write the day of the week and the date for quick reference.

Record memories of your vacation to share with others or to keep to yourself. You can jot these down as you go or reminisce at the end of the day.

Keep track of photos taken so you can find them later!

Watch your expenses to stay within a budget or to track your resort charge account balance.

Remember all those great (or not-so-great) meals and snacks by noting them here. You can even include the price of the meal or snack, too!

What did you forget? What do you want to do again? What would you like to try next time? What wouldn't you touch again with a ten-foot pole? Make a note of it here!

Use the Vacation-at-a-Glance page just in front of your PassPockets to record park hours, showtimes, meals, or anything that helps you plan your trip. If you prefer to travel light, don't be shy about removing a PassPocket and carrying it around for the day instead of toting your entire PassPorter. Just tuck it back in here at the end of the day! (If you have the spiral version and feel uncomfortable about tearing out a PassPocket, you may prefer our ring-bound Deluxe Edition with looseleaf pockets—see page 312.) You can also purchase extra PassPockets—visit http://www.passporterstore.com/store.

Finding Disney Information

PassPorter can act as your **first source** of information for the Walt Disney World Resort. It can also be a companion to other Disney books you may already own or purchase later. Either way, we like to think it packs a lot of information into a small package. Everything you need to know to plan a wonderful Disney vacation can be found within its pages.

Do keep in mind that the Walt Disney World Resort is constantly changing. We've taken every step to ensure that your PassPorter is as up-to-date as possible, but we cannot foresee the future. So to help your PassPorter remain current, we **make free updates available** to you at our web site (http://www.passporter.com/customs/bookupdates.htm). If you have ideas, questions, or corrections, please contact us—see page 308.

Oodles of **travel guidebooks** are available if you have a hankering for second opinions. We highly recommend *The Unofficial Guide to Walt Disney World* by Bob Sehlinger for its irreverence, sheer quantity of detail, and touring plans. *Birnbaum's Walt Disney World* offers the official line and plenty of cheerful Disney character graphics.

Call the **Walt Disney World Resort** at 407-WDW-MAGIC (407-939-6244) or e-mail them through their web site (http://www.disneyworld.com) when you need answers to specific questions. In our experience, their representatives are very friendly, but they rarely volunteer information and won't offer opinions. Prepare questions in advance. If the person you reach doesn't have an answer, call back—several times if necessary. Don't hesitate to ask for a manager if you can't get the information you need.

Travel agents you know and trust can be a great source of information—many have web sites, too. Also check with **membership organizations** that arrange travel, such as AAA (see page 11).

Magazines and newsletters about Disney are also available. Our own free weekly PassPorter News has Disney and other travel features, book updates, news, reviews, reports, contests, tips, and deals—subscribe at http://www.passporter.com/news.htm (subscribers are also entitled to a discount on PassPorter guidebooks). ALL EARS® Newsletter is a free unofficial weekly e-mail with Disney articles and news —subscribe at http://allears.net. Annual Passholders in the United States (see page 10) receive a quarterly newsletter from Disney. And, for the price of a gold membership fee ($74.99), D23 members receive the *Disney twenty-three* publication quarterly, which contains exclusive interviews with filmmakers and Imagineers, plus behind-the-scenes glimpses—all in glossy color (subscribe at http://www.d23.com).

Exploring a Whole New World Wide Web

The ultimate source of information, in our opinion, is the **Internet**. Of course, this requires access to a computer with access to the Internet, but with this you can connect to millions of vacationers happy to share their Disney knowledge.

The web offers hundreds of Disney-related sites. In fact, **PassPorter** has its own web site with updates, tips, ideas, articles, forums, and links. Visit us at http://www.passporter.com. We even have a special club—PassPorter's Club—just for vacation planners! More details are on page 316.

Disney's official web site at http://www.disneyworld.com is an excellent source for basic information, including hours, rates, and maps. Late changes to hours are best verified at 407-824-4321, however. Also check out the Disney Moms Panel at http://disneyworldforum.disney.go.com and the Disney Parks Blog at http://disneyparks.disney.go.com/blog.

We also recommend several **unofficial web sites**, which we frequent ourselves when planning a trip. We introduce these web sites as appropriate throughout the book (check pages 304–305 in the index for a full list). Two special sites deserves mention now: AllEars.net® is a comprehensive and up-to-date guide at http://www.allears.net, and MousePlanet.com has great articles and weekly updates at http://www.mouseplanet.com.

Another source of information (and camaraderie) is **discussion groups**. PassPorter has its own set of message boards with an active, supportive community of vacationers at http://www.passporterboards.com/forums—come chat with us, ask your questions, and share the fun! Fans also gather at **Tagrel.com** at http://www.tagrel.com, at Pete Werner's **Unofficial Disney Information Station** at http://www.disboards.com, as well as at **Intercot** at http://www.intercot.com and **DisneyEcho** at http://disneyecho.emuck.com.

E-mail lists are yet another valuable Internet resource, allowing you to observe and participate in discussions from the safety of your e-mailbox. We have a newsletter list with regular feature articles—subscribe for free at our web site. Many other mailing lists are available, including **The Mouse For Less** for Disney fans on a budget—visit at http://www.themouseforless.com.

Podcasts are the latest way to learn about Disney online—they are similiar to talk radio shows and free to listen to on your computer or iPod. PassPorter has its own podcast with host "moms" Jennifer Marx and Sara Varney—listen to us weekly at http://www.passporter.com/podcast.

Top Photo Slice: Giant laptop at Pop Century Resort (①522) © MediaMarx, Inc.

Planning

Getting There

Staying in Style

Touring

Feasting

Making Magic

Index

Notes & More

Budgeting for Your Vacation

There's nothing magical about depleting your nest egg to finance a vacation. Too many Disney vacationers can tell you that money concerns overshadowed all the fun. Yet you can avoid both the realities and worries of overspending by planning within a budget. Budgeting ahead of time not only keeps you from spending too much, it encourages you to seek out ways to save money. With just a little bit of research, you can often get **more for less**, resulting in a richer, more relaxed vacation.

If you purchase a **vacation package**, you have the advantage of covering most of your major expenses up front. And while Disney's package prices haven't offered a real savings in the past, they've recently been offering decent deals. Consider adding the Dining Plan to your package (see pages 223–225). Can't find a package with a great deal? Planning each aspect of your vacation separately often saves you even more money, as we show throughout this book. You can learn about vacation packages on page 32 and inquire into prices with the Walt Disney Travel Co. at 407-828-8101 or online at http://www.disneytravel.com.

Your **vacation expenses** usually fall into six categories: planning, transportation, lodging, admission, food, and extras. How you budget for each depends upon the total amount you have available to spend and your priorities. Planning, transportation, lodging, and admission are the easiest to factor ahead of time, as costs are more or less fixed. The final two—food and extras—are harder to control, but can usually be estimated.

Begin your vacation budgeting with the **worksheet** on the following page. Enter the minimum you prefer to spend and the maximum you can afford in the topmost row. Establish as many of these ranges as possible before you delve into the other chapters. Your excitement may grow as you read more about Walt Disney World, but it is doubtful your bank account will.

As you uncover costs and ways to save money later, return to this worksheet and **update it**. Think of your budget as a work in progress. Flexibility within your minimum and maximum figures is important. As plans begin to crystallize, write the amount you expect to pay (and can afford) in the Estimated Costs column. Finally, when you are satisfied with your budget, **transfer the amounts** from the Estimated Costs column to the back of each PassPocket. Note that each PassPocket also provides space to record actual expenses, which helps you stay within your budget. Tip: This worksheet and many others are available in electronic, interactive versions, and some even do the calculations for you—see page 316 for details.

More at ⓘ saving-money-for-disney-world

Budget Worksheet

Use this worksheet to identify your resources, record estimated costs, and create a budget for your vacation. When complete, transfer the figures from the Estimated Costs column to the back of each PassPocket.

	Minimum		Maximum		Est. Costs	
Total Projected Expenses	$		$		$	
Planning:						
📠 Phone Calls/Faxes:						
📓 Guides/Magazines:						
Transportation:	*(transfer to your Journey PassPocket)*					
🚗 Rental Car:						
🚗 Fuel/Maintenance/Tolls:						
🚗 Airfare/Travel Tickets:						
🚗 Luggage/Seat Fees:						
🚗 Shuttle/Town Car/Taxi:						
🚗 Stroller/Wheelchair/ECV:						
🚗 Parking:						
Lodging:	*(transfer to your Rooms PassPocket)*					
🏨 En Route Motel/Other:						
🏨 Resort/Hotel:						
Admission:	*(transfer to appropriate PassPocket)*					
🎟 Theme Park Passes:						
🎟 Water Park Passes:						
🎟 DisneyQuest Passes:						
🎟 Golf/Recreation:						
🎟 Guided Tours/Other:						

Food*:	Daily	Total	Daily	Total	Daily	Total
🍳 Breakfast:						
🍔 Lunch:						
🍽 Dinner:						
🍿 Snacks:						
☕ Groceries/Other:						
	(transfer to each daily PassPocket)					

Extras:						
🛍 Souvenirs/Clothing:						
💸 Gratuities:						
👕 Vacation Wardrobe:						
📷 Internet Access/Photos:						
📝 Other:						
Total Budgeted Expenses	$		$		$	

* If you're on the Disney Dining Plan package (see pages 223–225), you may want to check off your included meals in the worksheet so you don't budget money for them.

Top Photo Slice: Filling out a PassPorter worksheet © MediaMarx, Inc.

Planning
Getting There
Staying in Style
Touring
Feasting
Making Magic
Index
Notes & More

Money-Saving Programs

You can save real money on a Walt Disney World Resort vacation by taking advantage of the following money-saving programs. Some require a membership fee, but they often pay for themselves quite quickly.

Disney Rewards Visa Card—This credit card from Chase gives cardholders special discounts on Disney resorts, packages, and tours, plus onboard credits on the Disney cruise. The card itself has no annual fee and earns "Disney Dream Reward Dollars" equal to 1% or more of your purchases. You can redeem your dollars relatively quickly for Disney travel, entertainment, and merchandise. Exclusive cardholder benefits are also typically offered, such as special character meet and greets. Another perk is the "pay no interest for 6 months" offer on Disney packages and cruises, but keep in mind initial deposits and all payments must be made with the card or you can lose the deal. Be sure to read the fine print carefully, too—if you carry a separate balance while floating a 0% vacation deal, your payments may apply to the higher interest balance first and you could end up paying some steep interest. Also, double-check exactly when you need to pay off the balance and be careful about confusing terminology. We have a Disney Visa ourselves and we think the "rewards" are just average, interest rates are high, and the available discounts are sparse (but attractive when offered). Disney Rewards Visa is available to U.S. residents only. If you have a Disney Rewards Visa, be sure to mention this when making reservations so they can offer any available incentives or deals. There's also a Chase Visa Rewards Disney debit card which offers some theme park benefits (but no longer earns Reward Dollars)—this card is available to those who bank with Chase. For details, visit http://disneyrewards.disney.go.com or call 877-252-6576. Also see our in-depth article at http://www.passporter.com/credit.asp.

Annual Pass (AP)—An Annual Pass (regular or premium) saves big money on admission if you plan to visit for more than 10–14 days in a one-year period (depending on the pass)—this is the point at which it becomes less expensive than regular admission. It may also deliver discounts at selected resorts, meals, tours, and ticketed events, plus invitations to special events. And let's not forget Tables in Wonderland eligibility (see below). Florida residents can pay for their Annual Pass in monthly installments without extra fees. See pages 122–123 for details and call 407-WDW-MAGIC for prices.

Florida Residents—Those of you with proof of Florida residency (such as a valid Florida driver's license) can enjoy great savings on Disney tickets, resorts, cruises, and more. The deals are so good we're almost tempted to move to Florida. For more information, visit http://disneyworld.disney.go.com/florida-residents/.

Tables in Wonderland (formerly the Disney Dining Experience)—This program offers 20% discounts on food and alcohol (for up to 10 persons, paying with one credit card or with cash) at most Disney eateries, plus free theme park parking after 5:00 pm, and free resort valet parking when dining at the resort. Available to Annual and Seasonal Passholders and Florida residents ages 21 and up with a valid Florida driver's license or ID card. Membership is $75/year for Annual/Seasonal Passholders; $100/year for Florida residents without an Annual or Seasonal Pass (renewals are $75/year). A second membership for your spouse or partner is $50/year. Call 407-566-5858 to order (allow 4–6 weeks, or request a confirmation letter if traveling within 6 weeks). The card is also available for purchase at Guest Services at each theme park. This discount program cannot be combined with any other discount or package, and there are some blackout dates (e.g., major holidays like Mother's Day, Easter, July 4th, Thanksgiving, Christmas Eve/Day, and New Year's Eve/Day). An 18% gratuity is added to all Tables in Wonderland transactions (20% at Victoria & Albert's), regardless of party size. The person whose name is on the card must be present for the discount to be applied.

Disney Vacation Club (DVC)—This timeshare program may save money for families who plan ahead. DVC members also get discounts on select meals, admission, and backstage tours. See pages 108–109.

Disney "Postcard" Specials and Advertisements— Disney sometimes offers lodging discounts in direct mail and mass media advertisements. These offers may be sent to previous Disney guests and vacationers who've requested planning materials, or they may appear in newspaper or TV ads. These offers usually have eligibility requirements, such as residence in a particular state, or can only be used by the person who received the mailing. If you receive an offer, be sure to save it for your records. You'll need the "coupon code"

Kidani Village at Animal Kingdom Lodge, just one of many DVC resorts

and perhaps an ID number ("pin code") to make your reservation. Be sure you are eligible for the offer—if you show up at Disney and can't prove eligibility, you'll lose your "deal." Visit http://www.mousesavers.com for a listing of current offers. Tip: Be sure to check your "spam" e-mail folder for any wayward Disney offers that may wind up there.

Bounceback Offer—After you arrive at a Disney resort hotel, you may get an offer to return ("bounceback") to Walt Disney World at some point in the future at a great rate! Look for bounceback offers in your hotel room, or after you return home.

Orlando Magicard—This free card offers discounts on many non-Disney shows and park tickets, as well as rental cars and hotels. Call 888-416-4026 or visit http://www. orlandoinfo.com/magicard.

Entertainment Book—This annual discount book offers coupons for rental cars, off-property hotels and restaurants, and non-Disney theme parks like Universal Orlando, SeaWorld, and Busch Gardens. Cost is about $35 for a new edition (older editions may be less). Call 888-231-SAVE (888-231-7283) or visit http://www.entertainment.com.

American Automobile Association (AAA)—Members enjoy discounts ranging from 10% to 20%, including tickets (when purchased from AAA). Contact your local office, call 800-222-6424, or visit http://www.aaa.com.

🛑 Money-Saving Tips

✔ *MouseSavers.com is a web site dedicated to cataloging available Disney discounts and deals. Webmaster Mary Waring has built a huge following, both at http://www.mousesavers.com and through her free monthly newsletter.*

✔ *If you are flying, check newspapers and the Internet for fare sales—they occur more frequently than you might think and offer savings. Expedia.com (http://www.expedia.com) has great combo deals on fares and hotel rooms!*

✔ *If you are driving or arriving late in the evening, consider staying a night at a less expensive motel your first night.*

✔ *You can save money on meals by sharing entrees or by eating only two meals a day, as Disney portions tend to be quite large. Bring quick breakfast foods and snacks from home to quell the munchies and keep up your energy.*

✔ *Always ask about discounts when you make reservations, dine, or shop. You may discover little-known specials for AAA, Disney Visa Card, Florida residents, Annual Passholders, or simply vacationers in the right place at the right time.*

✔ *Join The Mouse For Less community for more money-saving tips—you can subscribe for free at http://www.themouseforless.com.*

More at ① catching-deals

Planning

Getting There

Staying in Style

Touring

Feasting

Making Magic

Index

Notes & More

Planning

Getting There

Staying in Style

Touring

Feasting

Making Magic

Index

Notes & More

Plan It Up!

Use these tips and stories to make planning your vacation fun:

66 If you have access to the **Internet**, make it a point to get online once a week for the latest news. We have many trip reports from fellow vacationers posted on our message boards at http://www.passporterboards.com/forums. MousePlanet also offers trip reports at http://www.mouseplanet.com/wdwtr. 99

66 When planning our trip, we make a 'Family Favorites' list for each park. It's impossible to cover all of Walt Disney World in a single trip, and knowing what is most important to each of my family members helps me set some priorities so that everyone leaves each park happy. I pass around a map or list of the rides and attractions in each park (after marking out any that will be closed), and each family member marks their top two or three choices. I use that information to create a list of the 'must do' favorites for each park. I tuck the lists into my Deluxe PassPorter's pocket, so that they're handy as we tour. Even if we don't make it to every ride in a park, we can at least be sure that we all get to visit our top favorites! 99

— Contributed by Bonnie McCarty, a winner in our Reader Tip Contest

66 To enhance the excitement and anticipation before a trip, we celebrate Disney Days. Every month leading up to a trip, on the day of the month we are scheduled to leave, we do as many Disney things as we can think of, such as wearing Disney T-shirts, listening to our Disney music, watching a movie or planning video, looking at pictures of past trips, or making a special Disney themed meal. After a concentrated day of Disney magic, we can hardly wait to head to the airport! 99

— Contributed by Suzanne Sevier, a winner in our Reader Tip Contest

Magical Memory

66 *When my sister's 40th birthday rolled around, I wanted to do something really special for her—she is the most generous, sweetest person. So I teamed up with her husband and my mother to secretly plan a trip to Walt Disney World. Keeping it a surprise was tough, but we managed to keep it from her and all the kids until the actual day of our departure. To reveal the big news to her, I led her and the whole family on a treasure hunt around town, eventually taking them toward the airport. When she got to the airport, I had her stop just outside at a cell phone lot. I then gave her the final clue and told her she had to go there. She was dumbfounded for a moment, but just then a plane flew overhead ... and she realized we were flying to Florida right then and there! The kids screamed in excitement and my sister was completely floored! It was a great day, and we had an amazing trip! Happy Birthday, Kim. I love you!* 99

...as told by author Jennifer Marx

© MediaMarx, Inc.

My sister when she realized we were going to Disney!

| Disney's Animal Kingdom Area | Epcot Area | Downtown Disney Area | Magic Kingdom Area |

Chapter 2: Getting There (and Back!)   Topic: Introduction to Traveling   13

Getting There (and Back!)

So, you promised your family a trip to visit the Mouse, or for the tenth time today you've gleefully thought, "I'm going to Disney!" Eventually the moment of truth arrives: Just *how* are you going to get there?

Traveling in this age of tightened security requires more planning and patience, but you'll discover it is quite easy to get to the Walt Disney World Resort. The path to Orlando is well traveled by cars, planes, trains, buses, and tours. On the other hand, "easy" isn't always convenient or inexpensive. Choosing the best and most affordable way to get to Disney can take some doing. We can help!

FIND many ways to get to Disney

In this chapter, we walk you through the process of making your travel arrangements. We brief you on weather, attendance levels, park hours, and seasonal rates so you can pick the best time to go or make the most of the dates you've already chosen. You'll find descriptions of each major path to the Walt Disney World Resort and a worksheet to help you pick a route and make your reservations. Then it's time to get packing, with the help of our special packing lists. Finally, we help you smile and enjoy your journey with tips for having fun along the way.

DISCOVER the best times to visit Disney

What we won't do is take up space with the phone numbers of airlines and car rental companies or travel directions from every city. You can find that information on the Internet or in your phone book. Just jot down numbers and notes on the worksheet, and transfer the winners to the appropriate PassPocket in the back.

CHART your journey and make travel plans

It's important to note that due to reservation change penalties, air and rail travel is generally less flexible than lodging. Thus, we find it works much better to make traveling decisions before finalizing hotel arrangements. However, you may prefer to skip to the next chapter and shop for your lodging first. Just return here to tailor your travel plans to your lodging choice.

PACK just what you need to bring to Disney

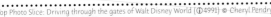

Top Photo Slice: Driving through the gates of Walt Disney World (①4991) © Cheryl Pendry

Planning — Getting There — Staying in Style — Touring — Feasting — Making Magic — Index — Notes & More

| Magic Kingdom Area | Downtown Disney Area | Epcot Area | Disney's Animal Kingdom Area |

14   Chapter 2: Getting There (and Back!)   Topic: Deciding When to Go

The Best of Times

Most Disney veterans can tell you, in no uncertain terms, that some times are much better than others to visit the "World." We wholeheartedly agree, but there's more to it. While there are certainly times of the year that are less crowded or more temperate, only you can decide the best time to visit. To help you decide, we charted the **fluctuating factors** for each month below. If you ask us, the best time to visit is November–February, but avoid the holidays, when parks fill to capacity. Three-day weekends are also to be avoided whenever possible. The latter half of August and September are less crowded, though you'll battle the heat. For links to more temperature and rainfall data, visit http://www.passporter.com/wdw/bestoftimes.htm.

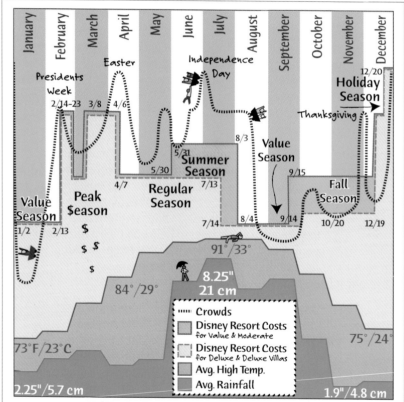

2013 Disney resort cost seasons are as follows:

Value Season is Jan. 2–Feb. 13 (all), Jul. 14–Sep. 26 (moderate, deluxe), Aug. 5–Sep. 6 (campsites), Aug. 4–Sep. 14 (value); *Peak Season* is Feb. 14–23 (value, moderate), Feb. 14–Apr. 6 (campsites), Mar. 8–Apr. 6 (value, moderate), Mar. 10–Apr. 6 (deluxe), Dec. 13–19 (all); *Regular Season* is Feb. 24–Mar. 7 (all but campsites), Mar. 8–9 (deluxe), Apr. 7–May 30 (all), Jun. 1– Aug. 3 (campsites), Sep. 27–Oct. 19 (moderate, deluxe); *Summer Season* is May 31–Aug. 3 (value), May 31–Jul. 13 (moderates); *Fall Season* is Sep. 15–Dec. 12 (value), Oct. 20–Dec. 12 (moderate, deluxe); *Pre-Holiday Season* is Oct. 7–Dec. 21 (campsites only); and *Holiday Season* is Dec. 20–31 (all).

Top Photo Slice: Walt Disney World Railroad station on a bright, sunny day © MediaMarx, Inc.

(Side tabs, top to bottom:) Planning · Getting There · Staying in Style · Touring · Feasting · Making Magic · Index · Notes & More

(Right margin:) More at ① peak-season | last-minute-trips | taking-kids-out-of-school (tip: enter this keyword at http://www.passporter.com/ℹ for more information!)

Getting There

One of the major hurdles to a Walt Disney World Resort vacation is figuring out how to get there in the first place. Many of us think along the traditional (and expensive) lines first and become discouraged. It doesn't have to be like that. There are **more ways** to get to Disney than you probably realize. Below we describe each, beginning with the most popular. At the end of the list, on page 23, a worksheet gives you space to make notes, jot down prices, and note reservation numbers. When your travel plans are finalized, record them on the first PassPocket.

By Car, Van, Truck, or Motorcycle

Many vacationers arrive at Disney in their own vehicle. It's hard to beat the **slowly rising sense of excitement** as you draw closer or the freedom of having your own wheels once you arrive. Driving may also eliminate the concerns you or family members may have with air travel. Additionally, driving might be less expensive than air travel for large families. Be sure to compare the costs of driving versus flying before you decide. On the down side, gas is very expensive these days and you may spend long days on the road, which cuts deeply into your time with Mickey.

If you opt to drive, carefully **map your course** ahead of time. You can do this with an AAA TripTik—a strip map that guides you to and from your destination. TripTiks can be created for free at the http://www.aaa.com web site, and AAA will print and mail them to members. If you're driving, we heartily recommend *Along Interstate-75* (http://www.i75online.com) and/or *Drive I-95* (http://www.drivei95.com). I-95 drivers should also visit http://www.usastar.com/i95/homepage.htm. Or try a trip routing service, such as http://www.mapquest.com or http://maps.google.com. **Tip**: Have exact change ready for the unmanned toll booths along the Florida toll roads on your route. Check toll prices at http://www.floridasturnpike.com/TRI/index.htm and http://epass.oocea.com.

If you live more than 500 miles away, **spread out your drive** over more than one day, allotting one day for every 500 miles. Arriving at Walt Disney World overly road-weary is no way to begin a vacation. If your journey spans more than one day, decide in advance where to stop each night and make reservations accordingly. Check that your air-conditioning is in good working order and your cell phone is charged before heading out (bring a cell phone charger and headset, too). Secure rest areas are available once you hit the Florida border, making it a bit easier to drive at night. Also see our in-depth articles on driving at http://www.passporter.com/driving.asp.

More at ① driving | driving-with-kids | driving-at-night

Top Photo Slice: Tomorrowland Indy Speedway at the Magic Kingdom (①9514) © Cheryl Pendry

By Airplane

Air travel is the fastest way for most vacationers to get to Orlando. In fact, air travel may be less expensive than you think if you know the tricks to getting an **affordable flight**.

Be flexible on the day and time of departure and return. Fares can differ greatly depending on when you fly and how long you stay. Consider flying on Tuesdays, Wednesdays, and Saturdays, which are historically lower-fare days. Also include a Saturday night stay in your travel dates, when possible, as it may produce a lower fare. And try to avoid traveling during holidays, as this results in significantly higher fares (though flying on the actual day of a holiday can sometimes be a money-saver).

Take advantage of the many "**fare sales**." To learn about sales, visit airlines' web sites or travel sites such as Expedia (http://www.expedia.com), Orbitz (http://www.orbitz.com), Travelocity (http://www.travelocity.com), or Kayak (http://www.kayak.com). Note that not all airlines are represented on these travel sites. Subscribe to e-mail fare alerts from travel sites and from the airlines that serve your home airport(s). If Southwest Airlines is an option, be sure to check out DING! (see http://www.southwest.com). Tip: It pays to book at least 21 days in advance in most cases, but when you're not ready to book, check out Bing's FareCast (http://www.farecast.com) —it offers airfare price predictions, shows you when fares are rising or dropping, and tells you if you should buy now or wait.

Be sure to include **luggage and/or seat assignment fees** when you compare fares. You'll find handy fee charts at http://www.kayak.com.

Try **alternate airports**, such as Orlando Sanford or Tampa, when researching fares. It may be less expensive to fly to another airport and rent a car to drive to Walt Disney World.

Be persistent. Ask for their lowest fare if you call the airline directly. When you find a good deal, put it on hold immediately (if possible), note your reservation number on page 23, and cancel later if necessary.

Consider **Priceline.com** (http://www.priceline.com), where you name your own price for a round-trip ticket (but once your price is met, you can't cancel).

Finally, **don't stop shopping**. If your airline offers a cheaper fare later, you may be able to rebook at the lower rate (watch out for penalties).

Once you reserve a flight, **make a note** of the reservation numbers, flight numbers, seat assignments, and layovers on your first PassPocket. To arrange **ground transportation** from the airport, see pages 21–22.

More at ① flying-with-kids | waiting-to-take-off | surviving-long-flights | surviving-bumpy-flights

Our Top 10 Flying Tips & Reminders

It may be fastest to fly, but it's certainly not less complicated these days. Here are our top 10 flying tips, reminders, and warnings:

1. Visit http://www.tsa.gov for **travel security news and updates**. You can also use this web site to check security waitpoint times the day before you leave, and to check the status of your flight before departing for the airport. Speaking of web sites, we also suggest you use online check-in if it is offered by your airline, which most now do. Some airlines are also testing an "e-boarding pass" which is sent to your mobile device—you just bring it up on your cell phone or PDA and show it at the security checkpoint.

2. Be aware that many airlines **charge extra fees** for baggage and certain seats, and that you may get a discount if you pre-pay these.

3. Pick up a **meal and drinks** for the flight after you pass through security, as most domestic flights have discontinued meal service.

4. Pack **sharp or potentially dangerous items** in checked luggage (or just leave them at home). This includes pocket knives and sport sticks. Cigarette lighters, scissors with blades under 4" and nail clippers without knives are allowed. For details, visit http://www.tsa.gov.

5. Remember the **3-1-1 rule** for liquids/gels in carry-ons: They must be in 3.4 oz. **or less** bottle(s), all in **1 quart-sized, clear, zip-top bag**, and **1 bag per person**, placed in a screening bin. Limit your carry-ons to one bag and one personal item (e.g., purse)., though note that medical devices (like a CPAP) are not counted in the limit for carry-on items.

6. Keep your **luggage unlocked** for inspections to avoid damage. Or buy TSA-approved luggage locks at any retail store—they are typically the same price as regular locks.

7. Plan to arrive at the airport at least **two hours prior to departure**. Add an extra 30–45 minutes if you are dropping off a rental car.

8. **Curbside check-in** may be available (fees may apply), but you may need to obtain a boarding pass from your airline's desk anyway.

9. E-ticket holders should bring a **confirmation and/or boarding pass**. If you don't have one, print it from your airline's web site (your hotel's front desk should also be able to print boarding passes within 24 hours of departure).

10. Keep your **photo ID handy**. We carry ours in PassHolder Pouches (see page 311).

More at ⓘ airline-security

Top Photo Slice: Checking in at the Orlando International Airport (ⓘ15637) © Cheryl Pendry

Orlando International Airport

Orlando International Airport is a large, sprawling hub and one of the better (and cleaner) airports we've flown into. When you arrive, your plane docks at one of the **satellite terminals** (see map below). From there, follow the signs to the automated **shuttle** that takes you to the main terminal—there you'll find **baggage claim** and ground transportation. Once you reach the main terminal (Level 3), follow the signs down to baggage claim (Level 2). Shuttles, taxis, town cars, rental cars, and buses are found down on Level 1 (take the elevators opposite the baggage carousels). Disney's Magical Express (see page 21) check-in is located on Level 1, Side B. Each shuttle and bus company has its own ticket booth. If you get lost, look about for signs or an information desk that can get you back on track.

As your authors used to live in different cities, we became quite good at **meeting up at the airport**. It's best to meet your party at their baggage claim area as you won't be allowed past security without a valid boarding pass. The trick is knowing which airline and baggage claim area. Use the map and airline list below, or call the airport directly at 407-825-2001. Be careful when differentiating between Side A's and Side B's baggage claims. Gates 1–29 and 100–129 use Side A, while gates 30–99 use Side B. Check the arrival/departure boards in the terminal for flight status, too! Other terminal meeting spots are the Disney Stores (see stars on map below) or an eatery. Be sure to exchange cell phone numbers, too.

For **more details** on the Orlando International Airport, call 407-825-2001 or visit http://www.orlandoairports.net. Page travelers at 407-825-2000.

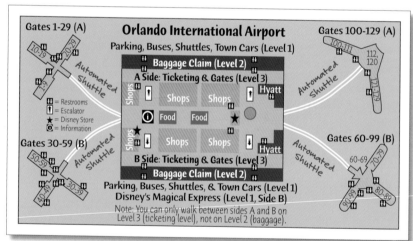

Aer Lingus, Air Canada, Air Transat, Alaska Airlines, Allegiant, American Airlines, Copa, Continental, Interjet, Martinair, Mexicana, MiamiAir, and SunWing use Gates 1–29; BahamasAir, Frontier, Midwest, Spirit, Sun Country, United, and US Airways use Gates 30–59; AirTran, Delta, and JetBlue use Gates 60–99; AeroMexico, British Airways, Lufthansa, TAM, Virgin Atlantic use Gates 80–89; and JetBlue and Southwest use Gates 100–129.

Orlando Sanford Airport

Travelers flying to Orlando **from Europe or via group charter** may arrive at the smaller Orlando Sanford International Airport (FSB), located about 18 miles northeast of Orlando and 67 miles from Port Canaveral. Airlines with scheduled service into Sanford include Allegiant Air, Direct Air, ArkeFly, Iceland Express, SST Air, Vision Airlines, and Icelandair, as well as three international charter services with flights from the United Kingdom and Ireland (Monarch, Thomas Cook, and Thomson Airways).

Alamo/National, Avis, Dollar, Enterprise, Hertz, and Thrifty all operate **in-terminal car rental desks**. Budget has an off-site rental office. Mears Transportation and several shuttle services provide bus/van service from Sanford to Orlando-area attractions and Port Canaveral.

International passengers arrive and depart from Terminal A, while domestic travelers use Terminal B. A Welcome Center is located across the street from Terminal A and is home to ground transportation services.

Dining options here include the Budweiser Tap Room (terminal A) and basic food courts (terminals A & B).

For more details on the Orlando Sanford International Airport, phone 407-585-4000 or visit http://www.orlandosanfordairport.com. If you plan to rent a car at the airport and drive to the Walt Disney World Resort, use a map routing service such as MapQuest.com before you leave home to get directions (the airport is located at 1200 Red Cleveland Blvd., Sanford, FL 32773).

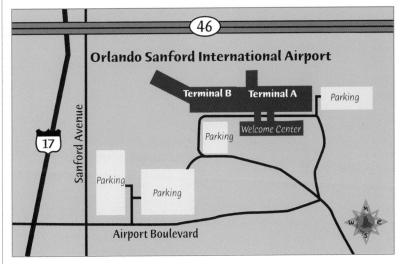

Planning | Getting There | Staying in Style | Touring | Feasting | Making Magic | Index | Notes & More

More at ⓘ sanford-airport

By Train, Bus, Tour, and Boat

By Train

The train is a uniquely relaxing and fuel-saving way to travel to the Walt Disney World Resort. **Amtrak** serves the Orlando area daily with both **passenger trains** and an Auto Train, which carries your family and your car. The **Auto Train** runs between suburban Washington, DC (Lorton, VA) and suburban Orlando (Sanford, FL). Other trains go through to Kissimmee, which is a closer, less-crowded station. Prices vary depending upon the season, the direction, and how far in advance you make your reservation. The Auto Train is also available one-way, and in many seasons, one direction is less expensive than the other direction. You may need to take a taxi or town car (see page 22) from the train station to the Disney property. Hertz rental cars are available from the Sanford (Orlando) station, but not the Kissimmee station. For Amtrak reservations, call 800-USA-RAIL or visit them at http://www.amtrak.com. Also see the in-depth PassPorter article at http://www.passporter.com/autotrain.asp.

By Bus

Buses make good economic and environmental sense. **Greyhound** serves Orlando and Kissimmee. You can take the local LYNX buses from there, but it's not fast or easy (for more information on LYNX, see page 22 under "Riding a Bus"). Buses often take longer to reach a destination than cars or trains do driving the same route. Fares are lowest if you live within 10 hours of Walt Disney World. For fares, schedules, and tickets, call Greyhound at 800-231-2222 or visit them at http://www.greyhound.com.

By Tour

A number of **special tours** go to the Walt Disney World Resort, which you may want to consider if you prefer to go with a large group or with like-minded folks. Check with the associations, organizations, and societies you belong to, or contact a travel agent.

By Boat

If you book passage on the **Disney Cruise Line**, your package may include a stay at the Walt Disney World Resort. The boat doesn't pull up to the Magic Kingdom, but Disney offers optional, prearranged transfers to and/or from the Walt Disney World Resort—this transportation may be included in your cruise package, or you may add it for an additional fee. See pages 106–107 for details on the Disney Cruise, and see page 313 to learn about our award-winning, detailed guide to the Disney Cruise Line.

By Everything Else!

The list of ways to get to Disney is really endless. You could even combine business with pleasure, as many others do!

More at ① auto-train

Are We There Yet?

Once you reach Orlando Airport, you need to continue about 20 miles before you actually reach Disney property. Your options are to take advantage of Disney's Magical Express shuttle service, use a shuttle or town car, rent a car, ride a bus, or call a taxi. Here's the details of each:

Disney's Magical Express (DME)

Disney's Magical Express is a free perk for Disney's resort hotel guests, providing **free ground transportation** to and from Orlando International Airport. Included with this service is luggage "intercept" on arrival in Orlando—properly tagged luggage is pulled off the conveyor and is delivered directly to your Disney resort hotel room (if your flight arrives between 5:00 am and 10:00 pm). If you arrive between 10:00 pm and 5:00 am, get your own checked baggage off the luggage carousel. Now just head directly to Disney's Welcome Center (Level 1, Side B)—if you have the booklet mailed to you in advance by Disney, proceed directly to the bus lines. (No booklet? Go to the check-in desk here and they will print vouchers.) For the return trip to the airport, you may be able to check in for your flight (and check your bags) before you leave your Disney resort. Disney's Magical Express is efficient, with guests being whisked to their resort with little wait and few (if any) stops at other hotels (though long waits and delays can still occur during peak arrival times). Nonetheless, Disney's Magical Express does take extra time. If you want another hour or two of park time on your first or last day, we suggest you pay for a town car service (see next page).

Arrival Tip: Travel with a **carry-on containing all your necessities**, including your park passes, a swimsuit, and a change of clothes. It may be many hours before your checked luggage arrives at your resort or before you're aware of any lost luggage.

Return Trip Note: You may **check your bags at the resort** on the day of your departure between 5:00 am and 1:00 pm (hours may vary). Check with your airline to learn if any baggage fees apply and, if so, pay them in advance. Guests on AirTran, Alaska, Delta, JetBlue, Southwest, United Airlines, and US Airways may only check one bag per passenger—if you have additional bags, you must check them at the airport or call BAGS at 407-284-1231 to pre-pay for excess luggage. Guests on American Airlines must pre-pay at the above number for all bags. All bags must be 50 pounds or less and must fit within the airline's dimension requirements. No oversize or overweight bags will be accepted.

You must **make reservations** for Disney's Magical Express at least one day prior to your arrival in Orlando (but do it at least ten days prior to allow time to receive your materials in the mail). To add this service, call Disney's regular reservations phone line or your travel agent, or visit http://www.disneyworld.com. Disney will need your airline flight numbers. Once reserved, Disney will send guests who reside in North America special luggage tags (one per person age 3 and above; more available by calling 866-599-0951) and an instruction booklet. If your flight is changed or delayed, notify Disney's Magical Express Guest Services at 866-599-0951.

Only **guests at Disney-owned resorts** can use Disney's Magical Express. Swan, Dolphin, Shades of Green, and all hotels on Hotel Plaza Boulevard (Regal Sun Resort, DoubleTree Suites, Hilton, etc.) are not included, and neither are travelers using Sanford Airport. Disney Vacation Club members wishing to use this service should contact DVC Member Services.

More at ⓘ magical-express

Planning · Getting There · Staying in Style · Touring · Feasting · Making Magic · Index · Notes & More

Magic Kingdom Area | Downtown Disney Area | Epcot Area | Disney's Animal Kingdom Area

22   Chapter 2: Getting There (and Back!)   Topic: Getting to the Resort and Parks

Are We There Yet?
(continued)

Taking a Shuttle or Town Car

A number of companies stay in business largely by transporting guests to and from Disney. Shuttle stands are located at the Orlando International Airport (Level 1), but all other pickup locations require advance notice. The major shuttle operator is Mears (800-759-5219). We prefer a **town car**, however. The town car driver greets us at baggage claim, carries our luggage, drives us to our hotel, and charges less than it costs a family of four to use a shuttle, taxi, or rental car. If you'd like to stop at a grocery store or if you need a car/booster seat, request this at reservation. We use Quicksilver Tours (888-468-6939, http://www.quicksilver-tours.com) and Happy Limo (877-642-7791, http://www.happylimo.com).

Driving a Car

If you're driving to Walt Disney World, you'll need specific directions. You can find detailed directions through a trip routing service (see page 15) or Disney (call 407-939-4636). Fliers planning to drive a car while in Orlando should rent at the airport. We don't feel a rental car is needed if you stay only on Disney property, as their internal transportation system works well (see pages 124–125) and even an occasional taxi fare can be cheaper than a rental car. If you plan to go off-property often, you may find a rental car helpful. Alamo (Disney's official rental car agency), Avis, Budget, Dollar, Enterprise, Hertz, Thrifty, and National are located right at the airport on Level 1 (in-airport rentals incur a 10% fee). Economy and many others are off-site, and you'll need to take a shuttle on Level 1 to reach them (off-site rentals carry an 8.67% fee). The Dolphin Resort and several off-property hotels offer rental car desks, too. Inquire about all taxes and surcharges. See our rental car tips at http://www.passporter.com/rentalcars.asp. Tip: Vacationers using I-75/Florida Turnpike can arrive via the Western Beltway (FL 429 Toll) and Disney's Western Way—see maps on cover flaps.

Riding a Bus

The regional bus system, LYNX, has limited service to the Walt Disney World property. Call 407-841-LYNX or visit http://www.golynx.com. Please note that it takes about three hours to get from the Orlando Airport to Walt Disney World via LYNX. If you need to get from your hotel to many other theme parks in the Orlando area, Mears offers transportation ($16 and up for a round trip)—call a day in advance.

Using a Taxi

While taxis are available, we don't recommend them for airport travel due to the cost. Large parties may be able to ride in a taxi minivan economically, however, especially for occasional travel within Walt Disney World.

Electronic, interactive worksheet available—see page 316

Travel Worksheet

Use this worksheet to jot down preferences, scribble information during phone calls, and keep all your discoveries together. Don't worry about being neat—just be thorough! When everything is confirmed, transfer it to your first PassPocket in the back of the book. ✏ Circle the names and numbers once you decide to go with them to avoid confusion.

Arrival date: _____ Alternate: _____
Return date: _____ Alternate: _____

We plan to travel by: ❏ Car/Van ❏ Airplane ❏ Train ❏ Bus ❏ Tour
❏ Other: _____

For Drivers:
Miles to get to Orlando: _____ ÷ 500 = _____ days on the road
We need to stay at a motel on: _____
Tune-up scheduled for: _____
Rental car info: _____

For Fliers:
Airline phone numbers: _____
Flight preferences: _____
Flight availabilities: _____
Reserved flight times and numbers: _____

For Ground Transportation:
Magical Express/town car/shuttle/rental car reservations: _____
_____
Package ground transportation details: _____
_____

Additional Notes:

Reminder: Don't forget to confirm holds or cancel reservations within the allotted time frame.

Top Photo Slice: Filling out at PassPorter worksheet © MediaMarx, Inc.

Side tabs (top to bottom): Planning | Getting There | Staying in Style | Touring | Feasting | Making Magic | Index | Notes & More

Packing List

Electronic, interactive worksheet available—see page 316

Packing for a vacation is fun when you feel confident you're packing the right things. Over the years, we've compiled this packing list for a great vacation. Just note the quantity you plan to bring and check off items as you pack. Consider carrying items in magenta on a daily basis as you tour.

The Essentials

❑ Casual clothing you can layer—the dress code nearly everywhere at Disney is casual, even at dinner. One "nice" outfit is usually enough.
___ Shorts/skirts ___ Pants/jeans ___ Shirts ___ Sweaters
___ Underwear ___ Socks ___ Pajamas ___ _____

❑ Jacket and/or sweatshirt (light ones for the warmer months)
___ Jackets ___ Sweatshirts ___ Sweaters ___ Vests

❑ Comfortable, well-broken-in shoes ... plus a second pair, just in case!
___ Walking shoes ___ Sandals/Crocs ___ Sneakers ___ _____

❑ Swim gear (bring one-piece suits for water slides)
___ Suits/swim diapers ___ Cover-ups/towels ___ Water shoes ___ Goggles

❑ Sun protection (the Florida sun can be brutal)
___ Sunblock ___ Lip balm ___ Sunburn relief ___ Sunglasses
___ Sunhats ___ Caps ___ Visors ___ _____

❑ Rain gear (compact and light so you don't mind carrying it)
___ Raincoat ___ Poncho ___ Umbrella ___ Extra socks

❑ Comfortable bags with padded straps to carry items during the day
___ Backpacks ___ Waist packs ___ Shoulder bags ___ Camera bag

❑ Toiletries (in a bag or bathroom kit to keep them organized)
___ Brush/comb ___ Toothbrush ___ Toothpaste ___ Dental floss
___ Favorite soap, shampoo, and conditioner ___ Deodorant ___ Baby wipes
___ Aspirin/acetaminophen/ibuprofen ___ Bandages ___ First aid kit
___ Prescriptions (in original containers) ___ Vitamins ___ Fem. hygiene
___ Hair dryer/iron ___ Anti-blister tape ___ Makeup ___ Hair spray
___ Razors and gel ___ Nail clippers ___ Cotton buds ___ Lotion
___ Mending kit ___ Spare eyeglasses ___ Lens solution ___ Bug repellent
___ Medical/duck tape ___ Small scissors ___ Safety pins ___ Insect sting kit

❑ Camera/camcorder and more film/tape than you think you need
___ Camera ___ Camcorder ___ Film/tapes ___ Memory cards
___ Batteries ___ Chargers ___ Case/tripod ___ _____

❑ Money in various forms and various places
___ Charge cards ___ Traveler's checks ___ Bank cards ___ Cash

❑ Personal identification, passes, and membership cards
___ Driver's licenses ___ Other photo ID ___ Passports ___ Birth certificate
___ AAA card ___ DVC member card ___ Discount cards ___ D23 card
___ Tickets/passes ___ Insurance cards ___ Calling cards ___ Air miles card

Tip: Label everything with your name, phone, and hotel to help reunite you with your stuff if lost. Every bag should have this info on a luggage tag as well as on a slip of paper inside it. Use our Luggage Tag Maker at http://www.passporter.com/wdw/luggagelog.htm.

More at ① luggage-tips | carry-ons

For Your Carry-On

- ❏ Your PassPorter, tickets, maps, guides, and a pen or pencil! ✎ Remember to pack any sharp or potentially dangerous items in your checked luggage, not your carry-on.
- ❏ Camera and/or camcorder, along with film, memory cards, tapes, and batteries.
- ❏ Any prescriptions (medications and the written prescriptions), important toiletries, sunblock, sunglasses, hats, bug repellent—liquids/gels in your carry-on must each be 3.4 oz. or less and all fit in a single quart-size bag.
- ❏ Snacks, 🍬 gum, favorite books, toys, games, blankets, change of clothes.

For Families

- ❏ Snacks and juice boxes
- ❏ Books, toys, 🎮 and games
- ❏ Stroller, carrier, and accessories 🧸
- ❏ Autograph books and fat pens
- ❏ EarPlanes (earplanes.com) or lollipops

For Couples

- ❏ Corkscrew and wine glasses 🍷
- ❏ Candles and matches
- ❏ Evening wear for nights out
- ❏ Jacket (if going to Victoria & Albert's)
- ❏ Portable CD player and CDs

For Connected Travelers

- ❏ Laptop and power supply
- ❏ Extension cord/surge suppressor
- ❏ Phone/network cables, coupler, splitter
- ❏ Security cable with lock
- ❏ Cell phones/iPads and chargers
- ❏ Two-way radios
- ❏ iPod/MP3 players
- ❏ Wi-fi router

For Heat-Sensitive Travelers

- ❏ Personal fans/water misters
- ❏ Water bottles (frozen, if possible)
- ❏ Washcloth to cool off face and neck
- ❏ Loose, breezy clothing
- ❏ Hats with wide brims
- ❏ Sunshades (for baby strollers)
- ❏ Elastics to keep long hair off neck
- ❏ Sweatbands

Everyone Should Consider

- ❏ Big beach towels (for pools and water parks)
- ❏ Penlight or flashlight (for reading/writing in dark places and to alleviate kids' fears)
- ❏ Water bottles and personal fan/water misters
- ❏ Snacks for any time of the day (plus gum, if you chew it, as it is not sold at Disney)
- ❏ Plastic cutlery for snacks or leftovers 🍴
- ❏ Quarters and pennies (and a way to hold them) for the coin presses and/or laundry
- ❏ Plastic storage bags that seal (large and small), plus trash bags
- ❏ Address book, stamps, and envelopes ✉
- ❏ Laundry detergent/tablets, bleach, dryer sheets, stain stick, and a laundry tote
- ❏ Binoculars and magnifying glasses
- ❏ Collapsible bag or suitcase inside another suitcase to hold souvenirs on your return
- ❏ Spare pair of prescription eyeglasses and a copy of your eyeglass prescription

Your Personal Packing List

- ❏ _____
- ❏ _____
- ❏ _____
- ❏ _____
- ❏ _____
- ❏ _____
- ❏ _____
- ❏ _____

- ❏ _____
- ❏ _____
- ❏ _____
- ❏ _____
- ❏ _____
- ❏ _____
- ❏ _____
- ❏ _____

More at ⓘ must-pack-items | child-safety-seats | cares-harness

Planning

Getting There

Staying in Style

Touring

Feasting

Making Magic

Index

Notes & More

Magic Kingdom Area   Downtown Disney Area   Epcot Area   Disney's Animal Kingdom Area

26   Chapter 2: Getting There (and Back!)   Topic: Traveling Tips and Stories

Planning

Getting There

Staying in Style

Touring

Feasting

Making Magic

Index

Notes & More

Adventuring!

Your journey is more pleasant when you consider it an adventure rather than a tiring trek. Here are our tried-and-true adventuring tips:

66 Bring your own **snacks and beverages** (purchased after you pass through security) aboard the plane. We also suggest you bring chewing gum (to offset air pressure), 3 oz. lotion (to offset dry air), and a DVD/CD player/iPod/MP3 player (to offset boredom). 99

66 I love bringing along my PassPorters on my magical vacations, but find taking it into the parks can be a hassle, so I downloaded the e-book version to my iPod/iPhone. It is **much easier to carry** and you always have your phone with you. Also it is great for the kids who usually carry their iPods. You can get the e-book versions online at PassPorter.com. 99

— *Contributed by Paula Rogers, a winner in our Reader Tip Contest*

66 I recommend putting your children's souvenir money on a Disney Gift Card. I do this every time we go to Walt Disney World. And if you have an iPod, iPhone, or iPad, check out the free Disney Gift Card app—you can register any and all Disney gift cards onto the app, and it will keep track of every purchase made and current balance. And, in Disney fashion, it is very colorful and easy to identify each different card and its owner. Look for it in the Apple App Store on your iPad, iPhone, or iPad. 99

— *Contributed by Maggie Akers, a winner in our Reader Tip Contest*

Magical Memory

66 *In preparation for our family trips to Walt Disney World, we make each of our children their own giant-sized coloring book/trip journal. We start with a large binder and the kids then color or draw their own covers, complete with stickers, stamps, etc., as well as their names prominently on the spine. We then let each child choose their favorite subjects and characters. For the older kids, you can add activity and journal pages. This gives them something special to do during the trip, as well as during the "mellow-out" times at the resort. After the vacation is over, you can add favorite photos and even cherished autographs. Not only are these big handmade coloring book/journals fun during the trip, but they also serve as great keepsakes for years to come.* 99

...as told by Disney vacationer Joyce Kelly

Alexander shows off his personalized journal © MediaMarx, Inc.

More at ⊕ 10-travel-tips

Top Photo Slice: Flying and driving into the sunset © MediaMarx, Inc.

Staying in Style

Planning

Getting There

Staying in Style

Touring

Feasting

Making Magic

Index

Notes & More

Nowhere in the "World" is Disney magic more evident than at the resort hotels on Walt Disney World property. In fact, the resorts are so impressive that we do not often consider staying "off-property" (as hotels outside of Walt Disney World are known), and we frequently plan our visits around our favorite resorts rather than our favorite parks. Staying in a Disney resort is unlike any other hotel experience we've had, and we've visited both the exotic and the expensive. It isn't just that staying at a Disney resort provides total immersion in the Walt Disney World experience. The resorts offer hidden surprises and a remarkable attention to detail.

RESERVE the resort and room you want

With more than 31,000 guest rooms and campsites throughout the Walt Disney World Resort, it would take more than 85 years to stay once in each room. (Sign us up!) There's something for every taste and budget. Whether you want a romantic setting, space for a family reunion, disabled access, or bunk beds, you can find it somewhere in the "World." There are enough choices to preclude staying at a non-Disney hotel, but bargains off-property are also a factor. If you visit with friends or family, prefer to stay in another hotel, or even take a cruise, your PassPorter still serves you well—you can record your arrangements here with the same ease. We include basic information on the Disney Cruise Line, Disney Vacation Club, and off-site hotels at the end of this chapter, too.

EXPLORE your resort in detail with info and maps

UNLOCK the door to resort basics, information, and tips

If you've already decided to stay at a Disney resort, your PassPorter puts you a step ahead! Our Walt Disney World resort descriptions are the most comprehensive of any guidebook, and our resort maps, photos, floor plans, tips, notes, and recommendations can help the veteran vacationer, as well as the novice, get the most out of their resort.

CHART each resort's facts & features in a checklist

To help you find your way through the staggering array of choices, we've prepared a detailed guide to choosing your resort. We heartily recommend you turn the page and take advantage of it.

Top Photo Slice: Our son Alexander asleep in a Mickey-themed bedroom at an ALL STAR Vacation Home © MediaMarx, Inc.

Choosing a Resort

Ah, this is the fun part! Deciding which resort to stay at reminds us of choosing a dessert from a tray laden with every imaginable, mouth-watering goodie. Some are too rich for us, others aren't quite sweet enough, but there are enough choices left over to make us feel spoiled. Sometimes we stay at two or more resorts in one visit. Are you surprised?

Start with the exhaustive **resort checklist** on the next page. Compare it with your preferences to uncover the resorts that meet your needs. Then carefully read the resort descriptions, beginning on page 37. Each description follows the same format, allowing you to find exactly what you seek as you **compare resorts**. The first and second pages of each description list resort essentials, along with floor plans and transportation times. The third page lists the best tips, notes, and ratings for each resort—this is the "good stuff" to help you make the most out of your experience. In the Ratings section, we and our readers grade each resort for value, magic, and satisfaction. An explanation of the ratings is at the bottom of this page. The fourth page features a detailed resort map and our ideas for the best rooms in the resort. Rates, addresses, and phone/fax numbers are listed at the end of each description. **Tip**: When researching resorts, use the darkest "stamp" (tab) at the top of the page to locate parks and eateries in the vicinity, which will have the same "stamp" at the top of their pages.

When you're ready, use the Lodging Worksheet on pages 116–117 to record your dates, preferences, and reservation options.

Resort Ratings Explained

We offer a variety of resort ratings in PassPorter to help you make the best decisions. Even so, we recommend you use these ratings as a guide, not gospel.

Value Ratings range from 1 (poor) to 10 (excellent) and are based on **quality** (cleanliness, maintenance, and freshness); **accessibility** (how fast and easy it is to get to attractions); and **affordability** (rates for the standard rooms)—**overall value** represents an average of the above three values. **Magic Ratings** are based on **theme** (execution and sense of immersion); **amenities** (guest perks and luxuries); and **fun factor** (number and quality of resort activities)—**overall magic** represents an average of the above three values. We use a point accumulation method to determine value and magic ratings.

Readers' Ratings are calculated from surveys submitted by experienced vacationers at our web site (http://www.passporter.com/wdw/rate.htm).

Guest satisfaction is based on our and our readers' experiences with how different types of guests enjoy the resort: ♥♥♥♥♥=love it ♥♥♥♥=enjoy it ♥♥♥=like it ♥♥=tolerate it ♥=don't like it

More at ① choosing-a-resort (tip: enter this keyword at http://www.passporter.com/⌐ for more information!)

Resort Comparisons

* Kitchen facilities are present only in the villas or family suites of indicated resorts	All-Star Resorts	Animal King. Lodge/Villas	Art of Animation	Beach Club/Villas	BoardWalk Inn/Villas	Caribbean Beach	Contemporary/Villas	Coronado Springs	Fort Wilderness	Grand Floridian	Old Key West	Polynesian	Pop Century	Port Orleans	Saratoga Springs	Shades of Green	Swan/Dolphin	Wild. Lodge/Villas	Yacht Club
Deluxe		✓		✓	✓		✓			✓		✓				✓	✓	✓	✓
Disney's Deluxe Villas		✓		✓	✓		✓			✓	✓				✓			✓	
Moderate						✓		✓	✓					✓					
Value	✓		✓										✓						

Rooms and Amenities

	All-Star Resorts	Animal King. Lodge/Villas	Art of Animation	Beach Club/Villas	BoardWalk Inn/Villas	Caribbean Beach	Contemporary/Villas	Coronado Springs	Fort Wilderness	Grand Floridian	Old Key West	Polynesian	Pop Century	Port Orleans	Saratoga Springs	Shades of Green	Swan/Dolphin	Wild. Lodge/Villas	Yacht Club
Total Rooms	5568	1293	1984	785	910	2112	963	1967	1195	1147	761	853	2880	3056	1260	586	2267	864	634
Occupancy	3-6	3-12	3-6	3-8	3-12	3-4	3-12	3-6	3-10	3-8	3-12	3-5	3-4	3-5	3-12	5-8	3-5	3-8	3-5
Mini-Bars																✓			
Coffeemakers		✓		✓	✓	✓	✓	✓	✓	✓	✓	✓		✓	✓	✓	✓	✓	✓
Hair Dryers	✓	✓	✓	✓	✓	✓	✓	✓	✓	✓	✓	✓	✓	✓	✓	✓	✓	✓	✓
In-Room Safes	✓	✓	✓	✓	✓	✓	✓	✓	✓	✓	✓	✓	✓	✓	✓	✓	✓	✓	✓
Kitchen Facilities*	✓	✓	✓	✓	✓		✓				✓				✓			✓	✓
Turndown (on req.)		✓		✓	✓		✓			✓	✓	✓			✓	✓	✓	✓	✓
Wireless Internet	✓	✓	✓	✓	✓	✓	✓	✓	✓	✓	✓	✓	✓	✓	✓	✓	✓	✓	✓

Eating and Drinking

	All-Star Resorts	Animal King. Lodge/Villas	Art of Animation	Beach Club/Villas	BoardWalk Inn/Villas	Caribbean Beach	Contemporary/Villas	Coronado Springs	Fort Wilderness	Grand Floridian	Old Key West	Polynesian	Pop Century	Port Orleans	Saratoga Springs	Shades of Green	Swan/Dolphin	Wild. Lodge/Villas	Yacht Club
Restaurants/Cafes	–	3	–	3	7	1	3	1	2	4	2	3	–	1	2	4	9	3	3
Character Meals				✓			✓		✓	✓		✓					✓		
Lounges	3	5	1	3	4	1	6	2	1	3	1	2	1	4	2	1	4	2	2
Food Courts	3	1	1	–	–	1	1	1	–	1	–	1	1	2	1	–	1	–	1
Room Service		✓		✓	✓		✓	✓	✓		✓					✓	✓	✓	✓
Pizza Delivery	✓		✓									✓		✓	✓				

Recreational Activities

	All-Star Resorts	Animal King. Lodge/Villas	Art of Animation	Beach Club/Villas	BoardWalk Inn/Villas	Caribbean Beach	Contemporary/Villas	Coronado Springs	Fort Wilderness	Grand Floridian	Old Key West	Polynesian	Pop Century	Port Orleans	Saratoga Springs	Shades of Green	Swan/Dolphin	Wild. Lodge/Villas	Yacht Club
Beach (no swim)				✓	✓	✓	✓	✓	✓		✓				✓		✓	✓	✓
Pools	6	2	3	2	3	7	3	4	2	2	4	2	3	7	5	2	2	2	2
Kid Pool	3	2	1	1	1	1	2	1	1	1	1	1	1	2	1	1	1	1	1
Spa (Hot Tub)	–	4	–	5	3	1	3	1	1	1	2	–	–	2	6	1	1	3	5
Spa (Services)				✓	✓		✓			✓					✓		✓	✓	✓
Health Club		✓		✓	✓		✓			✓						✓	✓	✓	✓
Marina		✓		✓	✓	✓	✓	✓	✓	✓	✓	✓		✓	✓			✓	✓
Tennis		✓					✓		✓	✓	✓				✓		✓		✓
Jogging Path	✓	✓	✓	✓	✓			✓		✓	✓	✓	✓	✓	✓		✓	✓	✓
Kids' Program		✓					✓		✓	✓		✓			✓		✓	✓	✓

Access and Facilities

	All-Star Resorts	Animal King. Lodge/Villas	Art of Animation	Beach Club/Villas	BoardWalk Inn/Villas	Caribbean Beach	Contemporary/Villas	Coronado Springs	Fort Wilderness	Grand Floridian	Old Key West	Polynesian	Pop Century	Port Orleans	Saratoga Springs	Shades of Green	Swan/Dolphin	Wild. Lodge/Villas	Yacht Club
Monorail							✓			✓		✓							
Disabled Rooms	288	66	96	10	51	22	6	99	8	5	67	17	126	34	16	22	51	46	10
Conf. Center				✓	✓												✓		✓

Your Favorites

Top Photo Slice: Panoramic of the Epcot area resorts (①3964) © Rick Wagner

Planning · Getting There · Staying in Style · Touring · Feasting · Making Magic · Index · Notes & More

Reserving a Room

Once you have an idea of where you want to stay at the Walt Disney World Resort, it's time to **make reservations**. A travel agent is not needed, but if you have a great travel agent, by all means consult him or her (they do not generally charge any fees for their services). Here's the lowdown on making Disney resort reservations:

Before you make your reservations, **use the worksheet** on pages 116–117 to jot down the dates you prefer to visit along with any alternates. Even a one-day change in your travel dates can open the door to availabilities. Be familiar with all resorts in your price range. We also suggest you finalize resort reservations after you make your flight reservations. Hotel room reservations may be changed or canceled without fees up to a certain date, but flight changes at any time almost always incur a fee.

You can make reservations for all Walt Disney World resort hotels at **407-WDW-MAGIC** (407-939-6244)—alas, all known toll-free numbers for Disney have been de-activated. Note that Walt Disney Travel Company agents answer the above number. Disney representatives can offer assistance in English, Spanish, Japanese, French, Portuguese, and German. If you have Internet access, you can research room rates and make reservations online at http://www.disneyworld.com (click on "Resorts")—discounts are sometimes available on the web site, but you must follow the specific links for the specials or you'll be charged regular rates. You may also want to try Travelocity or Expedia, both of which are popular Internet reservation systems—you can visit them at http://www.travelocity.com and http://www.expedia.com. Be sure to look for promotional rates while you're there, too! If you prefer, you can also make reservations through the mail by writing to Walt Disney World at Box 10100, Lake Buena Vista, Florida 32830.

Reservations can be made for just **lodging ("room only")** or for **vacation packages**, which include lodging, admission, and more (see page 32 for more details on the types of packages available). Prices and policies differ for each type of booking, which we describe on the next page.

Research **special deals or packages** by visiting MouseSavers.com (see page 11) or by calling Disney Reservations. If you have a Disney Visa card or Annual Pass, or if you are a Florida resident or military family, ask about those discounts, too. (The Swan and Dolphin offer discounts to nurses, teachers, and government employees.) If your dates aren't available, ask about alternates. Sometimes you can get a discount for part of your stay. Lock in whatever discount you can get, and book at the full price for the remainder. Keep calling back, as canceled reservations are released every morning. If a lower rate comes out later, you may be able to call back and get it applied.

Make any **special requests** at the time of reservation and again when you check in. If you need a barrier-free room, a refrigerator, or a crib, request this now. If you have a particular location or room in mind (we make many suggestions later), make sure to tell the reservations agent. It's best to make your request as general as possible. You'll have better luck requesting a "high floor with views of fireworks" than simply "room 5409." If Disney doesn't know why you want room 5409, they can't choose a suitable substitute. Disney will not guarantee a particular room or view, but if your request is "in the system," they will try their best to make your wish come true. Call your resort about three days before your arrival to confirm any requests you made.

More at ① reserving-a-room

Planning

Getting There

Staying in Style

Touring

Feasting

Making Magic

Index

Notes & More

In need of **ground transportation** between the Orlando International Airport and your Disney-owned resort? Disney's Magical Express provides free shuttle bus service from and to the airport, as well as luggage handling. If your reservation agent doesn't mention it, be sure to ask. If you forget, the service can be added to your reservation at least one day before your scheduled arrival. See page 21 for the full details on Disney's Magical Express.

Miles of smiles on a Magical Express motorcoach

You may be able to hold more than one reservation for the same date, but eventually you have to put down a deposit or lose the reservation. Typically, Disney resort reservations are held 7 days without confirmation as a courtesy, but only if you have at least 45 days until your stay. **Deposit and cancellation policies do differ** between packages and room-only reservations. Room-only reservations have a more liberal deposit policy—the cost of one night's lodging is all that's required (due in 7 days), with a no-penalty cancellation possible up to six days prior. With less than six days' notice, you forfeit the full one-night deposit. Packages require a deposit of $200, also due in 7 days, and full payment for your vacation is due 45 days in advance. Package reservations made online can be cancelled without a penalty at least 46 days before your arrival, or incur a $100 charge if made between 6 and 45 days prior, and $200 for cancellations made less than 6 days prior. There's a $50 charge for modifying package reservations within 46 days of your arrival, unless your change increases your package price.

Be sure to **pay your deposit** by 10:00 pm ET on your due date, or your reservation will be canceled. Your deposit can be made over the phone with American Express, MasterCard, Visa, Discover, JCB, Diner's Club, through mail or fax with the same credit cards or a personal check, or online in most cases. The Lodging Worksheet at the end of the chapter (pages 116–117) has spaces to check off confirmations and deposits made, too! **Tip**: You may be able to request an extension on your deposit if needed—inquire with Disney.

Once you've made your reservations, **record the details** on your Room(s) PassPocket, including the name of the resort, dates, type of room, price, reservation number, and any special information you want to note. This is also an ideal place to note any special requests you want to check on at check-in. Use a pencil if plans aren't final.

Higher Rates on Weekends, Holidays, and More

You should know that Disney charges higher room rates on weekends and some holidays. And if a stay straddles two lodging seasons, whenever the "season" changes, the rate changes, too. The weekend and holiday rates bump up by about $5–$30 per night at the value, moderate, and deluxe resorts. Affected holidays include Martin Luther King weekend, President's Day weekend, Easter week, Independence Day weekend, Columbus Day weekend, Thanksgiving weekend, and the week between Christmas and New Year's Day. It's possible that Disney may extend this practice to any period when demand for resort rooms is particularly high (or low), such as during a major convention or special event. You can learn the nightly rate for a given time period by calling Disney at 407-939-6244 or going online at http://www.disneyworld.com.

Choosing a Package

Disney's vacation packages offer the promise of peace of mind and luxury. Package rates may be lower than the list price for each component, but may include more components than you can possibly use. A good number of veteran vacationers tell us they love these packages! Note that everyone in your room must be on the same package and plan. For more information and reservations, ask your travel agent, call 407-939-6244, or visit http://www.disneyworld.com. Below are the 2013 packages:

Magic Your Way Basic Package—Get one or more nights at a Disney resort; an upgradeable Magic Your Way Base Ticket (see page 122); 100-point arcade game card; $15 Planet Hollywood certificate and souvenir keepsake; a free round of miniature golf; 15% off Niki Bryan spa treatments, boat rentals, bass fishing, and select childcare centers; 10% off Sammy Duvall's water sports; and one luggage tag/person. Three-night package starting at $143/adult (based on double occupancy).

Magic Your Way Quick Service Dining Plan—Everything in the basic package plus two meals at participating quick-service eateries (see page 223) and one snack per day, and one refillable drink mug/person. About $37/adult, $13/child per night above basic package.

Magic Your Way Dining Plan—Everything in the basic package above plus one resort refillable drink mug/person and dining at more than 100 participating Disney table-service restaurants* (see pages 223-225 for dining plan details). About $55-$57/adult or $16-$17/child per night above basic package cost.

Magic Your Way Deluxe Dining Plan—Everything in the above package, except you get three dining credits (good at table-service or counter-service) and two snack credits, plus one refillable mug/person. About $91-$95/adult or $24-$27/child per night above basic package cost.

Magic Your Way Premium Package—Everything in the basic package, plus breakfast, lunch, and dinner at more than 100 participating restaurants,* unlimited recreation, unlimited admission to Disney childcare clubs, Cirque du Soleil tickets, PhotoPass portrait session, preferred fireworks viewing, and unlimited admission to selected theme park tours**. About $168/adult or $119/child per night above basic package cost.

Magic Your Way Platinum Package—Everything in the premium package listed above, but you can eat at any Disney eatery, including Victoria & Albert's (premium menu only), character meals, and dinner shows. You also receive two "magical evenings"—reserved seating at one showing of Fantasmic! and one fireworks cruise. Additional benefits include one selected spa treatment, a specially created keepsake, and itinerary planning services. About $229/adult or $160/child per night above basic package cost.

Magic Your Way Wine and Dine Plan is no longer offered.

Annual Passholder Package with Dining—Annual passholders can purchase packages that include lodging (which may or may not be discounted) and the Quick Service Dining Plan, the standard Dining Plan, and/or the Deluxe Dining Plan.

* Participating Disney restaurants include all restaurants described in chapter 5 (see pages 221-270) **except the following eateries, which are excluded**: Victoria & Albert's (Grand Floridian); Bistro de Paris (Epcot); Rainforest Cafe (Animal Kingdom); Ghirardelli, Rainforest Cafe, T-Rex, Wolfgang Puck Dining Room, Fulton's Crab House, Portobello, Bongos, House of Blues, and Wetzel's Pretzels (Downtown Disney). Note that this list is subject to change at any time—be sure to check with Disney before making plans. Kids ages 3-9 must order off the children's menu when available. Dining Plan credits may also be used for in-room private dining.

** Selected theme park tours include all tours described on pages 272-273 except Mickey's Magical Milestones, Keep Moving Forward, Backstage Magic, and VIP Tours.

Resort Key

Resort Locations—The Disney resorts described in your PassPorter are all located within minutes of the theme parks. We organize them into four areas: Magic Kingdom, Downtown Disney, Epcot, and Disney's Animal Kingdom (use the map on the inside back cover for reference). Each resort's area is identified in its description. You can also use the blue "stamps" at the top of each page to locate all resorts in a neighborhood.

Room Locations—Room locations, such as a building or room number, can be requested, but are not guaranteed. However, if you note your preferences when you make your reservation, via phone about three days before arrival, and again when you check in, there is a chance you will get the room you want. Resort maps and suggestions are given for each resort in this chapter. If you don't like the particular room you've been assigned, do as you would with any hotel and politely ask for another.

Room Occupancy—All resorts have rooms that hold at least four guests, plus one child under 3 in a crib. Port Orleans Riverside (Alligator Bayou) rooms allow up to five guests with an optional trundle bed for a child. Many of the deluxe resorts have a day bed. Ft. Wilderness Cabins, All-Star Music family suites, and Art of Animation suites allow up to six. Treehouse Villas at Saratoga Springs and the two-bedroom villas in Disney's Deluxe Villa Resorts allow up to nine, and Grand Villas allow up to 12. There is an extra charge of $2–$25 per adult for more than two adults in a single room, except at Disney's Deluxe Villa Resorts.

Amenities—All rooms have the basics: television with remote control, phone, drawers, clothing rod with hangers, small table, and chairs, as well as simple toiletries. **Tip:** If your room doesn't have a coffeemaker or iron/ironing board, request it from housekeeping.

Check-In Time—Check-in time is 3:00 pm or 4:00 pm (varies by resort), although rooms may be available earlier (inquire upon your arrival). You can also check-in online at http://www.disneyworld.com within 10 days of your arrival! If you arrive early (as early as 8:00 am) and your room is not ready, you can register, leave your luggage, and go play in the parks while your room is being prepared. Tip: You can request a voice or text message be sent to your cell phone—ask about this Mobile Room Ready Notification service when you check-in!

Check-Out Time—Check-out time is 11:00 am. If you need to check out an hour or two later (up to 1:00 pm), ask the Front Desk the morning of check-out. If the resort isn't busy, they may grant your request at no extra cost. Extended check-out may also be available for an extra fee. You can also leave your bags with Bell Services and go play in the parks.

Childcare—Children's childcare "clubs" for ages 3–12 are available in many of the deluxe resorts (refer to the chart on page 29). In-room sitting is also available. Fees apply to all childcare. See pages 284–285 for details and opinions on childcare.

Concierge—Not to be confused with Lobby Concierge (see page 35), all of the deluxe resorts offer concierge services with extra perks like a continental breakfast, afternoon snacks, and planning services. Concierge services are associated with certain rooms (often on the higher floors) that come at a higher rate. Also known as Club Level service.

Convention Centers—Several resort hotels are popular among convention-goers due to their excellent facilities, including the BoardWalk, Contemporary, Coronado Springs, Grand Floridian, Swan, Dolphin, and Yacht Club. For more details on convention facilities, call 407-828-3200. Business Centers are available at each of the above resorts.

Data Services (Internet)—All Disney resorts have free w-fi available in guest rooms and some public areas. Fort Wilderness has free wired Internet access. If you need technical support, call 407-827-2732 or 407-938-4357. The front desk will also receive and send your faxes for a fee.

Planning | Getting There | Staying in Style | Touring | Feasting | Making Magic | Index | Notes & More

Resort Key: Disabled Access to Information

Disabled Access—All resorts offer accommodations and access for differently abled guests. For details and reservations, call Disney's Special Requests Department at 407-939-7807 (voice) or 407-939-7670 (TTY). Be sure to ask that "Special Needs" be noted on your reservation. See page 29 for the number of barrier-free rooms at each resort.

Extra Magic Hours—Guests at Disney resorts and the Swan, Dolphin, Shades of Green, and Downtown Disney Hilton can enter the parks up to one hour earlier or stay two hours later. Disney resort ID (room key) is required for entry, along with a valid admission. Only certain parks and attractions are open for Extra Magic Hours on any given day, however. The schedule changes from week to week (check http://www.disneyworld.com for the schedule during your visit), but here's a sample Extra Magic Hour schedule:

	Sunday	Monday	Tuesday	Wednesday	Thursday	Friday	Saturday
am	none	Animal Kingdom	Epcot	none	Magic Kingdom	none	Disney's Hollywood Studios
pm	Magic Kingdom	Disney's Hollywood Studios	none	Animal Kingdom	none	Epcot	none

Extra Magic Hour Attractions (underlined attractions are open only during evening Extra Magic Hours)—In the **Magic Kingdom**, this usually includes Space Mountain, Buzz Lightyear's Space Ranger Spin, Big Thunder Mountain, Stitch's Great Escape, Tomorrowland Indy Speedway, Haunted Mansion, Pirates of the Caribbean, Splash Mountain, Magic Carpets of Aladdin, and most of Fantasyland. **Epcot** opens Soarin', Mission: SPACE, Spaceship Earth, Test Track, The Seas With Nemo & Friends, Journey Into Imagination, "Honey, I Shrunk the Audience," Living with the Land, Gran Fiesta Tour Starring The Three Caballeros, American Adventure, and Maelstrom. **Disney's Hollywood Studios** opens Rock 'n' Roller Coaster, Tower of Terror, Star Tours, Muppet*Vision 3-D, The Great Movie Ride, Voyage of the Little Mermaid, and Toy Story Midway Mania. **Disney's Animal Kingdom** opens Expedition Everest, It's Tough to be a Bug!, Kali River Rapids, Festival of the Lion King, Dinosaur, TriceraTop Spin, Primeval Whirl, The Boneyard, Pangani Forest Exploration Trail, and Kilimanjaro Safaris. Attractions are subject to change.

Food—Every resort has places to eat, such as food courts, cafes, fine dining, and room service. All resort eateries are noted in each resort's dining section later in this chapter. Details on the table-service restaurants start on page 230. If you are looking for snacks or groceries, each resort has a store with a small selection of food and drinks. No gum is sold on property. Special dietary requests can be made (see page 228).

Housekeeping Services—Every Disney resort has daily "mousekeeping" services and will happily provide you with extra towels, pillows, and blankets upon request, as well as a hair dryer, iron, and ironing board. If you require extra toiletries, just ask for them. For tipping suggestions, see page 36. Note: Disney's Deluxe Villa Resorts provide reduced services to DVC members using their points.

Ice and Soda—All resorts have ice machines within easy walking distance. Most, but not all, also have soda machines. The rule seems to be the more plush the resort, the harder it is to find a soda machine. If soda is important, pick up some before you arrive (it's cheaper anyway). Another option is to purchase a refillable souvenir mug (offered at most resorts) for free (or low-cost) refills of soda, coffee, tea, and cocoa at your resort—see page 36.

Information—Check the Walt Disney World information channels on your in-room TV. These channels are available at every resort and offer a nice introduction for newcomers, plus a peek at what's new. You can touch "0" on any resort phone for more information.

Resort Key: Laundry to Recreation

Laundry—Every resort has either coin-operated/coinless machines in a laundry room near the pool (expect to pay at least $2/load) or a washer and dryer in your room. **Tip**: Most of Disney's Deluxe Villa resorts offer complimentary self-service laundry facilities (no coins needed). Laundry bags and forms are available in your resort room for same-day service (it's very expensive). **Tip**: Store your dirty laundry in the laundry bags.

Lobby Concierge—Each resort has a Lobby Concierge desk near the registration desk where you can buy park passes, make dining reservations, and find answers.

Mail and Packages—Purchase stamps in the resort shops; mail can be dropped off at Lobby Concierge or placed in mailboxes. Federal Express also picks up and drops off packages. A full-service Post Office is at the Shoppes at Lake Buena Vista at 12133 Apopka-Vineland Rd., about one mile north of the Crossroads Shopping Center.

Merchandise Delivery—Resort guests staying on Disney property can have park and Downtown Disney purchases delivered free to their resort, usually by the next afternoon or the day after. Inquire before your purchase is rung up. Your package is delivered to your resort's gift shop or front desk for pick-up, not your room (unless you're in concierge).

Money—Cash, Disney Dollars and Gift Cards, traveler's checks, MasterCard, Visa, American Express, Discover, Diner's Club, and JCB are accepted. Personal checks are accepted only at the resort where you are a guest. ATMs are near the front desk. Make your room deposit over the phone, Internet, or fax with the above credit cards or by mail with a credit card or check.

Parking—Secured, free, gated parking lots are available at all Disney resorts. The deluxe resorts also offer valet ($10/day, free to those with handicap parking permit/tags); Swan & Dolphin valet is $16/day. Show your resort ID or confirmation at the security gate—parking is reserved for resort guests and those using a resort's restaurants or recreation.

Pets—Pets are not allowed in the parks or resorts (except for a few campsites at Fort Wilderness—see page 67) unless you travel with a companion (service) animal. You may board your pet for the day or overnight at the Best Friends Pet Care resort, located across from Port Orleans Resort. Daycare fees are $16-$69, while overnight boarding is $21-$69/night per animal for Disney resort hotel guests ($23-$76/night for non-Disney resort hotel guests). The pet resort can accommodate dogs, cats, and "pocket pets" (anything that's not a dog, a cat, a primate, or venomous). Special features and upgrades include bedtime stories, private dog park, grooming, and more. Get details and make reservations at 877-4-WDW-PETS (877-493-9738) or http://wdw.bestfriendspetcare.com.

Pools—Every Disney resort has at least one swimming pool. Hours vary, but usually the "themed" pools close in the evenings while the "leisure" pools may stay open all night. Only guests staying at a resort can use its pool, though some resorts share pools and Disney Vacation Club members using their points have access to all but Stormalong Bay, Bay Cove Pool, and the pools at Disney's Animal Kingdom Lodge (unless they are staying there).

Preferred Rooms—Disney's value and moderate resorts offer preferred rooms with better locations and higher rates.

Recreation—Every resort has something to do, with many offering a wide variety of outdoor activities. You can visit another resort to use its recreational facilities (with the exception of swimming pools). Be sure to note the operating hours upon arrival or by phoning ahead.

© MediaMarx, Inc.

A themed pool

Resort Key: Refillable Mugs to Voice Mail

Refillable Mugs—All resorts sell thermal mugs that can be refilled free for the length of your stay at the resort in which you purchased the mug. If you drink a lot of soda, tea, coffee, or hot chocolate, these are a blessing—and they make fun souvenirs. Mugs are $14.49 + tax and can be refilled at a resort's food court or snack shop. In 2011, Disney tested a drink station that would only dispense drinks for mugs that have active RFID chips, but no word on if it will be implemented. Neither milk nor juice is a refill option unless it appears on the soda fountain.

Refillable mugs

Refrigerators—In-room refrigerators are provided free in Disney's deluxe, moderate, and value resorts. In most cases, these are mini-fridges, without a freezer. One-bedroom and larger Disney Vacation Club villas and Fort Wilderness cabins have full-size refrigerators.

Room Service—The deluxe resorts and some of the moderate resorts offer in-room dining. Most resorts offer a pizza delivery service in the afternoon and evenings.

Security—A gatehouse guards entry into every resort. If you arrive by car, plan to show your resort ID or photo ID and explain that you are checking in, dining, or using the resort's recreational facilities. All resort rooms have electronic locks that open with your resort ID for added security. In addition, you can store small valuables in your in-room safe (most, though not all, rooms have them) or with the front desk.

Smoking—All Disney resort guest rooms (including patios/balconies) are now nonsmoking. Designated outdoor smoking areas are indicated on resort maps.

Spa—Disney-speak for a hot tub. There's at least one spa at every Disney resort, with the exception of the All-Stars, Polynesian, and Pop Century. Traditional spa facilities (massages and manicures) are available in some resorts.

Tax—Sales tax is 6.5% in Orange County (most of Walt Disney World) and 7% in Osceola County (Pop Century, Art of Animation, and some parts of All-Star Resorts); sales tax is charged on all purchases and lodging. An additional lodging tax is 6% in both Orange and Osceola Counties.

Telephones—All rooms have a phone and information on how to use it. Local and toll-free calls are free; long-distance calls are the cost of the call plus a 50% surcharge. Use calling cards or cell phones instead. Incoming calls are free.

Turndown—Available at the deluxe resorts—request it from housekeeping.

Tipping—It's customary to tip valet parking attendants $1–$2 upon arrival and departure, bell services $1–$2/bag upon delivery and pick-up, and housekeeping $1/person/day. **Tip:** Leave your housekeeping tip daily with the housekeeper's name card so it's recognized.

Transportation—Every resort provides free transit to and from the parks via bus, boat, monorail, and/or pathway. We list each resort's options and in-transit times in this chapter.

Wheelchairs—You can borrow a wheelchair from any resort (inquire at Bell Services). A deposit may be required; availability is limited. Motorized wheelchairs (ECVs) may be rented at the parks for in-park-only use. You can rent ECVs at the BoardWalk Resort for use anywhere from Buena Vista Scooters (866-484-4797, http://www.buenavistascooters.com)—they also deliver to resorts. Other sources are Care Medical (800-741-2282–http://caremedicalequipment.com) and Walker Mobility (888-726-6837–http://walkermobility.com).

Voice Mail—Every resort offers free voice mail that can be retrieved from your room or any other phone in or outside of the Walt Disney World Resort. You can even personalize the message callers hear when they are connected to your room. If you are on the phone when a call comes in, the voice mail system still takes your caller's message.

Top Photo Slice: Turndown at an Animal Kingdom Lodge room (①3256) © Melissa Loflin

Disney's All-Star Resorts

Both economical and magical, the All-Star Resorts bring movies, music, and sports to life in three independent yet connected resort hotels. The All-Star Movies, All-Star Music, and All-Star Sports Resorts are located near Disney's Animal Kingdom theme park and the Blizzard Beach water park (use the blue tab at the top of the page for parks and eateries in the vicinity).

AMBIENCE

A star-studded production awaits you at the All-Star Resorts. From the painted stars everywhere you look to the autographed photos of famous celebrities lining the lobby walls, each resort greets you as a star in its **main hall**—Cinema Hall in All-Star Movies, Melody Hall in All-Star Music, and Stadium Hall in All-Star Sports. The halls house the registration desks, food courts, general stores, and arcades. Outside, the stars give way to larger-than-life movie, music, and sports icons, such as a towering Buzz Lightyear, a four-story-high conga drum, and a Coke cup that could hold 240 million ounces. Music plays in the background, providing you with an ever-changing soundtrack as you stroll through the grounds.

RESORT LAYOUT & ROOMS

The 5,568 guest rooms (1,728–1,920 in each resort) are situated in 15 differently themed areas encompassing a total of 30 buildings. **All-Star Movies Resort** showcases 101 Dalmatians, Fantasia and Fantasia 2000, The Love Bug, Toy Story, and Mighty Ducks; **All-Star Music Resort** features Calypso, Jazz Inn, Rock Inn, Country Fair, and Broadway; and **All-Star Sports Resort** sports Surf's Up!, Hoops Hotel, Center Court, Touchdown!, and Home Run Hotel. Each of the 15 areas features a themed courtyard flanked by two of the T-shaped buildings. The energetic and colorful themes are echoed in the guest rooms, with themed bedspreads, drapes, wallpaper, and a vanity area with one sink. Standard rooms have either two double beds or one king bed, a TV, a small table with two chairs, and drawers. Rooms with king-size beds are also the barrier-free rooms; thus, some of these rooms have only showers (no tubs). Rooms are small—260 sq. feet—but we find them adequate with the simple furnishings. 192 Family Suites are also available in All-Star Music—see page 39. No private balconies or patios, but each room has individual climate controls.

Standard Room Layout

Family Suite Layout

Double

Double

Queen

Sleeper chair and ottoman

Sleeper Sofa

Staying in Style · Planning · Getting There · Touring · Feasting · Making Magic · Index · Notes & More

Planning

Getting There

Staying in Style

Touring

Feasting

Making Magic

Index

Notes & More

Using the Amenities at Disney's All-Star Resorts

EATING & DRINKING

Food courts: World Premiere (Movies), Intermission (Music), and End Zone (Sports), each with four food stations plus a snack shop. Breakfast (6:00 am to 11:00 am) menu items typically include a Breakfast Platter for $8.29, a Western omelet for $7.29, and Mickey waffles for $5.69. Lunch and dinner (11:00 am to midnight) items include an individual pepperoni pizza for $6.09, chicken nuggets for $7.89, a taco salad for $7.69, a bacon cheeseburger for $8.79, and child meals for $4.99. Souvenir mugs ($14.49) offer unlimited soft drink refills. **Pizza delivery** is from 4:00 pm to midnight. **Walk-up bars** are at each food court and main pool.

© MediaMarx, Inc.

Family Suite at All-Star Music
500+ more photos at http://www.passporter.com/photos

PLAYING & RELAXING

For Athletes: Well-marked paths are ideal for walks and jogs.
For Children: Quiet playgrounds are located within each resort (locations vary—see map on page 40 for playground locations).
For Gamers: Each resort's main hall has an arcade—some games reward players with tickets that can be redeemed for small prizes.
For Shoppers: Donald's Double Feature (Movies), Maestro Mickey's (Music), and Sport Goofy (Sports) offer gifts and sundries.
For Swimmers: Each resort offers a main pool and a smaller pool. Movies' main pool conjures up the fun of Fantasia, Music's main pool is in the shape of a guitar, and Sports' main pool is styled after a surfing lagoon. All main pools have children's wading pools nearby.

GETTING ABOUT

Buses (see chart below for in-transit times) are found outside the main halls in each resort. Stops are well-marked and offer benches. We find the bus service efficient, but some guests complain of waiting too long. Destinations other than those below can be reached by changing buses at Disney's Animal Kingdom (daytime) or Downtown Disney (evening). Guests may find a car useful at this resort, and ample parking is freely available around the resort.

Magic Kingdom	Epcot	Disney's Hollywood Studios	Disney's Animal Kingdom	Downtown Disney
direct bus ~20 min.	direct bus ~10 min.	direct bus ~10 min.	direct bus ~10 min.	direct bus ~15 min.

Approximate time you will spend in transit from resort to destination during normal operation.

Top Photo Slice: The Calypso Pool at Disney's All-Star Music Resort © MediaMarx, Inc.

Making the Most of Disney's All-Star Resorts

All-Star Music boasts **192 "Family Suites"** (see photo on previous page). These 520 sq. ft. rooms sport two full bathrooms, a kitchenette, a queen bed, a full sofa bed, and two convertible twin beds. Each suite sleeps up to 6 people, plus one child under 3 in a crib. We love them!

Walk around the resorts to catch all the neat props and details that make these resorts so fun. Even the walkways have fun designs.

If you need an escape from the activity of the All-Stars, look for the **quiet spots** around the resorts. Relax in a hammock behind a stand of palm trees in Fantasia at All-Star Movies, or try the picnic tables in Country Fair's courtyard in All-Star Music for a leisurely lunch.

Watch for **activities and movies** at the main pools in the evenings!

Mini-refrigerators without freezers are included in all rooms and suites at no extra charge.

Plan to either carry your own luggage or wait a while (often 45–60 minutes) for their **luggage assistance service** to drop it off at your building. Unlike other Disney resorts, luggage is delivered at their convenience, not yours. Arrangements to pick up luggage on your departure day should be made the night before. You can borrow a luggage cart from the luggage assistance desk in the main hall, and you may need to leave your ID while you use the cart.

Toiletries are limited to a bar of facial soap at the sink and bath soap and shampoo in the shower/tub. You may want to bring your own.

Towels are not provided near the pools, so bring your own or use your room **towels**. Contact housekeeping for extra towels.

Check-in time is 4:00 pm. Check-out time is 11:00 am.

Ratings are explained on page 28.

Our Value Ratings:		Our Magic Ratings:		Readers' Ratings:
Quality:	6/10	Theme:	6/10	42% fell in love with it
Accessibility:	5/10	Amenities:	4/10	35% liked it well enough
Affordability:	9/10	Fun Factor:	2/10	12% had mixed feelings
Overall Value:	**7/10**	**Overall Magic:**	**4/10**	11% were disappointed

The All-Stars are enjoyed by...		(rated by both authors and readers)	
Younger Kids: ♥♥♥♥♥	Young Adults: ♥♥♥♥	Families: ♥♥♥♥
Older Kids: ♥♥♥♥♥	Mid Adults: ♥♥♥	Couples: ♥♥
Teenagers: ♥♥♥	Mature Adults: ♥♥	Singles: ♥♥♥

Sidebar tabs: Planning / Getting There / Staying in Style / Touring / Feasting / Making Magic / Index / Notes & More / TIPS / NOTES / RATINGS

ALL-STAR RESORT MAP

Finding Your Place at Disney's All-Star Resorts

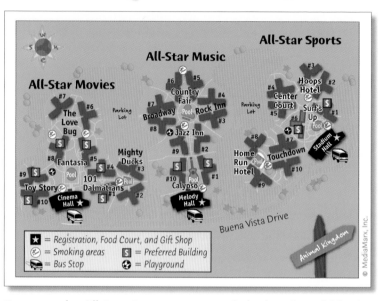

© MediaMarx, Inc.

BEST LOCATIONS

Rooms at the All-Star Resorts vary mostly by location within the resorts and floor. For convenience, we recommend **101 Dalmatians**, **Fantasia**, or **Toy Story** (at All-Star Movies), **Calypso** (at All-Star Music), and **Surf's Up!** (at All-Star Sports)—they are closest to the main pools, food, and transportation. Our personal preferences are **Fantasia** (at All-Star Movies), **Country Fair** (at All-Star Music), and **Home Run Hotel** (at All-Star Sports) as they are relatively quiet and have good views from most windows—the latter two are a good distance from the main hall, however. Quieter rooms are those that face away from the pools and are on the **top floor**.

RATES

2013 Sample Room Rates
Seasons are noted on page 14.

Room Type	Value	Fall	Regular	Summer	Peak	Holiday
Standard	$85–$99	$98–$118	$109–$134	$133–$158	$135–$165	$169–$176
Preferred	$101–$115	$114–$134	$132–$157	$149–$174	$151–$181	$184–$192
Family Suites	$202–$226	$224–$243	$259–$304	$305–$355	$309–$364	$375

13% tax not included in above rates. Preferred rooms are Fantasia, Toy Story, 101 Dalmatians, Calypso, and Surf's Up. Higher rate ranges are for weekend and holiday periods.

INFO

Disney's All-Star Movies/Music/Sports Resorts
✉ 1901/1801/1701 W. Buena Vista Dr., Lake Buena Vista, FL 32830
☎ Phone: 407-939-7000/407-939-6000/407-939-5000
✎ Fax: 407-939-7111/407-939-7222/407-939-7333
📋 For reservations, call Central Reservations: 407-939-6244

Disney's Animal Kingdom Lodge & Villas Resort

Disney's Animal Kingdom Lodge and Villas share the ambience of its neighboring park, Disney's Animal Kingdom (use the blue tab at the top of the page for nearby parks/eateries). Guests at this deluxe resort can watch grazing wildlife on 44+ acres of African savanna from their balconies.

AMBIENCE

Your trek is rewarded as soon as you step into the lobbies of the two Lodge buildings, **Jambo House** and **Kidani Village**, which offer dramatic views to the animal reserves and "kopje" (rock outcrops) beyond. Sunlight pours in through high windows, painting the lobby's thatched ceiling and carved wooden decorations in a warm, intimate glow. African artwork greets you at every turn. Designed by the architect behind Disney's Wilderness Lodge, the hotel shares its sister resort's **rustic appeal**, but adds a welcome warmth and intimacy. Then, of course, there are the animals, which add a sense of delight unique to this resort.

LAYOUT & ROOMS

Standard Room Layout

Two **horseshoe-shaped buildings**, inspired by African Kraal (corral) villages, give most rooms a view of the private wildlife reserve. Rooms feature hand-carved furniture, gauze hangings at the head of the beds, and Kente-inspired fabrics. Standard rooms (344 sq. ft.) have two queen beds; one king bed and a daybed; or one queen bed and bunk beds. See page 43 for more details on the deluxe villas here. All rooms have a balcony, ceiling fan, table and chairs, refrigerator, coffeemaker, armoire with TV and drawers, double sinks, in-room safe, iron and ironing board, hair dryer, voice mail, and newspaper delivery.

DINING

A casual yet upscale restaurant, **Jiko**, is open for guests who want an elegantly inventive dinner. **Boma**, which means "place of refuge," offers an exciting, African-flavored dining adventure with all-you-care-to-eat buffets at breakfast and dinner. **The Mara** is a quick-service cafe open all day—typical menu items include a croissant sandwich ($5.99), a breakfast platter ($6.79), a kid's breakfast ($4.99), African stew ($7.99), chicken Caesar salad ($7.79), and chicken flatbread ($8.79). Refillable mugs ($14.49) can be purchased at The Mara. **Sanaa** is a full-service restaurant over at Kidani Village serving lunch and dinner. Room service is also available. The table-service restaurants are reviewed on page 253.

Top Photo Slice: Disney's Animal Kingdom Lodge © MediaMarx, Inc.

Genuine PassPorter   Genuine PassPorter   Genuine PassPorter   Genuine PassPorter   Genuine PassPorter   Genuine PassPorter   Genuine PassPorter   Genuine

Using the Amenities at Disney's Animal Kingdom Lodge Resort

LOUNGING

Victoria Falls Lounge, which overlooks Boma, serves coffees, African wines, and beer. The **Cape Town Lounge and Wine Bar**, inside Jiko, serves great wines from South Africa. A small lounge is also near **Sanaa. Uzima Springs** and **Maji** are poolside bars offering beer and mixed drinks. Snacks, beer, and wine are at the **Zawadi Marketplace**, **The Mara**, and **Johari Treasures**.

©2021 © Elizabeth Ferris

Sunrise on Animal Kingdom Lodge
More photos at http://www.passporter.com/photos

PLAYING & RELAXING

For Animal Watchers: Bring plenty of film/memory cards for your camera—you may also want a tripod. Binoculars are handy, too.
For Athletes: Keep in shape in the Zahanati and Survival of the Fittest Fitness Centers near the pools. Massage treatments are also offered. There is also a jogging path between the buildings.
For Children: Simba's Cubhouse is a supervised club (see page 284). There are also the Hakuna Matata and Uwanja Camp playgrounds, storytelling at the fire pit, and daily activities at Boma.
For Gamers: Pumbaa's Fun and Games and Safari So Good Arcade.
For Shoppers: The festive Zawadi Marketplace and Johari Treasures have sundries, foodstuffs, books, clothing, and African crafts.
For Swimmers: Soak in the Uzima and Samawati Springs pools, and enjoy water slides (close at 10:00 pm), kids' pools, and four spas (hot tubs). Both pools feature zero-entry sections where you can wade into the water. A pool wheelchair is available.
For Tours: Inquire in advance about the Sunrise Safari (concierge only) and Sunset Safari (all welcome) experiences that tour the park savannas and include a breakfast at Tusker House or dinner at Jiko.

GETTING ABOUT

Buses to theme parks and Downtown Disney (see chart below for in-transit times) are a short walk out front of both buildings (see the map on page 44). Travel to other resorts via Disney's Animal Kingdom theme park (daytime) or Downtown Disney (evening). Ample parking is available, as is valet parking ($10/day). This is the only deluxe resort to lack boat or monorail access to a nearby park.

Magic Kingdom	Epcot	Disney's Hollywood Studios	Disney's Animal Kingdom	Downtown Disney
direct bus ~20 min.	direct bus ~15 min.	direct bus ~10 min.	direct bus ~7 min.	direct bus ~15 min.

Approximate time you will spend in transit from resort to destination during normal operation.

Top Photo Slice: Pond near the Samawati Springs Pool at Disney's Animal Kingdom Lodge © MediaMarx, Inc.

Making the Most of Disney's Animal Kingdom Lodge Resort

Disney Vacation Club has 134 studio and one-bedroom villas on the fifth and sixth floors of the original building ("Jambo House"), and Kidani Village has 324 studio, one-, two-, and three-bedroom villas, plus a full-service restaurant, savannas, pool, water play area, and a separate lobby area. Note that it is a 10-minute walk between the buildings, or you can take a bus (but it may take longer).

The Lodge has **44 acres of savanna**, which is distinct from the theme park, and is home to 36 species of mammals and 26 species of birds—more than 330 animals in all. Guests can see zebras, antelopes, giraffes, gazelle, wildebeests, ostriches, cranes, vultures, and storks. Animals may come within 15–30 feet from you, day or night. Each savanna has a few animal species that are unique to it. Each savanna closes daily for cleaning and animal care, but at least 2–3 savannas are always open. Best viewing times are typically early to mid-morning, and at dusk (ask about night-vision goggles).

African storytelling is held nightly around the firepit. "Safari guides" are also on hand to educate guests.

Tour the resort's **African art collection** on a free self-guided tour or a daily guided tour in the afternoons. Inquire at the front desk.

Four separate savannas (each about 11 acres) can be viewed 24 hours a day. If your room doesn't have a view of the savanna, **watch the animals** from the kopje (the large observation area that extends into the savanna), the Sunset Overlook (a delightful room in the Jambo House lobby), the overlook near the Uzima pool, and the alcoves along Zebra Trail and Kudu Trail (visit the second floor for outdoor viewing platforms that feature rocking chairs and binoculars).

Check-in is 3:00/4:00 pm. Check-out is 11:00 am. No late check-outs.

Ratings are explained on page 28.

Our Value Ratings:		Our Magic Ratings:		Readers' Ratings:
Quality:	9/10	Theme:	10/10	70% fell in love with it
Accessibility:	5/10	Amenities:	5/10	23% liked it well enough
Affordability:	6/10	Fun Factor:	8/10	7% had mixed feelings
Overall Value:	**6/10**	**Overall Magic:**	**8/10**	0% were disappointed

Disney's Animal Kingdom Lodge is enjoyed by... (rated by both authors and readers)		
Younger Kids: ♥♥♥♥♥	Young Adults: ♥♥♥♥	Families: ♥♥♥♥♥
Older Kids: ♥♥♥♥♥	Mid Adults: ♥♥♥♥♥	Couples: ♥♥♥
Teenagers: ♥♥♥	Mature Adults: ♥♥	Singles: ♥♥♥♥

Top Photo Slice: Giraffes on the savanna at Disney's Animal Kingdom Lodge (①13190) © David Latoundji

Finding Your Place
at Disney's Animal Kingdom Lodge Resort

ANIMAL KINGDOM LODGE MAP

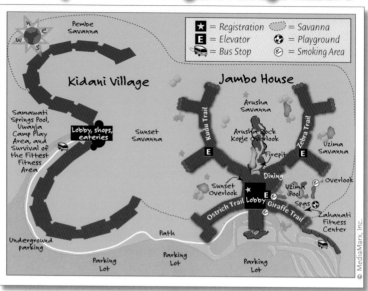

BEST LOCATIONS

At Jambo House, **standard rooms** are located on floors 1–4. Rooms come in three views: standard (Giraffe and Ostrich Trails), pool (Giraffe and Zebra Trails), and savanna (Zebra, Kudu, and Ostrich Trails). If animal-watching is your main draw, reserve a savanna-view room. Rooms on the far ends of the Zebra and Kudu Trails, and the far ends of Kidani Village, require a long walk. **Concierge rooms** (Jambo floor 5) are also available in pool and savanna views, as are several suites. **Villas** are located on floors 5 and 6 of Jambo House, also.

2013 Sample Room Rates
Seasons are noted on page 14.

Room Type	Value	Summer	Fall	Regular	Peak	Holiday
Standard View	$279–$299	$333	$316–$354	$340–$375	$407–$442	$486
Pool View	$290–$311	$344	$328–$367	$352–$388	$422–$458	$489
Savanna View	$358–$384	$422	$400–$448	$429–$473	$501–$544	$590
Concierge (Club)	$421–$450	$484	$463–$517	$482–$531	$578–$627	$654
Value Studio	$313–$320	$341	$326	$351	$428	$524
One-Bed. Savanna	$594–$610	$658	$623	$674	$775	$841

12.5% tax not included in above prices. Suites start in the high-$700s. Higher rates in price ranges are for weekends and holiday periods (see page 31).

Disney's Animal Kingdom Lodge & Villas Resort
✉ 2901 Osceola Parkway, Lake Buena Vista, FL 32830
☎ Phone: 407-938-4799   📠 Fax: 407-938-7102
📋 For reservations, call Central Reservations: 407-939-6244

More at ① animal-kingdom-lodge | animal-kingdom-lodge-villas | kidani-village

Disney's Art of Animation Resort

As the newest addition to Disney's resort collection, the Art of Animation Resort focuses on value-priced accommodations for families of up to 6 in a suite. Disney's Art of Animation is right across from Disney's Pop Century Resort in the Epcot area (use the blue tab at the top of the page for parks and eateries in the vicinity) on the northeast corner of Osceola Parkway and Victory Way. This new resort opened in May 2012.

Staying at Disney's Art of Animation Resort may be a bit like **stepping onto the screen** of your favorite Disney animated movies. Not unlike the All-Star and Pop Century resorts, the decor here is larger than life and vibrantly colored, reflecting the animated movies we all love. The resort features themed rooms and areas from four animated films: Finding Nemo, Cars, The Lion King, and The Little Mermaid. Look for Simba and friends on the African savannah, King Triton and Sebastian under the sea, Tow Mater and the Cozy Cone Motel, and Nemo and Marlin in their ocean home. The theme continues in the pools, play fountains, playgrounds, and food court!

Disney's Art of Animation Resort features 1,984 guest rooms and family suites. All rooms at this resort are themed after one of Disney's blockbuster animations—family suites are decorated in the style of The Lion King, Finding Nemo, and Cars; standard guest rooms have a Little Mermaid theme. The family suites feature a master bedroom with a queen bed, a living room with a double-size sleeper sofa and a double-size Inova "TableBed" (a table that converts into a bed), two full bathrooms, and a mini kitchen with small refrigerator, microwave, and coffeemaker. Standard guest rooms have either two double beds or one king bed, a TV, a small table with two chairs, and drawers. Rooms with king-size beds are also the barrier-free rooms; thus, some of these rooms have only showers (no tubs). Rooms are small—260 sq. feet for the standard guest rooms and about 525 sq. feet for family suites. There are no private balconies or patios, but each room has individual climate controls. Rooms have keyless entry; just wave your Key to the Word card near the pad.

Standard Room Layout

Family Suite Layout

AMBIENCE

RESORT LAYOUT & ROOMS

Planning | Getting There | Staying in Style | Touring | Feasting | Making Magic | Index | Notes & More

Planning

Getting There

Staying in Style

Touring

Feasting

Making Magic

Index

Notes & More

Using the Amenities at Disney's Art of Animation Resort

EATING & DRINKING

Art of Animation has a large food court called **Landscape of Flavors**, featuring a Mongolian grill and a design-your-own-burger station. It's open daily for breakfast, lunch, and dinner. Menu items include tandoori chicken ($9.99), pepperoni pizza ($9.49), and create your own smoothie ($5.49).

The chandelier in the Art of Animation main hall is made of concept art!
View more photos at http://www.passporter.com/photos

Purchase a mug for $14.49 for unlimited refills. A pizza delivery service is available in the afternoons and evenings, along with seasonal snack carts near the pool and beverages at The Drop Off pool bar in the Finding Nemo courtyard.

PLAYING & RELAXING

For Athletes: The 12' wide lakeside path is ideal for walks and jogs. The lake does not offer a marina.

For Children: Two quiet playgrounds and an interactive play fountain are here (see map on page 48 for locations).

For Gamers: The Pixel Play arcade is located in Animation Hall.

For Shoppers: The large Ink and Paint shop offers Disney logo merchandise, clothing, sundries, and some snack foods.

For Swimmers: Cool off in the large The Big Blue pool in the Finding Nemo courtyard (which also features a wading pool), and two smaller themed pools called the Flippin' Fins Pool (The Little Mermaid courtyard) and Cozy Cone Pool (Cars courtyard).

GETTING ABOUT

Buses (see chart below for in-transit times) are outside the main building of the resort. Stops are well-marked and offer benches and shelter. Bus service is prompt and efficient. Destinations other than those below can be reached by changing buses at Disney's Hollywood Studios or Epcot (daytime) or Downtown Disney (evening). Parking is freely available, though you should study the map to find the closest lot to your room.

Magic Kingdom	Epcot	Disney's Hollywood Studios	Disney's Animal Kingdom	Downtown Disney
direct bus ~25 min.	direct bus ~20 min.	direct bus ~15 min.	direct bus ~15 min.	direct bus ~20 min.

Approximate time you will spend in transit from resort to destination during normal operation.

Making the Most of Disney's Art of Animation Resort

Rooms at this resort have **"keyless" doors**. Guests need only to hold their Key to the World card near the door to unlock it (they even work if your key card is still in a PassHolder Pouch). Walt Disney World plans to retrofit all of its resorts with these locks by the end of 2013.

Originally, this resort was to be an extension of Disney's Pop Century Resort (see pages 81–84) representing the first half of the 20th century, and would have been known as the **Legendary Years**!

The **33-acre lake** beside this resort is an added perk for a value resort—the other value resorts have no ponds, lakes, or rivers. Frequent park benches line the path, and you can see huge, colorful icons at the Pop Century across the lake reflected in the water.

Wondering how you would sleep on the **Inova TableBed** in the family suites? It's really rather clever and space-saving! You can learn more at http://www.inovallc.com/cont_tablebed.html.

If you opt for a family suite and want a little **extra privacy** between sleeping quarters, you could try bringing a shower curtain and an extra-long tension-mounted shower rod. This should allow you to place a curtain between the room with the fold-down bed (table bed) and the sleeper sofa in the living room.

Epcot's **IllumiNations** fireworks is visible from some locations at this resort. Best views are from the northeast end.

Self-service laundries are located near each pool. Wash loads and dry cycles are $2.00 each.

Check-in time is 4:00 pm. Check-out time is 11:00 am.

Ratings are explained on page 28.

Our Value Ratings:		Our Magic Ratings:		Readers' Ratings:
Quality:	7/10	Theme:	6/10	65% fell in love with it
Accessibility:	5/10	Amenities:	4/10	22% liked it well enough
Affordability:	8/10	Fun Factor:	4/10	7% had mixed feelings
Overall Value:	**7/10**	**Overall Magic:**	**5/10**	6% were disappointed

Pop Century is enjoyed by...		(rated by both authors and readers)
Younger Kids: ♥♥♥♥♥	Young Adults: ♥♥♥F	amilies: ♥♥♥♥♥
Older Kids: ♥♥♥♥♥	Mid Adults: ♥♥♥	Couples: ♥♥
Teenagers: ♥♥♥♥	Mature Adults: ♥♥	Singles: ♥♥

Top Photo Slice: The "elephant graveyard" from The Lion King in an Art of Animation Courtyard (①37942) © Eddie Cabrera

Planning

Getting There

Staying in Style

Touring

Feasting

Making Magic

Index

Notes & More

Finding Your Place at Disney's Art of Animation Resort

ART OF ANIMATION RESORT MAP

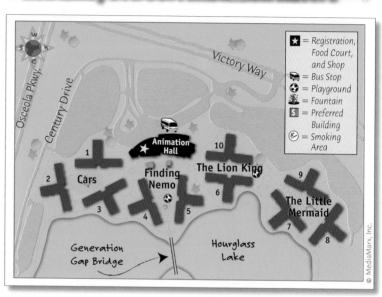

© MediaMarx, Inc.

BEST LOCATIONS

Much like other **value resorts**, the guest rooms and suites at Art of Animation differ mostly by proximity to Animation Hall and floor level. As always, if you seek a quieter room, request a room/suite on the third or fourth floors of a building. There are no preferred-rate buildings at this resort. Cars, Finding Nemo, and The Lion King house the family suites, while standard rooms fill The Little Mermaid. Thanks to the layout, however, no rooms are really a great distance from Animation Hall—only The Little Mermaid section seems "out there" and it really isn't that far. The layout here is very similar to Pop Century (see page 84).

RATES

2013 Sample Room Rates

Seasons are noted on page 14.

Room Type	Value	Fall	Regular	Summer	Peak	Holiday
Standard	$100-$114	$113-$133	$126-$151	$148-$173	$150-$180	$191
Family Suite	$252-$276	$269-$304	$309-$354	$348-$398	$359-$414	$433

12.5% tax is not included in above rates. There is a $10 per person charge for each additional adult in a room, but no extra charge for children under 18. Rooms may face parking lots, pools, the lake, or courtyards. Higher rates in price ranges are for weekends and holiday periods (see page 31).

INFO

Disney's Art of Animation Resort

✉ 1850 Century Drive, Lake Buena Vista, FL 32830

☎ Phone: 407-938-7000   📠 Fax: 407-938-4040

🗓 For reservations, call Central Reservations: 407-939-6244

Disney's BoardWalk Inn & Villas Resort

BoardWalk Inn & Villas Resort enjoys a favored location in the middle of the action, fronting Crescent Lake between Epcot and Disney's Hollywood Studios (use the blue tab at the top of the page for parks and eateries in the area). The Villas are affiliated with the Disney Vacation Club (see pages 108–109).

This **"seaside" resort** takes you back to the heyday of the Atlantic City Boardwalk in the 1920s and 1930s, where carefree days floated by on the summer breeze. Reminiscent of an elegant bed-and-breakfast inn, the BoardWalk continues this impression inside with its old-fashioned furnishings and soft, muted colors. Outside, a stroll along the vibrant promenade offers great views, family fun, and more eateries, clubs, and shops than you can visit.

The two different sides of this resort offer varying accommodations, ranging from 359 to 2,142 sq. ft. **BoardWalk Inn** has 378 rooms with one king or two queens plus a daybed or queen sofa bed, and suites. **BoardWalk Villas** feature 532 studios and one-, two-, and three-bedroom villas (suites)—studios have a kitchenette, suites have a full kitchen, big-screen TV, DVD player, and washer/dryer. All rooms in the resort have a balcony or patio, double sinks, a marble vanity, a table and chairs, a sofa, an armoire, TV, ceiling fan, toiletries, and a hair dryer. Also available are housekeeping, turndown service (on request), voice mail, and, in most rooms, an in-room safe.

Standard Room Layout (Inn)

Unique to this resort is a lively entertainment complex along the waterfront promenade. This innovative mini-park offers a variety of dining options. BoardWalk table-service restaurants, detailed on page 254, include **Big River Grille & Brewing Works**, a modern brewpub; **ESPN Club**, an All-American sports cafe; **Flying Fish Cafe**, fine dining with an ever-changing menu; and **Kouzzina by Cat Cora** features Greek cuisine. The **Belle Vue Room** offers a quick bite in the mornings. Two quick-service cafes round out the menu. **BoardWalk Bakery** tempts you with baked goods and coffee—try the chocolate croissant ($2.79), bacon, egg & cheese croissant ($5.99), or a Lunch Bag (sandwich plus salad or chips for $8.09). **Seashore Sweets** offers ice cream, cookies, fudge, saltwater taffy, and coffees.

Looking for the Beach Club and Villas? See pages 99–103.

Planning · Getting There · Staying in Style · Touring · Feasting · Making Magic · Index · Notes & More

AMBIENCE · LAYOUT & ROOMS · DINING

Using the Amenities at Disney's BoardWalk Inn & Villas Resort

LOUNGING

The BoardWalk is rich with lounges and clubs. **Atlantic Dance Hall** and **Jellyrolls** (see page 214) serve up drinks and fun. In the resort itself is the **Belle Vue Room**, perfect for a quiet drink and a game of chess. **Leaping Horse Libations** is the pool bar near Luna Park. 24-hour room service is also available.

The BoardWalk is beautiful at night

350+ more photos at http://www.passporter.com/photos

PLAYING & RELAXING

For Athletes: Muscles and Bustles Fitness is a fitness center with exercise equipment, steam room, sauna, and massage therapies (for an extra fee). Rent bikes at Community Hall (the resort's recreation center) and surrey bikes on the BoardWalk. There are also two lighted tennis courts and a walking/jogging circuit around Crescent Lake and along the path to Disney's Hollywood Studios.

For Children: A playground and wading pool is at Luna Park. Harbor Club kids' care club is closed—see other options on page 284–285.

For Gamers: Side Show Games Arcade has video games. Rent DVDs at Community Hall (free to DVC members, $5 for guests).

For Shoppers: Dundy's Sundries and Screen Door General Store offer the basics, while Thimbles & Threads and Disney's Character Carnival stock apparel and gifts. Wyland Galleries has collectibles.

For Swimmers: Of the three pools, the largest is Luna Park with a 200-ft. "wooden coaster" slide. All pools have spas (hot tubs).

GETTING ABOUT

Buses are boarded in the front of the resort, while **boats** depart from the marina (see the chart below for in-transit times). Travel elsewhere via a park (daytime) or Downtown Disney (evening). You can **walk** to Disney's Hollywood Studios, Epcot, Yacht & Beach Club, and Swan & Dolphin. If you miss the Disney's Hollywood Studios boat, just walk quickly to the Swan & Dolphin boat dock before your missed boat reaches it and hop on. Valet parking is a $10/day option.

Magic Kingdom	Epcot	Disney's Hollywood Studios	Disney's Animal Kingdom	Downtown Disney
direct bus ~20 min.	walk/boat ~10/~5 min.	walk/boat ~15/~20 min.	direct bus ~10 min.	direct bus ~15 min.

Approximate time you will spend in transit from resort to destination during normal operation.

Top Photo Slice: The coaster slide at BoardWalk Resort's Luna Park © MediaMarx, Inc.

Making the Most of Disney's BoardWalk Inn & Villas Resort

The guest rooms at BoardWalk Inn were last **refurbished** in 2010.

The **Belle Vue Room** is a marvel of nostalgia. It's tucked away in a corner down the hall from the lobby on the Inn side of the resort. You'll find backgammon, chess, and checkers tables (ask a cast member for game pieces), as well as a single-malt scotch menu.

Take a stroll through the grounds, away from the busy Promenade. The **landscaping** is a delight. If you prefer the bustle of the BoardWalk, rent a **surrey bike** and tour around the promenade and lake.

The BoardWalk Inn's **Garden Suites** have to be the most romantic in the "World." Each of the 14 suites looks like a two-story cottage. All suites have private entrances and most have a unique garden surrounded by a white picket fence with a trellised arbor gate. Suites have a separate living room, sleeper sofa, and a wet bar on the first floor, while the open second floor has a king-size bed, a separate shower, and a large whirlpool tub.

Look for several quaint **sitting areas** scattered about the resort.

Guests with rooms in the **small courtyard building** on the Inn side must use their room key to enter the building itself.

Noise and **light** levels are important considerations here due to the proximity of the BoardWalk Promenade. If these are concerns, request a room away from both the promenade and the pools.

Conference facilities are available at the BoardWalk.

Check-in time is 3:00 pm (BoardWalk Inn) or 4:00 pm (BoardWalk Villas). Check-out time is 11:00 am for both.

Ratings are explained on page 28.

Our Value Ratings:		Our Magic Ratings:		Readers' Ratings:
Quality:	9/10	Theme:	8/10	72% fell in love with it
Accessibility:	7/10	Amenities:	8/10	17% liked it well enough
Affordability:	3/10	Fun Factor:	6/10	8% had mixed feelings
Overall Value:	**6/10**	**Overall Magic:**	**7/10**	3% were disappointed

The BoardWalk is enjoyed by...		(rated by both authors and readers)
Younger Kids: ♥♥♥♥	Young Adults: ♥♥♥♥	Families: ♥♥♥♥♥
Older Kids: ♥♥♥♥	Mid Adults: ♥♥♥♥♥	Couples: ♥♥♥♥♥
Teenagers: ♥♥♥	Mature Adults: ♥♥♥♥♥	Singles: ♥♥♥

Top Photo Slice: Rocking chairs on the porch at Disney's BoardWalk Resort © MediaMarx, Inc.

Finding Your Place at Disney's BoardWalk Inn & Villas Resort

BOARDWALK RESORT MAP

© MediaMarx, Inc.

BEST LOCATIONS

It's hard to get a bad room here. Request a **water view** at the Inn if you want to watch the Promenade, but keep in mind it can be noisy. Water views in the Villas may overlook the canal leading to the Studios, but may also overlook the Promenade (you may request this). **Standard views** overlook attractive courtyards or the entrance driveway (not so bad as trees shield the parking areas). **Preferred views** in the Villas can overlook a pool, water, or garden view. Rooms around the leisure pools are more peaceful than those around Luna Park. Note that hallways on the Villas side can be very long.

RATES

2013 Sample Room Rates

Seasons are noted on page 14.

Room Type	Value	Fall	Regular	Peak	Holiday
Standard (Inn) or Studio (Villas)	$360–$385	$392–$422	$416–$455	$495–$535	$597
Water View (Inn)	$462–$494	$482–$519	$507–$555	$675–$730	$655
One-Bedroom (Villas)	$535	$548	$589	$685	$741
Two-Bedroom (Villas)	$737	$822	$939	$1,193	$1,284

12.5% tax not included in above prices. Concierge-level rooms begin in the low-$500s and suites begin in the high-$600s. Two-bedroom concierge suites begin in the $1,400s. Higher rates in price ranges are for weekends and holiday periods at the Inn (see page 31).

INFO

Disney's BoardWalk Inn & Villas Resort

✉ 2101 N. Epcot Resort Blvd., Lake Buena Vista, FL 32830
☎ Phone: 407-939-5100   📠 Fax: 407-939-5150
📋 For reservations, call Central Reservations: 407-939-6244

Disney's Caribbean Beach Resort

The free spirit of the tropics greets you at the Caribbean Beach Resort, Disney's original moderately priced resort. Within easy distance of both Epcot and Disney's Hollywood Studios (use the blue tab at the top of the page for parks and eateries in the area), this large and sprawling resort is popular with families.

AMBIENCE

The bright, sunny colors of the buildings and rooftops are your first sign of the **laid-back lifestyle** you'll find at the Caribbean. After you check in at the Customs House, you make your way to one of the six "islands" that encircle 45-acre Barefoot Bay. Lush tropical foliage, hidden courtyards, and white sand beaches are the setting for your lively Caribbean adventure.

RESORT LAYOUT & ROOMS

The 2,112 rooms are well spread out among the six exotic "**islands**" of the Caribe—Aruba, Barbados, Martinique, Jamaica, Trinidad North, and Trinidad South. Each island has a cluster of stucco, pitched-roof buildings without elevators that make up the "village centers," all painted in their own distinctive colors. The rooms in the two-storied buildings have bright colors and oak furnishings. The beds (one king or two doubles) have posts carved into pineapples, the symbol of hospitality. Guest rooms have double sinks in the separate vanity area with under-sink shelves and a privacy curtain, a table and chairs, an armoire with TV, a set of drawers, and a ceiling fan. There are no balconies or patios. Guest rooms here are the largest of all the moderate resorts at 340 sq. ft. Amenities include a coffeemaker, refrigerator, toiletries, housekeeping, limited room service, and voice mail.

Standard Room Layout

DINING

The Caribbean Beach offers a table-service restaurant, as well as a breezy food court and the ubiquitous pool bar. All are available in **Old Port Royale**, also called "Center Towne," housing the eateries, shops, main pool, and marina. The food court's hours are 6:00 am–11:30 pm. **Banana Cabana**, a pool bar located at Old Port Royale, offers a variety of specialty drinks ($6.50+) and beer ($4.00–$5.00) during pool hours. **Bluerunner** is a limited room delivery service—typical menu items include domestic beer ($5.75), wine ($10.95+ for 1/2 bottles), 16" pizza ($13.99–$17.99), and cheesecake ($3.59). **Shutters**, the table-service restaurant, serves Caribbean-flavored fare for dinner only—see the restaurant's description on page 255.

Planning | Getting There | Staying in Style | Touring | Feasting | Making Magic | Index | Notes & More

Top Photo Slice: Top of the Aruba guest house at Disney's Caribbean Beach Resort (①12215) © Kurt Ulrich

Planning · Getting There · Staying in Style · Touring · Feasting · Making Magic · Index · Notes & More

Using the Amenities at Disney's Caribbean Beach Resort

MORE DINING

A bustling village atmosphere sets the stage for **Market Street**, the resort's food court. The various food stations offer chicken, pasta, sandwiches, burgers, pizza, and baked goods. Menu items include French toast with bacon ($5.19), Oriental chicken salad ($6.69), bacon double cheeseburger with fries ($8.09), turkey BLT ($8.59), kids' grilled cheese ($3.99), and carrot cake ($2.99). Get refills at the beverage island with a mug ($14.49).

A Caribbean Beach pirate-themed room
150 + more photos at http://www.passporter.com/photos

PLAYING & RELAXING

For Athletes: The Barefoot Bay Boat Yard rents boats and "toobies" (motorized inner tubes). Rent a bicycle or surrey bike for a ride around the bay. Walkers and joggers enjoy the many beautiful paths and will really enjoy the circuit around Barefoot Bay and the footbridges to Caribbean Cay island.
For Children: There are playgrounds on the beaches in Barbados, Jamaica, and Trinidad South.
For Gamers: Goombay Games in Old Port Royale has video games.
For Shoppers: The Calypso Trading Post & Straw Market offers themed gifts, sundries, clothing, and Caribbean items.
For Swimmers: The recently refurbished themed pool near Old Port Royale features cannons and waterfalls, as well as a wading pool for kids, a spa (hot tub), and a water slide. Six leisure pools are among the resort's "islands." Note that there is no swimming in the bay.
For Sunbathers: Each "island" has a beautiful, white sand beach.

GETTING ABOUT

Transportation to the theme parks and water parks (see chart below for in-transit times) is via frequent **buses**. Other resorts are accessible by changing buses at a nearby theme park (daytime) or Downtown Disney (evening). You can also take an internal resort bus if you need to reach other areas within the resort. To go to the Customs House (lobby concierge/luggage services), get off at Barbados.

Magic Kingdom	Epcot	Disney's Hollywood Studios	Disney's Animal Kingdom	Downtown Disney
direct bus ~20 min.	direct bus ~15 min.	direct bus ~12 min.	direct bus ~20 min.	direct bus ~25 min.

Approximate time you will spend in transit from resort to destination during normal operation.

Top Photo Slice: Inside Old Port Royale at Disney's Caribbean Beach (①10988) © Marianne Swan

Making the Most of Disney's Caribbean Beach Resort

While you can't swim in the bay, the **white sand beaches** are great spots to relax. We found several hammocks set up along the beach—take some time to just kick back and watch the palm trees flutter.

You can catch a glimpse of the **Epcot globe** between Old Port Royale and Martinique—look in the evenings for a glimpse of IllumiNations.

There are "hidden" **courtyards** sporting tables with umbrellas in every "island" of the resort—these are now the designated smoking areas, but can still be very rewarding places to relax. Be sure to take a trip across the bridge to **Caribbean Cay** (formerly Parrot Cay) in the middle of Barefoot Bay. Beyond the lush foliage and dense bamboo stands, you'll find gazebos, picnic areas, and hammocks.

All rooms have **refrigerators**.

There are **no elevators**.

This is a sprawling resort, making it difficult to get to Old Port Royale to eat or shop. Consider **stocking up** on snacks and quick breakfast foods. Board the "Internal" bus to move around the resort.

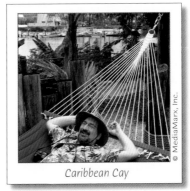
Caribbean Cay

All rooms in Martinique and Trinidad North are **preferred rooms**. Pirate-themed rooms are found in Trinidad South (see photo on previous page and prices on the next page), while the remaining rooms have a very subtle Finding Nemo theme.

Check-in time is 3:00 pm. Check-out time is 11:00 am.

Ratings are explained on page 28.

Our Value Ratings:		Our Magic Ratings:		Readers' Ratings:
Quality:	6/10	Theme:	6/10	47% fell in love with it
Accessibility:	5/10	Amenities:	6/10	43% liked it well enough
Affordability:	8/10	Fun Factor:	6/10	8% had mixed feelings
Overall Value:	**6/10**	**Overall Magic:**	**6/10**	2% were disappointed

Caribbean Beach is enjoyed by...		(rated by both authors and readers)
Younger Kids: ♥♥♥♥♥	Young Adults: ♥♥♥♥	Families: ♥♥♥♥
Older Kids: ♥♥♥♥♥	Mid Adults: ♥♥♥♥	Couples: ♥♥♥♥♥
Teenagers: ♥♥♥♥	Mature Adults: ♥♥♥♥	Singles: ♥♥♥

Side tabs: Planning / Getting There / Staying in Style / Touring / Feasting / Making Magic / Index / Notes & More

TIPS / NOTES / RATINGS

Finding Your Place at Disney's Caribbean Beach Resort

CARIBBEAN BEACH RESORT MAP

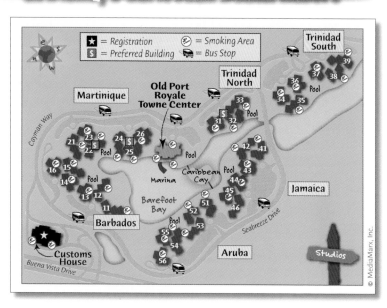

© MediaMarx, Inc.

BEST LOCATIONS

Your "island" can make or break your experience. Though more expensive, we suggest **Martinique** or **Trinidad North**, which are close to Old Port Royale. **Aruba** and **Jamaica**, across the Barefoot Bay bridge, are good choices for a bit of seclusion. You don't need a **water view** to enjoy your room here, but if you prefer one, we found the following rooms to have outstanding water views: 2524, 2525, 2556, and 2557 in Martinique; and 3117, 3149, 3225–3228, and 3257–3261 in Trinidad North. Corner rooms (available with either double- or king-size beds) seem larger as they often have an extra window.

RATES

2013 Sample Room Rates
Seasons are noted on page 14.

Room Type	Value	Fall	Regular	Summer	Peak	Holiday
Standard Room	$162–$177	$176–$191	$188–$213	$196	$211–$231	$252
Preferred, Water, or King	$187–$212	$201–$216	$213–$238	$221	$236–$249	$283
Pirate Themed Standard	$196–$211	$210–$225	$224–$249	$232	$247–$267	$297
Pirate Themed Water	$221–$236	$235–$250	$249–$274	$257	$272–$292	$322

12.5% tax not included in above rates. King-bed rooms come in both standard or water view, and both are the same rate as a water-view room. Preferred rooms (any view, any bed size) are located in Martinique and Trinidad North. Higher rates in price ranges are for weekends and holiday periods (see page 31).

INFO

Disney's Caribbean Beach Resort
✉ 900 Cayman Way, Lake Buena Vista, FL 32830
☎ Phone: 407-934-3400   🖨 Fax: 407-934-3288
📋 For reservations, call Central Reservations: 407-939-6244

More at ⓘ caribbean-beach

Disney's Contemporary Resort & Villas

The Contemporary Resort is one of the original and quintessential Walt Disney World hotels, built at the same time as nearby Magic Kingdom (use the blue tab at the top of the page for parks and eateries in the area). Bay Lake and the Seven Seas Lagoon surround the resort on three sides.

AMBIENCE

Every time we enter the Contemporary, we get the sense we've entered the **center of the "World."** It isn't just the soaring architecture, the massive steel and glass tower, or the monorail running right through it, though those are all a part of it. Rather, it is akin to the feeling city dwellers boast about: Everything you need, everyone you like, and every place that matters is right there. And that seems to be exactly the way Disney intended it, with the Grand Concourse housing many of the resort's services, restaurants, and shops.

RESORT LAYOUT & ROOMS

Standard Room Layout

The original 668 guest rooms are housed in the 15-story, A-frame **Tower** or within the three-story **Garden Wing**. These 436 sq. ft., modern rooms have Feng Shui-influences with flat-screen TVs, double closets, and dark cherry wood details with two queens or one king bed, and a daybed. Some rooms have large patios or balconies. Next door in the **Bay Lake Tower**, 295 Disney Vacation Club villas offer an "urban boutique" experience, with studios, one- and two-bedroom, and Grand Villas. Amenities include housekeeping, toiletries, safe, newspaper delivery, coffeemaker, refrigerator, hair dryer, turndown service (on request), voice mail, and valet parking.

DINING

The Contemporary has a wide variety of dining options. The two most popular table-service restaurants—**Chef Mickey's** (a character dining experience) and the trendy **California Grill** (the Contemporary's centerpiece)—are detailed on page 255. **The Wave** offers American cuisine with an international flair at breakfast, lunch, and dinner. The **Contempo Cafe** is a quick-service eatery open all day—typical menu items include a cheeseburger ($8.29), honey lime chicken sandwich ($8.89), pasta marinara ($5.99), and kid's meals ($4.99). Refillable mugs are available at the resort for $14.49. The **Sand Bar** by the pool also offers drinks ($2.39 & up), sandwiches ($8.79), and ice cream ($3.09).

Planning · Getting There · Staying in Style · Touring · Feasting · Making Magic · Index · Notes & More

Planning · Getting There · Staying in Style · Touring · Feasting · Making Magic · Index · Notes & More

Using the Amenities at Disney's Contemporary Resort

LOUNGING

The **Outer Rim Lounge** on the 4th floor of the main tower has fun drinks and comfy chairs in front of huge glass windows.
California Grill Lounge offers California wines and appetizers along with a magnificent view.
Contemporary Grounds is a coffee bar near the front desk. The **Top of the World** lounge at Bay Lake Tower is open for DVC resort guests only. There are also two pool bars. **Room service** is open 24 hours a day.

Bay Lake Tower at the Contemporary
300+ more photos at http://www.passporter.com/photos

PLAYING & RELAXING

For Athletes: The Olympiad fitness center has exercise equipment, sauna, and massage therapies. Boat rentals add to the fun. Sammy Duvall's Watersports Centre at the resort offers waterskiing and parasailing. Tennis courts are also available near Bay Lake Tower.
For Charmers: A full-service salon offers services by appointment.
For Gamers: A large resort arcade offers pinball and video games.
For Shoppers: The fourth-floor Concourse shops sell gifts and clothing. The marina pavilion offers swimwear and sun protection.
For Swimmers: The Bay Cove Pool (for Bay Lake Tower guests only) has a zero-entry, water slide, whirlpool spa, and an interactive children's water feature. There are also two more heated pools, two hot tubs, and another water slide, as well as a sand beach for sunbathers.

GETTING ABOUT

The Contemporary Resort offers myriad transportation options (see the chart below for in-transit times). For the Magic Kingdom, board the **monorail** on the fourth floor or walk the **path** on the north side (see map on page 60). For Epcot, monorail to the Transportation and Ticket Center (TTC) and transfer to the Epcot monorail. For other parks, take the **direct bus** just outside the lobby. For the Polynesian or Grand Floridian, take the monorail. For Fort Wilderness or the Wilderness Lodge, take the **boat**. For other destinations, go to the Magic Kingdom (daytime) or Downtown Disney (evening) and transfer to the appropriate resort bus. Valet parking is a $10/day option.

Magic Kingdom	Epcot	Disney's Hollywood Studios	Disney's Animal Kingdom	Downtown Disney
monorail/walk	monorail x 2	direct bus	direct bus	direct bus
~20/~10 min.	~5+10 min.	~20 min.	~20 min.	~35 min.

Approximate time you will spend in transit from resort to destination during normal operation.

Top Photo Slice: Entrance to The Wave restaurant at the Contemporary Resort © MediaMarx, Inc.

Making the Most of Disney's Contemporary Resort

The **Bay Lake Tower** is the newest Disney Vacation Club resort, but you don't have to be a member to reserve a room. The new tower offers dramatic views of the Magic Kingdom next door and Bay Lake. The Skyway Bridge connects the Bay Lake Tower to the original tower for access to the monorail and other resort services.

The Magic Kingdom fireworks can be watched from a **viewing patio** on the Bay Lake Tower rooftop (alas, it's only accessible to Disney Vacation Club members staying in Bay Lake Tower on cash or points), but there is a viewing patio on the 4th floor of the main tower—look for the door tucked in behind Fantasia Market.

The **Electrical Water Pageant**, a whimsical parade of lighted barges and music, can be seen from the shore of Bay Lake at 10:10 pm (or a bit later if the Magic Kingdom fireworks are at 10:00 pm).

The Contemporary Tower also offers one- and two-bedroom suites and two concierge levels, all with special amenities. Among the many amenities in the **suites** (bathrobes, triple sheeting, turndown service, etc.), the two-line speakerphones are great.

The obvious method of transportation to Magic Kingdom is via the monorail, but consider **walking** instead on busy mornings or when the park lets out—it's much faster! The monorail goes around the lagoon clockwise, so it can take a while to reach the Magic Kingdom.

Guest rooms in the **Garden Wing** can be a hike from the Tower's restaurants and services. If this is a concern, reserve a Tower room.

The Contemporary Resort has a **large convention center** also.

Check-in time is 3:00 pm/4:00 pm. Check-out time is 11:00 am.

Ratings are explained on page 28.

Our Value Ratings:		Our Magic Ratings:		Readers' Ratings:
Quality:	8/10	Theme:	4/10	50% fell in love with it
Accessibility:	9/10	Amenities:	9/10	24% liked it well enough
Affordability:	5/10	Fun Factor:	5/10	10% had mixed feelings
Overall Value:	**7/10**	**Overall Magic:**	**6/10**	16% were disappointed

Contemporary is enjoyed by...		(rated by both authors and readers)
Younger Kids: ♥♥♥	Young Adults: ♥♥♥♥♥	Families: ♥♥♥♥♥
Older Kids: ♥♥♥♥♥	Mid Adults: ♥♥♥♥	Couples: ♥♥♥♥
Teenagers: ♥♥♥♥♥	Mature Adults: ♥♥♥	Singles: ♥♥♥♥

Side tabs: Planning / Getting There / Staying in Style / Touring / Feasting / Making Magic / Index / Notes & More

TIPS · NOTES · RATINGS

Top Photo Slice: The striking windows in the Contemporary's original tower © MediaMarx, Inc.

Planning

Getting There

Staying in Style

Touring

Feasting

Making Magic

Index

Notes & More

Finding Your Place at Disney's Contemporary Resort

CONTEMPORARY RESORT MAP

© MediaMarx, Inc.

★ = Registration E = Elevator
☺ = Smoking area 🚌 = Bus Stop

LOCATIONS

If you are drawn to the Contemporary by its proximity to the Magic Kingdom and you want to **see the castle** from your room, be sure to reserve this specifically—only certain **Tower** rooms get this breathtaking view. The **Garden Wing** may lack the Tower's excitement, but we found the rooms delightful and serene, especially those facing the water. Very few of the Garden Wing rooms have **balconies**, but first-floor rooms have **patios**.

RATES

2013 Sample Room Rates

Seasons are noted on page 14.

Room Type	Value	Fall	Regular	Peak	Holiday
Standard View (Wing)	$330–$355	$362–$411	$367–$406	$407–$452	$551
Garden/Water View (Wing)	$378–$407	$417–$474	$426–$472	$483–$537	$595
Tower Room (Bay View)	$447–$492	$490–$557	$502–$556	$586–$651	$650
Tower (Magic Kingdom view)	$507–$545	$535–$607	$557–$616	$646–$718	$715
Bay Lake Tower Studio	$431–$441	$462	$492–$493	$571	$609
Bay Lake Tower One-Bedroom	$535–$545	$584	$597–$599	$695	$776
Bay Lake Tower Two-Bedroom	$726–$737	$832	$939–$945	$1,188	$1,299

12.5% tax not included in above rates. Concierge-level rooms (floors 12 and 14) start in the $600s. Suites come in a variety of views and start in the $1000s. Higher rates in price ranges are for weekends and holiday periods (see page 31).

INFO

Disney's Contemporary Resort

✉ 4600 North World Drive, Lake Buena Vista, FL 32830
☎ Phone: 407-824-1000 📠 Fax: 407-824-3539

More at ① contemporary

Disney's Coronado Springs Resort

Coronado Springs is located near Disney's Animal Kingdom and Disney's Hollywood Studios (use the blue tab at the top of the page for parks and eateries in the area). The resort offers moderately priced rooms and convention facilities. The resort surrounds a 15-acre lake known as Lago (Lake) Dorado.

The architecture and decor trace the travels of explorer Francisco de Coronado in colonial Mexico and the **American Southwest**. Adventure awaits around every corner, from the colorful, bustling market to the Mayan pyramid overlooking the main swimming pool. Your visit begins in a sunny plaza, which leads to the large, open lobby graced by beamed ceilings, elegant columns, and intricately inlaid floors. Around the corner, a festive market offers native foods, just the thing to eat on the lakeside terrace. The resort's buildings are clustered around sparkling Lago Dorado, including the stately main building, El Centro.

The renovated guest rooms in this 1,967-room resort are divided into three districts. Closest to El Centro are the **Casitas**, a bustling village of three- and four-story stucco buildings painted in soft pastels. Next around the lagoon are the rustic adobe-and-wood **Ranchos**. You could imagine Zorro dashing under the porch roofs and amid the cactus, while bubbling springs cascade into rock-strewn stream beds, ultimately to disappear into the parched desert earth. Finally, you reach the tropical **Cabanas**, vibrantly colored two-story buildings with the corrugated tin roofs of a rustic beach resort. Rooms are about 314 sq. ft. and offer two queen beds or one king bed, a separate vanity area with just one sink, table and chairs, armoire, and a TV. Amenities include toiletries, housekeeping, limited room service, hair dryer, iron and ironing board, coffeemaker, refrigerator, in-room safe, and voice mail. Newspaper delivery is available for $1.50/day. Concierge rooms and junior, one-bedroom, and executive suites are also available.

Standard
Room Layout

The large 190,000 sq. ft. **Conference Center** is quite modern and generally lacks the regional character of the resort. It boasts the largest ballroom in the Southeast (60,214 sq. ft.). An 85,000 sq. ft. exhibit hall, meeting rooms, another 20,000 sq. ft. ballroom, and patios round out the facilities. A full-service business center is also available.

AMBIENCE

RESORT LAYOUT & ROOMS

Planning
Getting There
Staying in Style
Touring
Feasting
Making Magic
Index
Notes & More

Top Photo Slice: Sunrise at Disney's Coronado Springs Resort (①2444) © Darren Mosher

Genuine PassPorter Genuine PassPorter Genuine PassPorter Genuine PassPorter Genuine PassPorter Genuine PassPorter Genuine PassPorter

Using the Amenities at Disney's Coronado Springs Resort

DINING

Coronado Springs' dining options are the real enchilada. **Maya Grill** (see page 256) is an upscale table-service restaurant open for breakfast and dinner. **Pepper Market** is an upscale food court dressed up like a festive, outdoor market for

Coronado Springs at dusk
75+ more photos at http://www.passporter.com/photos

breakfast, lunch, and dinner. Typical menu items include veggie frittata platter ($9.99), cheese omelet ($9.99), cheeseburger($9.99), chef's salad ($10.95), chicken quesadillas ($9.99), and kids' chicken nuggets ($6.50). An automatic 10% gratuity is added. **Siesta's** is the poolside bar serving sandwiches, nachos, fries, and various drinks. The **Rix Lounge** is a 300-seat lounge with music, appetizers, and specialty drinks. **Limited room service** is offered in the mornings and evenings. Refillable mugs ($14.49) are available at the Pepper Market.

PLAYING & RELAXING

For Athletes: La Vida Health Club has exercise equipment, whirlpool, and massage treatments. Boats, bikes, surreys, and fishing poles can be rented at La Marina, and there is a volleyball court. Enjoy a nature trail and a walk/jog around the lagoon.
For Charmers: Casa de Belleza offers beauty and hair treatments.
For Children: The Explorer's Playground is near the main pool.
For Gamers: Video games of all sorts are found at the Iguana Arcade near the main pool (note that the Jumping Bean Arcade closed).
For Shoppers: Panchito's has sundries, character items, and gifts.
For Swimmers: A leisure pool in each of the three districts, plus the Dig Site main pool, which is built around an ancient pyramid and features a water slide, spa (hot tub), and kids' pool.

GETTING ABOUT

Transportation to the theme parks is by frequent, direct **buses** (see chart below for in-transit times). There are four bus stops (see map on page 64). For other destinations, transfer at a nearby theme park (daytime) or at Downtown Disney (evening). A sidewalk connects the resort to Blizzard Beach, and it's a quick drive to both Disney's Hollywood Studios and Disney's Animal Kingdom.

Magic Kingdom	Epcot	Disney's Hollywood Studios	Disney's Animal Kingdom	Downtown Disney
direct bus ~15 min.	direct bus ~15 min.	direct bus ~15 min.	direct bus ~10 min.	direct bus ~25 min.

Approximate time you will spend in transit from resort to destination during normal operation.

Planning | Getting There | Staying in Style | Touring | Feasting | Making Magic | Index | Notes & More

Making the Most of Disney's Coronado Springs Resort

The **Dig Site** is really a miniature water park with delightful scenery and fun water attractions. The pool itself is huge (10,800 sq. ft.), and there's a large sandbox that masquerades as the "dig site" of the Mayan pyramid. The 123-foot-long water slide has a jaguar atop it that spits water. Oh, and they have the largest outdoor spa (hot tub) of any Disney resort—it fits 22 people!

Roll-away beds are available for $15/day (but rooms are still limited to four guests). Request a roll-away bed with your reservation and again at check-in.

The **Pepper Market** food court works a bit differently. Upon arrival, you are seated by a cast member and given a ticket. You then visit the various food stations, and when you find an item you want, your ticket is stamped. Drinks are refilled for you. You pay after your meal. A 10% gratuity is added (unless you get your food to go).

This resort goes for the sun-drenched effect and, in the process, seems to **lack enough shade** to protect you from the scorching Florida sun. Use caution if you are fair-skinned (as Jennifer is) or if you are going during the summer months.

Coronado Springs strikes us as a bit more **buttoned-down** than the other moderate resorts, no doubt due to the conference center and business facilities. While we have no major complaints, it also didn't delight us in the same way that other moderate Disney resorts have. On the other hand, some of our fellow vacationers are very impressed with the resort, especially its quality service. We definitely feel this is a great resort for business travelers.

Check-in time is 3:00 pm. Check-out time is 11:00 am.

Ratings are explained on page 28.

Our Value Ratings:		Our Magic Ratings:		Readers' Ratings:
Quality:	7/10	Theme:	8/10	35% fell in love with it
Accessibility:	6/10	Amenities:	5/10	47% liked it well enough
Affordability:	8/10	Fun Factor:	4/10	15% had mixed feelings
Overall Value:	**7/10**	**Overall Magic:**	**6/10**	3% were disappointed

Coronado Springs is enjoyed by...	(rated by both authors and readers)	
Younger Kids: ♥♥♥♥	Young Adults: ♥♥♥♥♥	Families: ♥♥♥♥
Older Kids: ♥♥♥♥	Mid Adults: ♥♥♥♥	Couples: ♥♥♥♥♥
Teenagers: ♥♥♥♥	Mature Adults: ♥♥♥	Singles: ♥♥♥

TIPS

NOTES

RATINGS

Planning · Getting There · Staying in Style · Touring · Feasting · Making Magic · Index · Notes & More

Planning

Getting There

Staying in Style

Touring

Feasting

Making Magic

Index

Notes & More

Finding Your Place at Disney's Coronado Springs Resort

CORONADO SPRINGS RESORT MAP

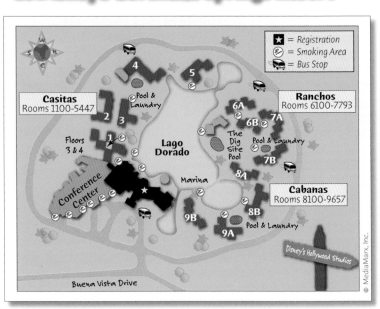

BEST LOCATIONS

The **Casitas** are the least interesting visually, but they are convenient to the Convention Center—in fact, they house the only rooms that you can reach from El Centro without leaving the protection of a roof or overhang. Building 1 is the closest to the Conference Center. The charming **Ranchos** are closest to the main pool and farthest from El Centro. We recommend building 6B for its view and proximity to the leisure pool. The **Cabanas** are convenient to El Centro. We loved our room in building 8B (close to pools and the bus); building 8A has good views, and 9B is next door to El Centro.

RATES

2013 Sample Room Rates
Seasons are noted on page 14.

Room Type	Value	Fall	Regular	Summer	Peak	Holiday
Standard Room	$167–$182	$181–$196	$193–$218	$201	$216–$236	$258
Preferred, Water, or King	$192–$207	$206–$221	$218–$243	$226	$241–$261	$288
Junior Suite (double beds)	$370–$400	$415–$445	$431–$476	$477	$515–$555	$608
One-Bedroom Suite	$680–$720	$739–$779	$759–$819	$800	$846–$901	$953

12.5% tax not included in above rates. Higher rates in price ranges are for weekends and holiday periods (see page 31).

INFO

Disney's Coronado Springs Resort

✉ 1000 W. Buena Vista Drive, Lake Buena Vista, FL 32830
☎ Phone: 407-939-1000   ✏ Fax: 407-939-1001
🖥 For reservations, call Central Reservations: 407-939-6244

More at ⓘ coronado-springs

Top Photo Slice: Pillows on a bed at Disney's Coronado Springs Resort © MediaMarx, Inc.

Looking for the Dolphin Resort? See page 105.

Disney's Fort Wilderness Resort & Campground

Much more than tents and hookups, Fort Wilderness is a resort in every sense of the word. It is pleasantly situated in a shady forest on Bay Lake, connected by a scenic waterway to the nearby Magic Kingdom theme park (use the blue tab at the top of the page for parks and eateries in the vicinity).

Enveloped by pine, cypress, and oak, this 700-acre campground is a **relaxing haven** after the noise and excitement of a long day at the parks. Rough-hewn log common buildings are nestled among towering pine trees and flowering meadows. Wilderness this is not, however. There are enough daily conveniences and services that the tents may be the only reminder that you are camping.

All types of camping are available—tent, pop-up, trailer, and motor home (RV)—throughout the 788 **campsites**. Located on small loop roads connecting to larger thoroughfares, each site is relatively secluded by trees and shrubs and offers its own paved driveway, Coquina rock bed, charcoal grill, picnic table, and 110V/220V electrical service. Of the three types of campsites, non-preferred, partial-hookup sites supply water, but are farthest from services, preferred sites are closer and have water, sewer, and free Internet access, and some provide cable TV as well, and premium sites offer larger pads for big RVs along with all other amenities. Each site fits up to ten people and one car; pets are welcome at certain sites. All sites are close to clean, air-conditioned Comfort Stations with restrooms, private showers, phones, ice machines (extra fee), and laundry facilities. For guests without a tent or trailer, the 407 **Wilderness Cabins** are roomy, air-conditioned "log cabins" (504 sq. ft.) that hold up to six guests plus a child under 3 in a crib. Each cabin has a living room, bedroom, a full kitchen, and bathroom. Charmingly rustic yet comfortable, each cabin comes with pots and utensils, plus a coffeemaker, stove, microwave, refrigerator, dishwasher, cable TV, DVD player, free high-speed Internet, phone, hair dryer, and safe. The living room has a pull-down double bed. The bedroom has a separate vanity, TV, a double bed, and bunk beds. Outside is a charcoal grill, picnic table, and deck. Amenities include voice mail and housekeeping. All guests at cabins must be accommodated within them; no tents are permitted outside the cabin.

Cabin Layout

AMBIENCE

RESORT LAYOUT & ROOMS

Top Photo Slice: Spanish moss and a covered wagon at Fort Wilderness Resort & Campground (①14549) © Cheryl Pendry

Genuine PassPorter   Genuine PassPorter   Genuine PassPorter   Genuine PassPorter   Genuine PassPorter   Genuine PassPorter   Genuine

Planning | Getting There | Staying in Style | Touring | Feasting | Making Magic | Index | Notes & More

Using the Amenities at Disney's Fort Wilderness Resort

DINING

Many guests cook at their sites or cabins. **The Chuck Wagon** is open during the nightly campfire and serves snacks. Typical menu items: a hot dog ($4.79), popcorn ($3.09), and s'more kit ($8.99). **Hoop-Dee-Doo Musical Revue** and **Mickey's Backyard BBQ** are dinner shows (see page 264). **Trail's End Restaurant** is a buffeteria (page 256). **Crockett's Tavern** serves drinks and snacks.

A Fort Wilderness Cabin
© MediaMarx, Inc.

PLAYING & RELAXING

For Athletes: You'll find two lighted tennis courts, plus volleyball, tetherball, basketball, and horseshoes. Rent a boat at the marina or a canoe or bike at the Bike Barn. Horseback rides ($42) at the livery (must be 9+ years, 48"+). Nature walks, too!

For Children: Pony rides ($5) and a nearby playground delight kids. Free nightly campfires with Chip and Dale and Disney movies, or go on a "hay ride" ($8/adult and $5/kids 3-9).

For Dogs: Enjoy the fenced, leash-free dog park near loop 300.

For Fishers: Try a bass fishing excursion in Bay Lake for $200–$230.

For Gamers: Two video arcades are within the resort.

For Romantics: Enjoy a relaxing, private carriage ride for $45.

For Shoppers: Gifts, sundries, and groceries at two trading posts.

For Show-Goers: Two dinner shows! See page 264 for details.

For Swimmers: The main Meadows pool has a slide, spa (hot tub), and children's play areas. The Wilderness Cabins have another pool. Beach is for sunbathing only. Child-size life vests are at the pools.

For Tours: A back trail Segway tour is offered here—see page 273.

GETTING ABOUT

Boats (see chart below) go to Magic Kingdom, Wilderness Lodge, and Contemporary. **Buses** to Disney's Hollywood Studios and Wilderness Lodge pick up/drop off at Settlement Depot. Buses for Epcot, Animal Kingdom/Blizzard Beach, and Downtown Disney/Typhoon Lagoon pick up/drop off at Outpost Depot. Three bus routes—Yellow, Orange, and Purple—serve locations within the resort and all stop at Settlement Depot and Outpost Depot. For resorts, transfer at Magic Kingdom or Downtown Disney. You can rent an **electric golf cart** to move about the resort easier.

Magic Kingdom	Epcot	Disney's Hollywood Studios	Disney's Animal Kingdom	Downtown Disney
boat	direct bus	direct bus	direct bus	direct bus
~15 min.	~25 min.	~30 min.	~30 min.	~35 min.

Approximate time you will spend in transit from resort to destination during normal operation.

Top Photo Slice: Marina and beach at Disney's Fort Wilderness Resort (①4631) © Amy Sellars

Making the Most of Disney's Fort Wilderness Resort

Electric golf carts are very popular for moving about the resort but are hard to get. To reserve one up to a year in advance, call the Bike Barn at 407-824-2742. Rates are $59 + tax per 24-hour period.

The **Electrical Water Pageant**, a light and music barge parade on Bay Lake, can be seen from the beach at around 9:45 pm.

Fort Wilderness offers **many special features** not found at other resorts, including the nightly campfire and movie (see previous page), trail rides, and more. See page 215 for details.

Seasonal, weekly, and monthly **discounts** may exist for campsites.

A **car** may come in handy at this resort, and there is 15-minute parking available at the Meadows Trading Post. Disney transportation to and from Fort Wilderness requires a transfer from internal to external transport, making it more time-consuming than most resorts. To reduce transit time, request a site in loops 100–800, as these are within walking distance of Settlement Depot and the marina.

Bring your **groceries**, or buy them at Winn-Dixie about a mile north of Downtown Disney. You can pick up some items from the trading posts.

Pets are allowed for $5/day in loops 300, 700–800, and 1600–1900 (request at booking). No pets in pop-ups or tents. Dogs may also visit the fenced-in Waggin' Trails Dog Park near loop 300.

Creekside Meadow offers rustic **group camping** with a Comfort Station, grills, and fire pits. Six-person tents and cots can be rented.

Campfires are not allowed at individual campsites.

Check-in time is 1:00 pm (campsites) or 3:00 pm (cabins). Check-out time for all is 11:00 am.

Note: The two Affordability Ratings below correspond to lodging and camping.   *Ratings are explained on page 28.*

Our Value Ratings:		Our Magic Ratings:		Readers' Ratings:
Quality:	7/10	Theme:	6/10	80% fell in love with it
Accessibility:	4/10	Amenities:	5/10	7% liked it well enough
Affordability:	6 & 10/10	Fun Factor:	8/10	10% had mixed feelings
Overall Value:	**6 & 7/10**	**Overall Magic:**	**6/10**	3% were disappointed

Fort Wilderness is enjoyed by...	(rated by both authors and readers)	
Younger Kids: ♥♥♥♥♥	Young Adults: ♥♥♥♥	Families: ♥♥♥♥♥
Older Kids: ♥♥♥♥	Mid Adults: ♥♥♥♥	Couples: ♥♥♥
Teenagers: ♥♥♥♥	Mature Adults: ♥♥♥♥	Singles: ♥♥

Planning   *Getting There*   *Staying in Style*   *Touring*   *Feasting*   *Making Magic*   *Index*   *Notes & More*

TIPS   NOTES   RATINGS

Planning

Getting There

Staying in Style

Touring

Feasting

Making Magic

Index

Notes & More

FORT WILDERNESS RESORT MAP

Finding Your Place
at Disney's Fort Wilderness Resort

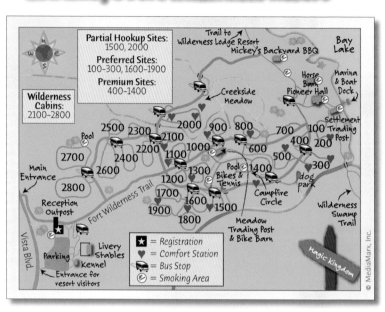

BEST SPOTS

Campsites and cabins are located on loops, circular drives with about 40 sites or cabins each. The most popular **cabin** locations are on loops 2500–2700 near the west pool, though we loved our cabin on loop 2100 near a bus stop. The most popular **campsites** are on loops 100 and 200. Most preferred and all premium sites are **close to Pioneer Hall** in the 100–800 and 1400 loops. **Full hookup campsites** are in loops 900–1300 and 1600–1900—we highly recommend loop 1300. **Partial hookups** are located in the 1500 and 2000 loops.

RATES

2013 Sample Campsite/Cabin Rates
Seasons are noted on page 14.

Room Type	Value	Fall	Regular	Peak	Pre-Holiday	Holiday
Partial Hookup Campsite	$48–$51	–	$70–$75	$80–$85	$54–$58	$97
Full Hookup Campsite	$65–$67	–	$89–$94	$107–$112	$69–$74	$113
Preferred Campsite	$72–$73	–	$97–$102	$113–$118	$75–$80	$121
Wilderness Cabin	$289–$329	$322–$327	$353–$368	$390–$420	–	$481

12.5% tax not included in above rates. There is an additional charge of $5/night for more than two adults in a cabin, or $2/night for more than two adults at a campsite. Higher rates in price ranges are for weekends and holiday periods (see page 31).

INFO

Disney's Fort Wilderness Resort & Campground

✉ 4510 N. Fort Wilderness Trail, Lake Buena Vista, FL 32830
☎ Phone: 407-824-2900   📠 Fax: 407-824-3508
📋 For reservations, call Central Reservations: 407-939-6244

More at ① camping

Disney's Grand Floridian Resort & Spa

The most luxurious of Disney's resorts, the Grand Floridian Resort & Spa is a breathtaking Victorian hotel with turrets and gabled roofs. It extends into the Seven Seas Lagoon between the Polynesian and the Magic Kingdom (use the blue tab at the top of the page for parks and eateries in the area).

AMBIENCE

From the moment you step into the **Grand Lobby**, you will feel as though you've been transported back to the 1890s and the days when the well-to-do wintered in style at grand seaside resorts. As in that unhurried time, the warm whites and marble floors draw you in, just as the towering lobby and stained glass skylights draw your eyes upward. It is the picture of charm, romance, and luxury.

RESORT LAYOUT & ROOMS

900 guest rooms are generously spread out among five **lodge** buildings and the Grand Lobby. The luxurious rooms are decorated in four different whimsical-yet-subtle themes: floral, cameo (fairies), swans (Wind in the Willows), and Alice in Wonderland. Rooms are about 400 sq. ft. and are resplendent with marble-topped double sinks and balconies or patios. Most guest rooms offer two queen-size beds and a daybed, accommodating five people. The lodge buildings also house the slightly smaller "dormer" rooms, plus suites. Amenities include signature toiletries, turndown service, mini-bar, large in-room safe, hair dryer, newspaper delivery, valet parking, 24-hour room service, free high-speed Internet—and best of all—comfy robes to relax in after a long day.

Standard Room Layout

DINING

Culinary delights await you in any of the restaurants and lounges, largely located on the first two floors of the Grand Lobby. Table-service restaurants, which are described on pages 256–257, include: **1900 Park Fare**, a festive character dining experience; **Cítricos**, sophisticated Floridian and Mediterranean cuisine; **Grand Floridian Cafe**, a sun-splashed cafe with traditional fare; **Garden View Lounge**, high tea in the afternoon; **Narcoossee's**, seafood with a view of Seven Seas Lagoon; and **Victoria & Albert's**, Disney's finest restaurant. Quick-service options include the **Grand Floridian Pool Bar** for snacks and **Gasparilla's Grill and Games** for light fare 24 hours a day. Typical menu items at Gasparilla's Grill include an egg croissant ($5.99), a cheeseburger ($7.59), a 16" cheese pizza ($13.99, toppings are $1.50), and a Reuben hot dog ($7.79).

Planning · Getting There · Staying in Style · Touring · Feasting · Making Magic · Index · Notes & More

Using the Amenities at Disney's Grand Floridian Resort & Spa

LOUNGING

Lounges at the Grand Floridian include the **Garden View Lounge**, which offers drinks in the evening. **Mizner's** serves cocktails and light snacks within earshot of the musicians who often perform in the Grand Lobby. The **Grand Floridian Pool Bar** also serves drinks and snacks, such as a cheeseburger with fries ($11.95) or a Cobb salad ($12.95). Visit **Gasparilla's Grill and Games** to buy refillable mugs ($14.49) and get refills.

Jennifer and Dave enjoy a Turret Suite

© MediaMarx, Inc.

PLAYING & RELAXING

For Athletes: Two clay tennis courts are available for a fee. Rent a variety of boats at the marina. You'll also find walking/jogging paths.
For Charmers: The Ivy Trellis Salon pampers you with hair and nail treatments. The Grand Floridian Spa & Health Club is closed for renovations until early 2013.
For Children: A playground is adjacent to the Mouseketeer Clubhouse, a supervised program for kids 4–12 (see page 285).
For Gamers: Gasparilla's Grill and Games has a video arcade.
For Shoppers: On the first floor, Sandy Cove stocks sundries and Summer Lace offers upscale women's clothing. On the second floor, M. Mouse Mercantile has gifts; Basin White offers upscale bath products; and Commander Porter's has men's and women's apparel.
For Swimmers: A moderately-sized leisure pool and hot tub are available, as is a themed, zero-entry pool near the beach with a slide and play fountain. Sunbathers enjoy the beach (no swimming).

GETTING ABOUT

A **monorail** goes to Magic Kingdom as well as the Contemporary, the Polynesian, and the Transportation and Ticket Center (TTC), where you can transfer to the Epcot monorail. **Boats** also take you to the Magic Kingdom and the Polynesian. For other parks (see chart below for in-transit times), use the **direct buses** in front of the resort. For other resorts, monorail to the Magic Kingdom (daytime) or bus to Downtown Disney (evening) and transfer to a resort bus.

Magic Kingdom	Epcot	Disney's Hollywood Studios	Disney's Animal Kingdom	Downtown Disney
monorail/boat ~3/~10 min.	monorail x 2 ~12+10 min.	direct bus ~10 min.	direct bus ~15 min.	direct bus ~20 min.

Approximate time you will spend in transit from resort to destination during normal operation.

Top Photo Slice: Monorail entering the Grand Floridian Resort station © MediaMarx, Inc.

Making the Most of Disney's Grand Floridian Resort & Spa

TIPS

The Grand Lobby is often filled with the sound of **live music**, ranging from solo pianists to full dance bands.

New **Disney Vacation Club villas** (147 to be exact) are coming to this resort at the end of 2013! They are being built on the beach between the resort and the Wedding Pavilion.

Many **children's activities** are offered, including scavenger hunts, arts and crafts, and story time (complimentary). Additional-fee activities like fishing trips, the Wonderland Tea Party, and the Pirate Cruise (see page 274) are also available.

Private dining is available for a quiet or romantic evening. You can have a meal on your balcony, on the beach, or even on a boat in the lagoon. Make arrangements in advance with room service.

For a touch of magic, end your day with a romantic, nighttime **stroll along the beach**. You may even catch the Electrical Water Pageant on the Seven Seas Lagoon around 9:15 pm.

NOTES

Four extra-special types of rooms are available. The **lodge tower** rooms have a separate sitting area, an extra TV and phone, and five windows. **Concierge** rooms offer personalized services, continental breakfast, evening refreshments, and a private elevator. Of the concierge rooms, special **turret rooms** (see our honeymoon photo on previous page) have wet bars and windows all around, while **honeymoon suites** pamper with whirlpool tubs!

The Grand Floridian Resort & Spa also has a **conference center**.

Check-in time is 3:00 pm. Check-out time is 11:00 am.

Ratings are explained on page 28.

RATINGS

Our Value Ratings:		Our Magic Ratings:		Readers' Ratings:
Quality:	10/10	Theme:	8/10	80% fell in love with it
Accessibility:	8/10	Amenities:	9/10	4% liked it well enough
Affordability:	2/10	Fun Factor:	6/10	11% had mixed feelings
Overall Value:	**7/10**	**Overall Magic:**	**8/10**	5% were disappointed

Grand Floridian is enjoyed by...		(rated by both authors and readers)
Younger Kids: ♥♥♥♥	Young Adults: ♥♥♥♥	Families: ♥♥♥
Older Kids: ♥♥♥♥	Mid Adults: ♥♥♥♥♥	Couples: ♥♥♥♥♥
Teenagers: ♥♥♥	Mature Adults: ♥♥♥♥♥	Singles: ♥♥♥

Top Photo Slice: Inlaid marble floor at the Grand Floridian Resort (①24373) © oldmom

Finding Your Place at Disney's Grand Floridian Resort & Spa

GRAND FLORIDIAN RESORT MAP

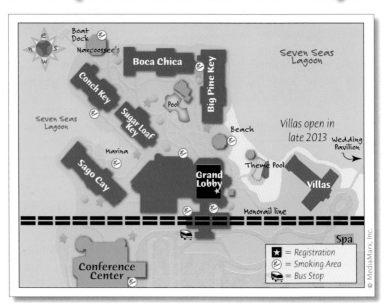

★ = Registration
Ⓢ = Smoking Area
🚌 = Bus Stop

© MediaMarx, Inc.

BEST SPOTS

The **dormer rooms** on the top floors of the lodge buildings may be a bit smaller (they only fit 4 rather than 5), but they feature vaulted ceilings, a secluded balcony, and a charming window above the French doors. The **best views of Cinderella Castle** come in the theme park-view rooms in Sago Cay and Conch Key lodges. Sugar Loaf Key is the closest lodge house to the Grand Lobby, but it also sees the most traffic and hears the most noise. Big Pine Key is near the beach, and its lagoon-view rooms offer picturesque vistas.

RATES

2013 Sample Room Rates
Seasons are noted on page 14.

Room Type	Value	Fall	Regular	Peak	Holiday
Garden View	$480–$515	$497–$557	$530–$580	$624–$684	$748
Lagoon View	$540–$579	$574–$644	$618–$676	$726–$796	$847
Magic Kingdom View	$585–$678	$619–$693	$702–$785	$786–$861	$912
Lodge Concierge (Sugar Loaf Key)	$597–$640	$641–$719	$675–$731	$820–$899	$932
Main Building Concierge	$793–$851	$946–$960	$873–$944	$1,033–$1,133	$1,170

12.5% tax is not included in above room rates. Honeymoon concierge rooms start in the $1400s. Suites, which are available in one- and two-bedrooms, are upwards of $1,000. Higher rates in price ranges are for weekends and holiday periods (see page 31).

INFO

Disney's Grand Floridian Resort & Spa
✉ 4401 Floridian Way, Lake Buena Vista, FL 32830
☎ Phone: 407-824-3000   📠 Fax: 407-824-3186
💻 For reservations, call Central Reservations: 407-939-6244

Disney's Old Key West Resort

Old Key West Resort caters primarily (but not exclusively) to Disney Vacation Club members. Old Key West is located roughly between Downtown Disney and Epcot (use the blue tab at the top of the page for parks and eateries in the area).

AMBIENCE

If Disney's Grand Floridian and BoardWalk set the pace for elegant turn-of-the-century seaside resorts, this is the dressed-down, laid-back antidote. Lush vegetation and low, white **clapboard buildings** with sky-blue eaves evoke authentic Key West style, and the public areas of the resort exude small-town intimacy. The quaint waterside shop, restaurant, and bar are connected by wooden walkways, and the Conch Flats Community Hall offers homey choices like table tennis and board games. The atmosphere is lively, friendly, and not at all hectic. Accommodations are spacious, comfy, and attractive.

RESORT LAYOUT & ROOMS

Intimate is not necessarily small. Old Key West is big enough to get lost in. (We speak from experience!) The resort's 761 guest "homes" range from **studios** (390 sq. ft.) with kitchenettes that sleep 4–5 adults, to spacious **one-bedrooms** (942 sq. ft.) with full kitchens that sleep 4–5 adults, **two-bedrooms** (1,395 sq. ft.) also with full kitchens that sleep eight adults, and the incredible three-bedroom/four-bath **Grand Villas** (2,375 sq. ft.) that sleep up to 12. All have a private patio or balcony perfect for breakfast, and all but the studios include a master suite with a large two-person whirlpool tub; a sprawling great room with full kitchen, dining area, and queen-size sleeper sofa; and washer and dryer. Villas sport views of the golf course, waterways, or woods. Amenities in all rooms include a TV, refrigerator, microwave, coffeemaker, free high-speed Internet, and voice mail. One-bedroom and larger villas boast a fully equipped kitchen, big-screen TV, DVD player, and in-room safe. These "homes" are excellent for groups and families who wish to stay together.

One-Bedroom (unshaded)

King

Queen

Queen

W/D

Shwr

Studio (shaded)

Entire layout represents a Two-Bedroom Home

Planning · Getting There · Staying in Style · Touring · Feasting · Making Magic · Index · Notes & More

Top Photo Slice: Sunset over Old Key West (①2540) ® Alison Hinsley

Genuine PassPorter · Genuine PassPorter · Genuine PassPorter · Genuine PassPorter · Genuine PassPorter · Genuine PassPorter · Genuine

Using the Amenities at Disney's Old Key West Resort

DINING & LOUNGING

Olivia's Cafe (see page 258) is a kind of casual, small-town place loved by locals. **Good's Food to Go** over by the main pool serves up breakfasts, burgers, and snacks—typical menu items include a tuna sandwich ($6.49) and a child's sandpail meal ($4.99). Refillable mugs are available for $14.49. Also by the main

Father, son, and grandma enjoy a one-bedroom villa at Old Key West

pool, the **Gurgling Suitcase** has drinks and appetizers like shrimp fritters ($5.99) and crab cake ($7.59). **Turtle Shack** by the Turtle Pond Road pool offers snacks seasonally. **Pizza delivery** is also available.

PLAYING & RELAXING

For Athletes: Tennis, basketball, shuffleboard, and volleyball courts are available. Rent boats and bikes at Hank's Rent 'N Return. Golf at the nearby course, or try the walking/jogging path. A health club has Nautilus equipment, plus a sauna and massages (extra fee).
For Children: The Conch Flats Community Hall offers games and organized events for kids. Playgrounds are near some of the pools.
For Gamers: The two arcades—Electric Eel Arcade and The Flying Fisherman—have plenty of video games to keep the kids happy.
For Shoppers: The Conch Flats General Store offers general and Disney merchandise, plus groceries and sundries.
For Swimmers: Three leisure pools and a large themed pool with a water slide, hot tub, sauna, and sandy play area round out the "R.E.S.T. Beach Recreation Department." A children's wading pool is near the main pool.

GETTING ABOUT

Direct **buses** to the four major parks and Downtown Disney (see chart below for in-transit times) stop at the resort's five bus stops. A **boat** from the marina also travels to Saratoga Springs and the Marketplace at Downtown Disney between 11:00 am and 11:00 pm—check the schedule. To get around the resort, hop on a bus, as they always stop at the Hospitality House before heading out. You can also take a (long) **walk** to Downtown Disney via a footpath.

Magic Kingdom	Epcot	Disney's Hollywood Studios	Disney's Animal Kingdom	Downtown Disney
direct bus ~25 min.	direct bus ~10 min.	direct bus ~10 min.	direct bus ~15 min.	bus/boat ~5/~15 min.

Approximate time you will spend in transit from resort to destination during normal operation.

Top Photo Slice: Sandcastle water slide at Disney's Old Key West Resort © MediaMarx, Inc.

Making the Most of Disney's Old Key West Resort

Some one-bedroom homes have a slight variation that can make a big difference if your party is large: There is a **second door to the bathroom** through the laundry room (see layout on page 73) that avoids the master bedroom. If this is important, request buildings 30 or higher at reservation and again at check-in.

Buildings 62–64 are the newest—they opened in early 2000. These are also the only buildings that have elevators.

Renovations to this resort brought a **sleeper chair** to all one-bedroom villas, bumping capacity up to five guests in those villas.

The **three-bedroom Grand Villas** are luxurious (and expensive). They are two-storied with private baths for each bedroom plus an extra bath for guests using the sleeper sofa. They have all the amenities of the other vacation homes, plus a 32" television and a stereo. They're very popular with families, so reserve as early as possible.

Hank's Rent 'N Return offers more than just bikes and boats. You can rent videos, board games, balls, and more. There are often daily activities and games—inquire when checking in.

Wildlife at Old Key West

If you stay in a studio, you won't have a washer and dryer in your room, but there are air-conditioned **laundry rooms** available near the pools at no extra charge. You can buy soap and bleach, too.

Check-in time is 4:00 pm. Check-out time is 11:00 am.

Ratings are explained on page 28.

Our Value Ratings:		Our Magic Ratings:		Readers' Ratings:
Quality:	7/10	Theme:	7/10	85% fell in love with it
Accessibility:	5/10	Amenities:	6/10	15% liked it well enough
Affordability:	4/10	Fun Factor:	5/10	0% had mixed feelings
Overall Value:	**5/10**	**Overall Magic:**	**6/10**	0% were disappointed

Old Key West is enjoyed by...		(rated by both authors and readers)
Younger Kids: ♥♥♥	Young Adults: ♥♥♥♥	Families: ♥♥♥♥♥
Older Kids: ♥♥♥♥	Mid Adults: ♥♥♥♥♥	Couples: ♥♥♥♥♥
Teenagers: ♥♥♥♥	Mature Adults: ♥♥♥♥♥	Singles: ♥♥♥

Planning · Getting There · Staying in Style · Touring · Feasting · Making Magic · Index · Notes & More

TIPS · NOTES · RATINGS

Top Photo Slice: Balcony at Disney's Old Key West Resort © MediaMarx, Inc.

Planning

Getting There

Staying in Style

Touring

Feasting

Making Magic

Index

Notes & More

OLD KEY WEST RESORT MAP

Finding Your Place at Disney's Old Key West Resort

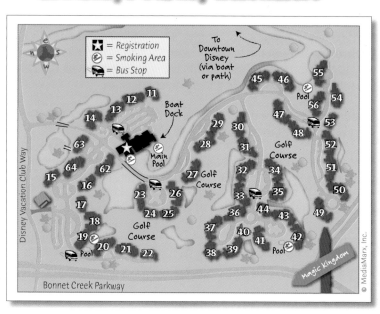

BEST LOCATIONS

Location is important in this sprawling resort. Though there are bus stops throughout the resort, we found staying near the **Hospitality House** to be a huge benefit. Buildings 11–14 and 62–64 are the closest (we loved our one-bedroom home in building 11), with buildings 15–16 and 23–26 also within reasonable walking distance. Most locations enjoy relative **peace and quiet**, but if you really want seclusion, 47–48 and 52–54 are nice as they are away from pools and roads, yet are near a bus stop. We suggest you avoid 30–44 as they feel remote, have traffic noise, and bus stops are often inconvenient.

RATES

2013 Sample Villa Rates
Seasons are noted on page 14.

Room Type	Value	Fall	Regular	Peak	Holiday
Studio Villa	$327–$343	$350	$370	$431	$472
One-Bedroom Villa	$452–$462	$477	$508	$586	$665
Two-Bedroom Villa	$618–$628	$680	$742	$903	$995
Grand Villa	$1,381–$1,391	$1,441	$1,517	$1,739	$1,822

12.5% tax is not included in the above rates. Three views are available—water, golf course, and woods—but with no difference in price.

INFO

Disney's Old Key West Resort
✉ 1510 North Cove Road, Lake Buena Vista, FL 32830
☎ Phone: 407-827-7700   📠 Fax: 407-827-7710
📋 For reservations, call Central Reservations: 407-939-6244

More at ⓘ old-key-west

Disney's Polynesian Resort

The Polynesian Resort is a lush, tropical paradise that brings the romance of the South Pacific to life. It rests tranquilly on the Seven Seas Lagoon between the Transportation and Ticket Center and the Grand Floridian Resort (use the blue tab at the top of the page for parks and eateries in the area).

AMBIENCE

The blooming gardens are your first hint of the beauty and color of the **tropics**, which are captured so splendidly here. You may not even notice that you've entered the main building, the Great Ceremonial House, with its atrium filled with falling waters and flowering tropical plants. "Aloha!" is more than a word here—it is a way of life—and you will be reminded of this again and again during your visit.

RESORT LAYOUT & ROOMS

853 guest rooms are arranged throughout **longhouses** on 11 "islands" of Polynesia. The longhouses are two or three stories; the first-floor rooms have patios, and many of the upper-floor rooms have balconies. The lush, laid-back feeling of the resort is carried into the recently renovated rooms with tropical blues and greens, dark, hand-carved wood furniture, and flat-screen TVs. Spacious rooms (409–448 sq. ft.) offer two queen beds and a daybed, accommodating five people. The roomy bathroom has a large mirror and toilet behind a partition. Suites and concierge-level rooms housed in the Tonga and Hawaii longhouses offer personal service and great views. Amenities for all rooms include toiletries, 24-hour room service, coffeemakers, refrigerators, housekeeping, turndown service (on request), and voice mail.

Standard Room Layout

DINING & LOUNGING

Paradise offers bounty in food, too. Two table-service restaurants (see page 258) are **Kona Cafe**, offering a filling breakfast and inventive lunch and dinner, and **'Ohana**, serving up food and fun with skewered meats. The 24-hour **Captain Cook's Snack Company** is a good place for a quick breakfast and light meals. Typical items are Mickey waffles ($4.59), Aloha pork sandwich ($8.89), and kids' chicken nuggets ($4.99). Refillable mugs are available for $14.49. A family-style **character breakfast** is served at 'Ohana, too. And let's not forget the Spirit of Aloha dinner show (page 265). **Tambu**, the lounge by 'Ohana, serves snacks and drinks, **Kona Island** is a coffee bar in the mornings, and the poolside **Barefoot Bar** has drinks.

Planning · **Getting There** · **Staying in Style** · **Touring** · **Feasting** · **Making Magic** · **Index** · **Notes & More**

Planning | Getting There | Staying in Style | Touring | Feasting | Making Magic | Index | Notes & More

Using the Amenities at Disney's Polynesian Resort

PLAYING & RELAXING

For Athletes: Boaters rent Sea Raycers and sailboats at the marina. Joggers enjoy the Walk Around the World that partially encircles the Seven Seas Lagoon, and a 1.5-mile path winds through the resort.

For Charmers: The Grand Floridian Spa is nearby (see page 215).

For Children: The Never Land Club is a childcare club (see page 285)—it's next to the arcade. A playground is near the main pool.

For Gamers: Moana Mickey's Arcade offers many video games.

For Shoppers: On the first floor, BouTiki has Polynesian-themed gifts and clothing and Wyland Galleries has collectibles. The second floor houses Trader Jack's (souvenirs and sundries) and Samoa Snacks.

For Show-Goers: Tucked in the back of the resort is Luau Cove, home to Polynesian-style dinner shows. More details on page 265.

For Swimmers: The Nanea Volcano themed pool features a large pool "fed" by a spring, a water slide, warm water areas, and a zero-entry section (pool wheelchair available). There's also a kids' play fountain, beach for sunbathing, and leisure pool, but no spa (hot tub).

Jennifer enjoys a spacious standard room at the Polynesian

GETTING ABOUT

A **monorail** shuttles you to the Magic Kingdom (see chart below for in-transit times), the Grand Floridian, and the Contemporary, as well as the Transportation and Ticket Center (TTC). A **boat** also goes to the Magic Kingdom. To reach Epcot, walk to TTC and board the monorail. To reach other parks and Downtown Disney, take **direct buses** (see map on page 80 for the bus stop). To reach most resorts, take a monorail to the Magic Kingdom and transfer to a resort bus (daytime), or bus to Downtown Disney and transfer to a resort bus (evening).

Magic Kingdom	Epcot	Disney's Hollywood Studios	Disney's Animal Kingdom	Downtown Disney
monorail/boat	walk + monorail	direct bus	direct bus	direct bus
~10/~5 min.	~10+10 min.	~15 min.	~15 min.	~25 min.

Approximate time you will spend in transit from resort to destination during normal operation.

Disney's Animal Kingdom Area

Epcot Area

Downtown Disney Area

Magic Kingdom Area

Chapter 3: Staying in Style   Topic: Polynesian Tips and Ratings   79

Planning

TIPS   Getting There

Staying in Style

Touring

NOTES   Feasting

Making Magic

RATINGS   Index

Notes & More

Making the Most of Disney's Polynesian Resort

On the beach in front of the Hawaii and Tahiti longhouses are several **bench swings** and **hammocks**. Not only are these heaven after a long day, they make ideal spots to watch the fireworks.

A **night stroll** here is sublime. A very secluded spot over the rise on the beach's point (Sunset Point) is pure magic (it's where your authors were wed), and a great spot to watch the Magic Kingdom fireworks and the Electrical Water Pageant (see below).

The **Electrical Water Pageant** passes right by the Polynesian around 9:00 pm. If you don't have a water-view room, take a stroll down to the beach or to the end of the dock near the marina.

The resort's guest rooms recently got a **facelift** with new designer bedding in tropical colors, new furniture (including a desk that can be extended out), and large flat-screen TVs (see photo on previous page). The public areas also received a fresh, new treatment.

Families love the Polynesian and it may get a bit **noisy** in the pool areas (near Samoa, Niue, Hawaii, Rarotonga, and Tokelau).

Walk to the Transportation and Ticket Center for the **Epcot monorail**. The monorail around the lagoon adds 20 minutes otherwise.

The Polynesian sometimes shares **bus routes** with the Contemporary and Grand Floridian resorts, picking up/dropping off guests at the Contemporary first and Grand Floridian last.

Daily activities are available for kids of all ages, such as coconut races, torch lightings, and hula lessons. Inquire at Lobby Concierge.

Check-in time is 3:00 pm. Check-out time is 11:00 am.

Ratings are explained on page 28.

Our Value Ratings:		Our Magic Ratings:		Readers' Ratings:
Quality:	8/10	Theme:	9/10	62% fell in love with it
Accessibility:	9/10	Amenities:	7/10	29% liked it well enough
Affordability:	3/10	Fun Factor:	8/10	7% had mixed feelings
Overall Value:	**7/10**	**Overall Magic:**	**8/10**	2% were disappointed

The Polynesian is enjoyed by...	(rated by both authors and readers)	
Younger Kids: ♥♥♥♥	Young Adults: ♥♥♥♥♥	Families: ♥♥♥♥♥
Older Kids: ♥♥♥♥♥	Mid Adults: ♥♥♥♥♥	Couples: ♥♥♥♥♥
Teenagers: ♥♥♥♥	Mature Adults: ♥♥♥♥♥	Singles: ♥♥♥

Top Photo Slice: Drums at Disney's Polynesian Resort © MediaMarx, Inc.

Planning

Getting There

Staying in Style

Touring

Feasting

Making Magic

Index

Notes & More

POLYNESIAN RESORT MAP

Finding Your Place
at Disney's Polynesian Resort

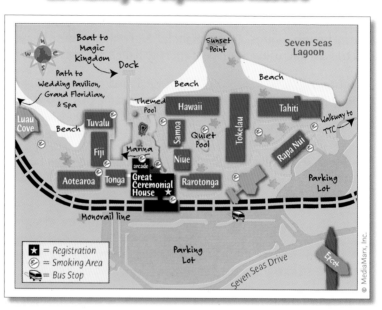

© MediaMarx, Inc.

BEST LOCATIONS

All **first-floor rooms** have patios, and all **third-floor rooms** have balconies. Most **second-floor rooms** have no balconies, with the exception of Tahiti, Rapa Nui, Tokelau, and Tonga, which do. Particularly nice water views can be found in Tuvalu, Hawaii, Tahiti, and Fiji. The first-floor rooms in Tahiti facing away from the water have pleasant, secluded patios, as do those in Rapa Nui and Rarotonga. If you opt for a garden view, we recommend Aotearoa with beautiful landscaping and an up-close view of the monorail. For added **privacy**, request a room on the top floor.

RATES

2013 Sample Room Rates
Seasons are noted on page 14.

Room Type	Value	Fall	Regular	Peak	Holiday
Garden View	$422–$452	$446–$502	$472–$511	$558–$608	$665
Lagoon View	$530–$567	$566–$637	$584–$654	$706–$769	$797
Garden View Concierge (Club)	$566–$606	$597–$672	$624–$676	$753–$821	$852
Lagoon View/Suite Concierge	$706–$756	$746–$840	$787–$852	$913–$995	$1,000
One-Bedroom Suite Concierge	$945–$1,000	$1,030–$1,129	$1,081–$1,151	$1,248–$1,338	$1,382

12.5% tax is not included in the above. Two-bedroom suites start in the $1600s. Higher rates in price ranges are for weekends and holiday periods (see page 31).

INFO

Disney's Polynesian Resort
✉ 1600 Seven Seas Drive, Lake Buena Vista, FL 32830
☎ Phone: 407-824-2000   📠 Fax: 407-824-3174
📋 For reservations, call Central Reservations: 407-939-6244

More at ① polynesian

Disney's Pop Century Resort

Auld acquaintance shall be remembered at Pop Century, one of the Walt Disney World Resort's value-priced resorts. At this innovative resort, you'll find the last half of the 20th century immortalized for its contribution to popular culture—icons and references to the 1950s–1990s are everywhere. Pop Century Resort is located in the Epcot area (use the blue tab at the top of the page for parks and eateries in the vicinity) on the northeast corner of Osceola Parkway and Victory Way.

AMBIENCE

Whether you're 8 or 80, a **blast from your past** awaits at Pop Century. Pop Century sits beside a 33-acre lake with a scenic bridge that leads to Disney's Art of Animation Resort, which opened in 2012. Go from the rockin' days of sock hops "to infinity and beyond" in eye-popping style with a uniquely themed check-in lobby, food court/shop/lounge, and pool bar. Outside, giant cultural icons fill the senses, including a monumental Rubik's Cube®, a huge foosball field, and a billboard-sized laptop computer. The themes continue with three imaginative themed pools. Each guest lodge building is festooned with cultural icons and "groovy" catch phrases. This resort's plans originally called for an expansion across the lake (representing the decades of the first half of the 20th century), but that fell by the wayside when the Art of Animation Resort was announced in its place.

RESORT LAYOUT & ROOMS

The 2,880 guest rooms in Pop Century are situated in five differently themed areas encompassing a total of 10 guest lodges. **Pop Century** celebrates the decades of the 1950s, '60s, '70s, '80s, and '90s. Themed courtyards are formed between two or more of the ten T-shaped guest lodges. Each decade's theme is reflected in the guest room decor, but rich, wood-grain furniture adds elegance to the fun. Rooms have either two double beds or one king bed, a large TV with remote, a small table with two chairs, and a roomy chest of drawers. Rooms hold up to four guests plus one child under three in a crib (a folding crib is available on request). Rooms are small—about 260 sq. ft.—but as with the All-Star Resorts, furnishings allow adequate floor space. Rooms have no private balconies or patios, but each offers climate controls. Amenities include soap, housekeeping, large in-room safe, mini-refrigerator, free wireless Internet, table-side modem jack, iron and ironing board, and voice mail.

Standard Room Layout

Planning | Getting There | Staying in Style | Touring | Feasting | Making Magic | Index | Notes & More

Planning · Getting There · Staying in Style · Touring · Feasting · Making Magic · Index · Notes & More

Using the Amenities at Disney's Pop Century Resort

EATING & DRINKING

Pop Century has a large **food court** with a variety of food stations. It's open daily for breakfast, lunch, and dinner. Menu items include a breakfast platter ($8.29), a bacon cheeseburger ($8.79), and a

A standard guest room at Pop Century
400+ more photos at http://www.passporter.com/photos

chicken Caesar salad ($8.09). Purchase a mug for $14.49 and get unlimited refills from the beverage bar. A pizza delivery service is available in the afternoons and evenings, along with seasonal snack carts near the pool.

PLAYING & RELAXING

For Athletes: The 12' wide lakeside path is ideal for walks and jogs. The lake does not offer a marina.
For Children: A quiet playground and play fountain is located within the resort (see map on page 84 for locations).
For Gamers: An arcade is located in the resort's main building.
For Shoppers: The resort offers a large shop with Disney logo merchandise, clothing, sundries, and some snack foods.
For Swimmers: Cool off in the main pool (which also features a wading pool), and two smaller themed pools. The fun pools are shaped like a bowling pin, a flower, and a computer. There are no spas (hot tubs) at this resort.

GETTING ABOUT

Buses (see chart below for in-transit times) are outside the main building of the resort. Stops are well-marked and offer benches and shelter. Bus service is prompt and efficient. Destinations other than those below can be reached by changing buses at Disney's Hollywood Studios or Epcot (daytime) or Downtown Disney (evening). Parking is freely available, though you should study the map to find the closest lot to your room.

Magic Kingdom	Epcot	Disney's Hollywood Studios	Disney's Animal Kingdom	Downtown Disney
direct bus ~25 min.	direct bus ~20 min.	direct bus ~15 min.	direct bus ~15 min.	direct bus ~20 min.

Approximate time you will spend in transit from resort to destination during normal operation.

Top Photo Slice: Kids water play fountain at Disney's Pop Century Resort © MediaMarx, Inc.

Making the Most of Disney's Pop Century Resort

The **33-acre lake** beside this resort is an added perk for a value resort—the equivalent All-Star Resorts have no ponds, lakes, or rivers. Frequent park benches line the path, and "roadside" signs note landmark cultural events of each era.

The other side of the lake is Disney's Art of Animation Resort, which features 2000 new rooms, more than half of which are **family suites** with living rooms and bedrooms. Themes include The Lion King, Cars, Finding Nemo, and Little Mermaid. This resort opened May 2012. To learn more, see photos, read tips, and get rates, see our description on pages 45–49 and visit http://disneyworld.disney.go.com/resorts/art-of-animation-resort

Epcot's **IllumiNations** fireworks are visible across the lake. Best views are from the '50s buildings—try the fourth floor!

Food court patrons are treated to a **dance routine** performed by the resort's cast members at breakfast and dinner! They do the Twist at 8:00 am and the Hustle at 6:00 pm. Be there or be square!

A **children's pop-jet fountain** is tucked away in a corner between the '60s and '70s—look for a statue of Goofy and a red Corvette.

Plan to either **carry your own luggage** or wait a while (perhaps 45–60 minutes) for the resort's luggage service to drop it off at your building. Arrangements to pick up luggage on your departure day should be made the night before.

Coin-operated laundries are located near each pool. Bring lots of quarters—wash loads and dry cycles are $2.00 each.

Check-in time is 4:00 pm. Check-out time is 11:00 am.

Ratings are explained on page 28.

Our Value Ratings:		Our Magic Ratings:		Readers' Ratings:
Quality:	6/10	Theme:	6/10	63% fell in love with it
Accessibility:	5/10	Amenities:	4/10	18% liked it well enough
Affordability:	9/10	Fun Factor:	4/10	11% had mixed feelings
Overall Value:	**7/10**	**Overall Magic:**	**5/10**	8% were disappointed

Pop Century is enjoyed by...	(rated by both authors and readers)	
Younger Kids: ♥♥♥♥♥	Young Adults: ♥♥♥♥	Families: ♥♥♥♥
Older Kids: ♥♥♥♥♥	Mid Adults: ♥♥♥	Couples: ♥♥
Teenagers: ♥♥♥	Mature Adults: ♥♥	Singles: ♥♥♥

TIPS
NOTES
RATINGS

Planning
Getting There
Staying in Style
Touring
Feasting
Making Magic
Index
Notes & More

Top Photo Slice: The Pop Century laundry room looks like a huge bowling shoe shelf! © MediaMarx, Inc.

Planning | Getting There | Staying in Style | Touring | Feasting | Making Magic | Index | Notes & More

Finding Your Place at Disney's Pop Century Resort

POP CENTURY RESORT MAP

Disney's Art of Animation Resort

Hourglass Lake

Generation Gap Bridge

★ = Registration, Food Court, and Shop
🚌 = Bus Stop
☺ = Playground
🎆 = Fountain
S = Preferred Building
☺ = Smoking Area

'60s | '70s | '50s | '80s | '90s

Classic Hall

5101-5472 | 4101-4472 | 3101-3472 | 6101-6472 | 2101-2472 | 1101-1472 | 0101-0472 | 7101-7472 | 9101-9472 | 8101-8472

Downtown Disney

© MediaMarx, Inc.

BEST LOCATIONS

Rooms at Pop Century **vary only by location** within the resorts and floor level. For convenience, we recommend the '50s, '60s, or '70s as they are closest to pools, food, and transportation. Our personal pick is the '70s as it is relatively quiet and has good views from most windows. Note that several buildings offer excellent views of Hourglass Lake, notably '50s, '60s, and '70s. If you seek quiet, request a room on the third or fourth floors. Note that rooms in the '60s are extra because they are the closest to Classic Hall, but we don't feel this resort is so spread out that you need to stay there.

RATES

2013 Sample Room Rates
Seasons are noted on page 14.

Room Type	Value	Fall	Regular	Summer	Peak	Holiday
Standard	$95-$109	$108-$123	$121-$146	$143-$168	$145-$175	$186
Preferred	$110-$135	$123-$143	$143-$168	$158-$183	$160-$190	$201

12.5% tax is not included in above rates. Preferred rooms are in the guest lodges closest to the main building. There is a $10 per person charge for the third and fourth adult in a room, but no extra charge for children under 18. Rooms may face parking lots, pools, the lake, or courtyards. Higher rates in price ranges are for weekends and holiday periods (see page 31).

INFO

Disney's Pop Century Resort
✉ 1050 Century Drive, Lake Buena Vista, FL 32830
☎ Phone: 407-938-4000   📠 Fax: 407-938-4040
📋 For reservations, call Central Reservations: 407-939-6244

Disney's Port Orleans Resort

In 2001, sister resorts Port Orleans and Dixie Landings merged into one resort known as Port Orleans. The large, moderately priced resort is located along the banks of the Sassagoula River, north of Downtown Disney (use the blue tab at the top of the page for other places in the same vicinity). Port Orleans is popular with young couples, families, and children, both for its value and for its fun atmosphere.

AMBIENCE

The romance of the Old South awaits you at Port Orleans. The resort is divided into two separate districts: the French Quarter (the smaller district and the original Port Orleans) and Riverside (the former Dixie Landings). The **French Quarter** recaptures the feeling and flavors of historic New Orleans as it prepares for Mardi Gras. The Mint is your first stop in the French Quarter, a large building with wrought ironwork details and a soaring glass atrium that safeguards the district's front desk, Lobby Concierge, and shop. A step outside reveals narrow cobblestone lanes, complete with "gas" lamps, wrought iron benches, and grand magnolia trees. A leisurely 10-minute walk along the Sassagoula River takes you over to **Riverside**. Banjo music and southern hospitality greet you as you enter Riverside's Sassagoula Steamboat Company, a replica of an old riverboat depot. The depot is the crossroads of this quaint settlement, housing the district's front desk and services. Venture out along meandering paths and wooden bridges to antebellum mansions in one direction or the quaint bayou dwellings in the other.

RESORT LAYOUT

The resort's 3,056 guest rooms are scattered among the two districts, with 1,008 in the French Quarter and 2,048 in Riverside. Rooms in the French Quarter are housed in seven large buildings (see map on page 89), each designed to resemble **rows of townhouses** with differing architectural styles, varying rooflines, and facades bricked or painted in shades of blue, cream, or peach. Most buildings have their own yards and gardens in front, which are charmingly fenced with wrought iron. Up the Sassagoula in Riverside you'll find 1,024 rooms gracing "Gone With the Wind," plantation-style mansions in an area called **Magnolia Bend**. These three-storied, elegant buildings are situated majestically along the Sassagoula River. An equal number of rooms are housed within crackerbox-style dwellings in the **Alligator Bayou** section. These two-storied, rough-hewn, elevator-less dwellings peek through the trees, with quaint paths winding through the "bayous." Alligator Bayou has a more intimate feel to it than its neighbor, Magnolia Bend.

Planning | Getting There | Staying in Style | Touring | Feasting | Making Magic | Index | Notes & More

Lodging and Dining at Disney's Port Orleans Resort

RESORT ROOMS

Rooms are 314 sq. ft. in size and **decorated in three styles**. In the French Quarter, you find faux French Provincial furniture, gilt-framed mirrors, and Venetian blinds. In Riverside's Magnolia Bend, antebellum rooms delight with cherry furniture and brocade settees.

A standard guest room at Port Orleans Riverside
300+ more photos at http://www.passporter.com/photos

Riverside's Alligator Bayou rooms sport beds made of hewn "logs" and patchwork quilts. All rooms accommodate up to four and come with either two queen beds or one king bed (king bed rooms are located on building corners); 963 Alligator

Standard Room Layout

Bayou rooms house up to five guests by offering a complimentary trundle bed in rooms with queen beds (trundle beds slide out from under the queen bed and fit a child or small adult). Rooms include a TV, armoire, table and chairs, ceiling fan, and a separate vanity area with double pedestal sinks and privacy curtain. Every room has a window (corner rooms have two), but none have private balconies. Amenities include toiletries (soap and shampoo only), hair dryers, coffeemakers, housekeeping, limited room service, in-room safe (most rooms), refrigerator, and voice mail.

DINING & LOUNGING

Port Orleans plays host to one of the more popular resort eateries: **Boatwright's Dining Hall**. This table-service restaurant in the Riverside district offers dinner only—see page 258. Two large food courts—**Sassagoula Floatworks and Food Factory** in the French Quarter and the **Riverside Mill** at Riverside—offer breakfast, lunch, and dinner. Typical menu items are beignets ($2.99), French toast with eggs ($5.19), cheesecake ($3.89), grilled chicken sandwich ($8.59), pasta with meatballs ($8.09), and kids' chicken nuggets ($4.99). Purchase a mug for $14.49 and get free refills at both food courts. The French Quarter's **Scat Cat's Club** is a full-service bar with live music on the weekends, while **Mardi Grogs** pool bar has drinks and snacks. In Riverside, the **River Roost** offers specialty drinks, appetizers, and music in the evenings, and **Muddy Rivers Pool Bar** has drinks and snacks. **Limited room service**.

Using the Amenities at Disney's Port Orleans Resort

For Athletes: The Dixie Levee marina in Riverside rents pedal boats, rowboats, canopy boats, and bikes (including surrey bikes). Be sure to check the rental hours early on to avoid disappointment later. Both districts offer plenty of paths for walkers and joggers, too.

For Fishers: An old-fashioned fishin' hole on Ol' Man Island in Riverside lets you hang a cane pole over a pond stocked with catfish, perch, bass, and bluegill (catch and release only). For more adventure, you can book a fishing excursion down the Sassagoula.

For Children: Two playgrounds are near the two themed pools.

For Gamers: South Quarter Games (French Quarter) has plenty of video games, as does the Medicine Show Arcade (Riverside).

For Romantics: Enjoy a relaxing, private carriage ride for $35.

For Shoppers: Jackson Square Gifts & Desires (French Quarter) and Fulton's (Riverside) stock sundries, souvenirs, and snacks.

For Swimmers: The French Quarter's Doubloon Lagoon is a moderately sized themed pool with a huge dragon housing the water slide (you slide right down its tongue). A Mardi Gras band of crocodiles shoots water at unsuspecting swimmers. The French Quarter also has a wading pool for the young ones and a hot tub (spa) nearby. In Riverside, Ol' Man Island offers a particularly nice "swimmin' hole" with a large free-form pool, complete with a water slide, a waterfall cascading from a broken sluice, and a fun geyser. A hot tub and kids' wading area are also here. Riverside also has five quieter pools spread throughout the resort.

Direct **buses** to the major theme parks and Downtown Disney stop regularly (see chart below for in-transit times). Buses usually pick up guests at French Quarter's single bus stop first, then go on to the four stops in Riverside. To get to other resorts and destinations, take a bus to Epcot (daytime) or to Downtown Disney (evening), and transfer to the appropriate bus. A **boat** also picks up guests from Riverside and the French Quarter and goes to and from Downtown Disney Marketplace until 11:00 pm (weather permitting). Boats run about once an hour until 4:00 pm and every 15 minutes thereafter. The trip is leisurely and relaxing. A **shuttle boat** also operates between the French Quarter and Riverside on a frequent basis, especially at meal times. Parking is available throughout the resorts.

Magic Kingdom	Epcot	Disney's Hollywood Studios	Disney's Animal Kingdom	Downtown Disney
direct bus ~10 min.	direct bus ~10 min.	direct bus ~15 min.	direct bus ~15 min.	direct bus/boat ~15/~20 min.

Approximate time you will spend in transit from resort to destination during normal operation.

Top Photo Slice: Rose-covered archways leading to Magnolia Bend at Port Orleans Riverside (①4163) © Michelle Clark

Making the Most of Disney's Port Orleans Resort

TIPS

The two **spas** (hot tubs) near the themed pools are heavenly after a long day at the parks. The spa in the French Quarter is a bit of a walk from the pool and quite secluded (look near the laundry), but large enough for several people to soak comfortably (and sociably).

Explore the **resort's grounds** for the quaint parks and gardens scattered throughout. The French Quarter's street and park names are a treat unto themselves, with names like Mud du Lac Lane and Beaux Regards Square. An evening stroll in the French Quarter when the "gas" lamps are lit is particularly magical.

Enjoy an **evening carriage ride** through the two sister resorts. Carriages depart from in front of Boatwright's in Riverside between 6:00 pm and 9:00 pm. Cost is $35 for a 25-minute ride for up to four adults or two adults and two to three children.

Small **refrigerators** are included in your room. Roll-away/trundle beds are also free of charge—request these at reservation time.

NOTES

The **beds** are pretty high off the floor. Watch young ones so they don't fall out, or request complimentary bed rails from housekeeping. If you are concerned, note that some rooms in Alligator Bayou at Riverside come with a pullout trundle bed, which you can request upon reservation and check-in. In fact, this trundle bed allows for a fifth person, making Port Orleans Riverside the only moderately priced resort to accommodate five people. Do note that the trundle is small and is really intended for a child or very short person.

Due to the resort merger, Port Orleans has **two front desks**, one in each district. Refer to your reservation to know whether to check-in at French Quarter or Riverside.

Check-in time is 3:00 pm. Check-out time is 11:00 am.

RATINGS

Ratings are explained on page 28.

Our Value Ratings:		Our Magic Ratings:		Readers' Ratings:
Quality:	7/10	Theme:	8/10	65% fell in love with it
Accessibility:	7/10	Amenities:	6/10	22% liked it well enough
Affordability:	8/10	Fun Factor:	6/10	4% had mixed feelings
Overall Value:	**7/10**	**Overall Magic:**	**7/10**	9% were disappointed

Port Orleans is enjoyed by...		(rated by both authors and readers)
Younger Kids: ♥♥♥	Young Adults: ♥♥♥♥♥	Families: ♥♥♥♥
Older Kids: ♥♥♥♥♥	Mid Adults: ♥♥♥♥	Couples: ♥♥♥♥♥
Teenagers: ♥♥♥	Mature Adults: ♥♥♥	Singles: ♥♥♥

Top Photo Slice: A horse and carriage passes a fountain at Disney's Port Orleans French Quarter Resort © MediaMarx, Inc.

Finding Your Place
at Disney's Port Orleans Resort

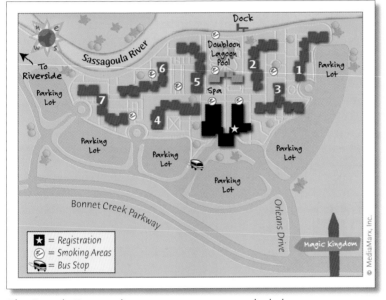

FRENCH QUARTER MAP

The French Quarter has a more compact, orderly layout.

RIVERSIDE MAP

Riverside is large and meandering, with an island in the middle.

Planning · Getting There · Staying in Style · Touring · Feasting · Making Magic · Index · Notes & More

Planning

Getting There

Staying in Style

Touring

Feasting

Making Magic

Index

Notes & More

BEST LOCATIONS

Choosing Your Room at Disney's Port Orleans Resort

Thanks to the merger of the two resorts, Port Orleans is exceptionally large and sprawling and **room location** can really make a difference in your resort experience. Each of Port Orleans' three distinctive sections is beloved by its fans. There's no right or wrong section. Request the style that suits you best.

Most rooms in the **French Quarter** are within easy distance of Lobby Concierge, the gift shop, and the food court. Buildings 2–5 are the nearest. The best views are of the Sassagoula River, as the opposite river bank is pristine—consider upgrading to a river view.

Riverside's Magnolia Bend features 512 **Royal Guest rooms** which let you "stay where royalty has stayed" featuring rooms with regal touches left behind by beloved Disney characters. Highlights include ornate beds with special optic effects, banners, and custom drapes.

The grand "mansions" and formal gardens of **Magnolia Bend** in Riverside add a luxurious air to your stay. The Magnolia Terrace building is a good pick for proximity to recreation and dining.

Our personal favorite is **Alligator Bayou** in Riverside. The buildings in Alligator Bayou are smaller (only two stories) and have lush landscaping. We often request building 14, which is near the main building, Ol' Man Island, a leisure pool, and a bus stop—it has no bad views. Buildings 15 and 18 are also good choices.

For a **quieter** room, request the second or third floor. Corner rooms are particularly nice as they provide two windows.

RATES

2013 Sample Room Rates
Seasons are noted on page 14.

Room Type	Value	Fall	Regular	Summer	Peak	Holiday
Standard Room	$162–$177	$176–$191	$188–$213	$196	$211–$231	$253
Preferred, Water, or King	$187–$217	$201–$216	$213–$238	$221	$236–$256	$283
Royal Guest Room	$192–$207	$206–$221	$220–$245	$226	$241–$261	$293

12.5% tax not included in above rates. River-view rooms are more than a water-/pool-view room and are about the same price as a Royal Guest Room. Higher rates in price ranges are for weekends and holiday periods (see page 31).

INFO

Disney's Port Orleans Resort
✉ 2201 Orleans Dr. and 1251 Dixie Dr., Lake Buena Vista, FL 32830
☎ Phone: 407-934-5000 (French Quarter) or 934-6000 (Riverside)
🖨 Fax: 407-934-5353 (French Quarter) or 934-5777 (Riverside)

More at ⓘ port-orleans

Disney's Saratoga Springs Resort & Spa

The largest of Disney's Deluxe Villa Resorts is just across the lake from Downtown Disney. Opened in May 2004 and completed in 2009, Disney's Saratoga Springs Resort and Spa offers deluxe villas for Disney Vacation Club members and nightly rentals for everyone.

Saratoga Springs stretches out over 65 acres adjacent to the Lake Buena Vista Golf Course and across Village Lake from Downtown Disney. This **Victorian-styled resort** is modeled on the historic vacation escape in Upstate New York. The fashionable elite of New York City journeyed up the Hudson on Commodore Vanderbilt's railroad to sip the health spa's waters, stroll its shady byways, and cheer their race horses to victory. Disney's architects soaked up the town's Arts and Crafts atmosphere to bring its essence to Walt Disney World. Saratoga Spring's 18 lodges cluster around the resort's lakes in six districts. Of those, Congress Park, The Springs, The Paddock, The Carousel, and The Grandstand represent the resort's theme of history, health, and horses. The new Treehouse Villas weigh in as the sixth district. The Carriage House check-in and hospitality building also offers dining and shopping.

Studio villas (355 sq. ft.) accommodate up to four guests with one queen bed, a sofa bed, sink, microwave, and a small refrigerator. The one-bedroom (714 sq. ft.) and two-bedroom (1,075 sq. ft.) villas hold up to 4 or 8 guests respectively and offer master suites with king beds and whirlpool tubs, DVD players, sofa beds, full kitchens, and washers/dryers. The Grand Villas (2,113 sq. ft.) sleep up to 12 on two levels and feature three bedrooms—the living room, dining room, and master suite (with its whirlpool tub) are on the first level, and on the second level are two more bedrooms with queen beds and private baths. The Treehouse Villas (1,074 sq. ft.) sleep up to 9 people in three bedrooms. All villas have a laptop-sized safe, and high-speed Internet access is available at no charge.

Studio Layout (shaded)

Entire layout represents a Two-Bedroom Villa

One-Bedroom (unshaded)

AMBIENCE

RESORT LAYOUT & ROOMS

Planning

Getting There

Staying in Style

Touring

Feasting

Making Magic

Index

Notes & More

Planning

Getting There

Staying in Style

Touring

Feasting

Making Magic

Index

Notes & More

Using the Amenities at Disney's Saratoga Springs Resort

DINING & LOUNGING

Hungry? The **Turf Club Bar & Grill** is a full-service restaurant (see details on page 259). **The Artists' Palette** is an eatery and market resembling an artist's loft. Open all day, it has pizzas, salads, sandwiches, bakery items, meals, groceries, gifts, and sundries. **The Rocks** and **Backstretch** pool bars are open daily.

Allie and Jennifer relax in their one-bedroom villa at Saratoga Springs

PLAYING & RELAXING

For Athletes: Rent surrey bikes at Horsing Around Rentals. There are also two clay tennis courts, basketball, shuffleboard, jogging path, and golf at the Lake Buena Vista Golf Course.

For Charmers: Saratoga Springs Spa (formerly The Spa at the Disney Institute) has a fitness center and a full range of spa treatments.

For Children: Organized activities are offered at Community Hall. Children's playground. "Pop-jet" play fountains are by the main pool and The Grandstand pool. Board games are in The Turf Club.

For Gamers: Win, Place, or Show Arcade games in Community Hall.

For Romantics: Enjoy a relaxing, 25-minute carriage ride for $35.

For Shoppers: Visit The Artists' Palette for groceries and sundries.

For Swimmers: The High Rock Spring pool features a zero-entry/ children's wading area, a 125-foot-long water slide, two free-form hot-tub spas, and an adjoining kids' play area. The Paddock has new 3,200 sq. ft. pool with zero entry, water slide, and play area. There are three other leisure pools with spas (hot tubs).

GETTING ABOUT

Direct buses to the four major parks, water parks, and Downtown Disney (see chart below for transit times) stop at the resort's five bus stops. These buses also provide internal transportation within the resort. A **boat** from the dock near the Carriage House goes to the Marketplace at Downtown Disney and Old Key West. **Walking paths** connect the resort with Downtown Disney Marketplace and West Side (West Side pathway crosses the footbridge near the boat dock). Parking is available next to each lodge building.

Magic Kingdom	Epcot	Disney's Hollywood Studios	Disney's Animal Kingdom	Downtown Disney
direct bus ~25 min.	direct bus ~10 min.	direct bus ~15 min.	direct bus ~20 min.	walk/bus/boat ~15/10/7 min.

Approximate time you will spend in transit from resort to destination during normal operation.

Making the Most of Disney's Saratoga Springs Resort

The **Main Street Railroad Station** at Magic Kingdom was modeled on the former station in Saratoga Springs, New York. The Carriage House, theater, and other nearby buildings were originally modeled on the architecture of Upstate New York resort, Chautauqua.

Want to **relax**? Barbecue pavilions, lakeside pavilions, formal gardens, and gazebos/fountains for "taking the waters" all add to the relaxed resort atmosphere.

A **refillable mug** ($14.49) is available for purchase at The Artists' Palette—you can refill it here and also at the pool bars.

The **Turf Club** is a full-service "bar and grill" serving creatively-prepared American favorites such as crab cakes ($13.49), a signature grilled romain salad ($5.49), root beer brined pork chop ($22.99), prime rib ($27.99). Kids meals are $8.59. Open 5:00 to 10:00 pm.

The **Treehouse Villas** are back! These old favorites were completely rebuilt and now feature three bedrooms (one bedroom with a queen-size bed and a whirlpool tub, another bedroom with a queen-size bed, a third bedroom with bunk beds), and a queen-size sleeper sofa and sleep chair in the living room. The Treehouse Villas also have two bathrooms, a fully-equipped kitchen, laundry, and a deck. The fun thing about the treehouses is that they are perched on pedestals, so you're sleeping on the second floor amidst all the trees! Note that these villas no longer have a downstairs bedroom as they did in their previous incarnation.

The classroom and meeting areas of the old Disney Institute are now the **main sales offices** and show-villas for Disney Vacation Club.

Check-in time is 4:00 pm. Check-out time is 11:00 am.

Ratings are explained on page 28.

Our Value Ratings:		Our Magic Ratings:		Readers' Ratings:
Quality:	6/10	Theme:	6/10	67% fell in love with it
Accessibility:	6/10	Amenities:	6/10	18% liked it well enough
Affordability:	6/10	Fun Factor:	5/10	10% had mixed feelings
Overall Value:	**6/10**	**Overall Magic:**	**6/10**	5% were disappointed

Saratoga Springs is enjoyed by...		(estimated by the authors)
Younger Kids: ♥♥♥♥	Young Adults: ♥♥♥♥	Families: ♥♥♥♥♥
Older Kids: ♥♥♥♥	Mid Adults: ♥♥♥♥♥	Couples: ♥♥♥
Teenagers: ♥♥♥	Mature Adults: ♥♥♥♥♥	Singles: ♥♥

TIPS

NOTES

RATINGS

Planning

Getting There

Staying in Style

Touring

Feasting

Making Magic

Index

Notes & More

Planning

Getting There

Staying in Style

Touring

Feasting

Making Magic

Index

Notes & More

Choosing Your Room at Disney's Saratoga Springs Resort

SARATOGA SPRINGS RESORT MAP

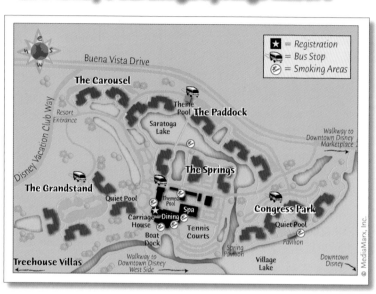

BEST LOCATIONS

Rooms in **Congress Park** have views of Downtown Disney and/or gardens and offer a short walk to the Downtown Disney Marketplace and a moderate walk to The Carriage House. Some garden views include parking lots. **The Springs** offers closest proximity to The Carriage House and themed pool, with views of Saratoga Lake or gardens/parking. **The Paddock** and **The Carousel** are the most spread out and distant from other facilities. Request to be close to the pool and/or footbridge if that's important. **The Grandstand** is close to the main facilities and has a superior pool area. The **Treehouse Villas** are secluded and a fair distance away from services. Requests for particular locations are honored when possible.

RATES

2013 Sample Villa Rates

Seasons are noted on page 14.

Room Type	Value	Fall	Regular	Peak	Holiday
Studio Villa	$327–$343	$350	$370	$431	$472
One-Bedroom Villa	$452–$462	$477	$507	$586	$665
Treehouse Villa	$709–$720	$782	$852	$1,035	$1,144
Three-Bedroom Grand Villa	$1,381–$1,391	$1,441	$1,536	$1,739	$1,822

12.5% tax is not included in the above rates.

INFO

Disney's Saratoga Springs Resort & Spa

✉ 1960 Broadway, Lake Buena Vista, FL 32830

☎ Phone: 407-827-1100   ✉ Fax: 407-827-1151

📋 For reservations, call Central Reservations: 407-934-7639

More at ⓘ saratoga-springs

Disney's Animal | Epcot | Downtown | Magic Kingdom Area

Looking for Shades of Green? Page 100. Swan Resort? Page 101.

Chapter 3: Staying in Style | Topic: Wilderness Lodge Introduction | 95

Disney's Wilderness Lodge & Villas Resort

The Wilderness Lodge and Villas are nestled in a dense forest of pines on Bay Lake, accessible by waterway from the Magic Kingdom (use the blue tab at the top of the page for parks and eateries in the area). The Lodge and Villas were inspired by the U.S. National Park lodges built in the 1900s.

Ah, wilderness! Rustic log buildings, swaying pines, babbling brooks, and the faintest whiff of wood smoke from the crackling fireplace. The Wilderness Lodge pays homage to the **grand log lodges** of the Pacific Northwest, with its towering lobby, 55-foot totem poles, and deluxe rooms. The Villas at Wilderness Lodge offer Disney's Deluxe Villa accommodations for Disney Vacation Club members (see pages 108–109) and all other guests. Architecturally, the Villas represent an earlier era than the main Lodge building and draw influences from the lodges created by America's railroad workers.

The Wilderness Lodge and the Villas offer varying accommodations, ranging from 340 to 1,071 sq. feet. The **Lodge** houses 728 guest rooms and suites, with some encircling the cavernous lobby but most in the two wings. The cozy Lodge rooms are outfitted with new furniture and bed spreads with Hidden Mickeys. Most Lodge rooms have two queen beds, but some offer a bunk bed in place of the second bed. The **Villas** feature 136 studios and one- and two-bedroom suites, each with a kitchenette or full kitchen, DVD player, and washer and dryer. All rooms have a balcony or patio, a small table and chairs, TV, double sinks, toiletries, in-room safe, refrigerator, turndown service (on request), newspaper delivery, voice mail, and valet parking.

Standard Lodge Room Layout

As you would expect from a Lodge, the food here is served in hearty, healthy portions. The two table-service restaurants (see page 260) are **Artist Point** for fine dining in the evening and **Whispering Canyon Cafe** for a fun, western-style adventure serving all-you-can-eat meals throughout the day. **Roaring Fork Snack Shop** is a self-service cafe serving breakfast foods, burgers, sandwiches, and snacks—purchase a refillable mug here for $14.49 and get free self-serve refills. Typical menu items include breakfast platter ($8.29), roast beef sandwich ($9.39), grilled veggie sandwich ($9.09), and wilderness salad ($9.19). **Miss Jenny's In-Room Dining** is available for limited room service at breakfast and dinner.

Sidebar labels: Planning · Getting There · Staying in Style · Touring · Feasting · Making Magic · Index · Notes & More

AMBIENCE

RESORT LAYOUT & ROOMS

DINING

Planning
Getting There
Staying in Style
Touring
Feasting
Making Magic
Index
Notes & More

Using the Amenities
at Disney's Wilderness Lodge & Villas Resort

LOUNGING

Territory Lounge, a saloon adjacent to Artist Point, serves up beers, wines, spirits, and snacks. The **Trout Pass Pool Bar** offers cocktails and light snacks you can enjoy at tables overlooking the main pool and Bay Lake. Beer and wine are also available from the resort shop.

Having fun at the Wilderness Lodge

PLAYING & RELAXING

For Athletes: Rent watercraft and bicycles at Teton Boat & Bike Rentals. A bike and jogging path extends about a mile to Fort Wilderness. A health club, Sturdy Branches, is available.

For Children: The Cub's Den is a supervised program for kids ages 4–12 (see page 285). A playground is located near the beach.

For Gamers: Buttons and Bells arcade, across from Cub's Den.

For Shoppers: The large Wilderness Lodge Mercantile in the Lodge carries clothing, sundries, foodstuffs, newspapers, and gifts.

For Swimmers: Cleverly designed to seem like part of Silver Creek, a free-form swimming pool is nestled among craggy rocks and waterfalls. A water slide and wading pool, as well as two hot tubs, are also available nearby. A leisure pool and another hot tub are located near the Villas. The white sand beach here on Bay Lake is ideal for relaxing upon, but swimming is not permitted.

GETTING ABOUT

You can take a direct **boat or bus** to the Magic Kingdom (see chart below for in-transit times). Boats also ferry you to Fort Wilderness and the Contemporary. **Buses** take you directly to Magic Kingdom, Epcot, Disney's Hollywood Studios, Disney's Animal Kingdom, Downtown Disney, and the water parks. To reach other resorts, go to the Magic Kingdom (daytime) or Downtown Disney (evening), and then transfer to a resort bus. Fort Wilderness and Wilderness Lodge share many of their bus routes, so travel to and from Fort Wilderness for the Hoop-Dee-Doo show (see page 264), horseback riding, etc., is quite convenient.

Magic Kingdom	Epcot	Disney's Hollywood Studios	Disney's Animal Kingdom	Downtown Disney
boat or bus	direct bus	direct bus	direct bus	direct bus
~8 or ~10 min.	~10 min.	~15 min.	~15 min.	~25 min.

Approximate time you will spend in transit from resort to destination during normal operation.

Top Photo Slice: Elevated wooden walkway at Disney's Wilderness Lodge Resort (①4394) © Amy Sellars

Making the Most of Disney's Wilderness Lodge & Villas Resort

Planning
Getting There
Staying in Style
Touring
Feasting
Making Magic
Index
Notes & More

TIPS

Guests staying in the **Villas at Wilderness Lodge** register at the main Lodge registration desk.

For good rainy day activities, ask for a **kids' activity/coloring book** at the bell station or a list of **Hidden Mickeys** at Lobby Concierge. You can also get a list of the resort's music at the Mercantile shop.

Explore the resort. Indian artifacts, historic paintings, and survey maps are displayed. Follow Silver Creek from its indoor origin as a hot spring and onward outside as a bubbling brook and waterfall, eventually making its way to Bay Lake.

Ask about becoming a **Flag Family**. Each morning, a family is selected to go on the Lodge roof to help raise or lower the flag! This is popular, so inquire at check-in for a better chance.

Inquire about the **"Wonders of the Lodge" tour** at Lobby Concierge. The walking tour explores the architecture, landscaping, totem poles, and paintings. Offered Wednesdays–Saturdays at 9:00 am.

Watch **Fire Rock Geyser**, modeled after Old Faithful, erupt like clockwork every hour on the hour from 7:00 am to 10:00 pm. The **Electrical Water Pageant** is visible from the beach at 9:35 pm.

NOTES

Courtyard-view rooms can be **noisy** with the sounds of children and rushing water. Opt for a Lodge view if you prefer serenity.

About 37 Lodge rooms with **king beds** double as the barrier-free (handicap-accessible) rooms and have a large shower with no tub.

Check-in time is 3:00/4:00 pm. Check-out time is 11:00 am.

RATINGS

Ratings are explained on page 28.

Our Value Ratings:		Our Magic Ratings:		Readers' Ratings:
Quality:	9/10	Theme:	10/10	79% fell in love with it
Accessibility:	6/10	Amenities:	6/10	17% liked it well enough
Affordability:	6/10	Fun Factor:	8/10	3% had mixed feelings
Overall Value:	**7/10**	**Overall Magic:**	**8/10**	1% were disappointed

Wilderness Lodge is enjoyed by...	(rated by both authors and readers)	
Younger Kids: ♥♥♥♥	Young Adults: ♥♥♥♥♥	Families: ♥♥♥♥
Older Kids: ♥♥♥♥	Mid Adults: ♥♥♥♥♥	Couples: ♥♥♥♥♥
Teenagers: ♥♥♥♥	Mature Adults: ♥♥♥♥	Singles: ♥♥♥

Top Photo Slice: Overhead lamps in the lobby at Disney's Wilderness Lodge (①3271) © Melissa Loflin

Planning

Getting There

Staying in Style

Touring

Feasting

Making Magic

Index

Notes & More

LODGE AND VILLAS RESORT MAP

Choosing Your Room
at Disney's Wilderness Lodge & Villas Resort

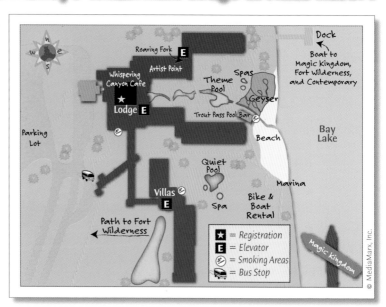

© MediaMarx, Inc.

BEST LOCATIONS

Standard rooms overlook the parking areas yet are close to the Lobby. **Lodge views** overlook woods (north side) or the Villas (south side). **Top-floor rooms** facing the woods on the Magic Kingdom (north) side may catch a glimpse of fireworks. Rooms facing the **courtyard or lake** offer panoramic views and cheerful resort sounds. If you seek privacy, consider a **honeymoon suite** at the top of the Lobby or a top-floor room with solid balcony railings. Concierge service is offered for suites and rooms on the seventh floor. **Villas** in the northeast corner offer views of the pool.

RATES

2013 Sample Room and Villa Rates

Seasons are noted on page 14.

Room Type	Value	Fall	Regular	Peak	Holiday
Standard View	$284–$304	$321–$356	$355–$380	$412–$447	$491
Woods View	$309–$332	$338–$376	$362–$400	$438–$476	$510
Courtyard View	$327–$351	$354–$394	$383–$423	$462–$502	$533
Studio Villa	$368–$378	$386	$420	$508	$543
One-Bedroom Villa	$503–$513	$533	$579	$706	$731

12.5% tax is not included in the above. Suites and concierge start in the $400s. Higher rates in price ranges are for weekends and holiday periods (see page 31).

INFO

Disney's Wilderness Lodge and Villas Resort

✉ 901 Timberline Drive, Lake Buena Vista, FL 32830

☎ Phone: 407-824-3200   ✏ Fax: 407-824-3232

🗒 For reservations, call Central Reservations: 407-939-6244

More at ① wilderness-lodge

Top Photo Slice: Bed headboard in guest room at Disney's Wilderness Lodge Resort (①4241) © Michelle Clark

Disney's Yacht and Beach Club & Villas Resorts

Offering luxury, convenience, and added amenities, the Yacht Club and Beach Club are sister resorts. Both resorts feature a relaxing atmosphere on Crescent Lake within walking distance of Epcot and Disney's Hollywood Studios (use the blue tab at the top for parks and eateries in the area).

AMBIENCE

These resorts evoke the charm of **bygone seaside resorts**. The Yacht Club is housed in a dove-gray clapboard building, exuding elegance and grace. The Beach Club atmosphere is casual, bringing to mind sun-filled days you might have found along the eastern seaboard generations ago. Windows in the sky-blue building may gaze out upon the "beach houses" nestled alongside the beach. The Beach Club Villas are housed in a separate building evoking the charm of Cape May, New Jersey. The Villas' clapboard walls are painted in seafoam green with white railings and columns, and gingerbread trim. Colorful pennants flap in the breeze from atop the roofs and turrets, and strings of light bulbs dangle gracefully between old-fashioned street lamps.

RESORT LAYOUT & ROOMS

Standard Room Layout

Each of the standard rooms at the Yacht and Beach Club is housed within five floors of one deceptively large yet creatively shaped building, while the villas are located within a free-standing addition. Covered walkways connect the Villas to the Beach Club lobby. Well-appointed and understated, the standard rooms are large (380 sq. ft.) and sunny. The 634 **Yacht Club** rooms are outfitted in ocean blues, floral patterns, and antiqued wood. The 580 **Beach Club** rooms are recently renovated and playfully decorated. Guest rooms have one king or two queen beds, a daybed, ottoman, double sinks, a make-up mirror, a small table and chairs, an armoire with a TV, and a small refrigerator. Some smaller rooms have a king-size Murphy bed and an extra sink and counter. Many rooms—but not all—have balconies or patios (all Yacht Club guest rooms have balconies). Amenities include room service, hair dryers (most rooms), iron, newspaper delivery, turndown service (on request—not available in the Villas), in-room safe, toiletries, and voice mail. Both the Yacht Club and the Beach Club offer concierge service with slightly larger rooms on the fifth floor. In addition, 40 special suites (20 in each resort) range in size from a junior suite to a two-bedroom suite to the ultimate Presidential Suite.

Side tabs: Planning | Getting There | Staying in Style | Touring | Feasting | Making Magic | Index | Notes & More

Planning | Getting There | Staying in Style | Touring | Feasting | Making Magic | Index | Notes & More

Lodging and Dining at Disney's Yacht and Beach Club Resorts

VILLAS

Added in mid-2002 are the 205 Beach Club Villas with studio, one-, and two-bedroom **villas** for Disney Vacation Club members (see pages 108–109) and the public at large. Studios accommodate up to four guests with one queen-size bed, a double-size sofa bed, and a kitchenette (with a sink, microwave, and a small refrigerator). The one- and two-bedroom villas accommodate up to four or eight guests respectively and offer full

Exploring the Beach Club

kitchens, DVD players, king-size beds, delightful whirlpool tubs in the master bathroom, double-size sleeper sofas in the living room, and washers/dryers. All villas are quite homey and feel like a cottage you might have on the beach. Amenities for all villas include room service, iron and ironing board, hair dryer, newspaper delivery, in-room safe, toiletries (shampoo and soap), and voice mail.

One-Bedroom (unshaded)

Queen

King

Shower

Studio Layout (shaded)

Entire layout represents a Two-Bedroom Villa

DINING

With the Yacht and Beach Club sharing restaurants, there are more dining options here than at almost any other resort. Table-service options (see page 261) include **Beaches and Cream**, a popular soda fountain (also serving breakfast); **Cape May Cafe**, a character breakfast and all-you-can-eat clambake; **Yachtsman Steakhouse** for dinner; and the **Captain's Grille** for breakfast, lunch, and dinner. The **Crew's Cup** offers a good snack menu. For a quick meal, try **Hurricane Hanna's**, a poolside grill, or the **Beach Club Marketplace**, offering breakfast items, baked goods, sandwiches, salads, gelato, coffee, and beverages (refillable mugs—$14.49) for eat-in or take-out.

Using the Amenities at Disney's Yacht & Beach Club Resorts

Several lounges will help you relax after a long day of playing. **Ale & Compass** and **Crew's Cup** in the Yacht Club serve drinks and munchies. At Beach Club, **Martha's Vineyard** features an award-winning wine list and appetizers. **Hurricane Hanna's** is a pool bar and grill—menu items include a hot dog ($6.79), cheeseburger ($8.29), and veggie wrap ($7.79). Room service is always available.

For Athletes: The Ship Shape Health Club is a complete fitness club offering a spa, sauna, and massage therapies. The resorts also sport two lighted tennis courts and a sand volleyball court. The Bayside Marina rents watercraft for cruises and surrey bikes to ride around the lake. Note that the Breathless II yacht is no longer operating.

For Charmers: Periwig's Beauty and Barber Shop is a full-service salon for hair, skin, and nail care.

For Children: A playground is near Stormalong Bay. Sandcastle Club offers supervised activities for children ages 4–12 (see page 284).

For Gamers: Lafferty Place Arcade has video games.

For Shoppers: The Beach Club Marketplace (Beach) and Fittings and Fairings (Yacht) offer sundries and resort wear.

For Swimmers: The three-acre Stormalong Bay water park is resort swimming at its best. Three free-form, sandy-bottomed pools create deceptively complex waterways with whirlpools, bubbling jets, "rising sands," a water slide in a shipwreck, and two hot tubs. Stormalong Bay is for Yacht and Beach Club and Villas resort guests only (bring your resort ID). Leisure pools are located at the far ends of the resorts. The Villas has its own leisure pool, called "Dunes Cove," and a hot tub.

Boats (see chart below for in-transit times) depart from the marina for Epcot and Disney's Hollywood Studios. **Buses** outside the lobby go to the Magic Kingdom, Disney's Animal Kingdom, and Downtown Disney. Reach other destinations by transferring at Disney's Hollywood Studios (day) or Downtown Disney (evening). Parking is available, as well as valet parking ($10/day). The BoardWalk, Dolphin, and Swan are all within **walking distance**, as is the International Gateway to Epcot. You could also walk to Disney's Hollywood Studios along the path beside the BoardWalk Villas (see map on page 52).

Magic Kingdom	Epcot	Disney's Hollywood Studios	Disney's Animal Kingdom	Downtown Disney
direct bus ~20 min.	walk/boat ~10/~10 min.	walk/boat ~20/~15 min.	direct bus ~20 min.	direct bus ~15 min.

Approximate time you will spend in transit from resort to destination during normal operation.

Top Photo Slice: Lounge chairs on the beach at Disney's Yacht and Beach Club Resort (①14386) © Cheryl Pendry

Side tabs: Planning · Getting There · Staying in Style · Touring · Feasting · Making Magic · Index · Notes & More

Section tabs: LOUNGING · PLAYING & RELAXING · GETTING ABOUT

Making the Most of Disney's Yacht and Beach Club Resorts

TIPS

Enjoy a **waterfront stroll** around Crescent Lake using the boardwalks and bridges encircling it. This is a very lively place!

Request **turndown service** from housekeeping before you go out for the evening, and return to find your bedcovers turned down with a chocolate. This service is not available in the Beach Club Villas.

A **bank of elevators** near each resort's lobby serves most rooms. If your room is at one of the far ends, look for a **single elevator or stairway** rather than trek down the hallways. If you're going to Epcot, the exit near Beach Club's leisure pool is convenient.

Yacht and Beach Club have **separate entrances** and **front desks**. Beach Club Villas guests check in at the Beach Club's front desk.

Explore the charming **public areas**, such as The Solarium (just off the Beach Club lobby), The Drawing Room (near the Villas' entrance), and The Breezeway (near the Dunes Cove pool).

NOTES

Bring **resort identification** with you to Stormalong Bay—it will be checked. It can be noisy with the sounds of happy children late into the night, so avoid it and places nearby if you seek peace.

All rooms on the first floor have pleasant patios. Most rooms on the top floor have full **balconies**, as do some on the intervening floors. Be aware that some balconies are standing room only, however. If a full-size balcony is important, request it.

A **conference center**, reminiscent of a town hall, is available.

Check-in time is 3:00/4:00 pm. Check-out time is 11:00 am.

Ratings are explained on page 28.

RATINGS

Our Value Ratings:		Our Magic Ratings:		Readers' Ratings:
Quality:	8/10	Theme:	8/10	55% fell in love with it
Accessibility:	8/10	Amenities:	9/10	34% liked it well enough
Affordability:	3/10	Fun Factor:	6/10	7% had mixed feelings
Overall Value:	**6/10**	**Overall Magic:**	**8/10**	4% were disappointed

Yacht and Beach Clubs are enjoyed by... (rated by both authors and readers)		
Younger Kids: ♥♥♥♥	Young Adults: ♥♥♥♥	Families: ♥♥♥♥
Older Kids: ♥♥♥♥♥	Mid Adults: ♥♥♥♥♥	Couples: ♥♥♥♥♥
Teenagers: ♥♥♥	Mature Adults: ♥♥♥♥	Singles: ♥♥♥

Finding Your Place
at Disney's Yacht and Beach Club Resorts

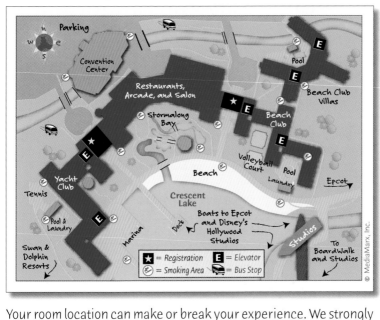

Your room location can make or break your experience. We strongly recommend you indulge in a room with a **water view** at either the Yacht or Beach Club. Specifically, try to avoid the standard-view, even-numbered Beach Club rooms between 3662–3726, 4662–4726, and 5662–5726, which overlook an ugly rooftop. You may also want to request a room **closer to the lobby** for easier access. Rooms with a king-size Murphy bed are slightly smaller than other rooms. The slightly larger rooms on the Beach Club's fifth floor are concierge. Rooms at the **Beach Club Villas** have views of Epcot, gardens, or the pool, but rates are the same for all.

2013 Sample Room and Villa Rates
Seasons are noted on page 14.

Room Type	Value	Fall	Regular	Peak	Holiday
Standard View or Studio Villa	$350–$375	$382–$421	$406–$448	$485–$525	$587
Water/Pool View	$436–$467	$477–$549	$497–$549	$558–$604	$650
One-Bedroom Villa	$519–$535	$548	$589	$685	$741
Two-Bedroom Villa	$726–$737	$822	$939	$1,193	$1,284

12.5% tax is not included in the above. Concierge rooms start in the high-$400's. Higher rates in price ranges are for weekends and holiday periods in non-Villa rooms (see page 31).

Disney's Yacht and Beach Club and Villas Resorts
✉ 1700/1800 Epcot Resort Blvd., Lake Buena Vista, FL 32830
🍽 Phone: 407-934-7000/8000   📠 Fax: 407-934-3450/3850

More at ⓘ yacht-club

Planning · Getting There · Staying in Style · Touring · Feasting · Making Magic · Index · Notes & More

RESORT MAP · BEST LOCATIONS · RATES · INFO

Shades of Green Resort

Shades of Green is a U.S. Armed Forces Recreational Center on Walt Disney World property, located near the Magic Kingdom theme park. Formerly The Disney Inn, this self-supporting resort is exclusively for active and retired military personnel in the Army, Navy, Air Force, Marines, and Coast Guard, as well as those in the Reserves and National Guard. Department of Defense civilians and U.S. Public Health Officers are also eligible. The resort was renovated in 2004 with bigger and better accommodations.

ROOMS

Nestled in the woods **between two golf courses**, Shades of Green offers 586 rooms with deluxe accommodations. Guest rooms remain among the largest on property at 450 sq. feet, accommodating up to five guests. Features include two queen-size beds, an armoire, and a TV, plus a sitting area with a daybed or sleeper sofa and table and chairs. Rooms have a refrigerator, coffeemaker, iron and ironing board, hair dryer, and an in-room safe. Free wireless Internet access is available throughout the resort. All rooms have either a balcony or patio. The resort (and all rooms) are smoke-free (smoking may be allowed on the balcony/patio). Eleven 1–3 bedroom suites are available, sleeping 6–8 guests each.

AMENITIES

Dining choices include the Garden Gallery family restaurant, Evergreens sports bar, a specialty Italian restaurant (Mangino's), the Express Cafe for quick meals, a coffee counter, and room service. There's also a lounge (Eagles). Resort amenities include two lighted tennis courts, two heated pools, wading pool, playground, exercise room, arcade, and laundry facilities. You can also purchase theme park tickets. Two **buses** are available, and you can take the 10-minute walk to the Polynesian and Transportation and Ticket Center. You must show your Shades of Green resort ID or military ID to board their buses. A car is helpful, and a multi-level parking structure is available ($5/day).

RATES

Rates are based on rank or pay grade and begin at **$95** (**$105** for pool views). Reserve up 53 weeks in advance (limit three rooms). **Tip**: Shades of Green is offering discounts on early bookings—visit http://www.militarydisneytips.com for news and announcements.

INFO

Shades of Green Resort
P.O. Box 22789, Lake Buena Vista, FL 32830
Phone: 407-824-3400   Fax: 407-824-3460
For more information, call 888-593-2242 or 407-824-3665
Web site: http://www.shadesofgreen.org

More at ⓘ shades-of-green

Walt Disney World Swan and Dolphin Resorts

Crowned by five-story-high sculptures of swans and heraldic dolphins, the Walt Disney World Swan and Dolphin resorts tower above the nearby Epcot area resorts. Westin and Sheraton, both of which are divisions of Starwood Hotels, jointly manage this pair of luxury hotels popular with business and international visitors.

Guest rooms feature either one king-size bed or two double-size beds, separate vanity and bath areas, two 2-line phones, mini-bar, hair dryer, iron, coffeemaker, weekday newspaper delivery, and in-room safe. The mandatory $12/day resort services fee gives you use the health club, Internet access, 60 minutes of local calls, 20 minutes of domestic long-distance calls, and two bottles of water daily. Some rooms have balconies, and 195 suites offer a bit more room. Guest rooms at both resorts sport a modern design by Michael Graves and "Heavenly Beds" with pillow-top mattresses and down comforters (delightful!). The sister resorts offer conference facilities, plus many of the same amenities found at Disney resort hotels.

Between the resorts, there are **15 eateries**, including Il Mulino, Garden Grove, Kimonos, Shula's Steakhouse, bluezoo (an upscale seafood restaurant by chef Todd English), and Fresh (an innovative market-style buffet)—see pages 259–260 for details. Picabu is a 24-hour quick-service buffet/cafeteria with a whimsical atmosphere. The BoardWalk entertainment district is just a stroll away, as is Fantasia Gardens miniature golf. Free **buses** serve Disney's parks and Downtown Disney, and boats run to Disney's Hollywood Studios and Epcot. Guests receive many of the benefits enjoyed at the Disney-owned resorts, including package delivery, Extra Magic Hours, and the option to purchase park tickets. The only thing guests can't do is charge Disney purchases to their room.

Rooms begin in the **high $200s**, but discounts and special rates are available—ask about discounts for AAA, Annual Passholders, teachers, nurses, and military. Great rates have been found on Sheraton.com, Westin.com, Hotwire.com, and Priceline.com (see page 16). Starwood members earn points (see http://www.spg.com).

Walt Disney World Swan and Dolphin Resorts

✉ 1200/1500 Epcot Resort Blvd., Lake Buena Vista, FL 32830
🖨 Phone: 407-934-4000 📠 Fax: 407-934-4884
📱 For reservations, call 888-828-8850 or 407-934-4000
💬 For more information, visit http://www.swandolphin.com

Top Photo Slice: The Walt Disney World Swan and Dolphin Resorts at sunset © Cheryl Pendry

Disney Cruise Line

The Disney Cruise Line set sail in 1998 with the same enthusiasm and energy you find at the Walt Disney World Resort. Each of the four ships (the Disney Magic, Disney Wonder, Disney Dream, and Disney Fantasy) have 5+ themed restaurants, including one or more for adults only. Experience Broadway-quality productions, first-run and classic Disney movies, and nightclubs. Separate areas of the ship were designed exclusively for adults and children.

ITINERARY

Cruises convenient for Walt Disney World guests depart Disney's own terminal in Port Canaveral at 4:00 pm. Four-night **cruises** spend the next day in Nassau, followed by a day at Castaway Cay, Disney's private island, then a full day at sea. Guests debark at Port Canaveral at 9:00 am the following morning. Three-night cruises follow the same plan, but skip the day at sea. Seven-night cruises offer different itineraries—one to the Eastern Caribbean (with stops at St. Maarten, St. Thomas/St. John, and Castaway Cay), one to the Western Caribbean (with stops at ports like Grand Cayman, Cozumel, and Castaway Cay), and some special cruises. In 2013, ships will sail to the Bahamas, Caribbean, Mediterranean, and Alaska in itineraries from 3- to 12-nights long.

STATEROOMS

Staterooms range from downright comfortable to out-and-out luxurious. Even the least expensive staterooms are decorated in glowing, warm woods and include a television, phone, cooler, and in-room safe. The bright and cheery bathrooms include a hair dryer and tub. Deluxe staterooms include a split bathroom, which makes family travel especially comfortable, and up to 44% of all staterooms offer a verandah. Staterooms that sleep four usually have one queen bed, a single daybed, and a single berth—great for families but not so great for two couples. At the high end, the two-bedroom Walter E. and Roy O. Disney suites are a feast for the eyes, decorated with exotic wood paneling and cut crystal—they include a whirlpool tub!

RATES

Many vacationers book add-on **packages** that combine a three- or four-night cruise and three or four nights at the Walt Disney World Resort. During the 2013 value season, three-night cruises start at $586/person (for double occupancy) for a standard inside stateroom to more than $5,000/person for a Royal Suite. Third, fourth, and fifth occupants pay much less. Airfare and ground transfers are extra. Add-on packages now allow you to stay at any of Disney's resort hotels, for any length of time.

More at ① preparing-to-cruise | cruising-for-adults

Top Photo Slice: The Disney Magic in St. Thomas, U.S. Virgin Islands © Janet Simonsen

Making the Most of the Disney Cruise Line

DINING

Your cruise includes all food onboard (including room service) and lunch at Castaway Cay. Soft drinks are free at meals and at the beverage station. Alcoholic beverages are extra. Each night you'll be assigned to a different dining room. **Royal Palace** (Dream), **Royal Court** (Fantasy), **Lumiere's** (Magic), or **Triton's** (Wonder) is the most formal dining room, which is also open daily to all for full-service breakfast and lunch. **Enchanted Garden** (Dream/Fantasy) and **Parrot Cay** (Magic/Wonder) are more casual, and also host the breakfast buffets. **Animator's Palate** is an extraordinary room, that transforms before your eyes. **Palo** is the ships' intimate, adults-only restaurant with an elegant Italian menu and marvelous service. You may reserve a table at Palo ($20/person surcharge) in advance online or in person on the afternoon that you board, and seats can go quickly. The Dream and Fantasy add adults-only **Remy**, a fine French restaurant, for $75. Breakfast and lunch buffets and snacks are served on Deck 9/11. Fountain drinks are complimentary from the beverage station on Deck 9/11.

NOTES

State any preferences at reservation time and again a month before you sail. Your **cruise documentation** with your room assignment arrives a few weeks before you sail, and you can check-in online.

Passports are not required for regular itineraries, but we still suggest them. Get your required **papers** in order long before you depart.

All shore-side food, transportation, and entertainment in every port of call except Castaway Cay is **at your own expense**. Unless you are especially adventuresome, we suggest you either book a shore excursion (listed in your cruise documentation) or stay onboard.

Dress is casual, but wear a dress/jacket at the Captain's reception, dinner at Royal Palace/Court/Lumiere's/Triton's, and Palo and Remy.

TIPS

To **save money**, book a cruise-only passage as early as possible. You can still book ground transfers through Disney.

Your day at **Castaway Cay** is short. Be sure to wake up early!

Need more details? We have a **400+ page guidebook** all about the Disney Cruise! See page 316 and visit http://www.passporter.com/dcl/guidebook.asp.

For more information, visit http://www.disneycruise.com or call 888-DCL-2500.

Top Photo Slice: The AquaDuck water coaster on the Disney Dream (①24887) © MediaMarx, Inc.

Looking for more information? Get details on our new Disney Vacation Club guide on page 313.

108 | Chapter 3: Staying in Style | Topic: Disney Vacation Club

Disney Vacation Club

Can you ever get enough of Walt Disney World? Disney Vacation Club (DVC) members are betting that they can't. DVC is Disney's kinder, gentler version of a vacation timeshare, and offers several enticing twists on the timeshare experience. The DVC offers the promise of frequent, reduced-cost Disney vacations in exchange for a significant up-front investment.

RESORTS

Disney operates **11 Disney's Deluxe Villa Resorts**: Old Key West (pages 73–76), Boardwalk Villas (pages 49–52), Villas at Wilderness Lodge (pages 95–99), Beach Club Villas (pages 99–103), Saratoga Springs (pages 91–94), Animal Kingdom Villas (pages 41–44), the Bay Lake Tower villas at the Contemporary (pages 57–60), Vero Beach (Florida coast), Hilton Head Island (South Carolina), Grand Californian Villas (Disneyland), and the new Aulani Resort (Hawaii). Coming next are 147 new villas at the Grand Floridian Resort, opening at the end of 2013. Studios, one-, two-, and three-bedroom villas with kitchen and laundry facilities are offered (studios have kitchenettes and access to laundry rooms). Housekeeping is limited, with full services every eight days.

THE PROGRAM

With a typical vacation timeshare, you buy an annual one-week (or multiple-week) stay during a particular time period in a specific size of accommodation. DVC uses a novel **point system** that adds far greater flexibility and complexity to the process. You can use your points however you wish to create several short getaways or a single, grand vacation—at any time of the year and at any DVC or other Disney resort. Here's how it works: You buy a certain number of points at the going rate (from $135–$160 per point as of press time). 100 points is the minimum—so every year you'd have at least 100 points to apply toward accommodations. You might need 20 points/night for a one-bedroom at Old Key West weeknights during the off-season. 90 points/night may be needed for a two-bedroom at BoardWalk weekends in peak season. Just as with a regular resort room, rates are affected by size, view, location, season, and day. You also pay annual dues based on the number of points purchased. Rates vary, depending on your "home" resort—from about $4.22 to $7.11 per point—so dues on a 160-point purchase would be about $675–$1,138. If you compare the combined cost of points and fees to renting comparable, non-discounted resort rooms, it takes about seven years to recover the value of the points purchased. After that, vacations might cost half the prevailing rental rates. Membership contracts at Saratoga Springs Resort expire in 2054; at Animal Kingdom Villas in 2057; at Bay Lake Tower and at Grand Californian contracts in 2060; at Aulani in 2062; most other contracts expire in 2042.

More at ① dvc-secret | hilton-head

Making the Most of the Disney Vacation Club

While you can reserve up to eleven months in advance at your **home resort**, you can only book seven months in advance at others.

You can **borrow points** from the next year or save unused points until next year. You can buy more points from Disney at the going rate, or buy/sell points on the open market—we heartily recommend DVC By Resale (http://www.dvcbyresale.com, 800-844-4099).

Don't let unused points expire! If you can't use all your points this year or prefer to use them later, you must contact DVC Member Services. Otherwise, those **points expire** at the end of your use year. If you can't use points, bank them or try "renting out" your points (and non-DVC members may consider "renting" points to try out DVC).

Use points to book **at most Disney resorts in the world**, Disney Cruise Line, Adventures by Disney, luxury hotels, and adventure travel vacations, or barter points for "swaps" at non-Disney resorts.

DVC members receive many **discounts** on items including annual passes, resort rooms, dining, guided tours, etc. They also qualify for the Tables in Wonderland dining discount program (see page 10).

DVC members staying at a DVC resort on points may purchase the **Disney Dining Plan** for the length of stay (see pages 223–225).

Anyone may **rent Disney Vacation Club points** from a DVC member, and this can be a great money-saver. For details and folks willing to rent points, visit http://www.mouseowners.com.

Vacancies at DVC resorts, called Disney's Deluxe Villa Resorts, are made available to **nonmembers**—they are booked just like regular Disney resort reservations, and daily housekeeping is included. Thus, it may be very difficult to use your DVC points at a resort if you are booking near to your intended arrival date.

Want to learn more? Get our 191-page DVC guide (paperback or e-book) at http://www.passporter.com/disney-vacation-club.asp and visit our DVC forums at http://www.passporterboards.com/forums/owning-magic-disney-vacation-club/

PassPorter's **Disney Vacation Club Guide**

✉ 200 Celebration Place, Celebration, FL 34747-9903
📞 Phone: 800-500-3990   📠 Fax: 407-566-3393
📋 DVC information kiosks are at most Disney parks and resorts.
✍ Sales offices and models are at Disney's Saratoga Springs.

TIPS

NOTES

INFO

More at ⓘ dvc-cruise

Planning · Getting There · Staying in Style · Touring · Feasting · Making Magic · Index · Notes & More

Planning

Getting There

Staying in Style

Touring

Feasting

Making Magic

Index

Notes & More

Hotel Plaza Resorts

Each of these hotels are located on Disney property across from Downtown Disney, but are independently owned and operated. A variety of discounts may be available. Some of the Disney resort hotel benefits mentioned earlier in this chapter do not apply (such as Extra Magic Hour and package delivery, except at the Hilton). All the Hotel Plaza Resorts offer scheduled buses to the parks (see next page) and are within walking distance of Downtown Disney. Visit http://www.downtowndisneyhotels.com.

Hotel Name (in alphabetical order)	Starting Rates	Year Built	Year Renovated
DoubleTree Guest Suites Resort	**$129+**	**1988**	**2008**

This all-suite hotel offers 229 one- and two-bedroom suites. All rooms come with dining areas, kitchenettes (refrigerator, microwave, and coffeemaker), separate living rooms with sofa beds, double-size or king-size beds, three TVs, two phones, in-room safe, hair dryer, iron and ironing board, and toiletries (no balconies). Suites accommodate up to six people (up to four adults). Amenities include a heated pool, wading pool, fitness center, arcade, one restaurant, one lounge, one pool bar, and room service. Look for the freshly baked chocolate chip cookies upon your arrival. Web: http://www.doubletreeguestsuites.com. Call 800-222-8733 or 407-934-1000.

Regal Sun Resort	**$99+**	**1972**	**2007**

Formerly the Grosvenor Resort, this recently-renovated hotel offers 626 rooms in a 19-story high-rise nestled beside Lake Buena Vista. All rooms come with standard two double-size beds or one king-size bed, flat screen TV, MP3 clock radio, coffeemaker, refrigerator, in-room safe, wireless Internet access, hairdryer, iron and ironing board, and toiletries (no balconies). Resort amenities include two heated pools, whirlpool spa, a new kids water playground, two tennis courts (as well as basketball, volleyball, and shuffleboard courts), scheduled kids activities, business center, fitness center, thermal spa, arcade, one restaurant (with character breakfasts thrice weekly), one casual dining cafe, one pool bar, one lounge, and room service. Note that the MurderWatch Mystery Theatre is no longer offered here. Web: http://www.regalsunresort.com. Call 800-624-4109 or 407-828-4444.

The Hilton	**$189+**	**1984**	**2008**

This newly renovated first-class business hotel is located right across the street from the Downtown Disney Marketplace. The 814 rooms are luxurious, each offering "Serenity" beds (two doubles or one king), overstuffed chair, flat screen TV, MP3 clock radios, two phones, hair dryer, iron and ironing board, coffeemaker, mini-bar, newspapers, Internet access ($9.95/day), and toiletries (no balconies or in-room safes). Amenities include two heated pools, kids water play area, two whirlpool spas, fitness center, arcade, shopping area, three eateries (one with character meals every Sunday), two cafes, and one lounge, one pool bar, and room service. The Hilton is the only Hotel Plaza Resort to offer the Extra Magic Hour perk (see page 34). Web: http://www. downtowndisneyhotels.com/Hilton.html. Call 800-445-8667 or 407-827-4000.

Holiday Inn	**$115+**	**1978**	**2007**

With 323 standard rooms and one suite, this renovated 14-story hotel offers clean, basic accommodations. Standard rooms come with two double beds or one king bed, balconies, satellite TV, hair dryer, iron and ironing board, coffeemaker, in-room safe, newspaper delivery, toiletries, and high-speed Internet. Additional amenities include Nintendo games (extra fee), two heated pools, wading pool, whirlpool spa, fitness center, arcade, one restaurant, one cafe, and room service. Web: http://www.downtowndisneyhotels.com/HolidayInn.html. Call 800-223-9930 or 407-828-8888.

DOWNTOWN DISNEY Resort Area Hotels

Hotel Name (in alphabetical order)	Starting Rates	Year Built	Year Renovated
The Royal Plaza	**$140+**	**1975**	**2006**

This hotel offers 394 standard rooms that each accommodate up to five guests and have a sitting area, balcony or patio, coffeemaker, and phone, in addition to the new "Royal Beds" (two double beds or one king bed), sofa bed, 27" cable TV, in-room safe, hair dryer, iron and ironing board, newspaper delivery, high-speed Internet access, and toiletries. Rooms in the tower are slightly larger and offer upgraded bathrooms. Hotel amenities include a heated pool, whirlpool spa, four tennis courts, arcade, a restaurant (kids 12 and under eat free with a paying adult), a lounge, a pool bar, and room service. Of all the Hotel Plaza hotels, this is the one that gets the most rave reviews from other vacationers. Note: This hotel is slated to become a B Hotel, fully renovated, in late 2013. Web: http://www.royalplaza.com. Call 800-248-7890 or 407-828-2828.

Lake Buena Vista Best Western Resort	**$159+**	**1973**	**2010**

This 18-story, Caribbean-themed hotel is on the shores of Lake Buena Vista. The renovated resort offers 321 standard rooms (345 sq. ft.) and four suites, all of which have balconies. Rooms come with two queen beds or one king bed, satellite TV, hair dryer, iron and ironing board, coffeemaker (with coffee and tea), in-room safe, newspaper delivery, wireless Internet, and toiletries. Other amenities include Nintendo games and premium movies for an extra fee, one heated pool, a wading pool, privileges to the DoubleTree fitness center, two eateries, two lounges, and room service. Web: http://www.orlandoresorthotel.com. Call 800-348-3765 or 407-828-2424.

Buena Vista Palace Hotel & Spa	**$299+**	**1983**	**2007**

A high-rise hotel with 1,014 luxury guest rooms and suites. This is the largest of the hotels on Hotel Plaza Boulevard. It's also the closest hotel to Downtown Disney Marketplace. All rooms feature balconies or patios, two double beds or one king bed, flat screen TV, Herman Miller chair, cordless phone, coffeemaker, in-room safe, hair dryer, iron and ironing board, newspaper delivery, and toiletries. Wireless Internet access, WebTV, Sony PlayStation games, and premium movies are available for an additional fee. Resort amenities include three heated pools, whirlpool spa, tennis and sand volleyball courts, full-service European-style spa with fitness center and beauty salon, arcade, three restaurants (one with character breakfasts every Sunday), a cafe, two lounges, a pool bar, and room service. Formerly known as Wyndham Palace Resort & Spa. Web: http://www.buenavistapalace.com. Call 407-827-2727.

Hotel Plaza Resort Transportation to the Parks

Guests staying at these Hotel Plaza Resorts get free bus transportation to the four major Disney parks, Downtown Disney, and the water parks. Hotel Plaza buses—which differ from the standard Disney buses—run every 30 minutes and typically start one hour before park opening and continue up to two hours after park closing. Note that buses to the Magic Kingdom drop you off at the Transportation and Ticket Center (TTC), where you can take a monorail or boat to the park entrance or transfer to another bus to another Disney destination. Disney's Animal Kingdom buses may operate only once an hour during the slower times of the day. Within walking distance is Downtown Disney, where you can also board Disney buses to other resorts. Those bound for the water parks should check with their hotel for bus schedules. Guests who want to venture off to Universal Studios/Islands of Adventure, SeaWorld, Wet 'n' Wild, or the Belz Outlet Mall can take a shuttle for $12/person round-trip—check with your hotel on pick-up times. Many guests who stay at these hotels recommend you get a rental car—all hotels but the Lake Buena Vista Best Western and Hotel Royal Plaza have a rental car desk.

Planning

Getting There

Staying in Style

Touring

Feasting

Making Magic

Index

Notes & More

Hotels Near Disney World

Below are several hotels and motels near Walt Disney World (but not on Disney property) that either we've stayed in and recommend or at which our readers report good experiences. More hotels are listed on following pages.

Hotel Name (in alphabetical order)	Starting Rates	Year Built	Year Renovated
Nickelodeon Family Suites	**$119+**	**1999**	**2005**

Besides the resort's close proximity to Walt Disney World (just 3 miles/5 km), the hotel offers unique and very convenient "KidSuites" with a living room, kitchenette, master bedroom, and kids' room. The kids get a bunk bed, TV, game system (fee applies), and a small table and chairs—decorated with SpongeBob SquarePants, Rugrats, The Fairly OddParents, Jimmy Neutron, or Danny Phantom. A three-bedroom KidSuite with an extra adult bedroom is also available. If you don't have kids, you can get a room with a different configuration, such as the Nick@Nite Suite (whirlpool tub and 50" TV) and the Kitchen Suite (full kitchen). A breakfast buffet and Nickelodeon character breakfast are available. The resort also has a huge pool complex with seven water slides, four-story water tower, zero-entry pool, water playground, two hot tubs, and a small miniature golf course. There is a free scheduled shuttle bus to Walt Disney World, but we found it more convenient to drive. Visit http://www.nickhotel.com or call 407-387-5437 or 866-462-6425. Hotel address: 14500 Continental Gateway, Orlando, FL 32821

Radisson Resort Orlando Celebration	**$118+**	**1987**	**2012**

We enjoyed our stay at this 718-room, 6-story deluxe hotel just 1.5 miles (2.5 km) from the gates of Walt Disney World. Guest rooms accommodate up to four guests with either one king-size bed or two double-size beds. Recently refurbished rooms come in either pool or courtyard views and feature modern Italian furniture and marble bathrooms. Amenities include a 25" TV, mini refrigerator, in-room safe, coffeemaker, iron and ironing board, hair dryer, make-up mirror, voice mail, and data ports. For a $11.30 daily service fee, you get scheduled shuttles to attractions, 24-hour access to the fitness center, high-speed Internet access (most rooms), use of lighted tennis courts, free local and toll calls, and free newspaper delivery. The resort has two pools, a water slide, a wading pool, and two hot tubs, as well as playground, and arcade. Food service includes a full-service restaurant (open for breakfast and dinner), a deli with Pizza Hut items, a sports bar, a pool bar, and room service. Note that kids under 10 eat free when accompanied by a paying adult. For the best rates, visit http://orlando.guestselectresorts.com or call 866-358-5609 or 407-396-7000. 2900 Parkway Boulevard, Kissimmee, FL 34747

Sheraton Safari Resort	**$161+**	**1994**	**2011**

While this isn't equivalent to Disney's Animal Kingdom Lodge, this safari-themed resort is a winner with kids and adults alike. The 490-room, 6-story hotel is located just $^1/_4$ mile ($^1/_2$ km) from the Disney property (you can't walk to it, but it is a short drive or ride on the scheduled shuttle). Guest rooms come in standard (one king-size or two double-sized beds), Safari Suites (with kitchenette and separate parlor), and deluxe suites (with full kitchens and large parlors). Standard rooms accommodate up to four guests, or five guests with the rental of a roll-away bed. All rooms have a balcony or patio, TV with PlayStation, two phones with voice mail, dataports, and high-speed Internet access, hair dryer, make-up mirror, coffeemaker, iron and ironing board, and in-room safe. The resort features a large pool with a 79-ft. water slide, wading pool, hot tub, fitness center, and arcade. One full-service restaurant (Casablanca's) offers breakfast and dinner (kids under 10 eat free with paying adults), along with the Outpost Deli (for lunch and dinner), the ZanZibar Watering Hole, and room service (6:30 am–10:00 pm). Visit http://www.sheratonsafari.com or call 407-239-0444 or 800-423-3297. Hotel address: 12205 Apopka-Vineland Road, Orlando, FL 32836

Hotels Near Universal Studios

Below are the three on-site hotels at Universal Studios Florida (about 7 miles/11 kilometers from Walt Disney World property). Note that guests staying in these hotels get special privileges at Universal Studios and Islands of Adventure, such as the "Universal Express" ride access system to bypass attraction lines, early admission to The Wizarding World of Harry Potter (one hour before the park opens), priority seating at some restaurants, complimentary package delivery, on-site transportation, and more. Each of these hotels accepts pets and offers pet-related services. All of these resorts are operated by Loews Hotels (http://www.loewshotels.com).

Hotel Name (in alphabetical order)	Starting Rates	Year Built
Hard Rock Hotel	**$244+**	**2001**

If you think Hard Rock Cafe is great, this 650-room hotel really rocks. Step inside a rock star's mansion filled to the rafters with a million-dollar rock memorabilia collection. Standard guest rooms (365 sq. ft.) feature two queen beds or one king bed, flat-panel TV, MP3 station, stereos, two-line cordless phones, mini-bar, coffeemaker, in-room safe, hair dryer, bathroom scale, iron and ironing board, and toiletries. There are 14 Kids Suites with a separate sleeping area for the kids. Hotel amenities include a heated pool with a water slide and underwater audio system, wading pool, two whirlpool spas, sand beach, fitness center, two restaurants (including a Hard Rock Cafe with a concert venue), a cafe, a lounge, a pool bar, and room service. Web: http://www.hardrockhotelorlando.com. Call 800-BE-A-STAR (800-232-7827) or 407-445-ROCK. Hotel address: 5800 Universal Blvd., Orlando, FL 32819

Portofino Bay Hotel	**$279+**	**1999**

Stay in this remarkably themed resort and get a big taste of the Italian Riviera. The hotel is a deluxe recreation of the seaside village of Portofino, Italy, developed with the help of Steven Spielberg. There may be cobblestone streets outside, but luxury abounds inside. 750 rooms and suites are available, including several Kids Suites. Standard rooms come with either two queen beds or one king bed and double sofa bed, cable TV, two phones, mini-bar, coffeemaker, in-room safe, hair dryer, iron and ironing board, and toiletries. Deluxe rooms offer a bit more space, an upgraded bathroom, a VCR, CD player, and fax machine. Resort amenities include three heated pools, a water slide, whirlpool spas, a full-service spa, fitness center, a Bocce ball court, four restaurants, three cafes, a lounge, and room service. Web: http://www.portofinobay.com. Call 407-503-1000 or 800-232-7827. Hotel address: 5601 Universal Blvd., Orlando, FL 32819

Royal Pacific Resort	**$224+**	**2002**

This hotel is Universal Studio's lowest-priced resort, boasting 1,000 guest rooms with a South Seas theme and lush landscaping. Standard rooms (355 sq. ft.) accommodate up to five guests (four adults) and feature two queen beds or one king bed, cable TV, mini-bar, coffeemaker, in-room safe, hair dryer, iron and ironing board, and toiletries. The Club Rooms add robes, bathroom scales, turndown service, newspaper delivery, continental breakfast, and afternoon beer/wine/snacks. Resort amenities include a huge pool, kids' water play area, wading pool, two whirlpool spas, sand beach, volleyball court, putting green, fitness center, arcade, a supervised children's program, two restaurants, a cafe, a lounge, a pool bar, and room service. Web: http://www.universalorlando.com/Hotels/Loews-Royal-Pacific-Resort.aspx. Call 888-322-5541 or 407-503-3000. Hotel address: 6300 Hollywood Way, Orlando, FL 32819

More Hotels Outside Disney

You may prefer to stay "off-property" to attend a conference, visit other parks, or pay a bargain rate. Below are several popular hotels, motels, and inns off property. We've included starting rates for standard rooms (off-season), driving distance to Downtown Disney, available transportation to Disney, the year it was built (plus the year it was renovated, if available), if it is a Disney "Good Neighbor Hotel" (able to sell multi-day passes), a short description, web site (if available), and a phone number.

Hotel/Motel Name (in alphabetical order)	Starting Rates	Distance to WDW	Trans. Avail.	Year Built	Good Neighbor
AmeriSuites LBV	$79+	3mi/5km	Bus	'00	

151-suite resort with free breakfast. http://www.amerisuites.com. 407-997-1300

| **Caribe Royale Resort** | $210+ | 4mi/6km | Bus($) | '97 | ✔ |

Ten-story suite hotel with living rooms and wet bars. AAA discount. 407-238-8000

| **The Celebration Hotel** | $260+ | 8mi/12km | Bus | '99 | ✔ |

Upscale business hotel within Disney's town of Celebration. 407-566-6000

| **DoubleTree Club Hotel** | $112+ | 1.5mi/2km | Bus | '86('99) | ✔ |

246 rooms and kid suites. http://www.doubletreeclublbv.com. AAA discount. 407-239-4646

| **Embassy Suites LBV** | $125+ | 3mi/5km | Bus | '85 | ✔ |

All-suite hotel with a Caribbean theme in Lake Buena Vista. 407-239-1144

| **Gaylord Palms** | $249+ | 1mi/1.5km | Bus | '02 | ✔ |

1,406-room luxury resort near Disney. http://www.gaylordpalms.com. 407-586-0000

| **Hawthorne Suites LBV** | $135+ | 1mi/1.5km | Bus | '00 | ✔ |

Rooms and suites, free breakfast. http://www.hawthornlakebuenavista.com. 407-597-5000

| **Holiday Inn Maingate East** | $69+ | 6mi/10km | Bus($) | '73('99) | ✔ |

Standard rooms and Kidsuites. Located in Kissimmee. 407-396-4488

| **Homewood Suites** | $90+ | 6mi/10km | Bus | '91('00) | ✔ |

Two-room suites with kitchen, living area, and bedroom. AAA discounts. 407-396-2229

| **Hyatt Regency Grand Cypress** | $260+ | 3mi/5km | Bus | '84('97) | |

750-room hotel with balconies, private lake, nature trails, and golf. 407-239-1234

| **Marriott Orlando World Center** | $275+ | 4mi/6km | Bus($) | '86('99) | |

28-floor, 2,000-room resort with four restaurants and a convention center. 407-239-4200

| **Quality Suites Maingate** | $92+ | 6mi/10km | Bus | '90('99) | ✔ |

One- and two-bedroom suites with living rooms and kitchenettes. 407-396-8040

| **Red Roof Inn** | $49+ | 5mi/8km | – | '89('97) | |

Basic budget lodging with a good reputation. Located in Kissimmee. 407-396-0065

| **Sheraton's Vistana Resort** | $239+ | 3mi/5km | Bus | '80('97) | |

One- and two-bedroom villas. Details at http://www.sheraton.com. 407-239-3100

| **Staybridge Suites** | $155+ | 2mi/3km | Bus | '93('98) | ✔ |

All-suite hotel with one- and two-bedroom suites and free breakfast. 407-238-0777

Tip: You really need a car when staying at off-property hotels. Even when shuttles to the parks are provided, the schedules and drop-off/pick-up points aren't accommodating. If you are flying to Orlando and staying off-site, be sure to factor in the cost of renting a car.

Top Photo Slice: The Celebration Hotel © MediaMarx, Inc.

Vacation Homes

Another off-property lodging option that can provide excellent value is a vacation home rental. Vacation homes are typically free-standing **houses or condos with several bedrooms, kitchens, and pool access** ... some vacation homes even have their own private pools and hot tubs. Vacation homes are ideal for large families and groups. Many vacation home rental companies operate near Walt Disney World, and choosing from among them can get confusing. Important points to look for in a vacation home rental company include proximity of homes to Walt Disney World, quality of customer service, prices, and extra fees. We've only tried one rental company—ALL STAR Vacation Homes—but we've been so impressed that we've been back several times. Below is their information, followed by general contact information for some other vacation home companies for which we've received positive reviews from our readers.

ALL STAR Vacation Homes really shines in our book. ALL STAR Vacation Homes has a full guest service center near their properties; more than 150 homes within four miles of Walt Disney World (we can see Expedition Everest from the patio of our favorite home at 8009 Acadia Estates); excellent amenities in clean, luxurious homes; and great deals on a wide variety of home sizes. Most homes have computers with Internet, and

all guests have free access to their Internet Cafe. Their customer service has always been helpful and friendly, and their vacation homes have secured and gated entrances. Vacation home rentals start as low as $119/night. We could go on and on ... actually, we have in the form of several feature articles (see http://www.passporter.com/asvh.asp). For more information and to make a reservation, phone 888-825-6405 or visit http://www.allstarvacationhomes.com and ask for the PassPorter rate deal (free standard rental car or $125 off a 7-night home rental).

Relaxing in our ALL STAR Vacation Home

Florida Spirit Vacation Homes—More than 100 vacation homes within six to ten miles of Walt Disney World, which you can pre-select online. http://www.floridaspiritvacationhome.com, 866-357-7474.

Mouse Pads Vacation Rentals—Offers homes and townhomes, all with private pools. http://www.mousepadsorlando.com, 866-668-7335.

More at ⓘ all-star-vacation-homes

Top Photo Slice: Playing in the private pool at an ALL Star Vacation Home in Windsor Hills © MediaMarx, Inc.

Planning

Getting There

Staying in Style

Touring

Feasting

Making Magic

Index

Notes & More

Electronic, interactive worksheet available—see page 316

Lodging Worksheet

Use this worksheet to jot down preferences, scribble information during phone calls, and keep all your discoveries together. Don't worry about being neat—just be thorough! Circle your final choices once you decide to go with them (to avoid any confusion) and be sure to transfer them to your Room(s) PassPocket.

Arrival date: _____   Alternates: _____

Departure date: _____   Alternates: _____

Total number of nights: _____   Alternates: _____

We prefer to stay at: _____

Alternates: _____

_____

Using your preferences above, call Disney's Reservations phone line at 407-939-6244 or visit http://www.disneyworld.com and jot down resort availabilities in the table on the next page. It works best for us when we write the available days in the far left column, followed by the resort, view/type, special requests, rate, and total cost in the columns to the right. Draw lines between different availabilities. Circle those you decide to use, and then record the reservation numbers, as you'll need them to confirm, cancel, or make changes later. The two columns at the far right let you note confirmations and room deposits so you don't forget and consequently lose your reservation.

Additional Notes:

Collect information on lodging in the table below. We've included some sample notes to show you how we do it, but you're welcome to use this space in any way you please.

Dates	Resort	View/Type/Requests	Rate	Total	Reservation #	Confirm by	Dep.
7/10 - 7/13	Port Orleans	Water View (Riverside)	$221	$663	2635 1419 8419	2/14/13 ✓	✓
7/11 - 7/14	All-Star Movies	Standard (Fantasia)	$133	$399		2/15/13	

Planning | Getting There | Staying in Style | Touring | Feasting | Making Magic | Index | Notes & More

The Last Resort

Your resort or hotel is your home-away-from-home, and deserves special consideration. Here are our some of our best lodging tips:

" We have stayed at Polynesian, Old Key West, Pop Century, All Star Music, and in a RV at Fort Wilderness, which all have **lobby concierge service**. I have found many people think this service is for 'deluxe' resorts only. The concierge service is great to help you find a character you can't find, assist with special dining reservations or shows, and answer questions when the front desk cast members are busy with check in and check outs. When our daughter was 4 (she's 22 now and still loves Pooh), we couldn't find Pooh Bear. We were leaving the next day. I went to the concierge desk and they found Pooh for us early the next morning. Our daughter walked up to Pooh with her Pooh Bear in her hands and gave Pooh a huge hug. I cried. If I hadn't gone to the concierge desk that one precious moment in time would have never happened. So don't be intimidated by the words, 'concierge desk'—just go up and talk to some wonderful folks that are there to help you. It's like magic! "
— *Contributed by Patricia Hunt, a winner in our Reader Tip Contest*

" One year my family, my brother's family, and my mother stayed at the Animal Kingdom Lodge. When I made the reservations I asked for adjoining rooms because my brother has four children and their family needed two rooms. When we arrived, we had room side by side but no door between the rooms. When I inquired the cast member at the front desk said that adjoining means side by side and connecting means an interior door between the two. So here's my tip: if you want rooms with interior doors that join the rooms, ask for **connecting not adjoining**. "
— *Contributed by Nancy Stansbury, a winner in our Reader Tip Contest*

" The best plan I made for our trip were our **'Do Nothing Days' at the resort**. On those days we would wake up late, dress slowly, and meander out to enjoy a full day at the resort's pool. It was nice to have quiet days to recooperate from the busy days and give us newfound energy for the next few days of Disney fun ahead. It allowed us to slow the busy Disney pace down a little bit so that we could truly enjoy every single Disney moment we could. I wouldn't plan a Disney trip without them. "
— *Contributed by Kimberley Abt, a winner in our Reader Tip Contest*

Magical Memory

" We brought my in-laws on a much deserved trip to Walt Disney World and stayed at Old Key West. Being elderly, they chose to opt out of certain plans, but thoroughly loved just hanging out at the resort. One evening, my husband and I decided to see IllumiNations, but my in-laws chose to hang back at the resort. After we returned to the room, they were almost giddy with their 'magical' adventure. They went to the Gurgling Suitcase for a treat, found a bench outside of Olivia's and sat there, holding hands, enjoying the IllumiNations fireworks that were visible above the trees. They acted like they found some secret that no one else knew about. "
...as told by vacationer Pam VanAustin

Top Photo Slice: Epcot area resorts at sunset © Amy Sellars

Genuine PassPorter Genuine PassPorter Genuine PassPorter Genuine PassPorter Genuine PassPorter Genuine PassPorter Genuine PassPorter

Planning | Getting There | Staying in Style | Touring | Feasting | Making Magic | Index | Notes & More

Touring the "World"

The Walt Disney World Resort has been called many things—a world-class resort, an endless playground for young and old alike, and even a mecca to capitalism—but we have never heard it called boring.

The "World" (as it is known to insiders) began in 1971. Opening on October 1st of that year, it offered a small fraction of what we enjoy today: the Magic Kingdom park and the Contemporary and Polynesian resort hotels. It was the dream of an All-American leader, Walt Disney, who didn't live to see opening day. Yet his legacy flourished, becoming the 43-square-mile wonderland we know and love today.

DECIDE what parks to visit and which attractions to see

One of the things that makes the Walt Disney World Resort so special is the attention to detail and service. It takes tens of thousands of people, known as "cast members," working together to stage the "show" we see as "guests." You'll notice that Disney often uses special words to describe their unique services and attractions. There's nothing mundane here.

LEARN the basics of having fun in the parks

To help you recognize these terms, we begin with Park Passwords, defining the "Disneyese" you'll hear and read, such as the much-touted "FASTPASS" ride reservation system. We then move on to practical matters, such as transportation and admission to the parks. Next come our expanded and detailed attraction descriptions for the four major theme parks, along with plenty of color photos and the largest theme park maps you'll find in any Disney guidebook. (They fold out!) Descriptions and maps of the smaller parks follow, along with hints, tips, and a Touring Worksheet to help you decide what to do. Don't overlook our at-a-glance attraction lists and theme park touring plans.

DISCOVER the parks and attractions of Disney

GET where you want to go with ease

So let's go around the "World" in 102 pages!

Planning | Getting There | Staying in Style | Touring | Feasting | Making Magic | Index | Notes & More

Park Passwords

Admission Media—Park passes (tickets). See pages 122–123 for pass details and rates.

Attraction—An individual ride, show, or exhibit.

Baby Care Centers—Special centers are found in each of the major parks. All restrooms (men's included) support diaper changing.

Cast Member—All Disney employees are "cast members"—they wear white name tags with their names.

Disney Dollars and Gift Cards—Disney's own currency, good throughout the Walt Disney World Resort.

ECV—Electric Convenience Vehicle. You can rent these four-wheeled scooters at the parks and elsewhere. See page 36.

Extra Magic Hour—Resort guests can enjoy certain parks earlier or later on certain days. See page 34 for details.

FASTPASS—Disney's ride "reservation" system (see below).

FASTPASSes from Frontierland

Making the Most of FASTPASS

Tired of waiting in long lines? Disney's FASTPASS system reduces the amount of time you spend in line—and it's free to all park guests! Just slip your park pass into a machine near an attraction with FASTPASS. Out pops your pass and a printed ticket (see sample below) that promises you a ride during a particular period some time later in the day. Depending on how many tickets have been issued to other guests, you may be able to return in 25 minutes, or hours later. When you receive your FASTPASS, look for the time you can get your next FASTPASS (you can usually get another immediately after the return time of your current pass, or in two hours, whichever comes first). The FASTPASS ticket also shows important information, such as height restrictions. When your FASTPASS return time arrives, walk up to the attraction's "FASTPASS Return" entrance, show your FASTPASS to the cast member, and walk on in. There's usually still a short wait, and you'll experience most or all "pre-show" activities. Every FASTPASS attraction has a "Standby" line, which is the regular wait-in-line queue—the wait time for the Standby queue is typically half as long as the FASTPASS return time.

We recommend you get your first FASTPASS early in the day for one of the more popular rides, as FASTPASS tickets can run out on busy days. Our attraction descriptions later in this chapter indicate if an attraction has FASTPASS (look for the **FP** icon), and our touring plans give recommendations on which FASTPASSes to get throughout a day. Note that FASTPASS isn't always available, especially later in the day.

At press time Disney is testing a new ticket-less system called FASTPASS+, which uses a plastic card with all of your FASTPASS selections programmed on it. No word yet on if this new system will become permanent.

> **Sample FASTPASS**
>
> Return Anytime Between
> **9:45 am**
> and
> **10:45 am**
> Riders must be at least
> 40" (102cm) to experience
> Splash Mountain
>
> Another FASTPASS' ticket will
> be available after 9:45 am
> **SUN JUN 17**
> 6/17/2007   8:49

Actual size: 2" x 3 ½"

More at ⓘ fastpass (tip: enter this keyword at http://www.passporter.com/i for more information!)

First Aid—First aid stations are at the four theme parks and two water parks (see maps).

Guest Relations—An information desk, located inside and outside the front gates of all four parks and Downtown Disney. Lobby Concierge at resorts provides a similar range of services.

Guidemaps—Free maps available at the parks. See also "Times Guide."

Lockers—Available for a fee ($7-$9 + $5 deposit) in each park and at the Transportation and Ticket Center. Save your receipt for a new locker at another park on the same day.

Lost & Found—Lost items or children can be claimed at a central location in each park. Consult a guidemap or a cast member. Also see page 281.

Money—Pay with Disney Dollars, Disney Gift Cards, cash, traveler's checks, American Express, MasterCard, Visa, Discover, JCB, Diner's Club, and Disney Visa Reward Vouchers. Disney Dollars and Gift Cards are sold at parks, resorts, and most U.S. Disney Stores. ATMs are in the parks, resorts, and Downtown Disney. Disney resort guests can charge to their room.

Packages—Purchases can be delivered and held for pick-up near the park exit at all major parks, and Disney resort guests can have packages delivered to their resort the next afternoon free of charge. Inquire about package delivery <u>before</u> purchasing.

Park—Disney's recreational complexes requiring admission, which include the four major parks (Magic Kingdom, Epcot, Disney's Hollywood Studios, and Disney's Animal Kingdom) and four minor parks (Blizzard Beach, Typhoon Lagoon, ESPN Wide World of Sports, and DisneyQuest). Descriptions begin on page 129.

Parking—Fee is $14 a day for cars, $15 for camper/trailers, and $18 for bus/tractor trailers. Parking is free to Disney resort guests; Swan/Dolphin, Shades of Green, and Downtown Disney Hilton guests; and Annual Passholders. Tables in Wonderland members park free after 5:00 pm. Tip: Save your receipt to park free at another park on the same day.

PhotoPass—This service lets you view all photos taken by Disney's photographers at http://www.disneyphotopass.com. No more waiting in long queues to view/buy photos.

Queue—Waiting area/line for an attraction or character meet.

Re-Entry—Guests may exit and re-enter the same park on the same day. Be sure to hold on to your pass and bring photo ID. Disney uses a safe finger scan (biometrics) rather than handstamps when you enter and re-enter a park (see photo).

Security—All bags are searched before entering parks.

Shopping—Shops sell Disney and themed items. We list the best shops in this chapter.

Smoking—Prohibited in resorts, buildings, queues, and parks, except in designated smoking areas (see park maps).

All guests get a finger scan upon park entry

Strollers & Wheelchairs—Strollers ($15/single stroller, $31/double, $13-$27/day for length-of-stay rental), wheelchairs ($12/day—no deposit, $10/day for length-of-stay rental), and ECVs ($50/day + $20 deposit) can be rented at the parks. Limited availability—arrive early, bring your own, or rent elsewhere (see page 36). Save your receipt for a free rental at another park on the same day, but there's no guarantee a rental will be available. Tip: Save money and get better strollers by renting from Orlando Stroller Rentals (http://www.orlandostrollerrentals.com).

Tax—Florida and county sales tax totals 6.5%.

Times Guide—Free listing of attraction hours and showtimes—pick up as you enter the parks.

More at ① first-aid-on-vacation | single-rider-lines

Park Passes

It's safest to budget **$95**/day for ages 10+ (**$88**/kids ages 3–9), the single-day/single-park base price with tax for the major parks (based on the last price increase in June 2012). The "Magic Your Way" multi-day passes deliver flexibility and savings (especially for stays of five days and longer), so you can do more at a lower price. The prices here include tax. Estimate a 4%–12% increase when rates go up again (sometime in mid-2013?).

Magic Your Way Tickets   *Actual 2012-2013 Rates*

*Magic Your Way tickets are available for 1-10 days. Guests can stick to basic admission or add one or more options at the time of purchase (see explanations below). Magic Your Way includes single-day passes and all varieties of Park Hopper passes. A Magic Your Way **Base Ticket** ($95-$339) is good for entry to a single major park (Magic Kingdom, Epcot, Disney's Hollywood Studios, or Disney's Animal Kingdom) for each day of the ticket. Multiday Base Tickets bring substantial discounts (see chart on the next page), so it pays to buy your admission all at once. Multiday Base Tickets expire 14 days after the first use, but they do not have to be used on consecutive days. More days—and options—can be added to a Base Ticket within 14 days of first use. The **Park Hopping** option (add $60.71) lets you visit more than one major park on the same day, for the length of your ticket. If you intend to visit more than one park a day, the Park Hopping option is indispensible because you cannot simply buy extra days of admission on a Base Ticket and then use more than one admission in a single day. The Magic Your Way **Water Parks Fun and More** option (add $60.71) adds a limited number of single-park admissions for the minor parks (Blizzard Beach, Typhoon Lagoon, DisneyQuest, Wide World of Sports, and Disney's Oak Trail golf course) to any Base Ticket. Each Water Parks Fun and More option is worth $13-$55, depending on where you use it. Purchase this feature with 1-day Base Tickets and you receive two Water Parks Fun and More options, while 2- to 10-day Base Tickets receive the same number of options as there are days on the pass. Regardless of how many options you receive, the cost to add this feature is always the same. As long as you make a minimum of two visits to the more costly minor parks, you'll get your money's worth. Combining park-hopping and water park fun and more options adds $84.14 to the price of an adult base ticket. The **No Expiration** option (add $32-$293) is best suited for those who plan to save the unused portion of a multiday ticket for a future trip. Prices for the various tickets are listed in the comparison chart on the next page.*

Annual Pass   *Actual 2012-2013 Rates*

Unlimited admission to the four major parks for a full year, plus special privileges. An Annual Pass ($611) costs less than two 3-day Magic Your Way Base Tickets with Park Hopping. Annual Passes also kick in great discounts on resorts (based on availability) and other privileges, such as a newsletter and events. There are also annual passes for the water parks ($106/$86), DisneyQuest ($95/$76), and water parks plus DisneyQuest ($137/$105). You cannot share an Annual Pass (or any other multiday pass).

Premium Annual Pass   *Actual 2012-2013 Rates*

A Premium Annual Pass ($744) offers the same privileges as the regular Annual Pass plus unlimited admission to the minor parks (including DisneyQuest) for $133 more than the regular. Five minor park visits cover the added cost. A Premium Annual Pass costs less than two 3-day Magic Your Way tickets with park-hopping, water parks, and no-expiration options.

Premier Annual Pass   *Actual 2012-2013 Rates*

The Disney Premier Passport ($797.69) offers premium annual pass benefits at both Walt Disney World and Disneyland Resort in California. Available only at park ticket booths.

Planning · Getting There · Staying in Style · Touring · Feasting · Making Magic · Index · Notes & More

Old Ticket Media: If you have an old Park Hopper with unused days on it, you may use those days, but you can no longer upgrade old ticket media if it has been used.

Upgrades and Exchanges: Within 14 days of your ticket's first use or before the admissions on the original tickets are used up (whichever comes first), upgrade or apply the unused value to a better ticket. Visit Guest Relations/Lobby Concierge before you go home.

Disney Vacation Club Discounts: Discounts of about $100 are available on Annual Passes for members of the immediate family residing in the same household.

AAA: Members (see page 11) can expect some sort of discount (historically 5%) on some passes. You must purchase tickets directly from AAA to get the discount.

Florida Resident Discounts: It pays to live nearby. Florida Resident Seasonal Passes work like Annual Passes, but with blackout dates in busy seasons and no free parking. There are some other special deals for Florida residents only, including discounted Annual Passes. A multi-day ticket for Florida residents is available with a small, advance purchase discount—check the Disney World web site for details.

Military Discounts: Discounts of roughly 7%-8% may be available on admission—check with your Exchange shop or MWR (Morale, Welfare, and Recreation) office. Some offices may need to pre-order your tickets, so we advise you check with them well in advance. Keep an ear out for special programs for active military personnel—in recent years, Disney offered all active military personnel a free five-day park hopper, with discounted admission for up to five people. To learn more, visit http://www.disneyworld.com/military, phone 407-939-4636, or visit Shades of Green (see page 104) upon arrival.

Online Ticket Brokers—These folks sell legitimate, unused tickets at excellent rates: http://www.ticketmania.com (877-811-9233), http://www.floridaorlandotickets.net (407-344-0030), or http://www.mapleleaftickets.com (800-841-2837). Be wary of others hawking tickets, including eBay and timeshares.

Kids Play Free (Well, Some Do): Kids under 3 are admitted into the parks for free (and get a free ride if the ride allows someone that small). Anyone 10 and over is considered an adult in the eyes of the ticket booth. Passes for kids ages 3-9 cost about 20% less than adult passes. Also, the option-filled pass you buy for yourself is usually more than your child needs, especially if you use childcare programs (detailed on pages 284-285).

Pass Comparison Chart: Options and prices for your number of days in the parks. *(2012/2013 prices for adult, nondiscounted passes purchased at the gate, including 6.5% tax.)*

Pass Type	Days: 1	2	3	4	5	6	7	8	9	10	11	12	13	14
Base (single day/park)	$95	$187	$258	$273	$285	$296	$306	$317	$328	$339				
Base + No Expiration		$219	$300	$363	$424	$472	$509	$546	$594	$632				
Base + Park Hopping (PH)	$132	$248	$318	$333	$346	$357	$367	$378	$389	$400				
Base + Park Hop. + No Exp.		$280	$361	$424	$485	$533	$570	$607	$655	$692				
Base + Water Parks & More	$155	$248	$318	$333	$346	$357	$367	$378	$389	$399				
Base + Water Parks + No. Exp.		$280	$361	$424	$485	$533	$570	$607	$655	$692				
Base + Water Parks + PH	$179	$272	$342	$357	$370	$380	$391	$402	$413	$423				
Base + PH + WP + No. Exp.		$304	$384	$447	$508	$556	$593	$630	$678	$716				
Annual Pass											$611	→		
Premium Annual Pass											$744	→		

Tip: Copy down or take a photo of the numbers on the back of your tickets, as you will need these to replace lost tickets. Record the numbers on the worksheet on page 317.

More at ① replacing-lost-passes

Top Photo Slice: Ticket windows at Disney's Animal Kingdom © MediaMarx, Inc.

Planning · Getting There · Staying in Style · Touring · Feasting · Making Magic · Index · Notes & More

Getting Around the Parks and Resort

The internal **transportation system** at the Walt Disney World Resort is quite extensive, with buses, boats, and the famed monorail all doing their part to shuttle guests around the property. Transportation hubs exist at each major theme park and Downtown Disney, where you can reach nearly any other place in the "World" by bus, monorail, or boat. The Transportation and Ticket Center (TTC) near the Magic Kingdom forms another hub, where you can get the monorail, ferryboat, and various buses. For current route information, see our property transportation chart on the right, check with a transportation cast member, or call 407-WDW-RIDE (407-939-7433).

Bus service is the cornerstone of the Walt Disney World transportation system. It is efficient, if occasionally confusing. With a few exceptions, bus routes run every 15 to 20 minutes, from about one hour prior to park opening until about one hour after closing. Bus stops are clearly marked. Travel times vary by route. Be sure to build in extra time for travel. Tip: Special early-morning buses visit all Disney resorts to pick up guests—ask about it at your resort. Most buses are lift-equipped to accommodate a limited number of wheelchairs and ECVs (usually two at a time).

A Disney bus passes under a monorail

Monorail trains run along two circular routes for the Magic Kingdom. The express route visits the park and the Transportation and Ticket Center (TTC), while the resort route also stops at the Contemporary, Polynesian, and Grand Floridian resorts. A separate line connects the TTC to Epcot. Monorails run from 7:00 am until one hour after park closing.

If you **drive**, you'll find ample parking at the parks. Use the map on the back flap of your PassPorter to get around the "World." **Tip:** Jot down your vehicle location in your PassPorter, or take a digital photo, so you don't forget where you parked. Also, if you intend to take advantage of Extra Magic Hour (EMH) mornings (see page 34), we recommend you avoid driving to the Magic Kingdom—it may be difficult to get into the park early enough. If you do drive, the gates at the TTC generally open 30–45 minutes before EMH time on EMH mornings.

From several locales, **boats** (also known as launches, ferries, cruisers, and Friendships) usher guests to the Magic Kingdom, Epcot, Disney's Hollywood Studios, Downtown Disney, and between some resorts. Boats generally depart every 15–30 minutes. At the Magic Kingdom, large ferries transport guests from the TTC to the gates, and a **railroad** encircles the park. Small boats run between the Magic Kingdom and the nearby resorts. At Epcot, "**Friendship**" boats shuttle you between points in the World Showcase.

By far the most reliable and common method of transportation within the "World" is **walking**. You can't walk between most parks and resorts—it's too far and there are few sidewalks, making it unsafe. You will, however, walk a lot around the parks, the resorts, and even between some parks and resorts. Bring comfortable, broken-in, walking shoes!

More at ① monorails

Disney Property Transportation Chart

Note: TTC = Transportation and Ticket Center (see previous page)

To get to the Magic Kingdom from...	Take the...
Polynesian or Grand Floridian	Monorail or boat
Contemporary	Monorail or walk
Wilderness Lodge or Fort Wilderness	Boat (or bus from Wilderness Lodge)
All other resorts	Bus
Disney's Hollywood Studios or Animal Kingdom	Bus to TTC, then monorail or boat
Epcot	Monorail to TTC, then monorail or boat

To get to Epcot from...	Take the...
Polynesian	Monorail (or walk) to TTC, then monorail
Contemporary or Grand Floridian	Monorail to TTC, then monorail
BoardWalk, Yacht/Beach Club, Swan/Dolphin	Boat or walk (to World Showcase)
All other resorts	Bus (to Future World)
Disney's Hollywood Studios or Animal Kingdom	Bus (or boat/walk from Studios)
Magic Kingdom	Monorail or boat to TTC, then monorail

To get to Disney's Hollywood Studios from...	Take the...
BoardWalk, Yacht/Beach Club, Swan/Dolphin	Boat or walk
All other resorts	Bus
Epcot or Disney's Animal Kingdom	Bus (or boat/walk from Epcot)
Magic Kingdom	Monorail or boat to TTC, then bus

To get to Disney's Animal Kingdom from...	Take the...
All resorts	Bus
Disney's Hollywood Studios or Epcot	Bus
Magic Kingdom	Monorail or boat to TTC, then bus

To get to Downtown Disney/Typhoon Lagoon from...	Take the...
Port Orleans	Boat (DD Marketplace only) or bus
Old Key West or Saratoga Springs	Boat (DD Marketplace only), bus, or walk
All other resorts	Bus
All parks (except Magic Kingdom)	Bus, boat, monorail to a resort, then bus
Magic Kingdom	Walk/monorail to Contemporary, then bus

To get to Blizzard Beach/Winter Summerland from...	Take the...
Disney's Animal Kingdom	Any resort bus going to Blizzard Beach
All resorts (or other theme parks)	Bus (or take resort bus and transfer)

To get to Fantasia Gardens from...	Take the...
All resorts (guests at Swan, Dolphin, BoardWalk, and Yacht & Beach Club can walk)	Travel to Disney's Hollywood Studios, boat to Swan, then walk

To get to Wide World of Sports from...	Take the...
All resorts	Go to Disney's Hollywood Studios, then bus

To get to Hoop-Dee-Doo Revue from...	Take the...
Magic Kingdom, Wilderness Lodge, or Contemporary	Boat to Fort Wilderness
Any other park	Bus to Fort Wilderness
Any other resort	Go to Magic Kingdom, then boat

To get to a Disney Resort Hotel from...	Take the...
Any resort (Swan, Dolphin, BoardWalk, Yacht & Beach Club are in walking distance of each other)	Go to nearby theme park or Downtown Disney, then bus, boat, or monorail

Top Photo Slice: A Friendship boat cruises through the International Gateway at sunset (①5395) © Amy Sellars

Planning | Getting There | Staying in Style | Touring | Feasting | Making Magic | Index | Notes & More

Park Tips and Ratings

Check **theme park hours** by calling 407-WDW-INFO (407-939-4636) or by visiting the web site at http://www.disneyworld.com. Resort guests may also consult the "News and Extras" update sheet, park maps, and Times Guides on arrival. Park hours are typically published six months in advance. Once you know the park hours for your trip, write them on the appropriate PassPocket. Don't be surprised if the park hours change on short notice. Fortunately, most changes are for longer hours.

Study the descriptions and maps to **familiarize yourself** with the names and themes of the lands before you arrive. We provide handy, fold-out, full-color maps for each major park in this chapter—on the inside of each map are our favorite touring plans and a list of attractions. Feel free to pull them out and take them along with you to the park for quick reference. Some readers even like to laminate them!

Studying the Magic Kingdom map

Check the **Tip Board** on the main thoroughfare in each major park and near the big slides at the water parks. These Tip Boards are continuously updated with wait times and closings—even openings or sneak peeks of new attractions.

Plan your visit around the things that are **most important** to you or require advance planning (like restaurant seatings or show times). If you're just not sure, you can use our favorite touring plans included in each major park description as a starting point. In general, though, we feel it is more enjoyable to "go with the flow" from attraction to attraction within each land. Relax and have fun!

Park Ratings

We rate each park to help you make the best decisions. Even so, our ratings may differ from your opinions—use the ratings as a guide only.

Value Ratings range from 1 (poor) to 10 (excellent) and are based on **quality** (cleanliness, maintenance, and newness); **variety** (different types of things to do); and **scope** (quantity and size of things to do)—**overall value** represents an average of the above three values. **Magic Ratings** are based on **theme** (execution and sense of immersion); **excitement** (thrills, laughs, and sense of wonder); and **fun factor** (number and quality of entertaining activities)—**overall magic** represents an average of the above three values. We use a point accumulation method to determine value and magic ratings.

Readers' Ratings are calculated from surveys submitted by vacationers at our web site (http://www.passporter.com/wdw/rate.htm).

Guest satisfaction is based on our and our readers' experiences with how different types of guests enjoy the park:

♥♥♥♥♥=love it   ♥♥♥♥=enjoy it   ♥♥♥=like it
♥♥=tolerate it   ♥=don't like it

More at ① overcoming-kids-fears

Understanding and Using the Attraction Descriptions and Ratings

PassPorter's custom-designed attraction charts include background, trivia, tips, restrictions, queues, accessibility details, enhanced ratings, and much more! We've organized this wide array of information into a consistent format so you can find what you need at a glance. Below is a key to our charts, along with notes and details. Enjoy!

Description Key

Icons[4] · Ratings[5]

1 Attraction Name [D-3[2]] (Bar Color[3]) FP ⚠ A-OK! # # #	
An overview of the attraction, what to expect (without giving too much away), historical background, trivia and "secrets," our suggestions for the best seating/viewing/riding, tips and tricks, waiting/queue conditions (e.g., covered, outdoor, etc.), wheelchair and stroller access, height/age restrictions, and **Alex's Toddler Tips** (ages 1–4), Kid Tips (ages 5–10), **Allie's Tween Tips** (ages 11–12), and **Allie's TeenTips** (ages 13–16)—hints and tips by kids for kids!	Type[6]
	Scope[6]
	Ages[7]
	Thrill Factor[8]
	Avg. Wait[8]
	Duration[8]

[1] Each chart has an empty **checkbox** in the upper left corner—use it to check off the attractions you want to visit (before you go) or those you visited during your trip.

[2] **Map coordinates** are presented as a letter and a number (i.e., A-5). Match up the coordinates on the park's map for the attraction's location within the park.

[3] The **bar color** indicates the attraction's target audience, as follows:

| Thrill Seekers | Family Friendly | Loved by Little Kids | Everything Else |

[4] Icons indicate when an attraction has FASTPASS (**FP**) or a height/age restriction (⚠).

[5] Our **ratings** are shown on the far right end. An **A-OK!** indicates that an attraction is approved as little kid-friendly by our kids Allie and Alexander Marx. The three boxes on the right side show ratings on a scale of 1 (poor) to 10 (don't miss!). The first is **Jennifer's** rating, the second is Dave's, and the third is our **Readers'** ratings. We offer our personal ratings to show how opinions vary, even between two like-minded people. You can also use our ratings as a point of reference—Jennifer appreciates good theming and dislikes sudden spins or drops, while Dave enjoys live performances and thrills. We both appreciate detail-rich attractions where we can learn something new.

[6] The boxes on the right below the numeric ratings give basic information. The first box is **attraction type**. The second box is always **attraction scope**, which we rate as follows:

- E-Ticket — Headliner attraction; the ultimate; expect long lines
- D-Ticket — Excellent fun, not-to-be-missed
- C-Ticket — Solid attraction that pleases most guests
- B-Ticket — Good fun, but easily skipped in a pinch
- A-Ticket — A simple diversion; often overlooked

[7] **Age-appropriate ratings**. For example, we may say "All Ages" when we feel everyone, from infant on up, will get something out of the experience. More common is "Ages 4 & up" or "Ages 8 & up" for attractions we think will be best appreciated by vacationers who are at least 4 or 8. This is only our guideline and not a Disney rule.

[8] **Thrill/scare factor, average wait**, and **duration** follow the age ratings, though we eliminate these if they don't apply or expand them if deserving. We did our best to format this information so you can understand it without having to check this key, too!

More at ⓘ how-young-is-too-young

Planning · Getting There · Staying in Style · Touring · Feasting · Making Magic · Index · Notes & More

The Parks

Disney's parks are quite spread out. To gain a better overall mental image of the parks, take a look the park map below. Note how the four major Disney parks form the **anchor of the resort**, with the smaller parks arrayed below it like treasures in an ocean. Each park in the map below has its own map (go to the page number in parentheses). A similar "property map" marked with all roads and hotels is on the back flap of your book.

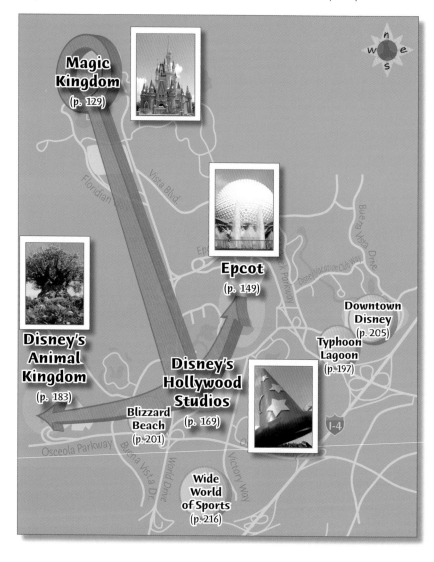

Top Photo Slice: Aerial view of Epcot as seen from the Characters in Flight by Aerophile balloon © MediaMarx, Inc.

Magic Kingdom

The Magic Kingdom is a true fantasyland, playfully painted in bold strokes upon the canvas of the imagination. This is quintessential Disney and often the first park guests visit. It is located the farthest north of all parks, on the shore of the Seven Seas Lagoon.

The Magic Kingdom conjures up fantasy, nostalgia, youth, and most of all, **magic**. One thing it does especially well is blend the ordinary with the unusual, enhancing both to make it all seem better than reality. This giant, 107-acre playground attracts people of all ages to its bygone boulevards, tropical gardens, western landscapes, living cartoons, and yesterday's vision of tomorrow. All roads lead to Cinderella Castle in the park's hub, the crown of the Kingdom.

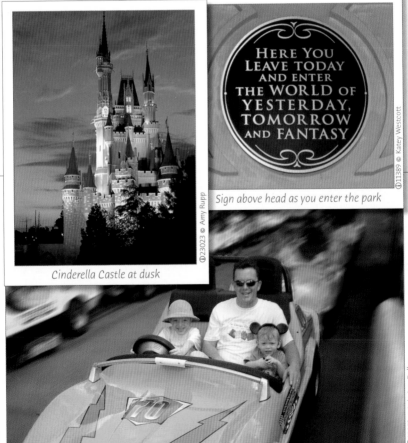

HERE YOU LEAVE TODAY AND ENTER THE WORLD OF YESTERDAY, TOMORROW AND FANTASY

Cinderella Castle at dusk

ⓣ23023 © Amy Rupp

Sign above head as you enter the park

ⓣ11389 © Katey Westcott

Driving in style down the Tomorrowland Indy Speedway

ⓣ15052 © Lois Ann Dolley

Top Photo Slice: Enchanting evening view of the Cinderella Castle looking down Main Street, U.S.A. (ⓣ14671) © Andrea Johnson

Side tabs: Planning · Getting There · Staying in Style · Touring · Feasting · Making Magic · Index · Notes & More

Orienting Yourself at the Magic Kingdom

Fold out the next page for touring plans and a handy attraction cha...

Five "lands" **radiate like spokes from the hub** of Cinderella Castle, located in the center of the park, with one more land added on for good measure (see the fold-out map on the facing page). Below are the lands in clockwise order, along with descriptions and headline attractions. Look behind the map to see our favorite itineraries and an at-a-glance list of attractions, and then turn to pages 137–148 for attraction details.

Main Street, U.S.A.
Walt Disney World Railroad Station
An early 1900s Main Street bustles with shops, eateries, a barbershop quartet, and City Hall.
Headline Attraction: Walt Disney World Railroad

Adventureland
Enchanted Tiki Room
Walk to the beat of jungle drums in a paradise filled with pirates, parrots, crocs, and camels.
Headline Attractions: Pirates of the Caribbean, Enchanted Tiki Room, Jungle Cruise, The Magic Carpets of Aladdin

Frontierland
Harper's Mill on Tom Sawyer Island
Journey back to the American Frontier, complete with a fort, mill, shootin' gallery, and "mountain range."
Headline Attractions: Splash Mountain, Big Thunder Mountain

Liberty Square
Liberty Belle Riverboat
Step back in time to Colonial America with her presidents, riverboats, and a haunted house.
Headline Attractions: The Haunted Mansion, The Hall of Presidents

Fantasyland
Teacups at the Mad Tea Party
An enchanted, brightly colored "small world" where elephants fly and teacups spin. Expanding in 2013!
Headline Attractions: Under the Sea ~ Journey of the Littler Mermaid, Winnie the Pooh, Dumbo, Mickey's PhilharMagic, Peter Pan's Flight

Tomorrowland
Entrance to Tomorrowland
The future as imagined in the 1930s, complete with space flights, aliens, and time travel.
Headline Attractions: Space Mountain, Buzz Lightyear's Space Ranger Spin, Monsters Inc. Laugh Floor

Magic Kingdom Map

Fantasyland

located on the lower level of Cinderella's Royal Table in Cinderella Castle

Enchanted Tales with Belle

Be Our Guest

Gaston's Tavern

"it's a small world"

Enchanted Tales with Belle

The Pinocchio Village Haus

Fort

The Haunted Mansion

Walt Disney World Railroad

Big Thunder Mountain Railroad

Tom Sawyer Island
Aunt Polly's Dockside Inn

Liberty Belle Riverboat

4:00

Peter Pan's Flight

Prince Charming Regal Carrousel

Mickey's PhilharMagic

Princess Fairytale Hall

Columbia Harbour House

The Hall of Presidents

Sleepy Hollow

Cinderella Castle

2:30

2:00

2:00

Splash Mountain

Raft 1:30

Frontierland

Liberty Square

3:00

Liberty Tree Tavern

1:30

2:00

Hub

Diamond Horseshoe Saloon

Pecos Bill Cafe

Country Bear Jamboree

Frontierland Shootin' Arcade

3:30

El Pirata Y el Perico

The Enchanted Tiki Room

The Magic Carpets of Aladdin

Aloha Isle

3:00

0:30

0:30

Tip Board

Swiss Family Treehouse

0:45

Pirates of the Caribbean

Jungle Cruise

The Crystal Palace

Casey's Corner

Ice Cream Parlor

Shrunken Ned's Junior Jungle Boats

3:30

Main Street Bakery

© MediaMarx, Inc.

Main Street, U.S.

Barber Shop

Main St. Vehicles

Tony's Town Square Restaurant

Adventureland

City Hall

Town Square Theater

Walt Disney World Railroad

Park Icon: Cinderella Castle

Monorail Station

Walk Around the World Path

Boat Docks

MAP COORDINATES	A	B	C	D

Magic Kingdom
Attractions At-A-Glance

(alphabetical order)

Attraction	Type	Allow	Page
☐ Astro Orbiter [F-4]	Ride	20+	146-T
☐ Big Thunder Mountain Railroad [A-2]	Coaster	50+	140-Fr
☐ Buzz Lightyear [F-4]	Track Ride	30+	146-T
☐ Carousel of Progress [F-4]	Show	30+	146-T
☐ Casey Jr. Playground [G-1]	Playground	20+	145-Fa
☐ Country Bear Jamboree [B-4]	Show	30+	140-Fr
☐ Diamond Horseshoe Saloon [B-3]	Pavilion	20+	141-LS
☐ Dumbo The Flying Elephant [F-2]	Ride	30+	142-Fa
☐ Enchanted Tales with Belle [D-1]	Show	30+	142-Fa
☐ Fairytale Garden [E-3]	Live Show	30+	142-Fa
☐ Frontierland Shootin' Arcade [B-4]	Arcade	15+	140-Fr
☐ Great Goofini [F-2]	Coaster	30+	145-TT
☐ Hall of Presidents, The [C-3]	Show	30+	141-LS
☐ Haunted Mansion, The [B-2]	Track Ride	30+	141-LS
☐ "it's a small world" [C-2]	Boat Ride	25+	143-Fa
☐ Jungle Cruise [B-4]	Boat Ride	40+	136-A
☐ Liberty Belle Riverboat [B-3]	Boat Ride	30+	141-LS
☐ Mad Tea Party [E-2]	Ride	20+	143-Fa
☐ Magic Carpets of Aladdin [B-4]	Ride	30+	138-A
☐ Main Street Vehicles [D-5]	Vehicles	30+	137-MS
☐ Mickey's PhilharMagic [D-2]	3-D Show	40+	143-Fa
☐ Monsters, Inc. Laugh Floor [E-4]	Show	45+	147-T
☐ Peter Pan's Flight [C-2]	Track Ride	40+	144-Fa
☐ Pirates of the Caribbean [A-4]	Boat Ride	30+	139-A
☐ Prince Charming Regal Carrousel [D-2]	Ride	15+	142-Fa
☐ Princess Fairytale Hall [D-2]	Character	30+	144-Fa
☐ Seven Dwarfs Mine Train [E-2]	Coaster	60–90+	144-Fa
☐ Space Mountain [G-3]	Coaster	40+	147-T
☐ Splash Mountain [A-3]	Coaster	60–90+	140-Fr
☐ Stitch's Great Escape! [E-4]	Show	50+	148-T
☐ Swiss Family Treehouse [B-4]	Walk-thru	30+	139-A
☐ Tiki Room, The Enchanted [B-4]	Show	20+	138-A
☐ Tom Sawyer Island [A-3]	Playground	60+	140-Fr
☐ Tomorrowland Arcade [G-3]	Arcade	20–40+	148-T
☐ Tomorrowland Indy Speedway [F-3]	Ride	50+	148-T
☐ Tomorrowland Transit Authority [F-4]	Track Ride	10+	148-T
☐ Town Square Theater [E-6]	Pavilion	30+	137-MS
☐ Under the Sea (Ariel's) [E-1]	Ride	60–90+	142-Fa
☐ Walt Disney World Railroad [D-6, A-2, G-1]	Train Ride	30+	137-MS
☐ Winnie the Pooh, Many Adv. [E-2]	Track Ride	30+	143-Fa

See page 151b for an explanation of this chart.

Touring

Our Favorite Touring Plans for the Magic Kingdom

NOTES

While we don't believe in the "commando" approach to fun, relaxing vacations, we realize that you may want guidance. Use these touring plans, which focus on the highest-rated attractions, as a starting point. You can do these plans in one day if you start by 9:00 am. If you can start earlier or stay later, add in additional attractions. The plans work best if you go in the same order, but feel free to re-order based on showtimes and wait times. Vacationers with infants and toddlers, or thrill-shy adults, may prefer to skip all attractions in blue.

ITINERARIES

Touring With Adults
Enter Tomorrowland
Get FASTPASS for Buzz Lightyear or Space Mountain
Visit Buzz Lightyear
Visit Stitch's Great Escape!
Visit Space Mountain
Enter Adventureland
Get FASTPASS for Jungle Cruise
Visit Enchanted Tiki Room
Visit Pirates of the Caribbean
Visit Jungle Cruise
Enter Frontierland (and have a snack)
Get FASTPASS for Splash Mountain
Visit Big Thunder Mountain
Visit Splash Mountain
Eat lunch at Liberty Tree Tavern or Columbia Harbour House (about 4 hours after entering park)
Enter Liberty Square
Visit Haunted Mansion
Visit Hall of Presidents
Watch parade from Sleepy Hollow
Enter Fantasyland (and have a snack)
Get FASTPASS for Peter Pan's Flight
Visit Under the Sea
Visit Mickey's PhilharMagic
Visit Peter Pan's Flight
Visit The Great Goofini (if open)
Take Walt Disney World Railroad from Fantasyland to Main Street, U.S.A. (if station open)
If the park is still open, do the following:
Eat dinner at Be Our Guest, Crystal Palace, or Tony's Town Square (about 8 1/2 hours into your day)
Watch nighttime parade from Main Street, Cinderella Castle, or Liberty Square
Watch fireworks from same spot
(Tour duration: About 10 1/2 hours)

Touring With Kids
Enter Fantasyland
Visit Under the Sea ~ Journey of The Little Mermaid
Visit Dumbo the Flying Elephant
Visit Peter Pan's Flight
Get FASTPASS for Mickey's PhilharMagic
Visit Winnie the Pooh
Visit Mickey's PhilharMagic
Watch Dream Along With Mickey (if showing)
Eat lunch at Pinocchio Village Haus
Enter Frontierland
Get FASTPASS for Splash Mountain or Big Thunder Mountain Railroad
Enter Adventureland
Visit Pirates of the Caribbean
Enter Frontierland
Visit Splash Mountain or Big Thunder Mtn.
Enter Adventureland (and have a snack)
Get FASTPASS for Jungle Cruise
Visit Magic Carpets of Aladdin
Visit Jungle Cruise
Enter Liberty Square
Watch parade from Sleepy Hollow
Visit Haunted Mansion
Enter Tomorrowland
Get FASTPASS for Buzz Lightyear
Visit Stitch's Great Escape!
Visit Monsters, Inc. Laugh Floor
Visit Space Mountain
Visit Buzz Lightyear
Eat dinner at Tony's Town Square, Crystal Palace, or Cosmic Ray's (about 8 hours after entering park)
Watch nighttime parade from Main Street
Watch fireworks from hub or Liberty Square
(Tour duration: About 9 1/2 hours)

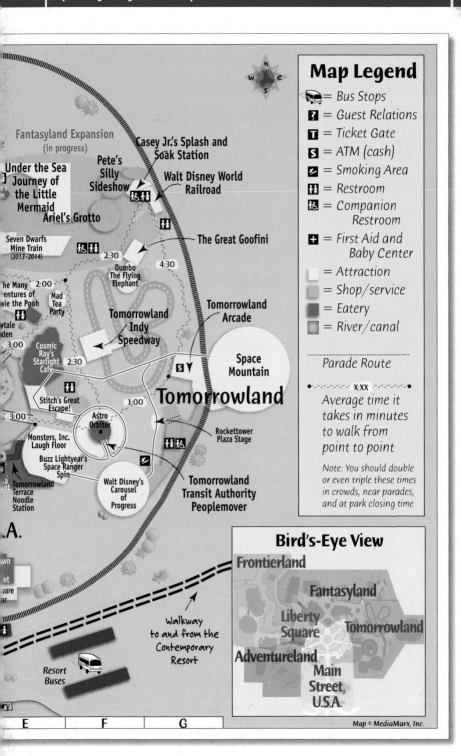

Fantasyland Expansion (in progress)

Under the Sea Journey of the Little Mermaid
Ariel's Grotto

Casey Jr.'s Splash and Soak Station

Pete's Silly Sideshow

Walt Disney World Railroad

Seven Dwarfs Mine Train (2013–2014)

2:30

The Great Goofini

Dumbo The Flying Elephant

4:30

The Many Adventures of Winnie the Pooh 2:00

Mad Tea Party

Fairytale Garden 3:00

Tomorrowland Indy Speedway

Tomorrowland Arcade

Cosmic Ray's Starlight Cafe 2:30

Space Mountain

Tomorrowland

Stitch's Great Escape!

3:00

1:00

Astro Orbiter

Rockettower Plaza Stage

Monsters, Inc. Laugh Floor

Buzz Lightyear's Space Ranger Spin

Walt Disney's Carousel of Progress

Tomorrowland Transit Authority Peoplemover

Tomorrowland Terrace Noodle Station

U.S.A.

Map Legend

🚌 = Bus Stops
❓ = Guest Relations
🎫 = Ticket Gate
💲 = ATM (cash)
🚬 = Smoking Area
🚻 = Restroom
♿ = Companion Restroom
➕ = First Aid and Baby Center
⬜ = Attraction
⬜ = Shop/service
⬜ = Eatery
⬜ = River/canal

Parade Route

•–––X:XX–––•
Average time it takes in minutes to walk from point to point

Note: You should double or even triple these times in crowds, near parades, and at park closing time

Bird's-Eye View

Frontierland

Fantasyland

Liberty Square

Tomorrowland

Adventureland

Main Street, U.S.A.

Walkway to and from the Contemporary Resort

Resort Buses

E   F   G

Map © MediaMarx, Inc.

Catching the Shows at the Magic Kingdom

Fun and excitement surround you in the Magic Kingdom. Live entertainment fills the streets with parades, performers, bands, and fireworks. Every afternoon, the 20-minute-long **Celebrate a Dream Come True Parade** highlights favorite Disney moments (see the parade route on the foldout map). We like to watch the parade from Frontierland or Liberty Square.

Mary Poppins in the daily parade

The dazzling **Wishes fireworks show** is generally held whenever the park is open after dark. Stand in front of Cinderella Castle to see Tinker Bell as she flies toward Tomorrowland during the 12-minute show. The fireworks are preceded by **"Celebrate the Magic,"** a show in which guest photos are projected on the castle. If you don't mind missing the castle show, Tomorrowland (near Indy Speedway) and Liberty Square are good viewing locations, too. Fantasyland is also possible, but it is very loud.

Cinderella Castle is the backdrop for live musical stage shows such as the Dream Along With Mickey stage show. In the evening, **Disney's Electrical Parade** (if showing) adds lights and music to the fun and follows the same route as the day parade. Disney characters make appearances throughout the park, especially at park opening and after some shows.

The glorious Wishes fireworks show over Cinderella Castle, as seen from the hub

More at ⓘ magic-kingdom-parades

Planning · Getting There · Staying in Style · Touring · Feasting · Making Magic · Index · Notes & More

Planning

Getting There

Staying in Style

Touring

Feasting

Making Magic

Index

Notes & More

TIPS

Making the Most of the Magic Kingdom

Take a **spin around the park** when you first arrive by boarding the train at the Walt Disney World Railroad station in Main Street, U.S.A. The 20-minute journey is a great introduction to the park.

Get a **haircut** at the Harmony Barber shop in Main Street. Try some colored hair gel at no extra charge, but watch out for the pixie dust! Young 'uns can get their very first haircut, too! Walk up or reserve at 407-WDW-STYLE.

Want a hairdo? The **Bibbidi Bobbidi Boutique** inside Cinderella Castle offers fancy do's for girls and boys ages 3 and up. Open from 8:00 am–7:00 pm—reserve up to 180 days at 407-WDW-STYLE.

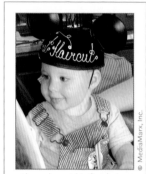

Alexander got his first haircut at the Harmony Barber Shop

Is your little prince or princess more of a pirate? Journey to the **Pirates League** in Adventureland for pirate "makeovers" for girls, boys, and even adults! Girls may also choose the "Mermaid Transformation" package! The "First Mate" package includes a bandanna, choice of facial effect (scar, tattoo, fake tooth, earring, or eye patch), sword and sheath, and personalized pirate oath for $29.95 plus tax. Reserve at 407-WDW-CREW.

Make time for the **Flag Retreat** in the Main Street town square, usually held at 5:00 or 5:30 pm daily. A color guard takes down the flag, and most days a marching band plays as well. Are you a veteran? Inquire at City Hall about assisting in the flag lowering, too.

Looking for something unique to do? Check out the new interactive game, "**Sorcerers of the Magic Kingdom**." This role-playing, trading-card game gives guests a chance to be the hero as they work to defeat the Disney Villains who are trying to take over the Magic Kingdom. This is a very fun, high-tech adventure in which you'll actually interact with the environment at the park as you battle the villains. Look for the "Sorcerer Recruitment Center" at the Firehouse on Main Street to pick up your quest, an activated Portal Key card, a pack of five random cards, and a map (all free of charge)! You can play as you tour the park, on your own or with your family/group.

Getting the Best at the Magic Kingdom

Sure stops for general Disney merchandise include much of Main Street, U.S.A.—shops here are open for 30–60 minutes after park closing. Here are some of our favorite **themed shops**:

Shop	Land	What makes it special
The Chapeau	Main Street, U.S.A.	Hats with embroidered names
Disney Clothiers	Main Street, U.S.A.	Upscale yet casual Disney clothes
Agrabah Bazaar	Adventureland	Themed, open-air marketplace
Plaza del Sol Caribe Bazaar	Adventureland	Pirate clothing and decor
Briar Patch	Frontierland	Great theme, Pooh and friends
Castle Couture	Fantasyland	Disney princess costumes
Mickey's Star Traders	Tomorrowland	Sci-fi toys and gadgets

Free wireless Internet is now available throughout the Magic Kingdom! Look for the "Disney-Guest" network on your wireless device and connect. Don't be surprised if it is a little slow.

Alcohol is now served in just one location at the Magic Kingdom: Be Our Guest restaurant (see page 231). If you're not dining here but want a drink, try one of the nearby resort hotels.

Need a **good place to meet**? The Liberty Bell in Liberty Square and the waterside seating across from the Plaza Restaurant are good choices. We recommend you avoid setting Cinderella Castle as your meeting point as it is sometimes inaccessible due to shows.

Main Street, U.S.A. closes a half hour later than the rest of the park. So while other folks fight the crowds in the parking lot, feel free to linger. Note that the stores are extremely busy at the end of the day.

Dining options abound, although table-service isn't as prevalent as at Epcot. There are six table-service restaurants and many counter-service cafes and carts. See pages 231–233 for details.

Ratings are explained on page 126.

Our Value Ratings:		Our Magic Ratings:		Readers' Ratings:
Quality:	7/10	Theme:	7/10	82% fell in love with it
Variety:	9/10	Excitement:	10/10	15% liked it well enough
Scope:	7/10	Fun Factor:	7/10	2% had mixed feelings
Overall Value:	**8/10**	**Overall Magic:**	**8/10**	1% were disappointed

Magic Kingdom is enjoyed by...		(rated by both authors and readers)	
Younger Kids: ♥♥♥♥	Young Adults: ♥♥♥♥	Families: ♥♥♥♥♥
Older Kids: ♥♥♥♥♥	Mid Adults: ♥♥♥	Couples: ♥♥♥♥
Teenagers: ♥♥♥♥	Mature Adults: ♥♥♥	Singles: ♥♥♥

SHOPPING

NOTES

RATINGS

Planning | Getting There | Staying in Style | Touring | Feasting | Making Magic | Index | Notes & More

Top Photo Slice: Windows above the Disney Clothiers shop in Main Street, U.S.A. (①9685) © Karen Majeau

Planning

Getting There

Staying in Style

Touring

Feasting

Making Magic

Index

Notes & More

Finding Your Way to the Magic Kingdom

BEST TIMES TO GO

The park tends to be the **busiest on Saturdays and Sundays**, and any day there are Extra Magic Hours scheduled (see page 34). We recommend you check the Extra Magic Hour schedule on Disney's web site and avoid those days if you prefer fewer crowds. Popular attractions such as Space Mountain and Splash Mountain are best done first thing in the morning to avoid long lines. Visit lands on the west (left) side of the park **earlier in the day**. Parents of young children are best off doing Fantasyland (particularly Dumbo) first as it gets busier later in the day. If you go to Splash Mountain and/or Big Thunder Mountain **during parade times**, note that the area can be very congested—use the riverside boardwalk or railroad instead. **Shop in the afternoon** to avoid crowds (ask about sending packages to the park exit or your resort).

GETTING THERE

By Monorail—From the Contemporary, Polynesian, or Grand Floridian resorts, take the monorail directly to the park. From Epcot, take the monorail to the Transportation and Ticket Center (TTC) and transfer to a Magic Kingdom express monorail or boat.

By Boat—From the TTC, ferry boats take guests to and from the Magic Kingdom. Guests at the Polynesian, Grand Floridian, Wilderness Lodge and Villas, and Fort Wilderness also have a boat service.

By Bus—From all other resorts, buses take you directly to the Magic Kingdom. From Disney's Hollywood Studios or Disney's Animal Kingdom, bus to the TTC and transfer to monorail or boat. From Downtown Disney, bus to the Contemporary and walk.

By Car—Take I-4 to exit 67 (westbound) or exit 62 (eastbound) and continue about four miles to the toll plaza. All-day parking is $14 (free to resort guests and annual passholders) and the pass is valid at other parks' lots on the same day. Park, take a tram to the Transportation and Ticket Center, and monorail or boat to the park.

By Foot—You can walk from the Contemporary Resort.

A ferry boat transports guests across the Seven Seas Lagoon

①22826 © Cam Matthews

More at ① most-magical-attractions

Charting the Attractions at Main Street, U.S.A.

Jennifer & Dave Readers

Planning | Getting There | Staying in Style | Touring | Feasting | Making Magic | Index | Notes & More

☐ **Main Street Vehicles** [D-5] A-OK!	3 2 5

Catch a one-way ride to or from the hub in vehicles fashioned after those popular at the turn of the century. We've seen horseless carriages, trolleys pulled by draft horses, and even a fire engine. These vehicles are fun to ride in if you're willing to wait in the slow, long lines. No time? Just walk instead. Vehicles tend to stop operating later in the day and during parades. Must transfer from wheelchair. **Alex's ToddlerTip:** "Look at the horses! ☺" **Allie's TeenTip:** "It's a bit boring."	**Vehicles**
	A-Ticket
	All ages
	Gentle ride
	Long waits

☐ **Town Square Theater** [D-6] FP A-OK!	3 5 5

Mouse fans gather in the theater's ornate lobby before being ushered into a backstage world of steamer trunks and whimsical theatrical props, where Mickey (and sometimes Minnie) graciously greet their guests. Wonderful details make this an above-average meet-n-greet. This is also the the park's PhotoPass Center.	**Exhibit**
	A-Ticket
	Ages 3 & up
	Simple fun

☐ **Walt Disney World Railroad** [D-6] A-OK!	5 5 7

Circle the Magic Kingdom on a popular steam train, with stops at Main Street, U.S.A., Frontierland, and Fantasyland. You'll catch glimpses of all but Liberty Square along the 1.5-mile journey. Ride the full route for fun, or disembark at any stop to travel through the park. Personal strollers must be folded before entering station. Replacement rental strollers may be available at other stops (hold on to your name tag!), but are not guaranteed. Attraction is closed during fireworks. Wheelchair and ECV friendly. **Alex's ToddlerTip:** "Choo choo! ☺" **Allie's KidTip:** "Kids like this train! It doesn't go too fast."	**Train Ride**
	B-Ticket
	All ages
	A bit loud
	Gentle ride
	Short waits
	20 min. ride (roundtrip)

Attraction descriptions and ratings are explained on page 127.

⚠ What Is and Isn't an Attraction?

We defined an "attraction" on page 120 as an individual ride, show, or exhibit. These are the destinations at the park and almost invariably come with a queue. We cover virtually all the attractions that Disney lists in their own guidemaps, plus a few that aren't listed but we still think are deserving of the "attraction" title (such as Main Street Vehicles). Like Disney, we don't consider things like talking trash cans (yes, they exist!) to be attractions as they rarely need a queue. We also don't consider outdoor stage shows, parades, or fireworks to be attractions, either—we cover these in the Entertainment sections in the park introduction pages of your PassPorter. Character greeting areas are less straightforward—if Disney considers one to be an attraction or we feel it offers more than simple character greetings, we include a description of it. For a list of character greeting locations, refer to the guidemap and Times Guide available upon your arrival. We also list popular spots to find favorite characters at Disney's Hollywood Studios on page 171b. For more specific information or hard-to-find characters, ask at Guest Relations in any of Disney's parks. Also check out our *Disney Character Yearbook*—details on page 314.

Alexander finds attractions everywhere

© MediaMarx, Inc.

Planning

Getting There

Staying in Style

Touring

Feasting

Making Magic

Index

Notes & More

Charting the Attractions at Adventureland

Jennifer Dave Readers

☐ Walt Disney's Enchanted Tiki Room [B-4]   A-ok! | 8 | 7 | 8 |

This classic attraction was recently "updated" back to a version closer to its original, which debuted at Disneyland in 1963. Updates include LED lighting and awesome audio! This is a perfectly cool place to sit and rest while Audio-Animatronics creatures sing and cavort above you. This is a fun musical revue, which grew from Walt Disney's notion for an unusually entertaining Chinese restaurant. Don't miss the new pre-show in the outdoor, covered queue area. Best views are on the left side. Wheelchair friendly. Assistive listening devices. **Alex's ToddlerTip:** ☺ **Allie's KidTip:** "Look for the Tiki gods." **TeenTip:** "It may seem lame, but it's not!"

ⓘ6889 © Joy Vodnik
Singing Tiki Gods

Show
D-Ticket
All ages
Dark, loud, angry gods
Short waits
3 min. intro
11 min. show

☐ Jungle Cruise [B-4]   FP   A-ok! | 6 | 6 | 7 |

See the sights along the "rivers of the world" in the company of a silly skipper. You and your fellow explorers will go chug-chugging up river in an open-air, awning-covered river boat inspired by the "African Queen." Every skipper tells a slightly different tale. Audio-Animatronics animals and "natives" liven things up. You may get damp. After-dark cruises are particularly fun. Outdoor, covered queue—lines can be deceptively long. Transfer from ECV to wheelchair. **Alex's ToddlerTip:** ☺ **Allie's KidTip:** "Lions, and tigers, and King Cobra!" **TweenTip:** "One of my favorites!"

ⓘ13623 © Janet Simonsen
Scenes along the Jungle Cruise

Boat Ride
D-Ticket
Ages 3 & up
Corny jokes
FASTPASS or long waits
10 min. ride

☐ The Magic Carpets of Aladdin [B-4]   A-ok! | 5 | 6 | 5 |

Take a spin through a whole new world. Colorful, rider-controlled carpets go around, up, and down—sit in the front to control the height, or sit in the back to tilt forward and back. Similar to Dumbo (see page 142). Water-spitting camels add to the fun. Transfer from ECV to wheelchair. **Alex's ToddlerTip:** "Wow! ☺" **Allie's KidTip:** "Sit in the front so you can zoom up and get sprayed by camels."

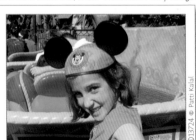
ⓘ13724 © Patti Kalal
Margaret anticipates her carpet ride

Ride
D-Ticket
Ages 3 & up
Med. waits
1½ min. ride

Charting the Attractions at Adventureland

Jennifer Dave Readers

Pirates of the Caribbean [A-4]   A-OK!   8 7 9

①13648 © Janet Simonsen

Dead men tell no tales!

"Yo ho, yo ho!" The ride that inspired the movies is a slow, dark cruise through a subterranean world of Audio-Animatronics pirates (including Jack Sparrow and Barbossa) and the townsfolk they plunder. Enjoy scene after riotous scene and fun special effects. Captain Blackbeard had replaced Davy Jones in 2011, and the Mermaids were introduced in October 2012. Lines can be long, especially on hot days because you get to wait in a cool cellar. Take the left line—it's shorter. You aren't likely to get wet, but seats can be damp. Transfer from ECV to wheelchair and transfer from wheelchair. **ToddlerTip**: "Scary! ☹" **TeenTip**: "Very cool! I love Jack!"

Boat Ride
E-Ticket
Ages 6 & up
Gentle drop, dark, scary to young kids
9 min. ride

Shrunken Ned's Junior Jungle Boats (closed) [B-4]   3 4 3

This very small "attraction," which involved driving tiny Jungle Cruise boats around a lagoon for $2, closed in autumn 2012. Not expected to re-open.

Arcade
A-Ticket

Swiss Family Treehouse [B-4]   5 5 4

Walk through the home of the shipwrecked family from the Disney classic "Swiss Family Robinson." The branches of the huge (and very fake) banyan tree, known as "Disneyodendron eximus," cradle the family's heirlooms and contraptions. The treehouse has multiple levels that you need to climb. Thus, this attraction is not wheelchair or stroller accessible, and it can be tiring for some. The line of guests winds through slowly. **Alex's KidTip**: "I love all the inventions in the treehouse!"

Walk-thru
B-Ticket
Ages 4 & up
Lots of stairs
Allow 15–30 min. to tour

Strollers: To Bring or Rent   See page 121 for more on rentals.

If you bring your own stroller (a boon for the airport and travel to and from the buses/parking lot), we recommend a compact, umbrella stroller, as it's easy to tote about. If you prefer to bring a larger, folding stroller (the kind with cup holders and serious cargo capacity), try to travel the buses at off-hours, when the stroller won't prevent you from getting onboard due to crowded conditions. Rentals in the parks are good for kids who only need an occasional ride and weigh less than the 70-lb. weight limit. All rental strollers in the parks are now either "jogging style" or molded plastic (see photo). Need an alternative? Rent a nicer stroller for a better price from a place like Orlando Stroller Rentals (http://www.orlandostrollerrentals.com), which we've used and recommend.

© MediaMarx, Inc.

Rental at Magic Kingdom

Top Photo Slice: Spitting "Liki Tiki" statues in Adventureland are fun on a hot day (①1870) © Brad K.

Genuine PassPorter Genuine PassPorter Genuine PassPorter Genuine PassPorter Genuine PassPorter Genuine PassPorter Genuine

Planning | Getting There | Staying in Style | Touring | Feasting | Making Magic | Index | Notes & More

Charting the Attractions at Frontierland

Jennifer · Dave · Readers

☐ Big Thunder Mountain Railroad [A-2]   FP 🧍 A-OK!   7 8 9

Be prepared to grin as you ride this not-so-scary roller coaster through a wild western landscape. There is plenty of speed and lots of curves, but no fearsome drops on this 4-min. mine train ride. You'll shake and rattle, though! Look around and enjoy Disney's lovingly built scenes. Night rides are extra fun! Lines can be long, but there will be fun, interactive things coming soon. 40"/102 cm height restriction, adult supervision required. Transfer from wheelchair. Health warning. **Allie's KidTip:** "Listen for the howls of the wolves. I loved this ride!

Coaster
E-Ticket
Ages 6 & up
Fast turns, dark caves
FASTPASS or long waits

☐ Country Bear Jamboree [B-4]   A-OK!   5 4 5

A troupe of Audio-Animatronics bears sings, dances, and jokes in this loving country music sendup. Grown-up city slickers might find the jokes and songs a bit corny, but the young 'uns just might take a hankerin' to 'em. This is another cool, dim place to duck out of the hot Florida sun. Wheelchair accessible. Reflective captioning. Assistive listening devices. **Alex's ToddlerTip:** ☺ **Allie's KidTip:** "Listen carefully for the words to the songs. They're funny!" **TeenTip:** "Boring."

Show
C-Ticket
Ages 2 & up
Loud
Med. waits
15 min. show

☐ Frontierland Shootin' Arcade [B-4]   4 6 3

Have fun shootin' targets with electronic rifles. Aim at cactus, tombstones, and bits of the landscape. Pay 1 dollar (four quarters) for about 35 shots. **Allie's KidTip:** "Shoot the red dots. But beware: The guns are heavy." **TweenTip:** "Awesome! Rest your elbow on the pad to get the best shot."

© MediaMarx, Inc.

Arcade
A-Ticket
Ages 9 & up

☐ Splash Mountain [A-3]   FP 🧍   4 6 9

Even bystanders can get soaked when riders slide down this five-story log flume into the Briar Patch. The first ten minutes of this attraction are a gentle ride through an Audio-Animatronics wonderland with all the "brer" creatures from "The Song of the South." Then, kersplash! 40"/102 cm height restriction, adult supervision required. Little ones can play in the charming Laughin' Place playground near the attraction's exit while big kids ride. Health warning. Transfer from wheelchair to ride. **Alex's ToddlerTip:** ☺ (for the playground) **Allie's KidTip:** "I love Splash Mountain. On the last big drop, you might want to lean back."

Coaster
E-Ticket
Ages 9 & up
Very steep drop at end!
FASTPASS or long waits
11 min. ride

☐ Tom Sawyer Island [A-3]   A-OK!   6 6 5

Young 'uns can explore caves, tunnels, and Fort Langhorn as they scamper over Tom and Huck's legendary hangout. Kids love the bridges; oldtimers wander the winding paths and play checkers. Caves are fun, but can be very dark and confining. Board a raft near Big Thunder Mountain to reach the island. This is a great place for a break—try Aunt Polly's Dockside Inn for a snack (seasonal). Must be able to walk. Closes at dusk. Tip: Look for the hidden whitewash brushes—if you find one, tell a cast member for a surprise! **Alex's ToddlerTip:** "Caves!" ☺ **Allie's KidTip:** "Follow the wolf howls to the fort."

Playground
C-Ticket
All ages
Dark, scary caves
Short waits
Allow 1 hr.

Tips: You can board the Walt Disney World Railroad (see page 137 for details) at the Frontierland Station [A-2]. Need a break? Look for the rocking chairs scattered about Frontierland and Liberty Square.

Planning · Getting There · Staying in Style · Touring · Feasting · Making Magic · Index · Notes & More

Charting the Attractions at Liberty Square

Jennifer Dave Readers'

☐ **Diamond Horseshoe Saloon** [B-3]   – – –

The Diamond Horseshoe Saloon is serving light refreshments most of the time; buffet meals in peak seasons. This attraction has had difficulty finding its place in recent years, and we wouldn't be surprised if it changes in the near future. Let's hope they bring back a live show. If it's open, it should remain wheelchair accessible.

Pavilion
A-Ticket

☐ **The Hall of Presidents: A Celebration of Liberty's Leaders** [C-3]   5 4 6

Ladies and gentlemen, the Presidents of the United States! The show begins with a 180° film presenting a patriotic, stirring view of our past. Every U.S. President is represented in full Audio-Animatronics glory—look for President Obama (see photo), who debuted here in July 2009. The revamped show focuses on the bond between a president and his people, and is now narrated by Morgan Freeman. A red brick colonial hall houses the large, 700-seat theater, a cool, quiet hideaway. Wheelchair accessible. Reflective captioning. Assistive listening devices. Shows are every half hour. **Allie's KidTip:** "You might like the movie—it talks about freedom." **TeenTip:** "I'd rather do something else."

Show
C-Ticket
Ages 10 & up
Dark theater
Short waits
23 min. show

President Obama joins the line-up

☐ **The Haunted Mansion** [B-2]   A-OK!   9 8 9

Go for a gore-free ride through a world of 999 grinning ghosts in this popular attraction. The spooky visual effects are astounding, but the scares are served up with a wink and lots of chuckles. There's a fun storyline, nifty special effects, and enough delicious detail here that you'll ride again and again. Just be sure to leave room in your two- to three-person "doom buggy" for hitchhiking ghosts! A new interactive queue is great fun, but you can bypass it for a quicker wait. May be too intense for young kids (though Allie liked it, she was a bit scared even at 12). Transfer from wheelchair to ride. Visit http://www.doombuggies.com for more details. **Allie's KidTip:** "Can you find the dog skeleton? Hint: It's on a cliff in the graveyard."

Track Ride
E-Ticket
Ages 6 & up
Mild scares, very dark
Medium waits
3 min. intro 7 min. ride

Spooky fun!

☐ **Liberty Square Riverboat** [B-3]   5 6 5

Take a cruise on a steam-driven sternwheeler. Mark Twain narrates your spin around Tom Sawyer Island, but the real joy is the attention to detail. The boat and its steam power plant are more interesting than the scenery—be sure to tour the decks. Dodge the sun in the middle deck salon. The "Liberty Belle" replaced the "Richard F. Irvine" in 1996. Wheelchair accessible. Adult supervision. Departs on the hour and half-hour. **Alex's KidTip:** "Ask if you can help steer the boat!"

Boat Ride
C-Ticket
All ages
Gentle rides
Med. waits
20 min. ride

Attraction descriptions and ratings are explained on page 127.

Top Photo Slice: The Liberty Bell in front of the Hall of Presidents (①9449) © Cheryl Pendry

Planning | Getting There | Staying in Style | Touring | Feasting | Making Magic | Index | Notes & More

Charting the Attractions at Fantasyland

Jennifer Dave Readers

Under the Sea ~ Journey of the Little Mermaid [E-1]   – – –

New! Enter Prince Eric's Castle and go under the sea to see Ariel and her friends. Board your two- to three-person Omnimover clamshell (a Doom Buggy by any other name) to be immersed in favorite scenes and music from the beloved film. Ariel, Eric, Sebastian, Scuttle, and evil Ursula are brought to Audio-Animatronic "life" using classic techniques and innovative lighting. The ride is identical to The Little Mermaid—Ariel's Undersea Adventure at Disney California Adventure, though the interactive queue is unique. Some dark and scary moments. Wheelchair and ECV accessible, transfer from ECV to wheelchair. Hearing disability services.

| Track Ride |
| E-Ticket |
| All ages |
| Expect long waits |
| 7 min. ride |

Dumbo The Flying Elephant [F-2]   A–Ok!   5 5 5

Improved! Every child wants to ride around, up, and down on Dumbo. Two-seater flying elephants take you for a short, fast spin. Show your child to lift the control lever to rise higher. Grown-ups will enjoy the pachyderm's-eye view. Dumbo has flown to a new location (see page 145) where a second ride system and innovative queue ease the historically long waits. Kids cavort in an indoor playground, parents sit in comfort, and the family is paged when it's time to ride. Adults must ride with small children. Must transfer from wheelchair.
Allie's Kid Tip: ☺ "Go as high as you can!"

| Ride |
| D-Ticket |
| All ages |
| Spins high in the air |
| Long waits |
| 2 min. flight |

Beloved by all ages!
①16974 © Jamie Slider

Enchanted Tales with Belle [D-1]   – – –

New! Explore Maurice's cottage and whimsical workshop, then step through a magic mirror into Beast's Castle. Madame Wardrobe is on hand to greet you, and to cast her guests for roles in a telling of the "tale as old as time." Then, an animtronic Lumière invites all into the Library, to await Belle's arrival and to watch or play their parts as she presents her famous story. The staging is similar to Storytime with Belle, which was formerly held in Fairytale Garden.

| Show |
| C-Ticket |
| All ages |
| Happy ending |
| 15 min. story |

Fairytale Garden [E-3]   A–Ok!   6 6 5

Rapunzel from "Tangled" started to "play and greet" guests here in October 2010 (and Storytime with Belle ended in 2010). Sit on stools and benches among the rose bushes and watch characters at various times throughout the day. Characters may take volunteers from the audience. Arrive about ten minutes early to get a seat. No shade. Wheelchair friendly. Allie's Kid Tip: "You might want to be in the show because it could be fun!!!"

| Live Show |
| B-Ticket |
| All ages |
| Happy ending |
| 15 min. story |

The Great Goofini (formerly Barnstormer) [F-2]   🚹 A–Ok!   7 7 6

Even grown-up coaster fans love this fast, swooping "flight" featuring The Great Goofini, a barnstorming pilot who came to town with Dumbo's Circus. This attraction was re-themed during the Fantasyland expansion (see page 145). Long lines move quickly through an uncovered queue, but take time to enjoy the Goofy artifacts. Cars may be small for big/tall adults. May close during wet weather. Transfer from wheelchair. Alex's Toddler Tip: "I like Goofy's plane! ☺"
Allie's Kid Tip: "Lift your hands in the air! You'll want to go on it again and again!"

| Coaster |
| D-Ticket |
| Ages 2 & up (35" and up) |
| Fast turns |
| Med. waits |
| 1 min. flight |

Charting the Attractions at Fantasyland

Jennifer Dave Readers

"it's a small world" [C-2]   A-OK! | 5 | 6 | 6 |

"It's a world of laughter, a world of tears..." Yes, these are Disney's famous singing and dancing dolls, who first debuted their act at the 1964-65 New York World's Fair. Their catchy song adapts to the local surroundings as your boat floats sedately past scenes depicting the world's continents and cultures. Must transfer from ECV to wheelchair to ride. **Alex's ToddlerTip:** ☺ **Allie's KidTip:** "Ask your grown-ups for a seat at the end of a row so you can see more."

Boat Ride
C-Ticket
All ages
Short to med. waits
11 min. cruise

Mad Tea Party [E-2]   A-OK! | 2 | 3 | 6 |

Spin and spin and spin some more inside a giant teacup. Young kids love to get dizzy, so this ride draws them like a magnet. Turn the metal wheel at the center of your teacup to make it spin even faster. You'll be as dizzy as the Mad Hatter.

This is one ride that lasts a bit longer than you'd like. Sit this one out if you're prone to dizziness. Adult supervision of children under 7. Must transfer from wheelchair to ride. **Alex's ToddlerTip:** "I want to ride the 'teacups' again ... and again! ☺" (this is his favorite ride!) **Allie's KidTip:** "Look for the dormouse!"

Ride
C-Ticket
Ages 4 & up
Scares adults
Short waits
2 min. spin

© MediaMarx, Inc.

Alexander and Dave twirl about in the teacups

The Many Adventures of Winnie the Pooh [E-2] FP   A-OK! | 6 | 5 | 7 |

Take a gentle ride through the world of that fabulously popular bear. Blow through the Blustery Day, bounce along with Tigger, dream of Heffalumps and Woozles, and float away in a mighty spring flood, all in a four-seat "honey pot" that moves along an indoor track. Pooh fans will exit feeling warm and fuzzy—the better you know Pooh's tales, the more you'll get from your tour through the cartoon cutout scenery. The covered queue winds through pages blown away from a huge storybook. Lines can be long—we suggest you get a FASTPASS soon after the park opens. Transfer from ECV to wheelchair. **Alex's ToddlerTip:** "Tigger and Pooh! ☺" **Allie's KidTip:** "Sit in the front."

Track Ride
D-Ticket
All ages
Kid-friendly; dark could be slightly scary
FASTPASS or long waits
3 min. ride

Mickey's PhilharMagic [D-2]   FP   A-OK! | 8 | 9 | 9 |

Trouble's brewing in Fantasyland in this 3-D movie experience, when Donald "borrows" (and loses) Mickey's sorcerer hat. The audience, assembled in front of a giant, 150-foot-wide screen in PhilharMagic Concert Hall, awaits a concert conducted by Mickey. Donald, naturally, gets into deep trouble. Soon he's scurrying through scenes from Disney classic films, trying to regain the lost hat. Along the way he meets Simba, Peter Pan, Lumiere, Aladdin, Ariel, and other favorite Disney characters. Look for Donald at the "end." The 3-D movie effects and sensations are kid-friendly. Best seats in middle or back of theater. Covered queue. Wheelchair accessible. Assistive listening devices. Reflective captioning. **Alex's ToddlerTip:** ☺ **Allie's TeenTip:** "Wow! Good for all ages."

3-D Show
E-Ticket
All ages
Intense effects may be scary
FASTPASS or med. waits
10 min. show

Attraction descriptions and ratings are explained on page 127.

Top Photo Slice: Mosaic of Cinderella and her prince in Cinderella Castle (①13571) © Janet Simonsen

Planning
Getting There
Staying in Style
Touring
Feasting
Making Magic
Index
Notes & More

Charting the Attractions at Fantasyland

Jennifer Dave Readers

Peter Pan's Flight [C-2]   FP   A-OK!   6 6 8

Climb aboard a flying, three-seat pirate ship that twists and turns sedately through the clouds. Follow Peter Pan and the Darling children from London to Neverland. Scenes featuring the Lost Boys, mermaids, Captain Hook's ship, and the crocodile unfold below, then you're safely home. Very dark, 4-minute ride. Covered queue area. Transfer from wheelchair to ride. **Alex's ToddlerTip:** ☺ **Allie's KidTip:** "Can you find the mermaids? One of them looks like Ariel!"

Track Ride
D-Ticket
Ages 3 & up
Dark, heights
FASTPASS or long waits

Prince Charming Regal Carrousel [D-2]   A-OK!   5 5 6

This colorful, lovingly maintained carrousel painted with scenes from Cinderella sits at the center of Fantasyland. Many of the 84 horses were rescued from a historic New Jersey carousel, but you'd have a hard time telling which ones. The horses closer to the perimeter tend to rise higher. A recently added chariot (an original) holds six. Look for Cinderella's horse with a golden ribbon on its tail. Disney tunes make it a joy for the ears! The carousel is particularly enchanting in the evening. Note that the name changed from Cinderella's Golden Carrousel in 2010 in anticipation of the Fantasyland expansion (see page 145). Guests must transfer from wheelchair to board. Adult supervision of children required. **Alex's ToddlerTip:** ☺ **Allie's KidTip:** "Sit carefully on the horse."

Ride
B-Ticket
Ages 2 & up
High horses can be scary
Short waits
2 min. ride

Princess Fairytale Hall (opening 2013) [D-2]   A-OK!   – – –

New! With the Seven Dwarfs Mine Train Ride soon to open across the way, Fantasyland didn't need a second Snow White-themed attraction, so the classic Snow White's Scary Adventure closed in early 2012 to make way for a new Princess meet-and-greet. Aurora, Cinderella, and other, less-traditional princesses like Tiana and Rapunzel will be on hand for autographs and photos. Expect moderate waits.

Pavilion
A-Ticket
All ages
Expect medium waits

Seven Dwarfs Mine Train (opening 2013–2014) [E-2]   – – –

Coming soon! This new, moderate roller coaster boasts an innovative ride vehicle that pendulum-swings from side to side as you ride the banked curves of the Seven Dwarfs fabled mine. Ride simulations suggest this will be a cross between Big Thunder Mountain Railroad and Splash Mountain. The journey will begin like any tubular-track coaster, up and into the mine. Inside, the track levels out and you pass Audio-Animatronics depicting scenes from Snow White. Then, emerge from the mine to finish up with short drops and fast turns. Accessibility and restrictions unknown at press time, but expect them to be similar to Big Thunder Mountain Railroad (see page 140).

Coaster
E-Ticket
Ages 4 & up
Fast turns, modest drops
FASTPASS ? or long waits
4 min. ride ?

Meet Your Favorite Characters

The new Fantasyland has more "character" than ever. Though Princess Fairytale Hall has yet to open (see above), there are three other character meet 'n' greets up and running in this part of the park. Most heralded is Enchanted Tales With Belle (see page 142). Ariel's Grotto has returned, in a new spot near the exit of the mermaid's ride—once more, her fans have a chance to chat and smile for some Ariel photos. Just around the corner in Storybook Circus is Pete's Silly Sideshow, where you can meet The Astounding Donaldo, The Great Goofini, Madame Daisy Fortuna, and Minnie Magifique!

More at ⓘ fantasyland-for-adults

Disney's Animal Kingdom Area | Epcot Area | Downtown Disney Area | Magic Kingdom Area

Chapter 4: Touring the "World" | Topic: Magic Kingdom Attractions | 145

Planning
Getting There
Staying in Style
Touring
Feasting
Making Magic
Index
Notes & More

Charting the Attractions at Fantasyland

Fantasyland Expansion in 2012–2014

The largest expansion in Magic Kingdom history is under way in Fantasyland. So big, that Mickey's Toontown Fair, Ariel's Grotto, and Pooh's Playful Spot playground were razed to make room, and Snow White's Scary Adventure was retired. In their places are (or will be) major new attractions dedicated to Beauty and the Beast, the Little Mermaid, and Snow White and the Seven Dwarfs; a Princess meet-and-greet will take over Snow White's old home; and Dumbo has flown to a new Circus-themed zone sporting two Dumbo rides and an innovative, interactive queue. Although early announcements promised Princesses and Pixies a-plenty, in early 2011 Disney made a mid-course correction, and in place of Pixie Dust, the Seven Dwarfs will be off to work, "In a mine, where a million diamonds shine." Let's tour the new construction, shall we? Just to the right of Pinocchio Village Haus is Belle's Village, a Beauty and the Beast-themed area featuring Maurice's Cottage/Enchanted Tales with Belle (see page 142), Be Our Guest restaurant, Gaston's Tavern, and Bonjour! Village Gifts. Be Our Guest, inside a hill topped by Beast's Castle, opened in late 2012 and seats 550 diners in the Ballroom, Gallery, and West Wing. Quick-service meals are served by day, switching to table service at dinnertime, and a time-honored Magic Kingdom tradition

Prince Eric's Castle at Under the Sea

©38140 © Amanda Nash

has fallen—wine and beer is offered at dinner! Next-door to Belle's Village and appropriately, in the general location of the old 20,000 Leagues Lagoon, is Under the Sea ~ Journey of the Little Mermaid (see page 144), a major dark ride packed with Audio Animatronic characters that's identical to the Little Mermaid ride at Disney California Adventure (though the queue differs dramatically). Prince Eric's Castle (yes, that's two new castles, though neither holds a candle to Cinderella's) stands guard on the hill housing the attraction. Near the ride's exit is an all-new Ariel's Grotto meet-and-greet. The Seven Dwarfs Mine Train (see page 144) will occupy a third low hill situated between Belle's Village and The Many Adventures of Winnie the Pooh. Next-door to Pooh, Snow White's Scary Adventure closed in mid-2012 to make way for Princess Fairytale Hall (page 144), a character meet and greet. Storybook Circus is in Toontown's old spot, featuring the new "double Dumbos." Flying alongside Dumbo is a re-themed Barnstormer roller coaster (see page 142). An all-new Fantasyland Station was built for the Walt Disney World Railroad; with the Casey Jr. Splash 'N' Soak Station water play area next door. The former Toontown Hall of Fame and Judge's Tent house Big Top Souvenirs, Big Top Treats, and Pete's Silly Sideshow character meet. The former Mickey character meet is now in Main Street's Town Square Exposition Hall (see page 137). The first part of the project opened in early 2012, with additional openings during that summer and fall. All that remains undone is the mine train ride and princess meet-and-greet, currently slated for 2013–2014.

Top Photo Slice: The "Floating Lights" above the Fairytale Garden (①29705) © Darlene Heidke

Charting the Attractions at Tomorrowland

Jennifer Dave Readers

☐ Astro Orbiter [F-4] A-OK! 1 3 3

Go for a short, fast spin in a two-seat rocket high above Tomorrowland. Often mistaken for a futuristic sculpture, the fanciful planets of Astro Orbiter go into motion with each launch. Think "Dumbo" with small, silvery space ships. Pull back on the stick to "soar" high. Get a dizzying view as your ship whirls. Must ride an elevator to board. Motion sickness warning. Outdoor, covered queue. Adults must accompany kids under 7. Transfer from wheelchair to ride. **Allie's KidTip:** "You can get a great view of the park." **TweenTip:** "Faster than Dumbo and Aladdin."

Michael , Victoria, Rick, and Miranda soar above Tomorrowland on the Astro Orbiter

Ride
C-Ticket
Ages 5 & up
Heights
Long waits
1 ½ min. flight

☐ Buzz Lightyear's Space Ranger Spin [F-4] FP A-OK! 8 8 8

All right, Space Rangers, it's time to help Toy Story's Buzz Lightyear defeat the evil Emperor Zurg! Buzz himself briefs new cadets before you're sent into battle in a Day-Glo, comic book world of planets and space creatures. Your two-seat space vehicle (an "XP-37 Space Cruiser") is equipped with a pair of "ion cannons" (laser pointers) mounted on the dashboard. Aim and shoot the electronic targets to accumulate points (aim for the higher targets for more points). Move the joystick to make your vehicle spin and home in on your targets. Compare your score at the end. Covered queue area is mostly indoors. Wheelchair accessible. **Alex's ToddlerTip:** ☺ **Allie's KidTip:** "Check your score. I made Space Cadet!"

Track Ride
D-Ticket
Ages 2 & up
Mild "space flight" effects
FASTPASS or med. waits
4 min. flight

☐ Walt Disney's Carousel of Progress [F-4] A-OK! 9 6 6

See the march of modern technology through the eyes of an American family. Each of the four scenes in this Audio-Animatronics show highlights another 20 years (or so) of progress in the 20th century. When the scene changes, the entire theater moves around to the next stage. One of Walt Disney's favorite attractions. (Jennifer loves it, too!) Limited hours. Outdoor, covered queue. Wheelchair accessible. Assistive listening devices. Closed captioning (pre-show only). **Allie's KidTip:** "Rover is cute."

Show
C-Ticket
Ages 6 & up
No scares
Short waits
22 min. show

The 1940s scene at Carousel of Progress

Progress is all around us!

Top Photo Slice: Astro Orbiter in Tomorrowland (①13392) © Janet Simonsen

Porter Genuine PassPorter Genuine PassPorter Genuine PassPorter Genuine PassPorter Genuine PassPorter Genuine PassPorter Gen

Planning

Getting There

Staying in Style

Touring

Feasting

Making Magic

Index

Notes & More

Charting the Attractions at Tomorrowland

Jennifer Dave Readers

Monsters, Inc. Laugh Floor [E-4]   A-OK!   6 7 7

Show
D-Ticket
All ages
Dark, playful monsters
12 minute show

This fun attraction picks up where the movie left off, inviting guests into a monster comedy club to collect their laughter and power Monstropolis. The fun show uses the same cool technology from "Turtle Talk with Crush" (see page 159), meaning the monsters onscreen like Mike Wazowski can interact with audience members. Expect some good natured ribbing, and some audience members even appear on screen. Indoor queue. Guests sit on hard plastic benches in the 458-seat theater. Wheelchair/ ECV accessible. Assistive listening. Handheld and video captioning for portions of show.

Monster vending machine ... how yummy!

①3864 © Michelle Clark

Space Mountain [G-3]   FP 🚹   6 8 9

Coaster
E-Ticket
Ages 8 & up
Dark, rough, jerky, fast
FASTPASS or long waits
2½ min. flight

Blast off into the blackness of space on the Magic Kingdom's most exciting roller coaster. You'll depart from 'Space Station Seventy-Five,' your gateway to the galaxies! This fast, indoor ride has sudden turns and short drops, but no big, stomach-in-your-throat drops. The darkness makes it scarier than it really is. The indoor queue and ride loading areas are rich with visual detail and interactive video games you can play while you wait (in the standby queue only). There are two slightly different coasters—go left for one, right for the other when you reach the loading area. Renovations in 2010 brought a smoother ride, more comfortable 'ships,' a darker 'flight' (with brighter 'stars'), better effects, new soundtrack, in-vehicle sound system, and a general sprucing up! Transfer from ECV to wheelchair, then transfer from wheelchair to ride. 44"/112 cm height restriction. Adult supervision. Health warning. Allie's Skid Tip: "I loved it! But it is bumpy. Try to sit in the middle. Ride it again if you can!"

Taking off into the star tunnel at Space Mountain

© MediaMarx, Inc.

Attraction descriptions and ratings are explained on page 127.

More at ① laugh-floor

Charting the Attractions at Tomorrowland

Stitch's Great Escape! [E-4]   6 5 6

Guests are recruited by the Grand Councilwoman, Captain Gantu, and Pleakley to guard "Experiment 626" (Stitch), and mischief ensues when that wily captive escapes into the theater. Even Skippy, from this attraction's previous incarnation, has a part. Animation, Audio-Animatronics, surround sound, lighting, and tactile effects combine to make an immersive experience. Alas, restrictive shoulder restraints, periods of total darkness, and a barrage of fire from "laser cannon" leave Stitch with too many scare factors and too little charm. Outdoor, covered queue. 40"/102 cm minimum height. Handheld captioning. Assistive listening. Wheelchair and ECV accessible. **Allie's TweenTip:** "I love it when the power goes out!"

Show	
D-Ticket	
Ages 7 & up	
May be scary for the young, yucky smells!	
Short to medium waits	
12 min. show	

Tomorrowland Arcade [G-3]   A-ok!   3 2 3

Play video games in this large, very loud arcade at the exit of Space Mountain. Spending money is required (change machines available). Wheelchair accessible. **Allie's KidTip:** "Play a Disney dancing game here!"

Arcade	
A-Ticket	
Ages 6 & up	

Tomorrowland Indy Speedway [F-3]   A-ok!   4 3 4

Every kid wants a chance to drive, and when they're tall enough they can at this popular attraction. Experienced drivers won't be as thrilled. Guide rails, shock-absorbing bumpers, and a low top speed (7 mph maximum) make these gas powered "race cars" safe. Family members can cheer from an enclosed grandstand (the entrance is to the right). Shortest waits are early in the morning. Covered outdoor queue. Transfer from wheelchair to ride. 52"/132 cm height restriction to drive solo. Health warning. Adult supervision required. **Allie's KidTip:** "Even if you're tall enough, make sure your feet can touch the pedals before you drive."

Ride	
C-Ticket	
Ages 4 & up	
Cars may bump yours from behind	
Long waits	
4 min. drive	

Tomorrowland Transit Authority Peoplemover [F-4]   A-ok!   6 6 6

Take a grand tour of Tomorrowland on an elevated, automated people mover. The four-seat vehicles move sedately along a route that takes you through Space Mountain and past nearly every other attraction in Tomorrowland. Along the way you can look down upon Tomorrowland's crowds and view a scale model of Progress City (formerly of Disneyland's Carousel of Progress). It makes a great introduction to Tomorrowland. Outdoor, mostly covered queue. Must be ambulatory to ride. Name changed to add Peoplemover in summer 2010. **Allie's KidTip:** "Look for the stars when you go through Space Mountain."

Track Ride	
B-Ticket	
All ages	
Dark	
Short waits	
12 min. grand tour	

Tip: Ever hear a talking trash can? Look for one called "PUSH" outside Mickey's Star Traders shop and throughout Tomorrowland.

Tomorrowland is a bright sight at night

Epcot

Triple the size of the Magic Kingdom, Epcot opened its doors (and many minds) in 1982. Epcot is the ultimate world's fair, showcasing a future where technology improves our lives, the countries of the world live in peace, and dreams really can come true.

Striving to educate and inspire as well as entertain, Epcot introduces millions to new **technological and international frontiers**. Epcot began as Walt Disney's dream of an "Experimental Prototype Community of Tomorrow;" it's a far cry from the ordinary communities where most of us live. The first of two "worlds," Future World greets you with its awe-inspiring, 180-foot-tall, geodesic sphere (Spaceship Earth). Streamlined structures and broad vistas transport you into the future of today's hopes and dreams. Beyond Future World is World Showcase, offering an inspiring glimpse into faraway lands, different customs, and exotic peoples.

ⓘ22887 © Heather Mahon

Gearing up for battle in Norway

ⓘ14939 © Scott Theus

Fish may not be food, but it looks like tourists are on the menu

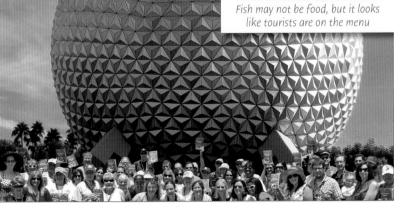

ⓘ16921 © MediaMarx, Inc.

PassPorter fans in front of Spaceship Earth during PassPorter's 10th anniversary

Top Photo Slice: Spaceship Earth at sunset (ⓘ2624) © Beth Borja

Planning

Getting There

Staying in Style

Touring

Feasting

Making Magic

Index

Notes & More

Orienting Yourself at Epcot

Fold out the next page for a touring plan and a handy attraction cha→

The **two worlds of Epcot** offer a variety of attractions, all housed in "pavilions"—nine in Future World and eleven in the World Showcase (see the fold-out map on the next page). Below are the headline attractions in the west and east sides of Future World and World Showcase. See the other side of the map for our favorite itinerary and an at-a-glance list of attractions, and pages 157–166 for attraction details.

Future World East
Science and technology take center stage with an up-close look at space travel, vehicle testing, communications, and energy.
Headline Attractions: Mission: SPACE, Test Track, Spaceship Earth, Universe of Energy

Mission: SPACE ☞

Future World West
Explore the nature of the world on land and in the sea, and the nature of imagination and perception in the recesses of our minds.
Headline Attractions: Soarin', The Seas with Nemo & Friends

The Seas with Nemo and Friends ☞

World Showcase East
Cruise a river in Mexico, experience a maelstrom in Norway, see the wonders of China, celebrate in Germany and Italy, and explore the American adventure.
Headline Attractions: Maelstrom, Gran Fiesta Tour, Reflections of China

Mexico pavilion ☞

World Showcase West
Hear drummers in Japan, view treasures in Morocco, see the sights in France, tour gardens in the United Kingdom, and explore the wonders of Canada.
Headline Attractions: Impressions de France, O Canada!

Japan pavilion ☞

Planning | Getting There | Staying in Style | Touring | Feasting | Making Magic | Index | Notes & More

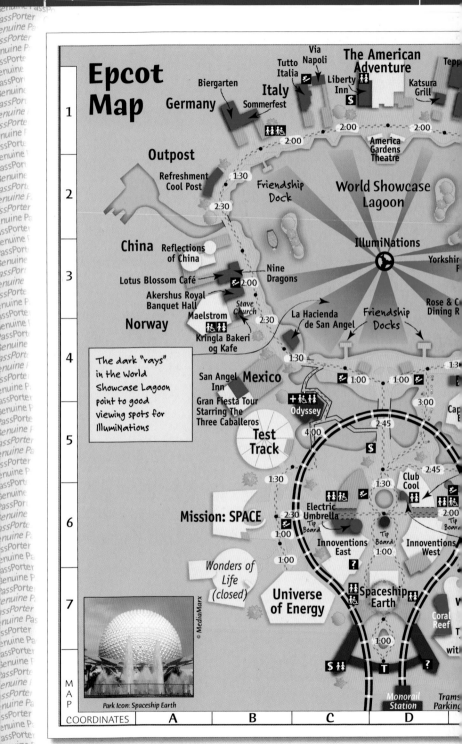

Epcot Map

Germany
Biergarten
Sommerfest

Italy
Tutto Italia
Via Napoli

The American Adventure
Liberty Inn
Teppa...
Katsura Grill

Outpost
Refreshment Cool Post

Friendship Dock

America Gardens Theatre

World Showcase Lagoon

IllumiNations

China
Reflections of China
Lotus Blossom Café
Nine Dragons
Akershus Royal Banquet Hall
Maelstrom
Stave Church
Kringla Bakeri og Kafe

Norway

Yorkshi...

La Hacienda de San Angel

Friendship Docks

Rose & C... Dining R...

The dark "rays" in the World Showcase Lagoon point to good viewing spots for IllumiNations

San Angel Inn
Mexico
Gran Fiesta Tour Starring The Three Caballeros
Odyssey

Test Track

Cap...

Mission: SPACE

Club Cool

Electric Umbrella
Tip Board
Innoventions East
Tip Board
Innoventions West

Wonders of Life (closed)

Universe of Energy

Spaceship Earth

Coral Reef
T...
with...

© MediaMarx

Park Icon: Spaceship Earth

Monorail Station

Trans... Parking

MAP COORDINATES

| A | B | C | D |

n Edo

Japan

Tokyo Dining

2:00

Morocco
Restaurant Marrakesh

Tangierine Cafe

Monsieur Paul

2:30

Chefs de France

Glacier

France

Boulangerie Patisserie

Impressions de France

World Showcase

To BoardWalk, Swan, Dolphin, and Disney's Hollywood Studios

Friendship Dock

Resort Boats

2:00

7:00

T

County sh Shop

1:00

International Gateway

To Yacht and Beach Club and Villas

wn om

2:00

United Kingdom

World ShowPlace Convention Center

Canada

Le Cellier

O Canada!

ain

Imagination!

Journey Into Imagination with Figment

1:00

Soarin'

Future World

Epcot Character Spot

1:00

The Land

Sunshine Seasons

The Garden Grill

Fountain View Ice Cream

:30

The Circle of Life

Living with the Land

The Seas ith Nemo & Friends

rtle alk Crush

To Buses

o Lot

Map Legend

= Bus Stops

? = Guest Relations

T = Ticket Gate

S = ATM (cash)

= Smoking Area

= Restroom

= Companion Restroom

+ = First Aid and Baby Center

= Attraction

= Shop/service

= Eatery

= River/canal

•----- X:XX -----•

Average time it takes in minutes to walk from point to point

Note: You should double or even triple these times in crowds and at park closing time

Bird's-Eye View

World Showcase East

World Showcase West

Future World East

Future World West

Map © MediaMarx, Inc.

E | F | G

Catching the Shows at Epcot

Epcot presents a rich medley of sounds and sights for the strolling visitor. Guests may encounter acrobats, dancers, actors, and musicians—more than **two dozen groups** in all. Most shows last about 10-20 minutes. Favorites include the Voices of Liberty and fife and drum corps at The American Adventure, Celtic rock and bagpipes in Canada, British rockers in the United Kingdom, brass bands in Germany, and a fun mariachi band in Mexico. You'll flip for China's acrobats, and Japanese and African drummers set your pulse pounding. The spectacular **Fountain of Nations** dances in time to the music (see page 167).

Fountain of Nations

Beyond casual entertainment, check your Times Guide for the open-air **America Gardens Theatre**, which offers half-hour performances, plus the Flower Power concerts in the spring, Eat to the Beat concerts in autumn, and Candlelight Processional in December (see page 289).

Crowds throng the World Showcase every evening at park closing for the popular **IllumiNations** fireworks and light show (see page 168 for all the details).

A reader joins in a skit as King Arthur in the United Kingdom

Planning · Getting There · Staying in Style · Touring · Feasting · Making Magic · Index · Notes & More

Planning · Getting There · Staying in Style · Touring · Feasting · Making Magic · Index · Notes & More

Making the Most of Epcot

TIPS

If you arrive at Epcot via the **monorail**, you get a wonderful aerial view of Future World and a glimpse of World Showcase.

Little ones adore the **Kidcot Fun Stops** at each World Showcase pavilion around the lagoon. Cast members offer kids various craft projects to color and decorate. Activities vary, sometimes giving kids something different to add to their creation at each country. Alexander loves it!

Kids also love the **play fountains** on the promenade between Future World and the World Showcase, and behind Innoventions East. Come prepared with suits under clothing and/or dry clothes and shoes.

Showing off a mask made at the Kidcot Fun Stops

Looking for **characters** at Epcot? Check out the Epcot Character Spot in Future World West, near Innoventions West.

Touring on a Segway

Consider an Epcot **guided tour**, such as the Keep Moving Forward Segway tour or Undiscovered Future World. See pages 272-273.

On your way out of the park in the evening, glance down at the path as you pass Innoventions—you'll discover **fiber-optic lights** embedded in the pavement that make beautiful patterns.

Epcot is the dining capital of the "World." Nearly all the good stuff encircles the lagoon in an **international dining extravaganza**, offering everything from the upscale Bistro de Paris to tacos at Cantina de San Angel. Future World offers less table-service dining, but it has some counter-service opportunities. See pages 234-241.

Epcot's main gate is at the **north end** of the park (the opposite of all the other parks), so east is to the right and west is to the left.

Getting the Best at Epcot

The World Showcase makes Epcot the center for unusual shopping, too. A wide array of **international gifts and crafts** grace every pavilion, from British woolens and Japanese silks to German cut crystal and Moroccan leather. Here are our favorite shops:

① 15300 © Lindsay Jones

Sombrero Love

Shop	Location	What makes it special
Art of Disney	Near Innoventions	Collectibles and animation cels
Disney Traders	World Showcase	Disney-themed merchandise
Mouse Gear	Future World	Huge store with clothes and gifts
ImageWorks	Imagination!	Unique photos and photo gifts
Plaza de Los Amigos	Mexico	Sombreros and tequila!
Yong Feng Shangdian	China	Huge store with a wide variety
Mitsukoshi Dept. Store	Japan	Authentic Japanese gifts, snacks
Tangier Traders	Morocco	Open-air, exotic shopping
La Maison du Vin	France	Two words: wine tastings!
The Crown and Crest	United Kingdom	Family name histories

SHOPPING

"**Friendships**" (boats) convey you to different points within World Showcase. You can usually get there faster if you walk, however.

Good viewing locations for **IllumiNations** go quickly. See page 168 for hints on getting the best possible view of the action.

After IllumiNations ends, step aside and wait for the crowds to thin. Take a **leisurely stroll** around the lagoon. Enjoy the music and the lights—you'll have a nice, quiet walk with very few people around. About 30 minutes after the show, you might even get to witness a huge fireball as cast members burn off excess fuel from the fire barges. As a bonus, you'll miss the traffic in the parking lot and bus queues.

NOTES

Ratings are explained on page 126.

Our Value Ratings:		Our Magic Ratings:		Readers' Ratings:
Quality:	8/10	Theme:	8/10	58% fell in love with it
Variety:	8/10	Excitement:	8/10	34% liked it well enough
Scope:	10/10	Fun Factor:	6/10	7% had mixed feelings
Overall Value:	**9/10**	**Overall Magic:**	**7/10**	1% were disappointed

Epcot is enjoyed by...		(rated by both authors and readers)
Younger Kids: ♥♥♥	Young Adults: ♥♥♥♥	Families: ♥♥♥♥
Older Kids: ♥♥♥	Mid Adults: ♥♥♥♥♥	Couples: ♥♥♥♥♥
Teenagers: ♥♥♥	Mature Adults: ♥♥♥♥♥	Singles: ♥♥♥♥♥

RATINGS

Sidebar tabs: Planning | Getting There | Staying in Style | Touring | Feasting | Making Magic | Index | Notes & More

Top Photo Slice: Hand-crafted wall tile in Morocco (①10669) © Melissa Potter

Finding Your Way to Epcot

Planning · Getting There · Staying in Style · Touring · Feasting · Making Magic · Index · Notes & More

BEST TIMES TO GO

The **best time to visit World Showcase** is when it first opens at 11:00 am, as most guests are still in Future World. It follows then that the **best time to tour Future World** is in the late afternoon and during dinner time (note attractions in Future World now stay open until 9:00 pm). World Showcase becomes congested in the evenings due to the many restaurants and IllumiNations show. Because of the focus on dining at Epcot, traditional lunch and dinner times are better spent at the attractions while others are eating. Along the same vein, you will find restaurants less busy and noisy if you dine before or after the normal lunch and dinner hour. **IllumiNations** is held nightly at park closing (usually 9:00 pm)—for a good view, start looking about one hour prior (see page 168). If you've already seen IllumiNations, consider **dining during it** for a quieter experience.

GETTING THERE

By Monorail—From the Magic Kingdom, Contemporary, Polynesian, or Grand Floridian, take the monorail to the Transportation and Ticket Center (TTC) and transfer to the Epcot monorail.

By Boat—From Disney's Hollywood Studios, Swan/Dolphin, BoardWalk, and Yacht & Beach Club, boats go to Epcot's International Gateway.

By Bus—From other resorts, Disney's Hollywood Studios, or Disney's Animal Kingdom, buses take you directly to Epcot. From Downtown Disney, take a bus to a nearby resort and transfer to an Epcot bus, boat, or walk. (Tip: Bus to BoardWalk and walk/boat to Epcot.)

By Car—Take I-4 to exit 67 (westbound) or exit 62 (eastbound) and continue on to the Epcot toll plaza. All-day parking is available for $14 (free to resort guests and annual passholders).

By Foot—From the BoardWalk Inn & Villas, Yacht & Beach Club and Villas, Swan & Dolphin, and Disney's Hollywood Studios, Epcot is within walking distance. Follow the paths toward International Gateway—it emerges between United Kingdom and France. Walk through United Kingdom and Canada to reach Future World.

A monorail glides over the water during the International Flower and Garden Festival

Charting the Attractions at Future World (East)

Jennifer Dave Readers

☐ Spaceship Earth [D-7] A-OK! 9 7 8

Go inside the huge geodesic sphere that towers above Epcot for a look at the development of communication technologies from cave paintings through the space age. Four-seat "time machine" vehicles take you up into the huge sphere past dozens of Audio-Animatronics reenacting milestones in communication. A renovation in 2007 added new ride scenes, changes to existing scenes, an interactive touchscreen in the "time machine" vehicle, and narration by actress Dame Judi Dench. At the end of the ride, you'll exit into a post-show exhibit, Project Tomorrow, sponsored by Siemens, where you can do things

Track Ride
E-Ticket
Ages 3 & up
Dark, steep incline, but gentle
Short waits
15 min. ride

such as "build a body" in 3-D, experience a driving simulation game, and check out an illuminated globe with a collage of futuristic images. Adults should accompany and sit beside children. We suggest you visit at park opening or in the evening for shorter waits. Outdoor queue is mostly covered. Guests must transfer from wheelchair. **Alex's Toddler Tip:** ☺ **Allie's Kid Tip:** "You'll love all the lights. And it's good for learning." **Allie's TeenTip:** "Really boring."

①4788 © Keith Stanton

An Audio-Animatronics Steve works on a computer prototype on Spaceship Earth

☐ Innoventions East [C-6] A-OK! 7 5 6

If gee-whiz technology pushes your buttons, pay a visit to Innoventions—Epcot's two-part, high-tech, hands-on trade exhibit. Innoventions East exhibits include The Sum of All Thrills (custom design your own 4-min. thrill ride, then ride it in a simulator), Internet activities (send electronic and video e-mail back home), Test the Limits Lab (test products like a real UL engineer), the "Don't Waste It!" exhibit (learn to recycle, reuse, and reduce trash with a mini dump truck), the StormStruck exhibit (experience a hurricane simulation), and the Agent P. signup area (see page 163 for information about Agent P.). Short queues in some exhibits. Wheelchair accessible. **Allie's TeenTip:** "Video e-mail is fun."

Playground
B-Ticket
All ages
Noisy
Short waits
Allow about 1 hour to explore

☐ Universe of Energy (Ellen's Energy Adventure) [B-7] A-OK! 5 6 7

Join Ellen DeGeneres for a humorous crash course in energy, the stuff that powers our world. Widescreen films, thunderous sound effects, and gigantic Audio-Animatronics dinosaurs help tell the tale. Ellen's cast includes Bill Nye the Science Guy, Jamie Lee Curtis, and Alex Trebek. Shows start every 17 minutes. Indoor queue with uncovered, outdoor, overflow queue. The queue moves quickly once the show begins. Effects may be too intense for small kids and some adults. ECV must transfer to wheelchair. Wheelchair accessible. Assistive listening. No flash photo or video lights. **Alex's Toddler Tip:** "Dinosaurs roar! ☺" **Allie's Kid Tip:** "Dinosaurs!!! Oh, and it has a movie about energy, too. May be loud." **Allie's TeenTip:** "It's still cool to me, and a fun way to learn."

Film/Ride
E-Ticket
Ages 4 & up
Dark, loud, dinosaurs
Med. waits
8 min. intro
37 min. ride

© MediaMarx, Inc.

Dinosaur topiaries

Attraction descriptions and ratings are explained on page 127.

Planning | Getting There | Staying in Style | Touring | Feasting | Making Magic | Index | Notes & More

Charting the Attractions at Future World (East)

Jennifer Dave Readers

Mission: SPACE [B-6] 🅵🅿 🕴 | 9 9 8

Prepare for space flight at the International Space Training Center. As a civilian "astronaut," you board a four-person training centrifuge to experience the sensations of liftoff and zero gravity. Guests can choose between the original, high-intensity version (Orange Team) or a low-intensity experience (Green Team). In the high-intensity version, sensations are intense—the simulator spins rapidly and you may get queasy. If you go for the full-octane experience, heed the warnings and don't close your eyes or look to the side during the ride. If you'd rather not take the chance of getting sick, try the milder version—it's the same ride but without the spinning. Save time to enjoy the post-show exhibits. Young kids enjoy the Space Base playground. Indoor, themed queue. 44"/112 cm height restriction. Young kids must be with an adult.

Thrill Ride
E-Ticket
Ages 8 & up
Disorienting
FASTPASS or long waits
7 1/2 min. pre-show
5 min. ride

Strapped in for take off!

The entrance to Mission: SPACE in the early evening

Test Track [B-5] 🅵🅿 🕴 A-ok! | 8 8 9

Do you feel the need for speed? How does 65 miles per hour in a rapidly accelerating six-seat, open-air test vehicle on a tightly banked track sound? Learn how GM tests (and tortures) new vehicles and experience some of those tests. This popular attraction was recently renovated and now has a new, interactive queue experience where you design a virtual car. You then board a "sim car" to try out your ideas on the track. The ride track remains the same as before, but now you test out your new car design in four scenes: capability (rough road and weather conditions), efficiency (your carbon footprint), responsiveness (maneuvering), and power (speed!). The attraction has even got a fresh new look with bright colors, reminding us of the movie "Tron." Get a FASTPASS early in the day, or use the "single-rider queue" on the left for the shortest wait. Front seat offers more leg room. Indoor/outdoor queue. 40"/102 cm height restriction. Young children must be accompanied by adult. Health warning. Must transfer from wheelchair to ride. Assistive listening. Closed captioning. Alex'sKidTip: "The test car only seems faster than your own car on the highway because the test car is open." Allie'sKidTip: "Sit in the middle of the car so you don't get sprayed!" TeenTip: "I love the end of the ride when you go SUPER fast!"

Thrill Ride
E-Ticket
Ages 7 & up
Fast, jerky
FASTPASS or very long waits or singles line
3 min. intro
5 min. ride

More at ⓘ mission-space

Charting the Attractions at Future World (West)

Jennifer Dave Readers

Club Cool [D-6]

| | | | 7 | 6 | 8 |

Sample free Coke beverages from other countries at this "clubby" diversion. This is a fun place to cool off and enjoy a soft drink, including an unusual aperitif called Beverly. You can purchase Coke merchandise here, including t-shirts, vintage-shaped bottles, and other "pop" art. Wheelchair accessible. **Allie's TeenTip:** "The drink from Japan is the best!"

| **Walk-thru** |
| A-Ticket |
| Ages 2 & up |
| Noisy, sticky floor |

Innoventions West [D-6]

| | | | 5 | 5 | 6 |

This is the other half of Innoventions (see page 157). Exhibits include Segway Central (guests ages 16 and older and less than 250 lbs. can test-drive the two-wheeled device), Smarter Planet (discover the power of computers),

the Great Piggy Bank Adventure (hands-on activities teach about saving), Where's the Fire? (a fire safety exhibit with an interactive game house), SlapStick Studios (fun with Velcro), and exhibits on computing and high-speed Internet technologies. Look for the e-mail postcards! Some short queues. Wheelchair accessible. **Alex's KidTip:** "Piggy banks are fun! ☺" **Allie's TeenTip:** "Video games are cool."

Great Piggy Bank Adventure

© MediaMarx, Inc.

| **Playground** |
| B-Ticket |
| Ages 6 & up |
| Noisy |
| Short waits |
| Allow about one hour |

The Seas with Nemo & Friends [E-7]   A-OK!

| | | | 6 | 7 | 6 |

Board "Clamobiles" and explore the world's largest saltwater aquarium tank and artificial coral reef. New technology allows your favorite characters from "Finding Nemo" to swim among the real marine life in the aquarium. View dolphins, sharks, manatees, and thousands of sea creatures. Check with a cast member for a demo schedule. For programs that explore the aquarium in more depth, see page 275. After the tame ride, don't miss Turtle Talk with Crush (see below). Indoor queue. Wheelchair accessible. Assistive listening. Reflective captioning. Closed captioning. **Alex's ToddlerTip:** "I found Nemo! ☺" **Allie's KidTip:** "I love the dolphins."

Takin' on the jellies!

(①11283 © Diana Barthelemy-Rodriguez

| **Pavilion/ Ride** |
| D-Ticket |
| All ages |
| Sharks! |
| Med. waits |
| Allow about one hour |

Turtle Talk with Crush [E-7]   A-OK!

| | | | 9 | 9 | 9 |

State-of-the-art technology allows guests to interact with Crush (the sea turtle from "Finding Nemo")—he can see and hear you, and talk back! This animated, interactive experience engages kids and impresses adults. Encourage young kids (ages 3-8) to sit up front for the best experience. Inside The Seas pavilion. Wheelchair accessible. **Alex's ToddlerTip:** ☹ (bored) **Allie's TeenTip:** "Totally awesome, dude! It's so cute to hear the little kids' questions and answers."

| **Show** |
| D-Ticket |
| Ages 3 & up |
| Long waits |
| 12 min. film |

More at ① the-seas

Attraction descriptions and ratings are explained on page 127.

Side tabs: Planning | Getting There | Staying in Style | Touring | Feasting | Making Magic | Index | Notes & More

Planning
Getting There
Staying in Style
Touring
Feasting
Making Magic
Index
Notes & More

Charting the Attractions at Future World (West)

Jennifer Dave Readers

The Land [E-6]	A-oK!	7	6	7

Agriculture and the environment take center stage, hosted by Nestlé. Rides, film, food court, and restaurant. "Behind the Seeds" guided greenhouse tour.

Pavilion
D-Ticket

The Circle of Life [F-6]	A-oK!	6	5	6

Timon and Pumbaa from The Lion King set out to build the Hakuna Matata Village Resort—without regard to their ecosystem. Simba reminds them (and us) how important it is to protect the environment. Great photography. Indoor queue with benches. Inside The Land pavilion. Wheelchair accessible. Assistive listening. Reflective captioning. **Alex's ToddlerTip:** "Simba! ☺" **Allie's KidTip:** "Simba tells us about the earth and how to take care of it." **TeenTip:** "Great for everyone!"

Film
C-Ticket
Ages 3 & up
Short waits
12 min. film

Soarin' [F-6]	FP 🧍	10	9	9

Soar over California's awesome scenery in a stunning copy of the headline ride at Disney California Adventure park. Guests are strapped into oversized porch swings and rise from the floor for a simulated hang glider tour of the Golden State. An eye-filling, IMAX-quality movie screen, gentle motion, stirring music, and scented breezes combine for an exhilarating journey that ends with fireworks over Disneyland. Queue is indoors and offers fun games to play while waiting. Inside The Land pavilion. 40"/102 cm height restriction. Transfer from wheelchair to ride. Closed captioning. **Alex's KidTip:** "It's like gliding! ☺" **Allie's TeenTip:** "Wow!"

Simulator
E-Ticket
Ages 7 & up
Heights
FASTPASS or very long waits
5 min. ride

Soarin' over Big Sur

© MediaMarx, Inc.

Readers did Soarin' eight times over eight days!

©13362 © Wendy Suchomel

Living With the Land [F-6]	FP	A-oK!	7	6	7

Learn how modern agriculture serves the needs of a hungry world and protects the environment. Your boat cruises through a multimedia exhibit and Disney's amazing experimental hydroponic greenhouses. See veggies that may be served for dinner upstairs (more than 30 tons are produced annually). Flash photos are only allowed in the greenhouses. Indoor queues. Inside The Land pavilion. Must transfer from ECV to wheelchair. Wheelchair accessible. **Alex's ToddlerTip:** ☺ **Allie's KidTip:** "They have American Alligators!" **TeenTip:** "Boring but educational."

Boat Ride
D-Ticket
Ages 4 & up
Dark
FASTPASS or med. waits
13 min. ride

Charting the Attractions at Future World (West)

Jennifer Dave Readers

Captain EO [E-5] `7` `6` `7`

In June 2010, Honey I Shrunk the Audience closed to make way for the return of Captain Eo, the "4D" film starring Michael Jackson and produced by filmmakers Francis Ford Coppola and George Lucas. The film graced Epcot from 1986–1994, the era of Michael Jackson's "Thriller," and Captain Eo is more of the same. Michael captains a spaceship with a cute, cuddly, and klutzy crew of aliens with a mission to deliver a gift to the Supreme Leader, a truly scary-looking female alien portrayed by Anjelica Huston. Music, of course, conquers all, and the Universe lives happily ever after. The "4D" in-theater effects are mostly limited to seats that shake to the music, and everything may seem a bit quaint and dated, but the pre-show "Making of..." film alone makes it worthwhile. Eo is in for an "indefinite" run, and there's no hint that Honey, I Shrunk the Audience will return (we think a new show is in development). Wheelchair accessible. Assistive listening.

3-D Film
E-Ticket
Ages 5 & up
Loud, intense
Medium waits
5 min. intro 17 min. film

Journey Into Imagination with Figment [E-5]   A-OK! `5` `5` `3`

Figment, the cute purple dragon, comes roaring back to Epcot in a reenergized version of Journey Into Your Imagination. Figment and Dr. Nigel Channing (Eric Idle) team up to stimulate our imaginations with sight, sound, smell, a bit of whimsy, and music from Disney legends Richard and Robert Sherman. Highlights include Figment's House and the final rendition of the theme song, One Little Spark. The ride still doesn't rate an "A," but you'll be charmed and tickled. Riders exit into the ImageWorks interactive playground. Indoor queue with outdoor overflow queue. Effects too intense for some children. Wheelchair accessible. **Alex's ToddlerTip:** "Ride again, please! ☺"

Track Ride
C-Ticket
Ages 5 & up
Portions are very dark, loud, with bright flashes
Med. waits
6 min. ride

ImageWorks: Kodak "What If" Labs [E-5]   A-OK! `6` `6` `7`

Hands-on sound and image exhibits and a gift shop, at the exit to Journey Into Imagination with Figment. Digital portraits (which can be sent via e-mail), inventive photo gifts, and a unique Kodak photo lab. "Backdoor" entrance through shop. **Allie's KidTip:** "It's cool! Check out the floor piano!"

Playground
B-Ticket
All ages
Allow 30 min.

The Imagination pavilion in the evening

☺5398 © Amy Sellars

Planning · Getting There · Staying in Style · Touring · Feasting · Making Magic · Index · Notes & More

Charting the Attractions at World Showcase
(clockwise order)

Jennifer Dave Readers

Mexico [B-4]   A-OK!   7 6 8

Enter Mexico's Mayan pyramid to find yourself in a magical, twilit village plaza with a volcano smoking ominously in the distance. Enjoy a fine exhibit of art and artifacts, eateries, a ride (see below), shops, and musicians. **Allie's KidTip:** "Don't worry, that's not a real volcano. Looks like it, though!"

Pavilion
D-Ticket
All ages
Low light

Gran Fiesta Tour Starring The Three Cabelleros [B-4]   A-OK!   6 6 5

Tour Mexico in this revamped boat ride (formerly El Rio del Tiempo) featuring Audio-Animatronics, music, and short film/animation clips with the Three Cabelleros (Donald Duck, Jose Carioca, and Panchito Pistoles). Jose and Panchito fly through Mexico in search of Donald for the big show. Don't miss

the cool fiber-optic fireworks display. Your boat floats past diners at the San Angel Inn restaurant. Indoor queue inside the Mexico pavilion. Transfer from ECV to wheelchair to ride. Wheelchair accessible. **Alex's KidTip:** "This is one of my favorite rides! ☺" **Allie's KidTip:** "Be sure to look up and see the fireworks on the ceiling!"

Skeleton fiesta seen on the Gran Fiesta Tour ⓒ8451 © Cheryl Pendry

Boat Ride
C-Ticket
All ages
Dark, but very tame
Short waits
7 minute cruise

Norway [B-3]   A-OK!   6 6 7

Castle in Norway ⓒ11398 © Katey Westcott

This taste of Norway features shops, the Maelstrom ride (see below), eateries, and an wooden Stave church. Peek inside the church for a history of the Vikings. **Allie's KidTip:** "If you see a troll, rub its nose for luck."

Pavilion
C-Ticket
All ages
Allow 30 min.

Spelmanns Gledje perform in Norway ⓒ1348 © Brad K.

Maelstrom [B-3]   FP   A-OK!   6 5 7

Board a boat for a refreshing ride through the Norway of fact and fancy. Trolls, Vikings, and a North Sea storm are all part of a fanciful ride that is much tamer than the name implies. The few "drops" are little more than a bounce. The Viking boats deposit you in an attractive indoor fishing village, prior to viewing a filmed travelogue. A new film is in production, set to debut sometime in the future—walk right through the theater if you decide to skip the film. Indoor queue. Must transfer from wheelchair to ride. Assistive listening. Reflective captioning (movie). **Allie's KidTip:** "Don't be scared of the life-size polar bears."

Boat Ride
D-Ticket
Ages 5 & up
Small drops and dark
FASTPASS or med. waits
15 min. ride

Planning | Getting There | Staying in Style | Touring | Feasting | Making Magic | Index | Notes & More

Charting the Attractions at World Showcase
(clockwise order)

Jennifer Dave Readers

☐ **China** [B-3]	A-ok!	4 5 6
Explore China through a film (see below), museum exhibits, gardens, eateries, and the Yong Feng Shangdian department store. Visit a half-scale model of Beijing's Temple of Heaven. Acrobats and gymnasts perform. **Allie's Kid Tip:** "When you walk into the temple to see the movie, look up."		**Pavilion**
		C-Ticket
		All ages
		Allow 20 min.

☐ **Reflections of China** [A-3]		7 6 7
Experience marvels of China in a sweeping, Circle-Vision 360° motion picture. Grand scenes of the Great Wall, the Yangtze Gorge, and Beijing's Forbidden City		**Film**
		C-Ticket
		Ages 6 & up
		Could cause dizziness
		Short waits
		13 min. show

alternate with views of bustling cities. The film—previously called "Wonders of China"—was improved in 2003 with vibrant new footage of modern China including Macau and Hong Kong. You must stand to view. Indoor waiting area with wooden benches. Wheelchair accessible. Assistive listening devices. Reflective captioning. **Allie's Kid Tip:** "Don't sit down or you'll miss part of the movie."

5131 © Amy Sellars

Temple of Heaven ceiling in China

☐ **Germany** [B-1]		3 4 7
Steep-roofed stone buildings, oompah bands, eateries, and shops evoke a quaint German square. Look for the model railroad, and listen for the glockenspiel that chimes on the hour. **Allie's Kid Tip:** "Find the train set in the toy shop."		**Pavilion**
		C-Ticket
		All ages

🔅 Agent P's World Showcase Adventure

Go on an interactive scavenger hunt with a little help from Agent P (from "Disney's Phineas and Ferb" show) and his "F.O.N.E." This high-tech and entirely free activity leads you through many of the countries of the World Showcase—when you find the answer to a clue, your F.O.N.E. will often trigger a special event, such as the ringing of the Glockenspiel in Germany. You should try this out, even if you're not a Phineas and Ferb fan! To sign up, visit one of the three kiosks early in the day (located in Innoventions East, Innoventions West, and the plaza between Future World and World Showcase) and you'll receive a mission time and starting location. Agent P's adventure replaced Kim Possible's mission in summer 2012.

© MediaMarx, Inc.

Agent P's F.O.N.E. can trigger the Glockenspiel in Germany

Planning | Getting There | Staying in Style | Touring | Feasting | Making Magic | Index | Notes & More

Planning | Getting There | Staying in Style | Touring | Feasting | Making Magic | Index | Notes & More

Charting the Attractions at World Showcase
(clockwise order)

Jennifer Dave Readers

☐ Italy [C-1]

Disney faithfully captures the spirit and architecture of Venice in this Italian piazza. Eateries, shops, jugglers, music, and entertainers in a Mediterranean garden set the scene at this pavilion. Look closely at the angel atop the 83-foot-tall bell tower—it is covered in real gold leaf. The tower itself is a replica of the Campanile in St. Mark's Square, Venice. While there are no rides or movies at this pavilion, it's still worth a visit. Allie's Kid Tip: "Make a good wish at King Neptune's fountain."

Maggie & Julianne

5	4	6

Pavilion
C-Ticket
All ages
Allow 15–20 minutes

☐ The American Adventure [D-1]

This all-American pavilion is halfway around the lagoon from Future World. Home to the American Adventure show, theater, art gallery, a hamburger joint, wonderful singers, and a shop. Allie's Kid Tip: "See the fife and drum corps."

6	5	7

Pavilion
D-Ticket
All ages

☐ The American Adventure Show [D-1]

Ben Franklin and Mark Twain take you on a patriotic tour of U.S. history. A large cast of Audio-Animatronics characters, including Thomas Jefferson and Susan B. Anthony. Martin Luther King Jr. takes center stage in updated filmed segments. Famous events are recreated and famous Americans share their ideas. Don't expect a critical view of history, however. The wide stage is easier to see if you don't sit in the front. See Epcot Times Guide for shows. Indoor queue. "Voices of Liberty" may sing. Wheelchair accessible. Assistive listening. Reflective captioning. Allie's Kid Tip: "Look on the walls for the statues."

7	7	7

Show
D-Ticket
Ages 5 & up
Dark at times
Med. waits
15 min. intro with singers
30 min. show

☐ America Gardens Theatre (seasonal) [D-1]

Live, musical entertainment is the hallmark of this outdoor theater on the edge of the lagoon. Check the Times Guide for show times—usually three half-hour shows daily. Seating is free, but the front rows may be reserved for "package" guests. Shows are visible from the promenade. Seating is on benches with sycamore trees providing some shade. Wheelchair accessible. Allie's Kid Tip: "Sit in the front because it's covered and the back is just trees."

6	7	6

Show
C-Ticket
Ages 2 & up
Short waits
Most shows 30 min.

Rainbow over The American Adventure on July 4th (really!)

Top Photo Slice: A golden eagle in front of the American Adventure pavilion (①2286) © Janet Simonsen

Charting the Attractions at World Showcase

(clockwise order)

Jennifer   Dave   Readers

Japan [D-1]   A-OK!   8 7 7

The sound of Taiko drummers may draw you to this pavilion, featuring traditional Japanese architecture and gardens, entertaining exhibits, updated eateries, and the Mitsukoshi department store. A beautiful and peaceful retreat. **Allie's Kid Tip:** "Go through the Japanese garden. The goldfish are neat."

| Pavilion |
| C-Ticket |
| All ages |
| Allow 20 min. |

Morocco [E-1]   A-OK!   7 6 7

Morocco's Moorish architecture, art exhibits, exotic cuisine, live entertainers, and crafts beckon to the adventuresome traveler. Much is hidden from the casual visitor—take the time to explore the museum and other areas. You'll find a character meet-and-greet area virtually hidden across from Restaurant Marrakesh, plus artisans and cultural representatives scattered throughout. Excellent shopping opportunities. **Allie's Kid Tip:** "You'll feel like you want to go to Africa. I like the entertainers here, too."

| Pavilion |
| C-Ticket |
| All ages |
| No scares |
| Allow about 20-30 min. to explore |

①8522 @ Cheryl Pendry

Twilight in Morocco

②2168 @ Janet Simonsen

Garden maze in front of the France pavilion

France [F-2]   A-OK!   7 7 7

The Eiffel Tower, cobblestone streets, renovated eateries, shops (including a Guerlain boutique), street performers, and a film (see below) evoke the essence of France. **Allie's TeenTip:** "I want to go to Paris, and this is almost as good."

| Pavilion |
| D-Ticket |
| All ages |

Impressions de France [F-2]   A-OK!   9 9 7

The beauty and romance of France's villages, cities, and countryside come to life in a breathtaking film. Fabulous scenery, wonderful 200° widescreen photography, and the best musical soundtrack at Walt Disney World (great French classical tunes) make this one of our favorites. Cool, dark theater offers seating and welcome relief. Shows on the hour and half-hour. Wrought-iron benches and small exhibits make even the indoor, air-conditioned queue enjoyable. Wheelchair accessible. Assistive listening. Reflective captioning. **Alex's Toddler Tip:** ☹ (bored) **Allie's Kid Tip:** "You get to see Notre Dame, like in 'Hunchback of Notre Dame.'"

| Film |
| D-Ticket |
| Ages 5 & up |
| Dark theater, loud music |
| Short waits |
| 18 min. film |

Attraction descriptions and ratings are explained on page 127.

More at ① japan-epcot

Charting the Attractions at World Showcase
(clockwise order)

Jennifer Dave Readers

Planning
Getting There
Staying in Style
Touring
Feasting
Making Magic
Index
Notes & More

☐ United Kingdom [E-3]   A-ok!   7 6 7

This is Florida's British Colony, full of quaint shops, gardens, a park with live entertainment (check the Epcot Times Guide for the British Revolution band—they're excellent!), a busy pub, and deliciously British eateries. Well-themed. **Allie's Kid Tip:** "You gotta play in the hedge maze! And there's really cool music."

Pavilion
C-Ticket
All ages will enjoy

Allie and Melanie in the classic British phone box

The large park nearly hidden in the back of the pavilion

© MediaMarx, Inc.
②2982 © Cheryl Pendry

☐ Canada [E-4]   5 5 7

The architecture and natural beauty of Canada are captured in a 360° movie (see below), nifty waterfall, gardens, shops, eateries, and live music.

Pavilion
C-Ticket

☐ O Canada! [E-4]   A-ok!   7 6 6

Experience the natural and manmade wonders of Canada in an updated Circle-Vision 360° film. Swooping aerials and dramatic scenery highlight this tour encompassing the Rockies and old-world Montreal. The updated film includes about 50% new footage and features Martin Short and Eva Avila. Shows start every 20 minutes. Stand to view. Indoor queue. Wheelchair accessible. Assistive listening. Reflective captioning. **Alex's Toddler Tip:** ☹ (bored) **Allie's Kid Tip:** "I got tired of standing for so long."

Looking out at Canada

© MediaMarx, Inc.

Film
C-Ticket
Ages 5 & up
Dark, a little dizzying
14 min. film

Canada at sunset

②3942 © Mark Zielberg

More at ① world-showcase

Top Photo Slice: The crenelated roofline of the United Kingdom pavilion (①8351) © Cheryl Pendry

Genuine PassPorter Genuine PassPorter Genuine PassPorter Genuine PassPorter Genuine PassPorter Genuine PassPorter Genuine PassPorter

Cooling Off at Epcot's Fountains

Water is everywhere at Epcot, but nowhere does it draw our attention more than the beautiful fountains throughout the park.

You can't help but notice Epcot's spectacular **Fountain of Nations** at the heart of Future World (see photo on page 153). You may even have been cooled (or chilled) by its drifting mists. But have you really taken the time to savor this carefully choreographed water ballet? Every 15 minutes, the fountain dances to another musical number, with special seasonal music during the Christmas holidays. Thousands of water jets and lights are computer-synchronized to the rhythms and melodies. 30,000 gallons of water course through the fountain, and 2,000 gallons can be airborne at one time, shooting up to 150 feet high. While the mists are more chilling at night, the fountain's lights make the display that much more magical. Enjoy a meal at the Electric Umbrella (see page 235) and catch the show!

Beyond this, nearly **every pavilion has its own water feature**, from the tidal splashes in front of The Seas with Nemo & Friends to the upside-down waterfall at the Imagination pavilion. Even the countries in World Showcase get into the watery act, with delightfully-detailed fountains that evoke each country's charms.

This water is flowing up, not down!

© MediaMarx, Inc.

Cooling off on a warm day

⊕3942 © Denise Lang

And let's not forget Epcot's **play fountains**, which are beloved by kids and kids-at-heart. You'll find two in Future World, one near the plaza as you pass into Future World and the other on the way to Test Track. If you intend to play in them, be sure to bring a change of dry clothing!

Planning | Getting There | Staying in Style | Touring | Feasting | Making Magic | Index | Notes & More

Top Photo Slice: The Fountain of Nations at Epcot (⊕10638) © Brigett Duncan

Planning

Getting There

Staying in Style

Touring

Feasting

Making Magic

Index

Notes & More

Making the Most of IllumiNations

IllumiNations: Reflections of Earth
brings every night to a spectacular
close. Brilliant fireworks and a rousing,
original musical score fill Epcot's World
Showcase Lagoon every evening at
park closing, heralding the creation of
Earth. A shower of sparkling comets
paves the way, a huge globe glides
across the lagoon to take center stage,
and a pageant of breathtaking scenery,
wildlife, and the peoples of the earth
plays across a giant video display
covering the continents of the globe.
Lasers, blazing torches, and more
fireworks tumble forth as the music
builds to a rousing climax.

①2811 © Cheryl Pendry

IllumiNations finale

Although the show is visible anywhere around the lagoon, there are definitely
better viewing sites. You can judge a viewing site well in advance of the
show as you stroll around the lagoon, or check our map on page 152. A clear
view of the water at the center of the lagoon is critical, as is a clear view of
the sky (watch those tree limbs). It also helps if the wind is to your back or
side (to avoid fireworks smoke). The bridge between France and the United
Kingdom is a prime (and popular) location. Italy and Norway are other good
viewing spots. Or try for a 7:30 pm advance reservation at the Rose & Crown.
Check in at the podium early and request a patio table. You may get lucky

with a great view. If not, enjoy
your meal anyway—diners
are invited outside to stand
and enjoy the show. Another
place to stay seated is at
La Hacienda de San Angel in
Mexico. Arrive at least 90 min.
early for a lagoon-side table.
We also highly recommend
the excellent views from the
lagoon-side patios in the
United Kingdom and France,
if they aren't already occupied
by private parties.

© MediaMarx, Inc.

IllumiNations lights up the sky

Disney's Hollywood Studios

This park's 154 acres spotlight the golden era of Hollywood and the glamorous silver screen. It's located southwest of Epcot and is connected to Epcot by Friendship boats and walkways. Disney's Hollywood Studios was renamed from Disney-MGM Studios in January 2008.

Tinseltown never looked so good. All the glamour, glitz, and pageantry of Hollywood come out to greet you at Disney's Hollywood Studios. Disney's rendition of Hollywood Boulevard is done up in 1930s art deco architecture, and an old-fashioned water tower (complete with Mickey ears) sets the stage. And you can't miss the 122-foot-tall version of **Mickey's Sorcerer's Hat** in the center of the park, representing the magic of show business and Disney animation. Disney's Hollywood Studios gives you a behind-the-scenes glimpse at movie-making as well as an opportunity to get involved in shows and tours. Celebrities may put in live appearances at Disney's Hollywood Studios as well, complete with a procession down Hollywood Boulevard and a handprint ceremony. The whole effect is of being a special guest at a major movie studio in the heart of Hollywood.

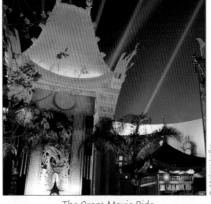
© Melissa Loftin

The Great Movie Ride

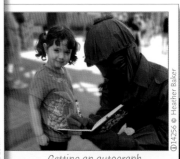
①14256 © Heather Baker

Getting an autograph

①2137 © Michael Dawson

Lights, Motors, Action! Extreme Stunt Show

Top Photo Slice: The Sorcerors Hat at night (①24427)© Sarah Mudd

Planning · Getting There · Staying in Style · Touring · Feasting · Making Magic · Index · Notes & More

Planning

Getting There

Staying in Style

Touring

Feasting

Making Magic

Index

Notes & More

Orienting Yourself at Disney's Hollywood Studios

Fold out the next page for touring plans and a handy attraction cha

Unlike other parks, Disney's Hollywood Studios' layout is free-form, much like Hollywood's artistic personalities (see the park map on the next page). See the inside of the fold-out map for daily touring itineraries and an attractions-at-a-glance list, and pages 177–182 for attraction details.

Hollywood Boulevard Area
Stroll among the stars—this is the "main street" of Tinseltown in its heyday.
Headline Attraction: The Great Movie Ride

The Great Movie Ride ☞

Sunset Boulevard Area
Step back in time to the Hollywood that never was on this famous, palm-lined boulevard.
Headline Attractions: Rock 'n' Roller Coaster, Tower of Terror, Beauty and the Beast

Tower of Terror on Sunset Boulevard ☞

Echo Lake Area
Learn the magic behind spectacular stunts and effects, vote for the next "American Idol," and go for a journey into outer space.
Headline Attractions: American Idol Experience, Star Tours, Indiana Jones Epic Stunt Spectacular

American Idol Experience ☞

Streets of America Area
Visit a movie set evoking famous urban skylines. It even has "towering" skyscrapers!
*Headline Attractions: Muppet*Vision 3-D; Lights, Motors, Action! Extreme Stunt Show*

Streets of America ☞

Pixar Place Area
Play with "the Toys" and peek behind the scenes in the "backlot," and animation exhibits.
Headline Attractions: Toy Story Midway Mania!, Voyage of the Little Mermaid

Green Army Men in Pixar Place ☞

Catching the Shows at Disney's Hollywood Studios

Ready Freddy gets around

Entertainment is simply a matter of course at Disney's Hollywood Studios. The unique **"streetmosphere"** performers make their home along famous boulevards of Hollywood and Sunset, as well as Echo Lake. Dressed in 1940s-style garb, they're responsible for all sorts of on-the-street shenanigans.

Check out the 20-minute-long **Disney Channel Rocks! show** on a traveling stage, featuring music from Disney Channel movies and shows.

The afternoon parade, **Pixar Pals Countdown to Fun**, features your favorite Disney*Pixar characters including Remy and Emile from "Ratatouille" and Carl and Russell from "Up." The parade route is marked on the map on page 172. Be sure to stake out your viewing spot along the parade route about 30 min. in advance.

Come evening, it's Mickey versus villains in **Fantasmic!** at the expanded Hollywood Hills Amphitheater. Fantasmic! is a spectacular 25-minute mix of live action, music,

Pixar Pals Countdown to Fun Parade

and fireworks. Schedule changes seasonally, so check the Times Guide.

Fantasmic Tip: Later shows have shorter waits and better seating. Fantasmic! is popular, though we can take it or leave it. A Fantasmic! Meal Package may be available with special seating—see page 243.

Fantasmic!

Planning / Getting There / Staying in Style / Touring / Feasting / Making Magic / Index / Notes & More

Making the Most of Disney's Hollywood Studios

TIPS

If you're interested in the **live shows**, check the Times Guide for showtimes and plan accordingly to avoid long waits or mad dashes.

Autograph seekers, be prepared! Characters come out in force for meet-and-greets in the park, especially at the Sorcerer Mickey's Hat. See page 171b for a "star" chart, and see page 276 for tips.

Look for the **well** near Indiana Jones Epic Stunt Spectacular (when you're facing the attraction entrance, it's located to the left). Just don't pull the rope. (You've been warned!)

Some of the shows involve **audience participation**. If you like this sort of thing, volunteer enthusiastically for the fun!

Waiting to meet Buzz Lightyear and Woody

If you love **Walt Disney and his legacy of animation**, plan to immediately follow your visit to Walt Disney: One Man's Dream with The Magic of Disney Animation (see page 180). The two attractions complement one another very well.

Seniors won't want to rush through Disney's Hollywood Studios—make enough time to slow down and enjoy the ambience of the park.

PassPorter readers picked to be extras at the Backlot Studio Tour

Lights, camera, action!

Top Photo Slice: American Idol Experience stage © MediaMarx, Inc.

Getting the Best at Disney's Hollywood Studios

SHOPPING

General merchandise shopping is on Hollywood and Sunset Boulevards. Many major attractions have a **themed shop**, too. All shops can be entered without going on a ride. Here are our favorites:

Shop	Location	What makes it special
Crossroads of the World	Hollywood Blvd.	Guidemaps, Times Guides, ponchos
Sid Cahuenga's	Hollywood Blvd.	One-of-a-kind movie memorabilia
Head to Toe	Hollywood Blvd.	Custom embroidery and engraving
Keystone Clothiers	Hollywood Blvd.	Quality Disney clothes
Villains in Vogue	Sunset Blvd.	Disney Villain clothing and gifts
Stage One Company Store	Streets of America	Quirky shop with Muppets!
Writer's Stop	Streets of America	Books! (We can't resist 'em!)
Tatooine Traders	Echo Lake	Star Wars items, fun theme
Hollywood Tower Hotel	Sunset Blvd.	Scary stuff and Tower of Terror gifts

NOTES

Disney's Hollywood Studios has several **unique restaurants** and cafes, and many participate in a Fantasmic! Meal Package. See pages 242–244 for dining and package details.

The focus at this park is on **independent shows and rides** rather than on a never-ending stream of entertainment. Be prepared for walking and waiting. Your reward is longer, lovingly produced shows, more intense rides, and fascinating backstage glimpses.

The pavement in front of Grauman's Chinese Theater (The Great Movie Ride) is full of **celebrity footprints** and handprints.

Kermit was here!

© 13284 © Wendy Suchomel

RATINGS

Ratings are explained on page 126.

Our Value Ratings:		Our Magic Ratings:		Readers' Ratings:
Quality:	8/10	Theme:	8/10	64% fell in love with it
Variety:	7/10	Excitement:	9/10	33% liked it well enough
Scope:	6/10	Fun Factor:	7/10	2% had mixed feelings
Overall Value:	**7/10**	**Overall Magic:**	**8/10**	1% were disappointed

Disney's Hollywood Studios is enjoyed by... (rated by both authors and readers)		
Younger Kids: ♥♥♥♥	Young Adults: ♥♥♥♥♥	Families: ♥♥♥♥♥
Older Kids: ♥♥♥♥	Mid Adults: ♥♥♥♥♥	Couples: ♥♥♥♥♥
Teenagers: ♥♥♥♥♥	Mature Adults: ♥♥♥♥	Singles: ♥♥♥♥

Top Photo Slice: Streetmosphere characters outside shops on Hollywood Boulevard (① 4412) © Melissa Potter

Genuine PassPorter Genuine PassPorter Genuine PassPorter Genuine PassPorter Genuine PassPorter Genuine PassPorter Genuine

Finding Your Way to Disney's Hollywood Studios

BEST TIMES TO GO

Disney's Hollywood Studios can be enjoyed in one day, although it is best to **visit the most popular attractions earlier** to avoid long lines. Arrive before the scheduled opening time for the best advantage. The most popular attractions—Toy Story Midway Mania!, Rock 'n' Roller Coaster, and The Twilight Zone Tower of Terror—generate very long lines. Make a beeline for these rides first thing, unless you've just eaten breakfast. Several of the shows have **limited seating capacity** (such as Voyage of the Little Mermaid) and can require a lengthy wait if busy. Whenever possible, get a FASTPASS! Check the entertainment schedule in the park Times Guide for show times. Take the length of show times into account when planning your route and keep in mind that several shows take a considerable amount of time. Many attractions and restaurants empty immediately before and during the parade, affording shorter lines or the chance to get a table without advance dining arrangements.

GETTING THERE

By Boat—From Epcot's International Gateway, BoardWalk Inn & Villas, Yacht & Beach Club & Villas, and Swan & Dolphin, take the Friendship boat.

By Bus—Take a direct bus from all other resorts, Epcot's main entrance, and Disney's Animal Kingdom. From the Magic Kingdom, catch a bus at the Transportation and Ticket Center (TTC). From Downtown Disney, Typhoon Lagoon, or Blizzard Beach, take a bus or boat to a resort and transfer to a Disney's Hollywood Studios bus.

By Car—Take I-4 to exit 67 (westbound) or exit 62 (eastbound) and continue on to Disney's Hollywood Studios parking. All-day parking is available for $14 (free to resort guests and annual passholders).

By Foot—You can walk from the BoardWalk, Swan & Dolphin, and Yacht & Beach Club, and even Epcot's International Gateway. Follow the marked pathways along the canal beside the BoardWalk Villas (see resort map on page 52 for path location).

Friendship boat dock at Disney's Hollywood Studios

2611 © Gayle Harteroad

More at ① disneys-hollywood-studios

Top Photo Slice: A stunt car drives on two wheels in Lights, Motors, Action! Stunt Spectacular (①4850) © Amy Sellars

Planning

Getting There

Staying in Style

Touring

Feasting

Making Magic

Index

Notes & More

Charting the Attractions at the Echo Lake Area

(in clockwise order starting from the left side of the park)

Jennifer Dave Readers

☐ Indiana Jones Epic Stunt Spectacular [D-5] *FP* A-ok! **7 6 8**

The Indiana Jones films set the stage for an action show of epic proportions. Disney has built a huge indoor/outdoor set to demonstrate the stuntperson's craft, including the famous rolling boulder, an Egyptian marketplace, and a flaming German airplane. Adults may be picked to join the show—arrive early and show enthusiasm if this interests you. Theater opens 25 minutes before the show and guests sit in a covered, outdoor theater. Loud explosions and hot flames may scare young children. Wheelchair accessible. Assistive listening. **Allie's TeenTip:** "It's a good show, but it's loud."

①2561 © Jyl Deshler
Saving the day!

Live Show
E-Ticket
Ages 4 & up
Loud, fire, violence
FASTPASS or med. waits
30 min. show

☐ ABC Sound Studio [C-4] **– – –**

This building previously housed Sounds Dangerous, an entertaining sound effects demonstration hosted by comedian Drew Carey, which closed in May 2012. Now you may find seasonal shows here during Star Wars Weekends or the holidays. No word yet on any permanent attraction for this location, but rumors that an extended version of the popular Jedi Training Academy show could appear here at some point in the future.

Show
Times, waits, and ages vary based on what's appearing

☐ Star Tours II: The Adventure Continues [B-5] *FP*   **8 8 8**

Take a flight to a galaxy far, far away in this "must ride" for all Star Wars fans, fully updated in 2011! The enhanced flight simulator at the heart of this ride never really goes anywhere, but through new high-definition video and a Disney Real-D 3D screen, you'll find it hard to believe as your StarSpeeder 1000 dives, banks, and speeds about. In the new story, C-3PO and R2-D2 take you on a wild ride with a "rebel" spy aboard—but where you fly and with whom you meet changes with each ride! There are 54 different random storylines you can experience, from visiting Tatooine to Naboo and meeting Princess Leia and Yoda. You'll want to ride this again and again! The attraction has an indoor queue with many new visual delights. Overflow queue outdoors is uncovered. 40"/102 cm height restriction. Young kids should be with an adult. Health warning. Guests must transfer from ECV to wheelchair, and from wheelchair to ride. Closed captioning. Non-moving rides may be available for ECV-bound and motion-sensitive—ask a cast member. **Allie's KidTip:** "This is good, but hold on tight!" **TeenTip:** "The back seats really are the best."

Thrill Ride
E-Ticket
Far-out fun
May be rough, rocky, may cause motion sickness
Expect FASTPASS or long waits
3 min. intro 4.5 min. flight

☐ American Idol Experience [C-4] **5 6 6**

Be part of the American Idol Experience! Wannabe "Idols" audition in the morning, and if they ace the two-stage tryouts they sing for a Studios audience. There are shows throughout the day, and the audiences vote for their favorites. The day's winners compete in the popular last show for the big prize—a "Dream Ticket," which is a front-of-line-pass to tryout at an American Idol TV regional audition. You can be 14 years old or over to perform at the park, but winners have to meet TV rules (the Dream Ticket can be transferred once to someone eligible to compete). Wheelchair accessible. Assistive listening. **Alex's KidTip:** ☺

Show
E-Ticket
Ages 5 & up
Loud
Long waits
25 min. show

Attraction descriptions and ratings are explained on page 127.

Top Photo Slice: Droid spotted in the queue for Star Tours (①3834) © Stephanie Fieldstad

Charting the Attractions in the Streets of America Area

Jennifer Dave Readers

Honey, I Shrunk the Kids Movie Set Adventure [B-3]   A-OK!   6 5 6

Kids climb, cavort, and caper amidst huge plants, insects, and spider webs in this playground based on the popular movies and TV show. Keep cool with various water sprays (it gets very hot here) and slide down giant rolls of film and leaves. Officially kids must be at least 4 years old to play, and adults must be with a child to enter. Wheelchair accessible.

Playground
B-Ticket
Ages 4 & up
Giant bugs
Short waits

①8724 © Elizabeth Key
Readers cavort in the playground

© MediaMarx, Inc.
Alexander plays on fungi

Lights, Motors, Action! Extreme Stunt Show [A-2]   FP   7 8 8

You'll be wowed by an epic display of the stuntperson's art in this updated show originally from Disneyland Paris. Villains in cars and motorcycles roar across the set in pursuit of the hero, as filmmakers shoot scenes for a spy movie. Giant video screens show how special effects action is turned into movie magic. Lightning McQueen and Mater, stars of Cars and Cars 2, have also joined the cast! A 5,000-seat partially shaded grandstand offers metal bench seats. With only 2–3 shows daily, plan to arrive early. FASTPASS offered in peak seasons. Brief, hot flames can make the front rows uncomfortable. Assistive listening. Wheelchair accessible. Unshaded queue. Lightning and Mater meet and greet available after the show.

Live Show
E-Ticket
Ages 3 & up
Loud!
Long waits or FASTPASS
25 minutes

Muppet*Vision 3-D [B-4]   A-OK!   7 7 9

Your 3-D glasses get a real workout as Kermit and his pals show you around the Muppet Labs. The Muppets are at their zany, pun-filled best in a frenetic good time that was Jim Henson's last production. The multiscreen videos and hilarious props shown in the pre-show area deserve your full attention. The digital projection theater is large and air-conditioned, with comfy seats. There's no need to sit in front to get a good view. Some effects may be scary for young kids. Indoor queue is fun. Wheelchair accessible. Assistive listening. Closed captioning. Reflective captioning. **Alex's ToddlerTip:** "I like Kermit! ☺" **Allie's KidTip:** "Keep your 3-D glasses on."

3-D Film
E-Ticket
Ages 4 & up
Intense, loud, some violence
Med. waits
15 min. intro
17 min. film

①6905 © Keith Stanton
Balloon atop the Muppet Labs

Charting the Attractions in the Streets of America Area

Streets of America Movie Set [B-4]

Readers: Jennifer Dave — 6 | 6 | 6

If you go to San Francisco, wear a flower in your hair

Whether or not you've been to the big city, you'll enjoy the movie set-style renditions of New York and San Francisco. The buildings are all facades, of course, but the detail is rich and pretty accurate. You'll find familiar bits of Chinatown and a London street in here, too. Disney entertainers may appear on the Plaza Hotel-like steps or roll down the streets in parade fashion. Look for the "Singin' in the Rain" umbrella (see photo), but don't be surprised if it gets a little damp! Wheelchair accessible.

| Walk-thru |
| A-Ticket |
| All ages |
| Few waits |
| Unlimited |

Singin' in the rain

Toy Story Pizza Planet Arcade [B-5]

A-Ok! — 2 | 3 | 6

This is a spacious, pleasantly themed arcade adjacent to the Pizza Planet cafe with a typical selection of video games and try-to-hoist-a-toy games. There's a depressing lack of Toy Story-themed arcade games, however. Tokens are needed to play. Most games require 2 to 4 tokens, and the tokens are 25 cents each. Not very magical. Wheelchair accessible. Allie's KidTip: "Fun games."

| Arcade |
| A-Ticket |
| Ages 5 & up |
| No scares |
| Few waits |

Osborne Family Spectacle of Dancing Lights

The late Jennings Osborne's Christmas lights were too much for his Arkansas neighbors, so Disney invited him to the studio backlot, where his lights became a Thanksgiving through New Year's tradition. The more than five million lights now grace the Streets of America Set, hopefully for many holiday seasons to come. Look for them early November through early January.

The Osborne Family Spectacle of Dancing Lights light up the holiday nights

More at ① osborne-lights

Charting the Attractions in the Pixar Place Area

JenniFer   Dave   Readers

The Magic of Disney Animation [F-2]   A-ok!   6 | 7 | 8

Animation fans enjoy this informative tour with hands-on exhibits. The "Drawn to Animation Theater" features Mulan's Mushu (Eddie Murphy) and a live animator. "Animation Academy" has 38 easels where a cast member teaches you to draw favorite characters. This is also a permanent character greeting spot, hosting characters from a recent film. **Allie's KidTip:** "The part with Mushu is funny!" **TeenTip:** "It sounds boring, but it's fun inside."

Walk-thru | D-Ticket | Ages 4 & up | No scares | Med. waits | Allow 45 min.

The Legend of Captain Jack Sparrow [D-2]   – | – | –

Fans of "Pirates of the Caribbean" movies can experience the story and history of Captain Jack Sparrow. The attraction is not yet open at press time, so watch our web site for more information. Outdoor queue. Wheelchair accessible.

Walk-thru | B-Ticket

Walt Disney: One Man's Dream presented by D23 [D-2]   8 | 8 | 8

This recently renovated attraction illustrates Walt's impact on his company and the world. Follow Walt's imaginings as they grow and learn how his boyhood experiences affected his lifelong accomplishments. Hundreds of priceless and never-before-seen artifacts are on display, as well as a showing of the moving "One Man's Dream" presentation at the end. Wheelchair accessible.

Walk-thru | D-Ticket | Ages 10 & up | Allow 30 min.

Walt talks about his dreams for Disney World on this display at One Man's Dream

Disney Junior—Live on Stage! [E-3]   A-ok!   7 | 6 | 8

Puppets gives a live version of Disney Channel favorites, including characters from "Mickey Mouse Clubhouse," "Little Einsteins," "Handy Manny," and the newest show, "Jake and the Never Land Pirates." Seating is on a carpeted floor. This attraction becomes a kid-friendly dance party on Extra Magic Hour evenings. Outdoor, covered queue. Wheelchair access. **Alex's ToddlerTip:** ☺ "Bubbles fall from the ceiling!"

Live Show | C-Ticket | All ages | 22 min. show

Charting the Attractions in the Pixar Place Area

Jennifer Dave Readers

Studio Backlot Tour [B-2]   A-OK!   6 6 7

This is the park's backstage movie magic blockbuster. See how sea battles and storms are stirred up, tour Disney's backlot, and brave Catastrophe Canyon, a special effects tour de force. Stand in long lines not once, but twice. Outdoor queue is covered. Wheelchair accessible. Closed captioning. 6 min. intro. **Allie'sKidTip:** "Sit on the left side to get wet!" **TweenTip:** "At the end you can view movie costumes." (Backdoor entry to exhibit via AFI Showcase Shop.)

Tram Ride
D-Ticket
Ages 6 & up
Fires, floods
Long waits
17 min. ride

Toy Story Midway Mania! [D-2]   FP   A-OK!   10 10 10

This dark ride is based on Pixar's Toy Story and is Disney's first interactive 3-D ride. It makes use of digital sets, effects like wind and water spray, and spring-action pointers to shoot virtual projectiles like eggs, darts, balls, and rings. Look for hidden targets to get extra points and enjoy different levels of play. The "Toy Story Trams" seat four guests each (two groups of two). Visit http://www.toystorymania.com. Indoor queue with interactive Mr. Potato Head (in standby queue only). Wheelchair accessible.

3-D Ride
E-Ticket
Ages 3 & up
Some fast spins
Very long waits
5 1/2 min. ride

Pixar Studios ... a sign of more attractions to come?

© 9992 © Alisa Niethammer

Toy Story Trams on the way to play!

© MediaMarx, Inc.

Mr. Potato Head in the queue

©22348 @ Jessibean1

Voyage of the Little Mermaid [E-2]   FP   A-OK!   8 7 8

Enjoy your favorite tunes while live action, puppets, falling water, and laser effects bring Ariel and her friends to life onstage, making you feel as if you're truly under the sea! Cool theater offers comfy seats. Middle rows are best for view of stage and effects. Stand to right during 5-min. pre-show for up-front seating. No flash photos or video lights. Covered outdoor queue. Wheelchair accessible. Assistive listening. Reflective captioning. **Alex's ToddlerTip:** "Ariel is here! ☺" **Allie'sKidTip:** "I love this! Look up!" **Allie's TeenTip:** "Boring!"

Live Show
E-Ticket
Ages 3 & up
Dark, strobe
FASTPASS or long waits
17 min. show

Planning | Getting There | Staying in Style | Touring | Feasting | Making Magic | Index | Notes & More

Charting the Attractions on the Hollywood & Sunset Boulevards

☐ Beauty and the Beast–Live On Stage [G-4]   A-oh!   6 | 7 | 8

Be Disney's guest! See Belle, Beast, Lumiere, Mrs. Potts, Chip, and that other beast, Gaston, live and on stage. An enthusiastic cast sings and dances its way through musical numbers from the animated film. The original story line all but disappears, but you'll hardly mind, thanks to the good performances, eye-filling costumes, and fine staging. Lines are long, but the theater opens 25 minutes prior to show. Live, pre-show entertainment on some days. Outdoor queue is uncovered. Wheelchair accessible. Assistive listening. Allie's KidTip: "This show skips some parts of the story."

Live Show	
E-Ticket	
Ages 5 & up	
Loud sound effects	
Med. waits	
10 min. intro 25 min. show	

☐ The Great Movie Ride [D-3]   A-oh!   6 | 6 | 8

Hollywood's famed Grauman's Chinese Theater sets the stage for a sedate ride through famous scenes from classic movies enacted by Audio-Animatronics characters. Some live-action excitement and two short films add a bit of Hollywood pizzazz. Long lines snake through a props and costumes exhibit. (Yes, that is a carousel horse from "Mary Poppins.") Following the pre-show film, the queue separates—each line sees a scene that the other does not. Indoor queue with overflow queue outdoors. Effects may be too intense for small children. Transfer from ECV to wheelchair. Wheelchair accessible. Allie's KidTip: "Snakes!"

Film/Ride	
D-Ticket	
Ages 4 & up	
Loud noises, scary scenes	
Long waits	
3 min. intro 18 min. ride	

☐ Rock 'n' Roller Coaster Starring Aerosmith [G-3] FP 🚶   8 | 10 | 9

Experience Disney's first high-speed coaster launch. Hurtle through twists, 4-5G turns, and three inversions (yes, upside down)—in the dark! Rock band Aerosmith invites you to take a limo crosstown and join them backstage. Aerosmith also provides the soundtrack for your ride—five different tunes are possible depending upon which "limo" you get. Upon boarding, we recommend you press your head against the headrest to prepare for the very fast start (0–58 in 2.8 seconds). Beyond that, this may be the smoothest coaster you ever ride—even the coaster-shy have enjoyed it. Interactive indoor queue area takes you through a recording studio's display of historic memorabilia. Take the single rider line for a shorter wait, or the "chicken exit" if you just want to enjoy the queue. 48"/122 cm height restriction. Transfer from ECV to wheelchair, and then transfer from wheelchair to ride. Allie's KidTip: "You won't believe how fast it goes! Make sure your stuff is safe." TweenTip: "The loops are my favorite!" TeenTip: "This ride rocks!"

Coaster	
E-Ticket	
Ages 8 & up	
Very fast, very dark, can cause motion sickness, headaches	
FASTPASS or long waits	
2 min. intro 3 min. ride	

☐ The Twilight Zone Tower of Terror [H-4] FP 🚶   3 | 9 | 9

Delight in the delicious spookiness of this haunted hotel, long before you ride its legendary "down and up and down and up again" elevator. The gut-wrenching drops are matched by wonderful visual effects. The queue splits in the basement—go left, it's typically shorter. To enjoy just the fabulous queue and pre-show, take the "chicken exit" before you board the elevator (ask a cast member). Outdoor queue is mostly shaded. 40"/102 cm height restriction. Health warning. Young children should be accompanied by an adult. Transfer from wheelchair to ride. Closed captioning. Allie's KidTip: "I like the up and down part, but the rest is scary." TweenTip: "There are handles to hold beside the seats if you're scared. (But I'm not scared!)" TeenTip: "This is the best ride at Disney World! And I got Jennifer to go on it with me finally!"

Thrill Ride	
E-Ticket	
Ages 8 & up	
Dark, scary, sudden drops	
FASTPASS or long waits	
10 min. intro 4 min. ride	

Attraction descriptions and ratings are explained on page 127.

More at ① rock-n-roller-coaster

Planning

Getting There

Staying in Style

Touring

Feasting

Making Magic

Index

Notes & More

Disney's Animal Kingdom

Disney's Animal Kingdom is the youngest and largest park (580 acres) at the Walt Disney World Resort. Part zoological park and part theme park, Disney's Animal Kingdom charms, delights, and thrills guests with a uniquely Disney look at the wild world. Disney's Animal Kingdom is located the farthest west of all the parks on the Walt Disney World property.

The Tree of Life towers above Disney's Animal Kingdom, reminding us of the wonder, glory, and fragility of nature's creations. This is the quietest of the parks out of respect to the animals who make their home here, but "quiet" doesn't mean "boring." Adventure awaits, as discoveries lurk around every bend. Like Epcot, Disney's Animal Kingdom is a place to explore with open eyes and eager minds. Lace up your boots, grab your safari hat, and load your camera—the adventure is about to begin!

D14336 © Denise Lang

Honorary "bug eyes" at It's Tough to Be a Bug!

D22855 © Amanda Hulse

Elephants spotted on a "two-week" safari

D8462 © Janice Kovacs

Broken tracks at the top of Expedition Everest ... evidence of the Yeti?

Top Photo Slice: The Tree of Life © MediaMarx, Inc.

Genuine PassPorter Genuine PassPorter Genuine PassPorter Genuine PassPorter Genuine PassPorter Genuine PassPorter Genuine

Planning

Getting There

Staying in Style

Touring

Feasting

Making Magic

Index

Notes & More

WELCOME

Orienting Yourself at Disney's Animal Kingdom

Fold out the next page for touring plans and a handy attraction cha→

To set the tone for the day, all guests pass through **The Oasis**, a lush jungle teeming with exotic wildlife, sparkling waters, and rocky crags. Then, standing on Discovery Island at the center, the **Tree of Life** binds the four lands of Disney's Animal Kingdom in a circle of life (see map). A new land, based on James Cameron's AVATAR films, is currently in development (see page 189). See the inside of the map for our favorite touring plans and a list of attractions, and pages 191–196 for attraction details.

Discovery Island
Journey to the center where the waters meet, the Tree of Life looms large, and the little creatures scurry.
Headline Attraction: It's Tough to be a Bug!
Tree of Life ☛

Camp Minnie-Mickey
Hike into an evergreen forest reminiscent of Adirondack fishing camps, catching "critters" like Mickey Mouse for hugs and autographs.
Headline Attraction: Festival of the Lion King
Camp Minnie-Mickey sign ☛

Africa and Rafiki's Planet Watch
Come together in the port town of Harambe, complete with thatched huts and baobab trees, and set off on safaris, treks, and adventures.
Headline Attractions: Kilimanjaro Safaris, Pangani Forest Exploration Trail
Sign at the entrance to Africa ☛

Asia
Step into the mythical kingdom of Anandapur (meaning "place of all delights") to experience the beauty, wonder, and peace of Asia.
Headline Attractions: Kali River Rapids, Maharajah Jungle Trek, Expedition Everest
Expedition Everest ☛

DinoLand, U.S.A.
Get tourist-trapped in the wacky world of an old dinosaur dig site, scattered with dino bones, then meet the "real" dinosaurs on a thrilling ride.
Headline Attractions: Dinosaur, Primeval Whirl, "Finding Nemo—The Musical"
Dino statue at Chester & Hester's! ☛

Catching the Shows at Disney's Animal Kingdom

The best entertainment at Disney's Animal Kingdom is its themed live **theater shows**, described in detail on pages 191–196. Roving entertainers take a back seat to the wildlife, of course. Fireworks shows don't fit in here, either—they would just scare the animals.

Finale of Festival of the Lion King

©2922 © Cheryl Pendry

Jammin' Jungle Parade

⑭14703 © Janet Simonsen

Mickey's Jammin' Jungle Parade features your favorite Disney characters as they set out "on expedition." The parade's "party animals" put on a wild street celebration and encourage guests to join in the action along the way!

Other entertainment includes **The Adventure Begins** show, which starts 15 minutes before park opening every day—Minnie, Pluto, and Goofy arrive in a safari truck to start your adventure!

In Africa's Harambe Village, **live bands** and acrobats keep the Dawa Bar and Tusker House's outdoor tables hopping. Visitors to Rafiki's Planet Watch may get lucky and catch **live animal acts** on the outdoor stage! Also be on the lookout for **DiVine**, a ten-foot-tall, towering and wandering "vine."

If you stay until park closing, you may get a little **"kiss goodnight"** from Donald, Goofy, Mickey and Minnie as they wave good-bye to all the guests leaving the park. Look for them in The Oasis just as you exit.

Simply DiVine

⑭23089 © Francis T. Tewey

Top Photo Slice: Friendly birds wait for their cue at Flights of Wonder in Asia (⑭14325) © Janet Simonsen

---

Making the Most of Disney's Animal Kingdom

TIPS

Disney's Animal Kingdom is a paradise, where delightful and often subtle details can work their magic if you **take the time** to notice. This is not a do-it-all-in-a-day-or-die park. Slow down, revel in the beauty, wonder at the animals, and enjoy yourselves!

Trails lead off in all directions—don't be afraid to explore them. A bridge and path connects DinoLand and Asia (see map on page 186). It's the perfect way to dodge afternoon parade crowds.

This park is one big photo op! Bring plenty of **memory cards/film** and **batteries**, and even **binoculars** for viewing animals.

Dining options here have seen some recent changes. A full-service and counter-service restaurant (Yak & Yeti) opened in Asia and Tusker House converted to a buffet with a character breakfast and lunch. See the listings on pages 245–247.

The outdoor, sheltered **seating** by Flame Tree Barbecue is a wonderful spot, whether you want to dine or simply rest. Tables and dining pavilions are set amidst lush tropical gardens.

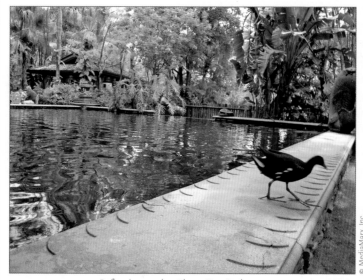

Reflecting pool at Flame Tree Barbecue

Getting the Best at Disney's Animal Kingdom

The best shopping at Disney's Animal Kingdom can be found in two places: Discovery Island around the Tree of Life and Africa's Village of Harambe. Of the two, Harambe offers more in the way of handcrafted and **imported goods**, while Discovery Island offers themed **Disney merchandise**. Here are our favorite shops:

Shop	Location	What makes it special
Outpost	Outside park entrance	Guidemaps, hats, sunglasses
Garden Gate Gifts	Inside park entrance	Film, stroller/wheelchair rentals
Beastly Bazaar	Discovery Island	Safari hats, logowear
Island Mercantile	Discovery Island	Disney-themed gifts
Disney Outfitters	Discovery Island	Upscale clothing, decorative items
Mombasa Marketplace	Africa	Crafts demonstrations
Out of the Wild	Rafiki's Planet Watch	Conservation-themed items
Chester & Hester's	DinoLand U.S.A.	Kitschy, quirky gifts (and junk!)

Not all **animals** can be seen all the time. On the plus side, you'll often see new ones each time, making subsequent visits unique.

Beverages sold in Disney's Animal Kingdom generally do not come with lids, for the animals' safety.

It always seems **hotter** at Disney's Animal Kingdom than at any other park. Be prepared with hats, sunglasses, sunscreen, and ways to keep yourself cool, like plenty of cold water and/or a personal misting fan ($16). Take advantage of the mist-spraying fans throughout the park when you need relief. Take frequent breaks in air-conditioned spots—try the eateries, shops, or attractions.

Disney announced in 2012 that they would bring the **fantasy world of AVATAR** to Disney's Animal Kingdom. Originally announced to start construction in late 2013, latest reports hint of delays. For more details, watch our web site and newsletter!

Ratings are explained on page 126.

Our Value Ratings:		Our Magic Ratings:		Readers' Ratings:
Quality:	8/10	Theme:	9/10	44% fell in love with it
Variety:	7/10	Excitement:	7/10	33% liked it well enough
Scope:	6/10	Fun Factor:	6/10	15% had mixed feelings
Overall Value:	**7/10**	**Overall Magic:**	**7/10**	8% were disappointed

Animal Kingdom is enjoyed by... (rated by both authors and readers)		
Younger Kids: ❤❤❤❤❤	Young Adults: ❤❤❤❤	Families: ❤❤❤❤❤
Older Kids: ❤❤❤❤	Mid Adults: ❤❤❤❤	Couples: ❤❤❤❤
Teenagers: ❤❤❤❤	Mature Adults: ❤❤❤❤	Singles: ❤❤❤❤

SHOPPING

NOTES

RATINGS

Planning / Getting There / Staying in Style / Touring / Feasting / Making Magic / Index / Notes & More

Planning
Getting There
Staying in Style
Touring
Feasting
Making Magic
Index
Notes & More

Finding Your Way at Disney's Animal Kingdom

BEST TIMES TO GO

Most guests arrive in the morning and leave in the afternoon, making **late afternoon** the best time to visit. Not only are the crowds thinner, but the park's animals prefer the cooler temperatures found in the earlier and later parts of the day, so you're more likely to see them. If possible, take advantage of Extra Magic Hours, especially in the cool of the evening. You may have more luck spotting animals during and after a rainstorm, too. When you **first arrive**, head for Expedition Everest or Kilimanjaro Safaris to pick up a FASTPASS (or just go ahead and ride if the wait is short enough). Another strategy is to ride one of the popular attractions early and then immediately get a FASTPASS for another attraction. Check the Animal Kingdom **Times Guide** for show times and durations, and plan your day accordingly—these shows can chew up more time than you'd expect. You can use our touring plans on page 185a to give you an idea of what you can expect to do in one day. Finally, if your park pass allows it, consider spreading out your visit over a **couple of days** rather than packing it all into one. Midday is best avoided due to the big crowds, the intense heat/sun, and sleeping animals.

GETTING THERE

By Bus—All resorts, Epcot, and Disney's Hollywood Studios have buses that take you directly to Disney's Animal Kingdom. From the Magic Kingdom, walk or monorail to the Contemporary and catch a bus. From Downtown Disney, take a bus to an Epcot-area resort and catch a Disney's Animal Kingdom bus.

By Car—From I-4, take exit 65 (eastbound or westbound) and follow signs to Disney's Animal Kingdom parking. All-day parking is available for $14 (free to resort guests with resort ID and annual passholders). The parking lot is some distance from the entrance. You'll appreciate the free trams to the front gate.

Note: There is no boat, path, or monorail access to this theme park.

④4978 © Cheryl Pendry

Parking lot tram at Disney's Animal Kingdom

More at ① animal-trekking

Charting the Attractions in The Oasis, Discovery Island, and Camp Minnie-Mickey

Jennifer Dave Readers

⬛ The Oasis [C-6]   A-Ok!   7 6 7

All guests pass through this lush jungle habitat of gurgling waters and exotic plants on their way in and out of the park. Many of the paths lead to small animal exhibits. Look for shady seats in a rocky grotto. Wheelchair accessible. **Allie's Kid Tip:** "Can you spot camouflaging lizards anywhere here?"

| Walk-thru |
| A-Ticket |
| All ages |
| Allow 20 min. |

⬛ Camp Minnie-Mickey Character Greeting Trails [A-5]   A-Ok!   4 4 6

Meet Mickey, Minnie, and other Disney characters in the shade of four rustic, open-air pavilions—each character has his/her own queue. Low-key atmosphere. Bring your autograph book and have your camera handy. Wheelchair accessible. **Alex's Toddler Tip:** ☺ **Allie's Kid Tip:** "Don't be shy."

| Pavilion |
| A-Ticket |
| All ages |
| Med. waits |

⬛ Festival of the Lion King [A-6]   A-Ok!   8 8 9

Broadway-caliber performance

①23090 © Francis T. Tewey

This colorful, dynamic pageant set to music from "The Lion King" features singers, dancers, acrobats, and floats, and really sets your hands to clapping! The 1,000-seat theater-in-the-round affords many great vantage points, but arrive early to sit down front. Try the first or last shows for shortest waits. Lots of audience participation and lots of fun! This theatre is fully air-conditioned. Outdoor queue is uncovered. No external video lights. Wheelchair accessible. Assistive listening. **Alex's Toddler Tip:** ☺ **Allie's Kid Tip:** "If you sit in the front you might get asked to play music!" **Tween Tip:** "Try to make the animal sounds."

| Live Show |
| E-Ticket |
| Ages 2 & up |
| Long waits (check showtimes in Times Guide) |
| 30 min. show |

⬛ It's Tough to be a Bug! [D-4]   FP   A-Ok!   8 8 9

Delve into the insect world beneath the Tree of Life on Discovery Island for a humorous show hosted by Flik from "A Bug's Life" and featuring a pint-sized cast of animated and Audio-Animatronics characters. 3-D effects, creepy sensations, and yucky smells can terrify the bug-wary. Queue offers close-up views of the tree's animal sculptures. Look for hilarious movie posters in the "lobby." Air-conditioned, 430-seat theater. Outdoor queue is uncovered. Special effects may be too intense for some. Wheelchair accessible. Assistive listening. Reflective captioning. The entrance is marked on the map on page 186. **Allie's Kid Tip:** "Sit between two grown-ups in case you get scared."

| 3-D Show |
| E-Ticket |
| Ages 6 & up |
| Dark, smells, bug noises, "stings" |
| FASTPASS or med. waits |
| 8 min. show |

⬛ The Tree of Life and Discovery Island Trails [C-3]   6 5 8

Tropical gardens and exotic animals surround the Tree of Life at the center of the park. Walk the winding paths, and get a close-up view of the tree, too. How many animals can you see in the trunk and roots? (Hint: 366, including a "hidden Mickey.") Wheelchair accessible. **Allie's Kid Tip:** "The animals are cool."

| Walk-thru |
| A-Ticket |
| All ages |
| Allow 30 min. |

Attraction descriptions and ratings are explained on page 127.

Side tabs: Planning · Getting There · Staying in Style · Touring · Feasting · Making Magic · Index · Notes & More

Planning | Getting There | Staying in Style | Touring | Feasting | Making Magic | Index | Notes & More

Charting the Attractions at Africa

Jennifer   Dave   Readers

☐ Kilimanjaro Safaris [B-1]   FP 🚹 A-oK!   8 | 8 | 9

Board a safari truck to explore 100 acres of African habitat with lions, giraffes, crocodiles, ostriches, gazelle, and many other live animals. Wildlife may be plentiful or scarce, since it's free to roam. Disney also includes a story line in case the animals are feeling shy. The ride gets very bumpy, so hang on tight. We recommend you ride first thing in the morning, late afternoon, or after it rains, when the animals are more active. Sit in outside seats for best views and photos. The safari closes at dusk. Outdoor queue is covered and has overhead monitors. Height restriction for children riding in front two seats. Young children should be accompanied by an adult. Health warning. Transfer from ECV to wheelchair to ride. Wheelchair accessible. Assistive listening. Closed captioning. **Alex's ToddlerTip:** ☺ **Alex's KidTip:** "It's more bumpy and more fun in back." **TweenTip:** "Look at the signs in the truck to identify the animals."

Ride
E-Ticket
Ages 4 & up
Bumpy, live birds and animals, "close escapes"
FASTPASS or long waits
19 min. vehicle ride

Wildebeest graze on the savanna as a safari truck passes by

①8284 © Cheryl Pendry

☐ Pangani Forest Exploration Trail [B-1]   A-oK!   6 | 8 | 7

This gorilla loves his blankie

①1834 © imadisneygirl

Animal lovers will stroll enthralled through this exhibit of African wildlife in an artfully built natural habitat. African birds, hippos, meerkats, and a troop of gorillas make their home here. Hands-on exhibits in the naturalist's hut add interest. A habitat—the Endangered Animal Rehabilitation Centre—calls attention to the African bushmeat crisis. The meerkat viewing area is especially popular, and plan to spend extra time in the aviary. Walk slowly or sit, and the wonders will unfold. Allow several hours if you love to watch animals. Early morning or late afternoon is the best time to visit. Wheelchair accessible. Closed captioning. **Alex's KidTip:** "The animals can't get close to you. It's ok!"

Walk-thru
D-Ticket
All ages
Live animals, birds flying overhead
Short waits
Allow at least 30 minutes

Charting the Attractions at Rafiki's Planet Watch

JenniFer, Dave, Readers

Wildlife Express Train to Rafiki's Planet Watch [C-1]   A-oK!   5 4 5

All aboard! This train at Harambe station is the only route into or out of Rafiki's Planet Watch (formerly called Conservation Station). Enjoy a ringside glimpse of the park's backstage animal care areas. A guide describes the sights as the train chugs slowly along the track. Note: Everyone must disembark at Rafiki's Planet Watch. As always, Disney's eye for detail shines forth around Harambe Station and onboard the train. The best seats are in the front row. Themed, outdoor queue is mostly covered. Wheelchair accessible. Assistive listening. **Alex's ToddlerTip:** ☺ **Allie's KidTip:** "Sit in the front row of the train to see better."

Train Ride
B-Ticket
All ages
Glimpses of backstage
Short waits
15 min. ride (each way)

Engine of the Wildlife Express Train to Rafiki's Planet Watch

⊕1721 © Brad K.

Rafiki's Planet Watch [off map]   A-oK!   5 6 5

This is the park's most remote and most underappreciated attraction, a must-visit for animal lovers of all ages. Formerly called Conservation Station, it was renamed and jazzed up with live animal encounter shows, more hands-on activities, and visits from Rafiki. The 5-min. walk from the train station to Rafiki's Planet Watch is interspersed with fun, conservation-themed exhibits and activities. See short films, use interactive video displays, and relax in darkened rain forest "soundscape" booths. View the park's nursery and veterinary hospital. Enjoy the cleanest, most animal-friendly petting zoo anywhere (it even has a hand-washing fountain at the exit). The Wildlife Express Train from Harambe is the only way into or out of Rafiki's Planet Watch. Wheelchair accessible. Assistive listening. **Alex's ToddlerTip:** ☺ **Allie's KidTip:** "Look for the fishes, lizards, and frogs. And go to the petting farm!"

Exhibit
C-Ticket
All ages
Backstage, educational fun
Live animals
Short waits
Allow at least 90 minutes for a good exploration

Petting a goat at Rafiki's

⊕7295 © Melissa Potter

Planning | Getting There | Staying in Style | Touring | Feasting | Making Magic | Index | Notes & More

Charting the Attractions at Asia

Jennifer Dave Readers

☐ Expedition Everest [G-3]   FP 🚹 | 9 | 10 | 9 |

Disney's newest "mountain" thrill ride takes guests on a rickety tea plantation train up and into 199-foot-tall Forbidden Mountain on the way to Mount Everest. Once inside the chilly mountain interior, you'll have a startling encounter with the fearsome Yeti—part god, part beast—and the largest and most complex Audio-Animatronics figure ever built. Banished, you'll hurtle through darkness and even ride backward. The coaster has several steep drops and sharp turns, and some parts are very intense. The incredibly detailed queue snakes through a Himalayan village filled with artifacts, a museum, and a Yeti shrine. Single rider line available. 44"/112 cm. height restriction. Health warning. Must transfer from wheelchair to ride. Visit http://www.disneyeverest.com.

| Coaster |
| E-Ticket |
| Ages 8 & up |
| Dark, drops, heights |
| FASTPASS or very long waits |
| 3 min. ride |

①10336 © Melissa Loftin
Yeti poster near Expedition Everest

☐ Flights of Wonder [D-2]   A-ok! | 7 | 7 | 7 |

Duck! Owls or hawks may fly right above your head during a show starring more than 20 species of free-flying exotic birds and their talented animal handlers. Guano Joe (or Jane), a tour guide from Anandapur Tours, adds some comic relief to this conservation-themed show. Guests are selected from the audience to join in the action. Afterward, everyone has a chance to come down to ask questions, view the "stars" up close, and take photos. Sit near the aisles for the closest animal encounters. Outdoor, shaded theater. Outdoor queue is uncovered. Theater opens 15 minutes beforehand. No food or drink allowed. Leave strollers at the door. Wheelchair accessible. Assistive listening. Allie's Kid Tip: "Volunteer to go on the stage! I'm too shy to do it, but it looks like fun."

| Live Show |
| D-Ticket |
| Ages 3 & up |
| Live birds overhead |
| Med. waits (showtimes listed in Times Guide) |
| 25 min. show |

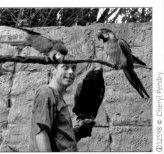
①12598 © Cheryl Pendry
Birds at Flights of Wonder

①10869 © Gina Pesca
This bird flew right overhead!

More at ① expedition everest

Charting the Attractions at Asia

Planning

Getting There

Staying in Style

Touring

Feasting

Making Magic

Index

Notes & More

☐ Kali River Rapids [F-2]   FP ♪ A-OK!   8 8 8

Jennifer Dave Readers

Drift through jungle mists, unexpected geysers, and smoking devastation on a somewhat daring ride in a 12-person raft. The roaring rapids boast one thrilling (albeit tame) drop. Just when you think it's all over, Disney tosses in one last little surprise. You will get wet—possibly damp, more likely soaked—and there's no way to predict (or control) how much. A small storage area is available on board, but it won't keep things very dry. Some guests wisely bring a poncho and a dry change of clothing—plastic ponchos are available for sale nearby. Shoes/sandals must be worn at all times. Long lines are common, but they snake through fascinating Asian architecture rich with fine detail. 38"/97 cm height restriction. Special effects may be too intense for some children and adults. Health warning. Must transfer from wheelchair to ride. **Allie's Kid Tip:** "If you go backward on the drop, be prepared to get soaked." **Tween Tip:** "It's good when it's really hot out!"

Raft Ride
E-Ticket
Ages 7 & up
Med. drop, flames, geysers, and you will get wet!
FASTPASS or long waits
5 min. cruise

Rafters getting squirted on Kali River Rapids

①4184 © Melissa Hasbrouck

☐ Maharajah Jungle Trek [E-1]   A-OK!   6 8 7

Walk a winding path through ancient ruins in a lush Asian setting. Tigers, tapir, fruit bats, deer, antelope, a Komodo dragon, and a walk-through aviary filled with tropical birds highlight this beautifully designed zoo. Artfully hidden barriers make you feel like you can reach out and touch the animals, but fortunately for them (and us) you can't. Cast members are on hand to enrich your animal-viewing adventure. We think the tigers, aviary, and bats are the highlights, but you'll find your own favorites. Be sure to pick up a guidemap on your way in. Animal lovers may be tempted to spend hours here—bring your camera! Wheelchair accessible.

Walk-thru
D-Ticket
All ages
Live animals, birds overhead
Short waits
Allow at least 30 minutes

Allie's Kid Tip: "Tigers! How many can you find?"

Tiger seen on the jungle trek

②2925 © Cheryl Pendry

Birdhouse

①14600 © Janet Simonsen

Planning
Getting There
Staying in Style
Touring
Feasting
Making Magic
Index
Notes & More

Charting the Attractions at DinoLand U.S.A.

Jennifer Dave Readers

The Boneyard [F-5] — A-OK! — 7 5 6

Kids can climb, slide, crawl, scamper, excavate, and explore to their hearts' content in a funky dinosaur dig. Parents are welcome, too. One of the places at Disney's Animal Kingdom with a water spray for hot days. Keep an eye on your young ones! Bring a towel and dry clothes. Wheelchair accessible. **Alex's Toddler Tip:** ☺ **Allie's Kid Tip:** "You can get wet here if you are hot. I love this place!"

Playground
B-Ticket
Ages 1 & up
Allow
30 min.

Dinosaur [E-7] — FP 🚹 A-OK! — 7 7 8

Intrepid riders are sent back through time to fetch a dinosaur before the dinos (and the riders) become extinct. Be prepared to be bounced, jostled, and scared as your Time Rover vehicle hurtles into the past and races through a dark forest. The "pre-show" and science exhibits in the indoor queue areas make the wait interesting. Front row "outside" seats for maximum thrills, inside seats for the less bold. No flash photography. 40"/102 cm height restriction. Young children should be accompanied by an adult. Effects may be too intense for some. Health warning. Must transfer from wheelchair to ride. Closed captioning (pre-show). **Allie's Kid Tip:** "Cover your eyes in the dark parts if you're scared. Ask your grown-ups to tell you when a dinosaur shows up so you can look."

Thrill Ride
E-Ticket
Ages 7 & up
Dark, loud, very scary, rough and bumpy ride
FASTPASS or long waits
3.5 min. ride

"Finding Nemo—The Musical" [G-5] — A-OK! — 7 8 8

The "Finding Nemo" themed stage show features original songs by a Tony Award-winning composer and the theatrical puppetry of the same artist who did the puppets for the Broadway version of "The Lion King." Joining the show are acrobats, dancers, and animated backgrounds. The covered, air-conditioned theater opens 20 minutes before show time. No external video lights. Uncovered outdoor queue. Wheelchair accessible. Assistive listening. **Alex's Toddler Tip:** ☺ **Allie's Kid Tip:** "Cool puppets!"

Live Show
E-Ticket
Ages 4 & up
30 min. show

Primeval Whirl [F-6] — FP 🚹 A-OK! — 7 7 8

Chester and Hester cooked up a dizzy bit of fun for Primeval Whirl, a totally whacky wild mouse coaster (with style). Your round "time machine" car spins as it goes around tight curves, over mild drops, and even through the jaws of a dinosaur. (What else?) Two identical coasters each boast 13 spinning, four-person ride vehicles. 48"/122 cm height restriction. Health warning. Must transfer from wheelchair to ride. **Alex's Kid Tip:** "This is a crazy ride! It goes so fast!"

Coaster
D-Ticket
Ages 7 & up
Fast, drops
FASTPASS
2.5 min. ride

TriceraTop Spin [F-6] — A-OK! — 5 5 7

Dumbo morphs into a Dino! Sixteen dinosaur-shaped, four-rider cars swoop around a huge, spinning toy top. Part of Chester & Hester's Dino-Rama! (see below). Must transfer from ECV to wheelchair to ride. **Alex's Toddler Tip:** ☺ **Allie's Kid Tip:** "Sit in the front and make the dinosaur tilt forward or backward."

Ride
C-Ticket
Ages 2 & up
1.5 min. ride

⚠ Chester & Hester's Dino-Rama!

Chester & Hester, the operators of DinoLand's crazy roadside-style gift shop, have created a roadside "carnival" with two attractions and about a half-dozen games of skill or chance. Play midway games for $2 a pop and maybe win a prize. Games include Mammoth Marathon, Bronto-Score, and Fossil Fueler.

Typhoon Lagoon Water Park

Typhoon Lagoon is a 56-acre water park with lush foliage, lazy rivers, roaring waterfalls, and a huge surfing "lagoon." The water park is located near Downtown Disney West Side.

Legend has it that this was once the Placid Palms Resort in Safen Sound, Florida, a **tropical hideaway** nestled on a sparkling lagoon. Disaster struck when a typhoon raged through the sleepy resort, flooding the lagoon and tossing ships about. In its wake, they discovered sharks in the harbor, a surfboard through a tree, and ships scattered everywhere. Most amazing was the Miss Tilly shrimp boat, impaled on a craggy mountain (Mt. Mayday) that kept trying to dislodge the boat with a huge plume of water. Water was everywhere, forming waterfalls, rapids, pools, and surf. In true Disney form, misfortune was turned into luck and the Typhoon Lagoon water park was born. Or so the story goes.

The park's attractions are arrayed around its focal point, the gigantic, 2½-acre **wave pool** at the foot of Mt. Mayday. The "mountain" offers the advantage of height to several tube and body slides that slither down it. Around the perimeter of the park is a "lazy river" called Castaway Creek, offering a relaxing retreat to swimmers drifting lazily along in inner tubes. Finding your way around the park can be confusing at first—the dense foliage and meandering paths recreate the tropical look quite convincingly. Just keep in mind that one path encircles the park, and you can see Miss Tilly perched atop Mt. Mayday from almost everywhere. This park is worth exploring, too— the lush Mountain Trail on Mt. Mayday presents photo opportunities, and many hidden groves and glens offer quiet getaways.

Leaning Palms is the largest of the cafes, offering combo meals with a bacon double cheeseburger ($8.79), chili dogs ($7.49), chicken nuggets ($8.19), pepperoni pizza ($7.29), Caesar salad ($8.19), and ice cream ($3.59). A kids' meal is $6.99 and includes your choice of a cheese pizza, hot dog, or turkey sandwich, plus chips, drink, and a sand pail. **Happy Landings** has ice cream and a fun water play area where you can take aim at the guests drifting by on Castaway Creek. **Typhoon Tilly's Galley & Grog** has fish & chips, snacks, ice cream, and beverages. **Let's Go Slurpin'** offers alcoholic drinks and snacks. **Low Tide Lou's** (seasonal) has sandwiches. **Surf Doggies** offers hot dogs and turkey legs. Look for a cart selling yummy donut holes, too! Three **picnic areas** have shade and tables.

Side tabs: Planning | Getting There | Staying in Style | Touring | Feasting | Making Magic | Index | Notes & More

AMBIENCE | PARK LAYOUT | EATING

Charting the Attractions at Typhoon Lagoon

Jennifer Dave Readers

Typhoon Lagoon Surf Pool [C-4] — A-OK! | 8 | 8 | 9 |

Waves in the world's largest inland wave pool at the base of Mt. Mayday change every half-hour, alternating between gentle bobs and 6-foot waves. Kids enjoy the two Bay Slides to the far left and the small tidal pools near the front. Observe the waves before entering. **Allie's Kid Tip:** "Don't scrape yourself on the bottom."

Pool / E-Ticket / Surfing waves scary to kids

Crush 'N' Gusher [E-5] — | 6 | 7 | 8 |

This "water roller coaster" has jets of water pushing you up hill, followed by short drops. Three slides: Pineapple Plunger and Coconut Crusher (1–3 riders), Banana Blaster (1–2 riders). 48"/122 cm restriction. Transfer from wheelchair/ECV.

Tube Slide / E-Ticket / Ages 7 & up

Castaway Creek [Entry points: A-3, A-4, D-2, D-3, D-5] — A-OK! | 9 | 8 | 8 |

Relax on a half-mile, 20-minute circuit around the park on inner tubes. Catch a free tube at one of five entrances. Note where you entered, too! **Allie's Kid Tip:** "This is nice and relaxing. Little kids will like the yellow inner tubes the best."

Pool / D-Ticket / Ages 3 & up

Ketchakiddee Creek [A-2] — | 6 | 6 | 7 |

Several fountains, two body slides, and a 30-sec. tube ride—just for little squirts (48"/122 cm or under). Shady, thatched-roof shelters. **Alex's Toddler Tip:** ☺

Playground / B-Ticket

Keelhaul Falls [B-1] — A-OK! | 6 | 7 | 7 |

A slow, solo tube ride with a surprise! (Warning—ride spoilers ahead.) Rafters plunge unexpectedly into a pitch-black tunnel about half the way down. **Allie's Kid Tip:** "The waterfall is fun! You don't get as wet as you think you will."

Tube Slide / C-Ticket / Ages 7 & up

Mayday Falls [B-1] — A-OK! | 5 | 6 | 7 |

Like Keelhaul Falls, this tube ride is solo. Unlike it, Mayday Falls is fast, twisting and turning through caves and waterfalls. **Allie's Kid Tip:** "This is very bumpy!"

Tube Slide / C-Ticket

Gang Plank Falls [B-1] — A-OK! | 8 | 6 | 6 |

Bring the family on this three- to five-person raft ride down the mountain. Watch out for waterfalls and those twisty-turny rafts! **Allie's Kid Tip:** "This is fun! Hold on tight because you go a little fast, but that's no problem."

Raft Slide / C-Ticket / Ages 4 & up

Humunga Kowabunga [C-1] — | 1 | 5 | 7 |

This is the ultimate thrill slide, shooting sliders down one of two slides in less than 10 seconds. Viewing bleachers at the bottom. 48"/122 cm height requirement. Health requirement. Ages 9 & up. **Allie's Kid Tip:** "It gave me a wedgie."

Body Slide / E-Ticket / Fast, steep

Storm Slides [D-1] — | 5 | 6 | 7 |

Three body slides (Stern Burner, Jib Jammer, and Rudder Buster) corkscrew through waterfalls and caves. Viewing bleachers at the bottom. Ages 8 & up.

Body Slides / E-Ticket

Shark Reef [E-1] — A-OK! | 9 | 8 | 8 |

Line up at Hammerhead Fred's Dive Shop for your snorkel (no charge), shower, 5-minute lesson, then snorkel across the small, chilly, saltwater lagoon. You may see a variety of fish, including three kinds of passive sharks. Bring an underwater camera. Scuba-assisted snorkel (extra fee). **Allie's Kid Tip:** "I love the sharks!"

Pool / E-Ticket / Ages 6 & up / Cold, salty

Making the Most of Typhoon Lagoon

A **refillable mug** ($9.99) uses barcode scanners so you can refill without cast supervision. Buy a new barcode ($5) on future visits.

Avoid **two-piece suits** on slides— they may come down the slide at a different speed than you. Also, swimsuits with rivets, buckles, or exposed metal are not permitted. Wear water shoes—the sand and pavement can get quite hot.

Ⓓ6950 © Alison Hinsley

A reader has fun at Castaway Creek

Want to go premium? Rent one of the **premium spaces**. The four spaces at Typhoon Lagoon are known as the "Beachcomber Shacks." Cost is $250 plus tax per day for up to six guests. Services include a personal attendant, private lockers, drink mugs, bottled water, lounge furniture, and towels. Available on a first come, first serve basis. Want something less pricey? You can rent "premium chairs" for $40 plus tax—this gets you two beach chairs, an umbrella, small table, and two towels.

Get your first taste of **scuba** in a special section of the Shark Reef. Cost is $20 for the first 30 min. and $15 for the rest of your party or for repeat dives. Pay at the booth near the dive shop.

You can rent lockers ($13-$15, with a $5 deposit) and towels ($2 each). Bring hotel towels rather than rent them—they're close to the same size. Changing rooms are also available. Life vests are free (refundable deposit). Some personal flotation devices may be permitted.

Park hours: generally open by 10:00 am, closed at 5:00 pm or later. A one-day pass (with tax) is $55.38/adults and $46.86/kids 3-9.

Ratings are explained on page 126.

Our Value Ratings:		Our Magic Ratings:		Readers' Ratings:
Quality:	7/10	Theme:	8/10	76% fell in love with it
Variety:	8/10	Excitement:	7/10	21% liked it well enough
Scope:	3/10	Fun Factor:	7/10	3% had mixed feelings
Overall Value:	**6/10**	**Overall Magic:**	**7/10**	0% were disappointed

Typhoon Lagoon is enjoyed by...	(rated by both authors and readers)	
Younger Kids: ♥♥♥♥	Young Adults: ♥♥♥♥♥	Families: ♥♥♥♥
Older Kids: ♥♥♥♥♥	Mid Adults: ♥♥♥	Couples: ♥♥♥
Teenagers: ♥♥♥♥♥	Mature Adults: ♥♥♥	Singles: ♥♥♥

Side tabs: TIPS / Planning / Getting There / Staying in Style / Touring / Feasting / NOTES / Making Magic / RATINGS / Index / Notes & More

Planning | Getting There | Staying in Style | Touring | Feasting | Making Magic | Index | Notes & More

TYPHOON LAGOON PARK MAP

Finding Your Way at Typhoon Lagoon

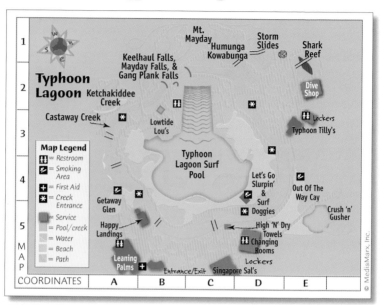

Map Legend
- = Restroom
- = Smoking Area
- = First Aid
- = Creek Entrance
- = Service
- = Pool/creek
- = Water
- = Beach
- = Path

Mt. Mayday, Humunga Kowabunga, Storm Slides, Shark Reef, Keelhaul Falls, Mayday Falls, & Gang Plank Falls, Typhoon Lagoon, Ketchakiddee Creek, Dive Shop, Castaway Creek, Lowtide Lou's, Lockers, Typhoon Tilly's, Typhoon Lagoon Surf Pool, Let's Go Slurpin' & Surf Doggies, Out Of The Way Cay, Getaway Glen, Crush 'n' Gusher, Happy Landings, High 'N' Dry Towels, Changing Rooms, Lockers, Leaning Palms, Entrance/Exit, Singapore Sal's

© MediaMarx, Inc.

MAP COORDINATES | A | B | C | D | E

BEST TIMES

Typhoon Lagoon is very popular during the **hot months** and gets crowded fast—arrive early, as gates close when the park reaches capacity. It's also wise to stake out your beach chairs early as the good ones are grabbed quickly. We prefer to visit when it's a bit **cooler** as crowds are lighter and the water is heated. The park closes for part of the year (usually November and December)—call 407-560-4141. If this park's closed, Blizzard Beach will be open. Beyond that, **weekdays** are better than weekends (locals love to visit the park). Visit in the **late afternoon** when the park empties a bit and the sun is less intense. The park may **close during storms**—when it reopens, it may be nearly empty. If you arrive when there are long lines, bypass them by getting your tickets at the Automated Ticket Vending Machines available here.

GETTING THERE

By Bus—All Disney resorts have direct buses to Typhoon Lagoon. From Magic Kingdom, Epcot, Disney's Hollywood Studios, and Disney's Animal Kingdom, take a bus or monorail to a nearby resort and transfer to a Typhoon Lagoon bus (which may also be the Downtown Disney bus). Allow about 30-60 minutes if you travel by bus.
By Car—Take exit 67 off I-4, take the first exit and turn right on Buena Vista Dr.—the park is on the right. From Downtown Disney, turn right to Buena Vista Dr. and the park is on the left. Free parking.

Top Photo Slice: Swimmers enjoy the huge surf pool at Typhoon Lagoon (①12219) © Cheryl Pendry

Blizzard Beach Water Park

Is it a water park, or a ski resort? The Blizzard Beach water park brings the chills and thrills of a Colorado winter to the warm Florida sun. Ski jumps, toboggan rides, and slalom runs zip you past snow that never melts in Disney's most action-oriented water park.

Disney's Imagineers scattered magic white stuff over the rocks and pines of towering Mount Gushmore to create a water park that'll make you shiver on the hottest August day. Oh, don't worry, the water is always a warm 80 degrees, but just a look at some of those water slides can freeze your insides. Luckily, Disney never abandons the idea of family fun—even the meekest snow bunny will have a ball!

Before you "hit the slopes" you'll discover the park's **"base lodge"** facilities—the major food, merchandise, and locker room areas. Then, as you face the mountain, the Tike's Peak children's area will be to your right. Straight ahead are two bridges over Cross Country Creek, the drift-along tube ride that encircles the mountain and most of the fun. Additional lockers can be found close to the action, near Downhill Double Dipper on the left and Ski Patrol on the right. Of course, Mount Gushmore dominates the park in every way. Its slopes are home to nearly two dozen lanes of slides and flumes. Most slides can be seen from the Lodge area, but Runoff Rapids is tucked away on the back slope of the mountain. You can also watch your daredevils in comfort, from shaded grandstands at the bottom of many slides. Three footpaths and a chairlift scale the 90-foot (9-story) mountain. After your first ascent on foot in the hot, Florida sunshine, you'll know why folks wait patiently for the chairlift, which takes you to the top in the comfort of a three-person, umbrella-shaded chair (32"/81 cm height restriction; under 48"/122 cm must be with an adult).

Water park meals are never fancy, which is fine when you're only wearing a swimsuit. **Lottawatta Lodge** serves up a bacon double cheeseburger combos ($8.79), chili dogs ($7.49), chicken wraps ($8.99), Caesar salads ($8.19), fresh fruit cup ($3.99), and kosher selections. A kid's meal is $6.99 with a choice of cheese pizza, hot dog, or turkey sandwich, plus chips, drink, and a sandpail. **Avalunch** and **The Warming Hut** offer hot dogs, sandwiches, ice cream, and usually close before dinnertime. The thirsty line up at **Frostbite Freddie's Frozen Freshments**, **Polar Pub**, and **The Cooling Hut**. There are also **picnic areas**.

AMBIENCE

ATTRACTIONS

EATING

Top Photo Slice: The "ski jump" atop Mount Gushmore at Blizzard Beach (⓪6244) © Cheryl Pendry

Charting the Attractions at Blizzard Beach

	Jennifer	Dave	Readers

Summit Plummet [D-2]   👤I | 2 | 5 | 9 |

Only the boldest ride the world's highest body slide, which drops 120 feet. Go feet first, cross your arms, and it's over in eight seconds. Be prepared for a steep drop and a wedgie! 48"/122 cm height requirement. Health requirement.

Body Slide / E-Ticket / Ages 9 & up

Slush Gusher [D-2]   👤I | 3 | 6 | 8 |

Ninety-foot-high double-bump slide is the second-tallest body slide in the park. One-piece suits recommended! 48"/122 cm height requirement. Ages 8 & up.

Body Slide / D-Ticket

Downhill Double Dipper [C-2]   👤I | 5 | 7 | 8 |

Race head-to-head on a half-enclosed innertube slide. Your race results are flashed on a scoreboard. 48"/122 cm height requirement. Ages 8 & up.

Tube Slide / D-Ticket

Snow Stormers [C-2]   A-OK! | 7 | 5 | 8 |

Zig and zag your way down this three-flume, family-friendly slalom mat slide. 12-second ride. **Allie's Kid Tip:** *"Fun, but it's a little bumpy." Ages 6 & up.*

Mat Slide / C-Ticket

Toboggan Racers [D-3]   A-OK! | 6 | 5 | 7 |

On your mark, get set, go! Race headfirst down an eight-lane mat slide. 10-second ride. **Allie's Kid Tip:** *"Push yourself off to go down." Ages 6 & up.*

Mat Slide / D-Ticket

Teamboat Springs [E-3]   A-OK! | 9 | 8 | 9 |

Whitewater-loving families can pack up to six in a large, round, river raft for a long, twisting ride—at 1,400 feet it is the longest ride of its kind anywhere. **Allie's Kid Tip:** *"Hold on to the bottom of the raft when you go down."*

Raft Slide / D-Ticket / Ages 4 up

Runoff Rapids [D-2] | 8 | 7 | 7 |

Ride a tube down this twisty, turny, family-friendly course. Three different open and enclosed slides. Up to two can share a tube on the open slides. **Allie's Kid Tip:** *"Pick up your behind over the bumps, or it won't feel good."*

Tube Slide / C-Ticket / Ages 6 & up

Cross Country Creek [Entry points: B-4, A-4, B-2, C-1, E-3, D-4]   A-OK! | 8 | 7 | 7 |

Float around the park on a moderately flowing creek. Enter and exit at any of six spots around the park. Return to your starting point in 20 minutes. **Allie's Kid Tip:** *"Don't get wet under the freezing waterfalls."*

Pool / D-Ticket / Ages 2 & up

Melt Away Bay [B-3]   A-OK! | 7 | 6 | 7 |

Bob in the sedate waves of a one-acre wave pool. Kids under 10 must be with an adult. **Allie's Kid Tip:** *"The tide pools are cool to play in!" All ages.*

Pool / C-Ticket

Ski Patrol Training Camp [D-3]   A-OK! | 8 | 7 | 7 |

Scaled-down area for kids 12 and under. Try Snow Falls slide, Cool Runners tube slalom, and Thin Ice Training Course—a walk across a field of "ice floes." **Allie's Kid Tip:** *"If an iceberg is far away, lean back to move toward it."*

Playground / D-Ticket / Ages 6-12

Tike's Peak [D-5]   👤I | 6 | 5 | 7 |

Even the littlest ones have a mini version of the park, with slides, wading pools, and fountains. Must be 48"/122 cm or shorter. Ages 0-6. **Alex's Toddler Tip:** ☺

Playground / C-Ticket

Top Photo Slice: Ski Patrol Training Camp at Blizzard Beach (Ⓟ6269) © Cheryl Pendry

Making the Most of Blizzard Beach

Save time—buy park passes at Guest Relations or Lobby Concierge.

There's **little shade** here—use waterproof sunscreen and cover-ups! Wear water shoes to ward off the heat of the sand and sidewalks.

Play **miniature golf** at Winter Summerland, adjacent to the water park. See page 214 for more on this imaginative mini golf course.

Pick up a **map** on your way in to locate the lockers ($13–$15) and towels ($2). Life jackets are free if you leave an ID and/or deposit.

Rent "**Polar Patios**" premium spaces here—see page 199.

You'll find **chaise lounges** wherever you go, but on busy days, follow the path around the back end of the mountain where you'll find secluded lounging areas and the main entrance to Runoff Rapids.

This is the "**big thrill**" water park, so it draws a young crowd. Typhoon Lagoon is a better choice for families.

If you ride the big slides, bikinis are a very risky fashion statement. You'll have better luck with a **one-piece suit**. Also, swimsuits with rivets, buckles, or exposed metal are not permitted.

The **Beach Haus** near the entrance sells just about anything you may have forgotten or lost, from sunscreen to swimsuits.

When the **summer weather** is at its hottest, the parking lots fill up early. Use Disney buses instead, which can always drive in.

Park hours: generally open by 10:00 am, closed at 5:00 pm or later. A one-day pass (with tax) is $55.38/adults and $46.86/kids 3–9.

Ratings are explained on page 126.

Our Value Ratings:		Our Magic Ratings:		Readers' Ratings:
Quality:	7/10	Theme:	8/10	94% fell in love with it
Variety:	8/10	Excitement:	8/10	2% liked it well enough
Scope:	4/10	Fun Factor:	7/10	2% had mixed feelings
Overall Value:	**6/10**	**Overall Magic:**	**8/10**	2% were disappointed

Blizzard Beach is enjoyed by...	(rated by both authors and readers)	
Younger Kids: ♥♥♥♥	Young Adults: ♥♥♥♥♥	Families: ♥♥♥♥♥
Older Kids: ♥♥♥♥♥	Mid Adults: ♥♥♥	Couples: ♥♥♥
Teenagers: ♥♥♥♥♥	Mature Adults: ♥	Singles: ♥♥♥♥

TIPS

NOTES

RATINGS

Planning

Getting There

Staying in Style

Touring

Feasting

Making Magic

Index

Notes & More

Finding Your Way at Blizzard Beach

BLIZZARD BEACH PARK MAP

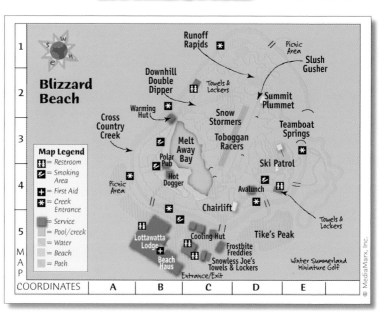

Map Legend
- 🚻 Restroom
- ♺ Smoking Area
- ➕ First Aid
- ✳ Creek Entrance
- Service
- Pool/creek
- Water
- Beach
- Path

BEST TIMES

Thanks to the heated waters, you'll be comfortable throughout the **cooler months**, and the sun is kinder. The crowds are thinner, but the days are shorter, and an overcast, rainy winter day can make life miserable. Note that the park may be closed on Fridays and Saturdays in the cooler months. Summer at Blizzard Beach brings **huge crowds** that arrive early in the day. If the park reaches capacity, the gates close to all. By **mid-afternoon**, the crowds have thinned, as those who are worst-wilted have packed it in. That's a good time to arrive, refreshing yourself after a long morning at nearby Disney's Animal Kingdom. Operating hours vary with the season, so check before you trek. Expect the park to be closed in early 2013 for its annual rehab (Typhoon Lagoon will be open).

GETTING THERE

By Bus—All resorts and Disney's Animal Kingdom have direct buses to Blizzard Beach. From Disney's Hollywood Studios, take the Coronado Springs bus. From Epcot, take the Disney's Animal Kingdom Lodge bus. From the Magic Kingdom and Downtown Disney, take a bus or monorail to a Disney resort and board a bus to Blizzard Beach. We recommend you take Disney transportation when you can, because the parking lot can fill up on busy days.
By Car—From westbound or eastbound I-4, take exit 65 (west on Osceola Parkway), exiting at Buena Vista Drive. Free parking.

Downtown Disney

If "heading downtown" is your idea of rest and recreation, the Walt Disney World Resort's Downtown Disney district is a major treat. From the world's largest Disney Store to mind-boggling Lego sculptures, super dining, and thrilling entertainment, you'll have a ball Downtown.

Downtown Disney has three unique **districts**. The **Marketplace** is a charming village of shops, **Pleasure Island** (its announced re-theming is now on hold) features shopping and dining (the clubs closed in 2008), and the **West Side** is the urban-style shopping, dining, and fun capital of the "World." Downtown Disney's pedestrian-only streets and sprawling layout avoid the "mall" feeling completely.

Downtown Disney satisfies the urge to "shop 'til you drop." There's no admission charge here, and you'll find much more than Disney merchandise. The **Marketplace** shops are the Design-a-Tee shop, The Art of Disney, Basin (bath products), Disney's Days of Christmas, Eurospain/Arribas Brothers (crystal shop), Goofy's Candy Co., Once Upon a Toy, Design-A-Tee (make your own t-shirts), Tren-D (latest fashions), Disney's Pin Traders, Lego Imagination Center, LittleMissMatched, Team Mickey's Athletic Club/Rawlins Making the Game, RideMakerz, the World of Disney (and its Bibbidi Bobbidi Boutique for little kids), Mickey's Mart (everything under $10), and Mickey's Pantry. **West Side** and **Pleasure Island** shopping feature the new Splitsville ("bowling, dining, music, nightlife"), Sunglass Icon, Disney's Candy Cauldron, DisneyQuest Emporium, Pop Gallery, Hoypoloi (sculpture gallery), Magnetron (magnets), Mickey's Groove (funky Disney gifts), Harley Davidson, Curl by Sammy Duvall, Planet Hollywood, Sosa Family Cigars, Starabilias (collectibles), Wetzel's Pretzels, and shops at House of Blues, Cirque du Soleil, and DisneyQuest. Magic Masters offers top-flight magic gear, demos, and even a hidden room. Packages can be delivered to your Disney resort!

Downtown Disney builds fun into nearly every shop and restaurant, but four spots put entertainment first. The **Characters in Flight by Aerophile** attraction is a tethered observation balloon that lifts riders up to 400 feet in the air—cost is $18/adult and $12/child age 3-9. Movie fans flock to the **AMC 24 Theatres Complex**, the Southeast's largest—their theaters sport stadium seating and new dining options and full bars in some theatres—tickets are $13/adults, $8/seniors, $10/students and kids ages 2-12. The innovative **Cirque du Soleil** also makes its home Downtown—see page 208. **DisneyQuest**, Disney's indoor "theme park," is detailed on pages 209-212.

Planning | **Getting There** | **Staying in Style** | **Touring** | **Feasting** | **Making Magic** | **Index** | **Notes & More**

Finding Your Way at Downtown Disney

DOWNTOWN DISNEY MAP

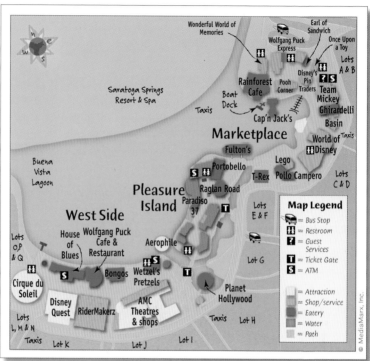

DINING

With the exception of Epcot, you won't find a more **diverse array** of dining in the "World" than at Downtown Disney. For a heaping serving of showbiz, head to Downtown Disney West Side. The House of Blues serves up fabulous live music, Wolfgang Puck Grand Cafe offers famously innovative California fare, and Bongos Cuban Cafe has sizzling Latin rhythm and foods. Downtown Disney's showplace is the famous Planet Hollywood, which drips with movie memorabilia. Fulton's Crab House serves upscale seafood on a riverboat, Cap'n Jack's Restaurant does seafood and steaks, the Rainforest Cafe cooks up imaginative fare, and T-Rex offers big portions alongside big dinos. On Pleasure Island, Portobello offers Northern Italian food, Raglan Road (Irish pub) and Cookes of Dublin offer authentic Emerald Isle fare, and Paradiso 37 features Mexican and South American cuisine. Busy shoppers like the lighter fare at The Earl of Sandwich, Wetzel's Pretzels, Wolfgang Puck Express, Ghirardelli Soda Fountain & Chocolate Shop, and Pollo Campero (fast food chicken) that replaced Ronald's Fun House (McDonald's). Complete descriptions of these eateries begin on page 248.

Making the Most of Downtown Disney

The World of Disney Store houses the popular **Bibbidi Bobbidi Boutique salon**, which offers hair styling and makeover services for both young girls ($55–$190) and boys ($16), ages 3–12. Appointments recommended (407-WDW-STYLE). Tip: Another location is inside Cinderella Castle—see page 134.

Kids can **play for free** at the Lego Imagination Center and in the water play fountain near the Marketplace bus stop entrance.

Little-known **discounts and specials** may be available. Be sure to ask! For example, movies at the AMC Pleasure Island 24 are just $6.00 before noon on weekdays.

Look for the **"Celebrate Tonight!" street party** in the West End Plaza of Pleasure Island. The nightly event features a DJ, dancers, and stilt walkers from 5:00–11:00 pm, Sunday through Thursday and 6:00 pm–midnight Friday and Saturday.

Every November, the **Festival of the Masters** at Downtown Disney offers art exhibits, food, performances, and kids' activities.

Christmas brings fun activities. There's also a year-round toy train ride (for a fee). Don't forget Disney's Days of Christmas shop, too.

Of the eateries here, only Cap'n Jack's is Disney-run, so **reservations policies** differ, although many offer reservations through Disney. Most eateries and shops let you charge to your Disney resort tab.

The Downtown Disney Marketplace and Pleasure Island **parking lots** are often packed. Try the huge West Side parking lot instead.

Most **shops** in the Marketplace open at 9:30 am, while West Side shops open at 10:30 am. Closing is at 11:00 pm, with seasonal variations.

For **more details**, call Downtown Disney at 407-828-3058.

By Bus—Buses are available from every Disney resort. From the parks, bus or monorail to a nearby resort and transfer.
By Car—From I-4, take exit 67, then take the first exit and turn right on Buena Vista Drive. Parking is free.
By Boat—Boats may shuttle between the Marketplace and West Side seasonally. Resort guests at Port Orleans, Old Key West, and Saratoga Springs can take a boat to the Marketplace, too.
By Foot—Guests at Saratoga Springs and Hotel Plaza Resorts may walk.

TIPS

NOTES

GETTING THERE

Planning

Getting There

Staying in Style

Touring

Feasting

Making Magic

Index

Notes & More

Cirque du Soleil

A circus has come to Walt Disney World, the likes of which you've probably never seen—magical, musical, a little mystical, and poetically graceful. Cirque du Soleil ("Circus of the Sun") from Montreal, Canada, has redefined the concept of "circus" for millions around the world and has a company-in-residence at Downtown Disney West Side.

SHOWS

Cirque du Soleil weaves its magic with acrobats, clowns, jugglers, dancers, aerialists, lights, original music, and fabulous costumes (and not one animal). The long-running show, **La Nouba** (from the French "to live it up"), weaves a continuous, dream-like thread. There's a story here, but many guests hardly notice or care. This isn't Big Top-style circus, either. It has as much in common with modern dance as it does with circus. It's not for everyone (Dave likes it, Jennifer doesn't), but it adds yet another dimension to the magic. Note that this 90-minute show has no intermission.

INFO

Housed in its own **1,671-seat theater** at the west end of the West Side, Cirque du Soleil offers its shows at 6:00 and 9:00 pm, Tues.–Sat. Tickets are $75–$146/adults and $60–$119/kids ages 3–9 depending on category—see chart below. If you are a DVC member or a Florida resident, inquire about possible discounts. Call 407-939-7600 or visit http://www.lanouba.com to reserve up to six months in advance or visit the box office. Seats within categories are assigned based on availability, but you might get your pick at the box office.

SEATING PLAN

Top Photo Slice: Cirque du Soleil building in Downtown Disney © MediaMarx, Inc.

More at ⓘ cirque-du-soleil

Planning · Getting There · Staying in Style · Touring · Feasting · Making Magic · Index · Notes & More

DisneyQuest

DisneyQuest is an indoor "theme park" housed in a big, blue, five-story building at Downtown Disney West Side. It features ride simulators, high-tech games, and hands-on activities for young and old alike.

Attractions run the gamut from simple video arcade games to a you-design-it, you-ride-it roller coaster simulator. Take the "Cyberlator" elevator to the Ventureport, where you can enter four zones: **Explore Zone**, **Score Zone**, **Create Zone**, and **Replay Zone**. Each zone organizes the attractions (described below) by theme. Each zone spans at least two floors, with various stairs and walkways linking them. This makes for a bewildering maze—study our map on page 212 to orient yourself before you go.

LAYOUT

Aladdin's Magic Carpet Ride [Floor 2] A-Ok!	6 4 6
Don virtual reality goggles for a wild, 4-min. ride on Aladdin's magic carpet. Swoop through Agrabah and the Cave of Wonder to search for jewels and free the Genie. Motion sickness warning. Explore Zone. Allie's Kid Tip: "Make sure your helmet is on tight so it doesn't fall off when you play."	**Virtual** D-Ticket Ages 6 & up Dizziness

Animation Academy [Floor 2] A-Ok!	7 7 6
Take your seat at a computer workstation as an instructor draws out your artistry. Hands-on lessons in drawing and/or animating characters. Several 20-minute lessons are offered. After the class, you can buy your creation. Create Zone. Allie's Kid Tip: "Check the schedule for a class that draws a character you like."	**Hands-on** D-Ticket Ages 6 & up Skill helps

Buzz Lightyear's Astroblasters [Floor 3] 🛝	7 5 7
Ride fully enclosed two-person bumper cars mounted with "cannons" that shoot large rubber balls. The driver pilots to scoop up ammo, and the gunner fires on other cars to make them spin out of control. 3-min. game. 51"/130 cm height restriction. Replay Zone. Allie's Kid Tip: "Try to hit a lot of cars so they spin around."	**Vehicles** D-Ticket Ages 9 & up Bumpy

CyberSpace Mountain [Floor 2] 🛝	9 8 9
Design and ride your own coaster! Start by choosing a theme and designing the coaster tracks on a computer screen. Then get strapped into a two-person flight simulator to experience your coaster, or choose from a ready-made coaster. Be prepared to be shaken, rattled, and rolled on a ride more dizzying than the real thing. Simulator seats are small. 51"/130 cm height restriction. Create Zone. Allie's Kid Tip: "If you feel sick, just hit the red stop button."	**Simulator** E-Ticket Ages 9 & up Upside-down during inversions

Invasion! An ExtraTERRORestrial Alien Encounter [Floor 5] A-Ok!	6 7 5
Dash across the galaxy to rescue Earth colonists from an invading horde in this simulator ride that borrows characters and fun from the former Magic Kingdom attraction. One teammate pilots the rescue vehicle, while three other teammates keep the bad guys at bay. Great pre-show film. Score Zone. Allie's Kid Tip: "I think kids will have more fun being a gunner than a pilot."	**Simulator** E-Ticket Ages 7 & up Mildly violent theme

Attraction descriptions and ratings are explained on page 127.

Planning | Getting There | Staying in Style | Touring | Feasting | Making Magic | Index | Notes & More

Charting the Attractions at DisneyQuest

☐ **Living Easels** [Floor 2]	A-OK!	5 4 4
Draw animated landscapes on a touch-sensitive screen. You can buy print-outs if you like. Create Zone. **Allie's Kid Tip:** *"Use your imagination!" Ages 3 & up.*	**Hands-on**	
	B-Ticket	

☐ **Midway on the Moon** [Floors 4 and 5]	A-OK!	6 8 5
Disney-themed versions of arcade games like Ursula's Whirlpool and traditional games like Skeeball. All games are free play, but prize redemption is no longer offered. Adults will love the classic games like Pac-Man, Frogger, and Donkey Kong. Replay Zone. **Allie's Kid Tip:** *"Look at all the games before you play."*	**Arcade**	
	A-Ticket	
	Ages 5 & up	

☐ **Mighty Ducks Pinball Slam** [Floor 3]	🧍	5 4 7
Use body motion/weight to move a "puck" around a huge screen and "body check" opponents on this simulator. 3-min. game. 48"/122 cm height restriction. Score Zone. **Allie's Kid Tip:** *"If you're tall enough but skinny, it might not work."*	**Simulator**	
	D-Ticket	
	Ages 9 & up	

☐ **Pirates of the Caribbean: Battle for Buccaneer Gold** [Floor 1]	🧍 A-OK!	8 8 9
Yo ho, yo ho! DisneyQuest's newest attraction pits you and up to four shipmates in a 3-D simulated sea battle in quest of pirate gold. Fire virtual cannonballs against your foes, and feel the deck shudder when you take a hit. 35"/89 cm height restriction. Explore Zone. **Allie's Kid Tip:** *"Shoot the ships that you pass!"*	**Simulator**	
	E-Ticket	
	Ages 7 & up	
	Violent theme	

☐ **Radio Disney SongMaker** [Floor 2]	A-OK!	6 6 4
Create your own hit song in a soundbooth. Combine styles and lyrics for laughs. You can buy a CD of it. Create Zone. **Allie's Kid Tip:** *"Don't be shy." Ages 4 & up.*	**Hands-on**	
	D-Ticket	

☐ **Ride the Comix** [Floors 4 and 5]		2 3 5
Swing your laser sword to battle comic strip villains in this 4-min., 3-D virtual reality game. Heavy goggles, sword-play, and motion sickness make this hard to play. Score Zone. **Allie's Kid Tip:** *"The monsters might scare you." Ages 8 & up.*	**Virtual**	
	D-Ticket	
	May feel dizzy	

☐ **Sid's Create-A-Toy** [Floor 2]		3 4 5
Create a demented toy from spare toy parts—on a computer screen. You can buy a real version of your creation. Create Zone. **Allie's Kid Tip:** *"Boring." Ages 4 & up.*	**Hands-on**	
	B-Ticket	

☐ **Virtual Jungle Cruise** [Floor 1]	A-OK!	9 6 6
Board a raft, grab a paddle, and take a 4-min. whitewater river cruise back in time on this motion simulator ride. Dr. Wayne Szalinski guides you and your teammates on this riotous journey over waterfalls and into the age of the dinosaurs. This is the only Jungle Cruise where you can see Walt Disney World's Cinderella Castle and Disneyland's Matterhorn at the same time! You may get a little damp. Explore Zone. **Allie's Kid Tip:** *"Paddle hard."*	**Simulator**	
	E-Ticket	
	Ages 6 & up	
	You must paddle on this ride	

Making the Most of DisneyQuest

DINING

You won't go hungry at DisneyQuest. Disney operates a satisfying **counter-service eatery** called FoodQuest spread over two levels (see page 250). FoodQuest offers an appetizing variety of pizzas, salads, burgers, sandwiches, and wraps, plus tempting desserts. All sorts of luxurious coffee concoctions are available as well. And while you sip your latté, you can browse the Internet on limited-use computer terminals. Note that the Cheesecake Factory no longer operates this eatery.

TIPS

First-time visitors should spend time exploring the entire place before splitting up. While you're at it, choose a **meeting place** and time. FoodQuest is a good choice with places to sit, and the Ventureport on the third floor is highly visible.

Allow about **three to four hours** to tour, more if you love arcades.

Be sure to wear a **wristwatch**—it's easy to lose track of time! Also, it's faster to use the stairs to go up or down one level. On the other hand, the elevators are less disorienting than the curving staircases.

The Wonderland Cafe sports tables with **free Internet access**, but the custom browser makes it tough to surf at will.

NOTES

Best times to visit are during the mornings and afternoons and on the weekends. It gets pretty busy in the evenings, after other parks are closed. Crowds are huge on foul-weather days.

Stop by the **tip board** on floor 3 for wait times and notes.

Discounted admissions may be available in the evening.

Ratings are explained on page 126.

RATINGS

Our Value Ratings:		Our Magic Ratings:		Readers' Ratings:
Quality:	6/10	Theme:	5/10	78% fell in love with it
Variety:	4/10	Excitement:	5/10	22% liked it well enough
Scope:	3/10	Fun Factor:	6/10	0% had mixed feelings
Overall Value:	**4/10**	**Overall Magic:**	**5/10**	0% were disappointed

DisneyQuest is enjoyed by...	(rated by both authors and readers)	
Younger Kids: ♥♥♥♥	Young Adults: ♥♥♥♥♥	Families: ♥♥♥♥
Older Kids: ♥♥♥♥♥	Mid Adults: ♥♥♥	Couples: ♥♥♥
Teenagers: ♥♥♥♥♥	Mature Adults: ♥	Singles: ♥♥♥♥♥

Sidebar (top to bottom): Planning | Getting There | Staying in Style | Touring | Feasting | Making Magic | Index | Notes & More

Planning

Getting There

Staying in Style

Touring

Feasting

Making Magic

Index

Notes & More

DISNEYQUEST MAP

Finding Your Way at DisneyQuest

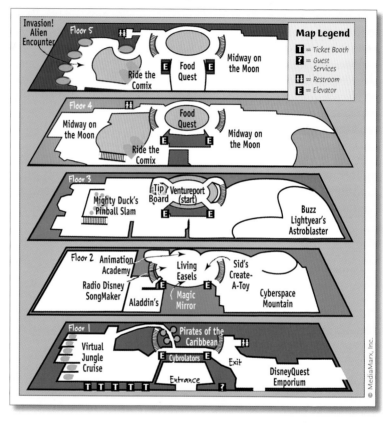

© MediaMarx, Inc.

ADMISSION

In keeping with Disney's approach to park admission, you pay a **single all-day price** and enjoy unlimited use of all rides, games, and activities. Adults pay $46.86 for a full-day admission, and kids ages 3-9 pay $40.47 (prices include tax). Children under 10 must be accompanied by an adult, but feel free to leave the older kids here while you shop elsewhere. Annual passes are available—see page 122. DisneyQuest **admission is included** in Magic Your Way tickets that have Plus options and Premium Annual Passes. DisneyQuest hours are 11:30 am-10:00 pm on Sundays-Thursdays, and 11:30 am-11:00 pm on Fridays and Saturdays (operating hours are subject to change).

INFO

For more DisneyQuest **information**, call 407-828-4600 or visit http://www.disneyquest.com. There is also a DisneyQuest kiosk in Downtown Disney Marketplace that offers information.

Top Photo Slice: Treasure map in the queue for Pirates of the Caribbean: Battle for Buccaneer Gold © Michelle Clark

More at ① disneyquest

Disney Celebrations in 2013

Nothing adds to a vacation like a **reason to celebrate**, and Disney knows this better than most. If you don't have a celebration of your own, Disney has one you can borrow. The 25th anniversary of Walt Disney World in 1996, the Millennium Celebration in 1999/2000, the 100th anniversary of Walt Disney's birth in 2001, and Disneyland's 50th birthday in 2005 all marked company or worldwide milestones. Sometimes, the celebratory focus has shifted to the guests themselves. "The Year of a Million Dreams" (well two years—2007 and 2008) started the trend. Then, "What Will You Celebrate?" promoted the "celebration vacation"—families that celebrate milestones like birthdays and anniversaries at Disney. In other words, your celebration became Disney's celebration. Regardless of focus, celebrations give Disney a chance to dress up its parks and introduce new rides and attractions, and give guests even more reasons to come visit.

In 2013, Disney Parks will present **"Limited Time Magic"** at both Walt Disney World and Disneyland. The idea is to host special events every week of the year. Some of announced festivities are obvious, such as Valentine's Week and Independence Week. (They haven't mentioned a Columbus Week, but you never know!) Of course, it's harder to find a theme for other weeks. "Long Lost Friends Week" (rarely-seen characters will be out to meet and greet, and guests will have a vote in who appears), and "Pirates Week" are among the gap-fillers. They've dedicated a Friday the 13th to the Villains—Disney Hollywood Studios will be open September 13th 'til the 13th hour (1:00 am) for a special dance party. Overall, we like the idea; no matter when you visit Walt Disney World (or Disneyland) during 2013, something special and unique will be happening. Of course, it's just a new wrapper for an old practice. The Disney Parks schedule is already crammed with special, short-term events. Why not weave them together into an all-encompassing theme? Some of these will be single-park events ("Dapper Dans Sing Boy Bands" can only happen on Main St. USA), while others may be resort-wide. Only time will tell.

Special celebrations come and go, but other events are **annual fixtures**, each spreading over many weeks. These include Epcot's Flower and Garden Festival, Epcot's Food and Wine Festival, Star Wars Weekends at Disney's Hollywood Studios, and the Thanksgiving/Christmas holiday season, which now begins about a week after Halloween. Then there are seasonal, after-hours parties—Mickey's Very Merry Christmas Party and Mickey's Not-So-Scary Halloween Party. Want to keep track of Disney's ever-changing lineup of celebrations? Subscribe to PassPorter News at http://www.passporter.com/news.htm.

Planning | Getting There | Staying in Style | Touring | Feasting | Making Magic | Index | Notes & More

More Places to Play

BoardWalk—The BoardWalk resort has its own entertainment complex with clubs, restaurants, and entertainment. Jellyrolls is a dueling piano bar that serves drinks and free popcorn ($10 cover, 21 and up, no smoking allowed). Atlantic Dance Hall serves specialty drinks while open-request DJ music lures you onto the floor (no cover, 21 and up, open Tuesday–Saturday from 9:00 pm to 2:00 am). ESPN Club (page 254) is a popular sports bar. Midway games and street performers add to the fun. For details and directions to the BoardWalk resort, see pages 49–52.

Celebration, Florida—Imagine what would happen if Disney created a real town and you've got the community of Celebration, located just a few miles from the parks. Disney has divested most of its control over the years, but it remains a quaint neighborhood. Visitors may stroll or shop, have a bite in a restaurant, take in a movie at the theater, or stay in the luxury hotel. Others dream of moving to this carefully planned development. For details, call 407-566-2200 or visit http://www.celebrationfl.com.

Golf—The Walt Disney World Resort boasts four championship courses and one nine-hole course, now operated by Arnold Palmer Gold Management, which will be redesigning the Palm course. The Palm will become designated as an Arnold Palmer Signature Course. All courses are open to the public and feature full-service facilities, including driving ranges, pro shops, cafes, and lessons. Walt Disney World resort hotel guests receive a free golf club rental when they purchase another club rental and a round of golf at any of the four golf courses. Disney resort hotel guests also get free transportation to the links for their scheduled tee times. For details and tee times, call 407-WDW-GOLF. Check out at http://www.wdwgolf.com.

Miniature Golf Courses—Disney has miniature golf, too! **Fantasia Gardens**, near the Swan Resort, has two 18-hole courses. One course is based on Disney's classic animated film, "Fantasia." The other is a "grass" course (Fantasia Fairways) with wildly undulating par-three and par-four holes from 40 to 75 feet long. Waits for tee times for this challenging course can be double the wait for the Fantasia course. **Winter Summerland** is a miniature golf park at Blizzard Beach with two 18-hole courses—one is blanketed in "snow," and the other celebrates the holidays in the tropics. Both are fun, and neither is very difficult. Tip: Ask about the "secret hole of the day" after you play at either course—if you get a hole-in-one in the secret hole, you may get a surprise. Cost with tax is $12.52 for adults and $10.39 for kids ages 3–9 (second round is half price), with discounts for Annual Passholders. Guests get one Disney logo golf ball for each round played! Hours: 10:00 am to 11:00 pm.

Disney's Animal Kingdom Area | Epcot Area | Downtown Disney Area | Magic Kingdom Area

Chapter 4: Touring the "World"   Topic: More Recreational Destinations   215

Planning
Getting There
Staying in Style
Touring
Feasting
Making Magic
Index
Notes & More

More Places to Play

Fort Wilderness Resort—Fort Wilderness is a respite from the bustle of the parks, offering canoeing, boating, fishing excursions, biking, tennis, horseback trail rides, horse-drawn carriage rides, wagon rides, and a back trail adventure on Segways (see tours on pages 272–273). You can also visit the horse barn (pony rides cost $4, and are for guests ages 2+, 45 inches or less, 80 lbs. or less), blacksmith shop, and a nightly campfire program (with character visits and free movies). The 45-minute guided trail ride is another hidden gem—we really enjoyed our horseback ride! Cost is $42 for ages 9+ (guests must be at least 48" tall and under 250 lb.). Phone 407-824-2832 for trail ride reservations (recommended). For more information on Fort Wilderness, see pages 65–68.

Health Clubs & Spas—Many of the deluxe resorts have Disney-owned health clubs with exercise equipment—some even offer massage treatments, steam rooms, and saunas. Use of a fitness center (excluding treatments) is complimentary to resort guests or $12/day/person for non-resort guests. If you've got relaxation in mind, we recommend the **Saratoga Springs Spa** and **Grand Floridian Spa & Health Club**. These world-class, full-service centers offer many beauty and wellness treatments, nutrition and fitness counseling, and lots of pampering. Call 407-827-4455 (Saratoga Springs) or 407-824-2332 (Grand Floridian Spa), or visit their web site at http://disneyworld.disney.go.com/spas.

Tennis—Tennis enthusiasts will find tennis courts at most of Disney's deluxe resorts, Fort Wilderness, Swan and Dolphin, and Shades of Green. For more information, call 407-939-7529.

Walt Disney World Speedway—Disney has its own speedway—a one-mile, tri-oval track for **auto racing**. The race track is home to the Richard Petty Driving Experience, in which participants get to drive or ride at speeds up to 145 mph! Even Dave strapped on his helmet and climbed in the passenger seat of a race car for a "ride around" experience. Teens ages 14-19 get a free three-lap ride along when accompanied by an adult who has purchased any drive or ride program that same day. And the new Exotic Driving Experience gets you behind the wheel of a Ferrari, Lamborghini, Corvette, or Porsche. For Richard Petty Experience details, call 407-939-0130 or 800-BE-PETTY, or visit the web site at http://www.1800bepetty.com.

Disney Nature Reserve—The Nature Conservancy runs this 12,000-acre hiking haven at the headwaters of the Everglades. For information, visit http://www.nature.org and search on "disney."

More at ⓘ richard-petty-experience

More Places to Play

Waterways (Boating, Fishing, etc.)—Water, water everywhere—and lots of things to do! You can rent boats at nearly every deluxe and moderate resort and Downtown Disney. Probably the most popular rentals craft are little, two-person speed boats called Sea Raycers—the old Water Mice have been replaced by these more up-to-date craft. They're available at most marinas around Disney for $32 per half-hour, $40 for 45 minutes; $45 for 60 minutes (driver must be 12+ and at least 60" tall to pilot with an adult, or 16+ with a driver's license to pilot alone; 320 lb. max, two persons per boat, weight limit per boat). Fishing excursions and cane pole rentals are also available in most of those same places. A bass fishing program allows guests to reserve two-hour, guided, catch-and-release bass expeditions at many Disney marinas. All equipment is provided (even a digital camera to document your catch), fishing licenses are not needed thanks to the state-licensed guide on board, and participants even get a free subscription to Bassmaster Magazine. Excursions accommodate up to five guests and cost $200–$230. Phone 407-WDW-BASS for info.

ESPN Wide World of Sports Complex—Disney's state-of-the-art **athletic center** features a 9,500-seat baseball stadium, 70,000- and 80,000-square-foot fieldhouses, a track & field complex, volleyball, tennis, baseball, softball, football, and more. In 2005, Disney added another 20 acres of baseball, softball, and multi-sport fields under the sponsorship of Hess. The complex hosts 180 youth, amateur, and professional sporting events annually. A new 100-lane bowling alley was slated to open at ESPN Wide World of Sports in 2010, but the progress seems to be stalled. General admission is $16/adults or $11/kids 3–9, but tickets for professional sporting events are typically more money. Note that the Multi-Sport Experience exhibit here has been closed. The 220-acre center is also the home of the Atlanta Braves Spring Training. The new PlayStation Pavillion offers high-end gaming, outside the admission gates. For more information, call 407-828-FANS (recorded information), or 407-939-1500 (to speak with a person), or visit http://www.disneyworldsports.com.

runDisney (Walt Disney World Running Events)—Disney's Wide World of Sports isn't just for spectators. Runners can register for the Walt Disney World Marathon, Half-Marathon, Family Fun Run 5K, and Goofy's Race and a Half Challenge (January 10-13, 2013). And Disney's Princess Half-Marathon Weekend will return again February 22-24, 2013. Jeff Galloway, a leading marathon trainer, is runDisney's official training consultant. Visit http://www.rundisney.com to learn more and to register.

Deciding What To Do

Whew! We bet you're now wondering how in the world (no pun intended) you'll find the time to **fit everything** at Walt Disney World into your vacation. It's simple: You can't do it. Even a month-long stay wouldn't be enough to do and see everything. Rather than try to fit everything into your vacation, make a practical plan.

Naturally, you can't plan everything in advance, nor should you try—spontaneity and discovery are two elements of a great vacation. Yet it is a good idea to get a feeling for the parks, attractions, and activities before you go and to make a note of the ones you simply "must" do. This helps you **create an itinerary** and keeps you from missing the things you've got your heart set on.

First, read the preceding pages carefully to gain a solid idea of what the Walt Disney World Resort is all about. Next, **make a list** of all the things you'd like to see and do. This can be a great family activity. Make it a free-for-all, no-holds-barred event—what we call a "blue-sky session." List everything, no matter how impractical, silly, or expensive. Once you've got a good list, pare it down to the things that are most important and copy them to the worksheet on the next two pages. List the activity, where in the "World" it is located (i.e., which park or resort), its approximate cost, and any notes (including why it's on the list).

When you're done with the list, take a good look at the locations. Are several located in the same park? If so, can you do them all on the same day? Go through the list and note other patterns. With luck, you'll have a better sense of where you're headed. Next, **assign the activities** to specific days of your vacation, using the Day/Date column on the far right. For example, on a recent trip, we wanted to visit Spaceship Earth, race around Test Track, and watch IllumiNations. All those activities are at Epcot, so we grouped them together on our third day. We wrote a "3" next to each of those items, but you could write "Wed" or the date instead. If you've planned too much for one day or place, your Cost and Notes columns may help you decide which activities to keep and which to throw out or schedule for another day.

Not all activities can be decided this way, nor should they. Some choices should be **spur of the moment**. Be sure to "schedule" some free time in your trip—preferably a whole day or two. Use these techniques as a general game plan to a great vacation!

Sidebar tabs: Planning | Getting There | Staying in Style | Touring | Feasting | Making Magic | Index | Notes & More

More at ⓘ planning-park-days | four-parks-in-one-day

Top Photo Slice: A bulletin board full of things to do in the now-closed Minnie's Country House (ⓘ6771) © Joy Vodnik

Electronic, interactive worksheet available— see page 316

Touring Worksheet

Use this worksheet to figure out the things you want to do most on your trip. Match up attractions to determine the parks you want to visit, noting the day/date (you may wish to refer to the Extra Magic Hour schedule on page 34). Fill in the park schedule grid at the bottom of the next page once you've picked days—the park schedule can help you complete your itinerary and choose eateries (in the next chapter).

Activity	Park	Land	Cost	Notes	Day/Date

Useful Abbreviations:

MK (Magic Kingdom)
EP (Epcot)
DHS (Disney's Hollywood Studios)
DAK (Disney's Animal Kingdom)
BB (Blizzard Beach)
TL (Typhoon Lagoon)
BW (BoardWalk)
DD (Downtown Disney)

DQ (DisneyQuest)
WWOS (ESPN Wide World of Sports)
DS (Disney Speedway)
FG (Fantasia Gardens)
WS (Winter Summerland)
DCL (Disney Cruise Line)
VB (Disney's Vero Beach)
OFF (Off-site)

USF (Universal Studios)
IOA (Islands of Adventure)
SW (SeaWorld)
COVE (Discovery Cove)
BG (Busch Gardens)
KSC (Kennedy Space Center)
CB (Cocoa Beach)
LF (LEGOLAND Florida)
FH (Friend/Family's House)

Activity	Park	Land	Cost	Notes	Day/Date

Write your park schedule in this calendar grid—note the date in the corners. You can get Disney park schedules online at http://www.disneyworld.com.

Planning

Getting There

Staying in Style

Touring

Feasting

Making Magic

Index

Notes & More

It's Not Such a Small World After All

If you've read this chapter, you know that touring Walt Disney World is no simple walk in the park. Here are some tips and tricks to help you:

> A great way to make magic for your family and for the cast members is to strike up a conversation! You have no idea how much a simple conversation with a guest can brighten a cast member's day. Pin trading can also be a great way to start these interactions. As a former college program Cast Member, I loved when families would stop to say hello, because everyone had great stories to tell. You might even find that the cast member is from the same area as you! Make some magic—chat with cast members!
>
> — Contributed by Chloe C., a winner in our Reader Tip Contest

> Whenever we go to a park we usually each bring in a water bottle, sunglasses, and various other items such as a camera, rain ponchos, fan spray bottle, etc. and we keep them in a draw string back pack. To avoid the long lines at the security bag check area, we unload the bag and carry all of our own belongings into the park and my husband stuffs the bag in his pocket. On the other side of the gates we put all the stuff back in the drawstring backpack and I carry it on my back!
>
> — Contributed by Lisa O'Meara, a winner in our Reader Tip Contest

Magical Memories

> When my oldest niece was about six years old, I asked her if she would like to go see the movie 'Cinderella' with me. Several weeks later, my father surprised our family with a trip to Orlando and a day of Walt Disney World fun. I had a wonderful day together with my father, sister, sister-in-law, niece, and nephew. In the afternoon my niece was getting tired so we walked around the Magic Kingdom by ourselves and then we took a rest on a bench near Cinderella Castle. Suddenly, my niece grabbed my hand and said, 'Oh Aunt Pammy! Cinderella! Did she know I was here and knows we went to see her movie?' Above us, Cinderella was walking around one of the turrets. I'd never seen her do this before! We waved and waved! To me, that is magic—it was not pre-planned, just spontaneous. Of course, nobody else in our family believed us when we told them, but Melanie and I know Cinderella is real.
>
> ...as told by Disney vacationer Pamela Pollaro

> A coworker and friend of mine, who has a little girl the same age as my daughter, had planned a trip to Walt Disney World at the same time as us. The magic of watching our two girls together was amazing. We had surprised both of them with matching outfits and an appointment at Bibbidi Bobbidi Boutique for a crazy hair style and make-up session. The magic continued througout the day with many cast member and guests commenting on how cute they both looked. They even made the big screen at Monsters Inc. Laugh Floor! Later in the day, a cast member saw them both looking at the Liberty Bell near Liberty Tree Tavern restaurant and then took their picture 'holding' the bell in their hands. The cast member told us to watch the castle at the Magic, Memories & You show that evening to see their picture on the castle! My friend and I were teary eyed as we watched the show realizing how truly magical this vacation was to us and the memories we made to take home to treasure forever.
>
> ...as told by Disney vacationer Jennifer Blain

More at ⓘ what-a-wonderful-world

Feasting and Snacking

You can't have a good vacation without a good meal (or two), and your Disney vacation is no exception. Disney knows how to make your mealtimes as entertaining, adventuresome, and satisfying as the rest of your vacation experience. Disney eateries go out of their way to give everyone a unique and delicious dining experience, so you'll find that even

the most exotic restaurant can please any taste, including the finicky eaters in your family. From the atmosphere to the service to the food itself, it has all been created to fill your imagination as well as your belly.

DISCOVER the fine points of dining at Disney

The choices can be awesome, ranging from basic hot dogs and burgers to once-in-a-lifetime elegance, from ultra-romantic dinners for two to foot-stompin' family hoedowns, and from exotic samplings of far-off places to the magic of a breakfast hug from Winnie the Pooh himself.

LEARN about character meals and dinner shows

For us, meal planning is more important than choosing which attractions to visit. It's easier to jump in an unexpectedly short line for a show than it is to get a table at the better eateries.

PLAN meals and reserve tables

The six basic types of Walt Disney World Resort meals are table-service restaurants, counter-service cafes, quick-service snack shops, "special experiences" (such as dinner shows and character meals), room service, and meals you fix yourself. We devote most of the space here to table-service and special dining experiences, which are more costly and require the most planning. We also include details on the counter service and snacks in the parks. Resort counter service and room service is discussed in the "Staying in Style" chapter. We can't say much about your home cooking until we're invited to your villa or campsite, though.

The chapter begins with a meal planning guide, then moves to mealtime tips, park-by-park and resort-by-resort eatery reviews, and the low-down on the big shindigs, and ends with worksheets to plan your meals.

READ our reviews of restaurants and cafés

Top Photo Slice: Alexander enjoys a Mickey ice cream bar at the Magic Kingdom © MediaMarx, Inc.

Vertical tabs (right margin): Planning · Getting There · Staying in Style · Touring · Feasting · Making Magic · Index · Notes & More

Planning

Getting There

Staying in Style

Touring

Feasting

Making Magic

Index

Notes & More

Deciding On Dining

If you thought selecting a restaurant in your hometown was tough, you haven't seen anything. The Walt Disney World Resort has more than **300 places to eat**. But before you go running for the exit, take heart. We've been to virtually every restaurant on property at least twice (often much more) and we offer easily digestible descriptions and yummy ratings for you in this chapter. Better yet, we have a tried-and-true system for deciding where and when to eat.

First, decide **how often** you want to eat out. Many folks (including ourselves) bring or buy some food for in-room snacks or meals, with light breakfasts being the most practical choice. All Disney resorts now supply a refrigerator at no charge, some include a coffeemaker, and Disney's Deluxe Villas resorts have kitchen facilities, too. You can, of course, eat out every meal. We like to eat a light breakfast in our room with food we've packed or purchased, such as peanut butter and jelly on English muffins. We then do one or two special breakfasts "out" (such as a character breakfast—see pages 262–263). We often eat lunch and dinner at the parks, resorts, or Downtown Disney. If you're doing the Disney Dining Basic or Quick-Service Plan (see the next three pages), you'll probably do about two meals a day. Some vacationers prefer to eat a big meal mid-morning and another mid-afternoon to save time and money (it's easy to fill up at many restaurants). More money-saving ideas are on page 229.

Once you have an idea of how often you want (and can afford) to eat out, your next task is to decide **when and where**. Revisit your Touring Worksheet (pages 218–219) and check the parks you want to visit—it is much easier to choose a restaurant in or near your day's destination. Every park offers table-service restaurants, counter-service eateries, and snack shops and carts. To help you choose from the overwhelming number of dining choices at Walt Disney World, this chapter offers descriptions of nearly all eateries. Descriptions are organized alphabetically within each park and resort to help you focus on your choices. Pick the eateries that fall within your budget, tastes, and needs—you may find it helpful to highlight or circle those eatery descriptions that interest you.

As you make decisions about your meals and the eateries you want to visit, jot them down on your **Meal Worksheet** at the end of the chapter on the next page. Make note of those table-service eateries for which advance reservations may be made. Continue on to the next page to learn the what, when, and how of advance reservations at the Walt Disney World Resort.

More at ① disney-dining (tip: enter this keyword at http://www.passporter.com/j for more information!)

Top Photo Slice: The tempting pastry case in Boulangerie Patisserie at Epcot (①15312) © Monica Gauvin

Disney Dining Plan

The hot buzz in recent years are the Disney Dining Plan packages. Available as an add-on to a Magic Your Way "package" (see page 32), and sometimes free as a promotional item, the Disney Dining Plan has **revolutionized the way many vacationers dine at Disney**. While a hands-down winner in the past, saving money and maximizing value is a challenge today.

Disney offers several Dining Plan packages in 2013. The most popular is the **Basic Dining Plan**, which can be added to any Magic Your Way "package" that includes at least one day of park admission. The add-on price is $59.20–$60.64/adult (includes tax) and $18.28–$19.34/ages 3–9 per night of your stay. The price is based on the time of year of travel, higher price during Peak, Summer and Holiday seasons. Those under age 3 may share their parent's meal. The Basic Dining Plan provides **three "credits" per person per night of your stay**: one table-service credit, one counter-service credit, and one snack credit, plus a resort refillable mug. This offers a very small savings over the average cost of dining. **To break even or "win,"** avoid all two-credit dining except for dinner shows and pizza delivery.

The **Deluxe Dining Plan** costs $106.47-$108.92 (includes tax)/guests ages 10 and up and $28.58-$30.79/guests ages 3–9 per night of your stay. The Deluxe Dining Plan includes three meal credits (use for either table or counter service) and two snack credits per person per night, plus one refillable mug. Savings and value can be very good on this plan if you avoid counter service meals, but it's easy to exceed your normal calorie count. (After paying tips, it can cost $110–$120/day per adult). For the **best value**, only dine at one-credit table-service restaurants. Three meals per day too much? A few two-credit meals won't destroy your savings. Pay out-of-pocket for all or most of your counter-service meals, and apply the extra credits to Signature Dining.

Disney also has a **Quick-Service Dining Plan**. For $40.02/adult and $15.25/ages 3–9, you get two counter-service meal credits (each credit is good for one entree or one combo meal, juice at breakfast, dessert at lunch/dinner, and one non-alcoholic beverage) and one snack per person per night, plus one refillable drink mug per person.

How do credits work? Table-service credits on the Basic Dining Plan include an entrée, dessert, regular soft drink, and sales tax. Meal credits on the Deluxe Plan add an appetizer. Most gratuities are not included. Counter-service meals on all plans provide an entrée, dessert, regular soft drink, and sales tax. Snack credits provide a single item, such as a soft drink, baked item, ice cream, or a Dole Whip (most items under $4). Disney affixes "DDP" icons to its menus to identify snack-credit items.

More at ⊕ dining-plans | dining-plan-tips | deluxe-dining-plan

Side tabs: Planning | Getting There | Staying in Style | Touring | Feasting | Making Magic | Index | Notes & More

Disney Dining Plan

(continued)

You can **use Disney Dining Plan credits at any time**, in any combination, for the duration of your stay (beginning at check-in). Table-service credits are good at more than 100 participating eateries (noted in this chapter), as well as in-room private dining, pizza delivery, and dinner shows (gratuities are included on these last three). All unused credits expire without refund at 11:59 pm on your check-out day; use 'em or lose 'em!

How do you get a Dining Plan? Add the plan to your reservation at least five days prior to your arrival. Disney Vacation Club members can purchase the Basic, Quick-Service, and Deluxe dining plans when staying "on points"—contact DVC for the details. Annual Passholders can purchase a special Dining Plan package that includes dining, lodging, but no admission—see details on page 32.

Dining Plan Tips:

Use your PassPorter! **It's packed with features** to help you maximize your dining plan. Our eatery descriptions include an "average price" figure that's great for comparing relative meal values on the plan. We also point out Disney Dining Plan participating eateries, as well as "Signature" dining restaurants (which require two table-service credits per meal). Our Meal Worksheet on page 269 includes columns for budgeting the use of your dining credits while you plan, and to keep track of how many are used as you vacation. You can also use the Meals and Snacks section of each PassPocket to keep track of these items.

Note that Disney Dining Plan participating eateries can **change around** a bit, so you should always re-confirm with Disney.

Consider **sharing meals** to stretch your Dining Plan credits.

The **computed cost** of Basic Dining Plan credits is $34.84 (table service), $15.70 (counter service), and $5.33 (snack)—barely lower than the price you'd pay off the plan. On the Basic and Deluxe Plans, you get decent "bang" from dinner shows and pizza delivery, as gratuities are also included. The two-credit Cinderella's breakfast is a money-waster under either plan.

According to our calculations, **average savings** on the counter-service dining plan are less than 1%, and, on the basic dining plan they're just 5%. Yet on the deluxe dining plan, average savings are around 20%, and it's even more if you use every meal credit for table service. You'd have to use one out of four deluxe plan credits for counter service meals to lose money.

Disney Dining Plan
(continued)

If you're eating counter service at your resort hotel and have the resort's **refillable mugs** (see page 36), use the soft drink portion of your counter-service credit on a bottled beverage from the Grab-n-Go, and save it for later.

On the Basic Dining Plan, it matters little if you dine at a la carte or **buffet/character table-service meals**—the value of each meal is similiar.

Want ice cream for your counter-service dessert? Ask the cashier if you can **get the frozen treat later on** so it won't melt. Generally, they'll mark your receipt so you can claim it later, maybe up to closing time that evening.

Watch your meal credits carefully. Each meal receipt lists the number of credits you have remaining, **but there can be errors**. Your resort's Lobby Concierge can print out a detailed accounting. Note the credits you've used (and plan to use) on our Dining Worksheet.

Your entire travel party's **credits are grouped together by type (adult and child)** so you can use your credits as you wish. You cannot, however, pay for someone else's meal with your credits, nor can you use adult credits for a child and vice versa.

You may **exchange two table-service credits** for selected dinner shows, Signature Dining, in-room dining, and pizza delivery—one pizza serves two adults. The average values (and quality) of many one-credit table-service restaurants are nearly as high as Signature Dining experiences, which can mean you'll get far **more bang for your buck** by avoiding the Signature establishments altogether.

Eateries participating in the Dining Plan can **change at any time**. You can download the most recent list of eateries at Disney's web site and/or request one at 407-WDW-DINE.

If you have **leftover snack credits**, use them to buy snacks for the trip home. You cannot use table-service or quick-service credits for snacks, however.

Here are some "**secret numbers**"—these are the average values of adult meals based on our calculations (includes tax and 18% gratuity):

Meal Type	breakfast	lunch	dinner
Counter-service	$12.26	$15.79	$15.79
Table-service - B(asic) Plan	$21.38	$36.80	$38.69
Table-service - D(eluxe) Plan	$27.38	$43.80	$46.69
Table-service Signature (B/D)	$52.07	$51.60/$59.60	$70.12/$78.12

Planning / Getting There / Staying in Style / Touring / Feasting / Making Magic / Index / Notes & More

Planning

Getting There

Staying in Style

Touring

Feasting

Making Magic

Index

Notes & More

Advance Reservations

With the popularity of the Disney Dining Plan (see pages 223–225), reservations have become essential at many restaurants. Virtually every table-service restaurant within Disney World allows anyone (whether or not you're on the Dining Plan) to make "Advance Reservations." Unlike traditional reservations, in which a table is held for your party at a designated time, Disney's advance reservations give you the **first table that becomes available**. Wait times for the first-available table vary, but we typically wait 10–30 minutes once we check-in at the eatery.

Most Disney table-service restaurants **accept advance reservations**, and we note this fact with each eatery description in this chapter. The only restaurants that don't accept advance reservations are some Downtown Disney restaurants, Big River Grille (24-hour reservations only), and ESPN Club (see detailed listings in this chapter). Additionally, some restaurants do take traditional reservations, such as Victoria & Albert's, the Swan & Dolphin restaurants (see pages 259–260), and the character meals at Cinderella's Royal Table and Akershus Royal Banquet Hall (see pages 262–263).

Advance reservations can be made **before your arrival** by calling 407-WDW-DINE (407-939-3463) from 7:00 am to 10:00 pm Eastern Time seven days a week. You can also make advance reservations online at http://disneyworld.disney.go.com/dining beginning at 6:00 am. Call or go online up to **180 days ahead of your visit** for reservations at most restaurants. Tip: Disney resort guests have the advantage of being able to book reservations for the first ten days of their trip at 180 days from their check-in date. Already at Disney? Search for table-service availability using your iPhone or Android—just download Disney's official (and free) Mobile Magic app. You can search for current availability and make your reservation, using either "list" or "Map" views—visit http://www.disneyparksmobile.com.

When you make an advance reservation, you will be asked to supply the name of your hotel, your phone number, your reservation number, and your date of arrival—you can record this information in your **Advance Reservations Worksheet** on page 269. If you aren't staying at a Disney resort, no problem—simply provide a daytime phone number. Many reservations now require a credit card guarantee, deposit, or full pre-payment. No-show penalties ($10/person or more) may be charged if you don't cancel a day prior. Emergencies are often excused, but be sure to call! If you are using the Disney Dining Plan for a meal, be sure to note this when you reserve it. You will get a **confirmation number** for each reservation. Record this in your worksheet, and later transfer it to your daily PassPockets. You may wish to call and confirm your reservations a few days before you arrive, too.

More at ① advance-reservations

If you don't get the advance reservation time and/or restaurant you want, **don't give up**—keep trying! Vacationers cancel their plans and spots open up all the time. We've gotten reservations for hot restaurants even on the day itself just by continuing to call and ask for any openings.

Want that **popular Le Cellier, 'Ohana, or Chef Mickey's reservation**? These are hot tickets and can be very difficult to get. Your best bet is to call exactly 180 days before the date you want to eat here. Get online by 5:55 am (online bookings begin at 6:00 am), or pick up the phone and start dialing 407-WDW-DINE at 6:55 am Eastern Time (phone lines open at 7:00 am). If you get a recording, listen carefully—if the recording indicates the office is closed, hang up and redial right away. Otherwise wait on the line and do not hang up—you're in a queue for the next available representative. When you get an actual representative on the line, tell them immediately (even if you have to interrupt them) that you need a reservation for the restaurant of your choosing—be sure to include the exact date and number of people. It is important to convey this information as quickly as possible, because hundreds of other people are doing the same thing right now and every second counts. We suggest you write down the line you will speak on your worksheet and simply rattle it off to avoid any delays. Do not specify a time—let the representative search for any available time.

You may also need a **credit card when you make your reservation**—payment in full is required at time of booking for character meals and dinner shows (unless you're using Disney Dining Plan credits), and a credit card guarantee may be needed for other meals. If you do not have a credit card, the reservation cannot be made.

If you decide not to eat at a particular restaurant, just call Disney again and **cancel your reservation**. (In the case of Signature dining, character meals, special dinner shows, and those meals that require a credit card guarantee, however, be aware that there are cancellation policies and fees.) If you are unable to get a reservation, call back about one week before the desired date and again on the morning you want to dine.

Check in at the restaurant's podium 15 minutes before your seating time. You may also need to wait anywhere from 5 to 30 minutes for a table to become available, depending upon how busy it is. Some restaurants issue a pager, and most have a comfortable waiting area or bar. If your restaurant opens before the park opens, simply tell the cast member at the park entrance turnstiles about your advance reservation—you may need to show your confirmation number. Daily bus transportation is available for these early advance reservations beginning at 6:30 am (Magic Kingdom area) and 7:00-7:15 am (all other parks). Be sure to tell the bus driver when you board where you need to go, and allow ample time to transfer if your reservation is at a resort.

Restaurant Menu

Alcoholic Beverages—Most eateries serve alcoholic drinks, though the only eatery in the Magic Kingdom that serves it is Be Our Guest. Bars and lounges are located around the "World." Legal drinking age is 21 and they do check your identification.

Character Dining—Dine with Disney characters! See pages 262–263.

Children's Meals—Nearly every eatery has a special menu for kids age 3-9. Kid staples like macaroni & cheese and chicken tenders can usually be had at the most exotic of restaurants even when they're not on the menu—ask your server. You may be able to substitute healthy choices such as carrots or fruit in the place of fries, too. Kids also get free refills on child-size beverages at table-service restaurants, including juice, milk, bottled water, and soda (but not including specialty drinks). All eateries also provide high chairs and booster seats, as needed. As you can imagine, Disney is one of the most kid-friendly places to eat in the world. (Special note to parents of infants and toddlers: Jars of baby food are not available in the eateries, but you can purchase them at the Baby Care Centers of each park if necessary—see page 120.)

Counter Service—Most food at Disney is sold fast-food style. The quality does vary—it's generally worse at the Magic Kingdom and best at Disney's Animal Kingdom. At Magic Kingdom, we like Pecos Bill Cafe in Frontierland and Columbia Harbour House in Liberty Square. Disney's Animal Kingdom only has three table-service restaurants, but the counter-service food is several cuts above the ordinary. We especially like Flame Tree Barbecue.

Coupons/Discounts—Don't plan on finding coupons for restaurants. We know only of AAA discounts at some Swan/Dolphin eateries. Discounts for annual passholders and Disney Vacation Club members (mostly at lunch) do exist—be sure to ask your server. You may qualify for the Tables in Wonderland program—see page 10 for details. See the money-saving tips on the following page for more information on available discounts.

Dietary Requirements—Low-cholesterol, low-salt, low-fat, and/or vegetarian meals are a regular part of the menu in most restaurants. With 72 hours of advance notice, gluten-free, kosher and other special dietary needs can be met. Cosmic Ray's at Magic Kingdom has a no-advance-notice kosher menu at the check-out (ask for this at other counter-service restaurants, too). You may contact Disney regarding your special dietary requirements by e-mail at specialdiets@disneyworld.com or phone 407-824-5967.

Dinner Shows—Disney offers several dinner shows, combining all-you-care-to-eat meals with live entertainment. See pages 264–266.

Dress—Casual clothing is appropriate for most eateries in the "World" except Victoria & Albert's (see page 257), which requires that men wear a jacket. Several spots also require "resort casual" dress (sometimes called "business casual"), which means that men should wear dress slacks, jeans, trousers, dress shorts, collared shirts, and/or t-shirts (jackets are optional) and women should wear skirts, jeans, dress shorts, dresses, blouses, sweaters, and/or t-shirts. Resort casual dress code prohibits hats, swimsuits, swim coveralls, tank tops, torn clothing, or flip flops. Resort casual restaurants include Artist Point, California Grill, Citricos, Flying Fish, Jiko, Narcoossee's, and Yachtsman Steakhouse.

Entertainment—Some restaurants supply entertainment, while others like the Whispering Canyon Cafe and 'Ohana provide activities for kids.

Menus—To see eatery offerings and prices before you arrive, visit Deb Wills' AllEarsNet web site (http://www.allears.net) for a wonderful collection of up-to-date menus.

Top Photo Slice: Front of the Restaurant Marrakesh menu (①2314) © Janet Simonsen

More at ① eating-healthy | food-allergies

Money—Cash, Disney Dollars and Gift Cards, traveler's checks, Disney Visa Reward cards, MasterCard, Visa, American Express, JCB, Discover, and Diner's Club. Disney Resort room charge cards are welcomed, even at some of the smallest snack carts. Note that the Disney Resort room charge card is not accepted at the Swan and Dolphin eateries. The Shopping & Dining Gift Card, which can be purchased in amounts between $5 and $1,500, is also accepted at select shops and eateries. Sales tax is 6.5%. Gratuities may be applied automatically to large parties (eight or more persons).

Peak Periods—Prices for character meals and some other popular eateries may increase by 10%-20% during peak periods and weekends, and Disney Dining Plan peak season rates are also higher.

Smoking—Florida law prohibits smoking in all enclosed restaurants and other indoor public spaces. Only outdoor establishments and freestanding bars (no restaurants or hotel lobbies allowed) can allow smoking, but Disney bans smoking at most of these, too.

⚠ Time- and Money-Saving Dining Tips

✔ If you're staying at a Walt Disney World resort hotel, you can make all of your advance dining reservations for the length of your stay (up to 10 days in advance) at 180 days from your arrival date.

✔ Inquire with Disney about Dining Plan add-ons to resort reservations (see pages 223-225). At press time, Disney is offering a free Dining Plan for select packages and dates into 2013. If the Dining Plan is not free, the Basic and Quick-Service Dining Plans only offer marginal savings. The Deluxe Dining Plan is a better deal, but only for those who normally eat three table-service meals a day and typically spend at least $90/day per adult.

✔ At counter-service eateries, there are usually several lines. The line farthest from the entry is often shorter. Look before you leap. Also note that counter-service eateries have lines on <u>both</u> sides of the cash register. If you see a short or nonexistent line on one side of an open register, jump in!

✔ Consider eating earlier or later than traditional mealtime hours. You'll be more likely to get a seat (if you haven't made reservations) or simply find the restaurant less crowded and noisy.

✔ Every item at counter-service restaurants can be ordered a la carte. If you don't want fries with that burger "meal," just ask, and you'll pay a reduced price.

✔ Landry's Select Club offers discounts at Rainforest Cafe, T-Rex, Yak and Yeti's, and 400 other Landry's locations. Get details at http://www.landrysinc.com. Annual passholder discounts may also be offered at these spots.

✔ The Tables in Wonderland program is for Florida residents and annual passholders. It offers 20% discounts on select restaurants in the parks and resorts, and more. See page 10 for details.

✔ Resort eateries are frequently less crowded than those in the parks. Consider a visit to a nearby resort restaurant before, during, or after a park visit. The Contemporary, Polynesian, and Grand Floridian resorts are close to the Magic Kingdom, the Yacht & Beach Club, BoardWalk, and Swan & Dolphin restaurants are close to Epcot and Disney's Hollywood Studios, and Disney's Animal Kingdom Lodge is a short drive/bus ride from Disney's Animal Kingdom.

More at ⓘ saving-money-on-dining

Planning · Getting There · Staying in Style · Touring · Feasting · Making Magic · Index · Notes & More

Understanding and Using the Eatery Descriptions and Ratings

PassPorter's popular capsule reviews cover all table-service restaurants, as well as counter-service eateries at the parks. Our reviews include all important details, plus ratings. Below is a key to our eatery charts. Dig in!

Description Key

Ratings[7]

[1] **Eatery Name** [D-2[2]] (Bar Color[3]) B $, L $, D $, S[4] DDP[5] 🎭[6] # # #	
Description offering an overview of the eatery, including comments on the theming, quality, and menu range. We try to give you an idea of what sort of foods you'll find at a particular eatery, along with typical prices and our recommendations. We also include information on the availability of lighter fare, children's meals, and alcoholic beverages. Whenever possible, we describe the type of seating (tables, booths, etc.) and whether it is indoor or outdoor.	Type[8]
	Cuisine[8]
	Noise Factor[8]
	Reservations[8]
	Avg. Wait[8]
	Hours[8]

[1] Each chart has an empty checkbox in the upper left corner—use it to check off the eateries that interest you (before you go) or those at which you ate (after your return).

[2] Map coordinates—match them up to park maps in "Touring the 'World'" for locations.

[3] The **bar color** indicates the eatery's main draw, as follows:

Gourmet Tastes	Eateries for Everyone	Fun Food	Character Meals

[4] Meals are indicated by letters: B (breakfast), L (lunch), D (dinner), and S (snack). The dollar figures that follow each meal type represent the average cost of a full adult meal. Table-service meal costs include appetizer, entree, dessert, soft drink, tax, and 18% tip. Average counter-service meal costs include entree, dessert, soft drink, and tax.

[5] The "DDP" symbol indicates that an eatery participates in the Disney Dining Plan (see pages 223–225) at press time. Note that the eateries are subject to change at any time—check with Disney before making plans. The color and letter in the lower right corner shows the type of Dining Plan eatery: blue "S" DDPS is snack, red "Q" DDPQ is quick service (counter service), purple "T" DDPT is table service, and gold "2" DDP2 is signature (because a Signature eatery requires two table-service credits). Verify participation at 407-WDW-DINE.

[6] Eateries with a reasonable selection of healthy items (low-fat/low-sodium/low-calorie) are indicated with a tape measure symbol. These are also friendly to weight watchers!

[7] The three white boxes on the right show ratings on a scale of 1 (poor) to 10 (loved it!). The first rating is **Jennifer's**, the second is Dave's, and the third is our **Readers'** rating. We offer our personal ratings to show how opinions vary, even between two like-minded people. You can also use our ratings as a point of reference—Jennifer likes eateries with extensive theming and well-prepared foods that aren't too exotic or spicy. Dave has more cultured tastes, enjoys unusual, spicy, and barbecue dishes, and loves seafood!

Kona Cafe

[8] The boxes on the right beneath the numeric ratings give basic information: eatery type (Table, Counter, or Buffet), cuisine, noise factor (from quiet to very noisy), seating (if reservations are accepted, needed, suggested, recommended, or required, and how many days in advance you can call), average wait time, and the eatery's hours.

Top Photo Slice: Windows in the atrium at Crystal Palace in the Magic Kingdom (Ⓟ14476) © Cheryl Pendry

Planning · Getting There · Staying in Style · Touring · Feasting · Making Magic · Index · Notes & More

Magic Kingdom Eateries

(park map on page 132)

Jennifer's Dave Readers

Be Our Guest [D-1]   L $15 DD PQ   D $46 DD PT   – – –

Step into the most delicious and beautiful part of Belle and Beast's world. This new restaurant has three themed wings: West Wing, Rose Gallery, and Ballroom. Lunch is counter service—order, find a table, and your food arrives on a cart! Sandwiches—carved turkey, steak, and grilled ham and cheese are $9, while Niçoise salad with tuna (or veggie-friendly with quinoa), vegetable quiche, and braised pork are $8–$11. Desserts are just $2.39. Dinner morphs to table service, and breaks Magic Kingdom tradition—beer and wine are served! Entrees are $16 to $30: pork chops, Cornish hen, salmon, steak, and seafood are dressed-up French style and the veggie choice is ratatouille (wrong movie!). Kids fare is "different"—pasta with tomato sauce and mozzarella is closest to "normal."

Counter and Table
French
Reservations required for table service
Call 180 days
Long waits

Casey's Corner [D-4]   L $14, D $14, S $4   DD PQ   5 5 7

Casey's at the bat, and there's a hot dog at the plate. Old-time stadium foods—Chili cheese dogs ($8.59), fries ($2.49), Cracker Jack ($2.39), and drinks ($2.59 & $2.89). Seating is outdoors; some indoor grandstands and tables near a big-screen TV.

Counter
American
11 am–closing

Cinderella's Royal Table [D-3]   B $52, L $56, D $66   DD P2   7 6 8

For Disney magic, you can't beat dining inside Cinderella Castle! The character meals at "Cindy's" are hot tickets and very expensive as a result—the pre-plated breakfast is $52.07 or $33.47/kids 3-9. And lunch is $55.81 or $34.71/kids (see pages 262-263). Dinner is $65.74 or $39.64/kids with your choice of appetizer, entree, dessert, and beverage. The price includes tax and gratuity, plus a six-print photo package (your photo is taken before you are seated). Cinderella appears at all meals. The food isn't quite as good as the better resort eateries, but the light through the stained glass windows makes it all worthwhile. If you'll be celebrating a special occasion, mention it at booking. Full payment is required at time of reservation (except for those on a dining plan). During holiday periods, meal prices are approximately an extra $6/adult and $4/kid.

Table
American
Med. noise
Advance reservations essential
Call 180 days
~8-11:15 am,
Noon-3:00 pm
4 pm-closing

Columbia Harbour House [C-2]   L $15, D $15, S $6   DD PQ   5 6 6

This cozy inn provides cool relief and attractive decor despite the inexpensive menu. Fried shrimp with fries ($9.99), fried fish with fries ($7.49), clam chowder ($4.69), garden salad ($8.59), and sandwiches ($8.99) dominate the menu, but several veggie dishes—such as the vegetarian chili ($4.49)—create a rare port in the storm at Magic Kingdom. Kids meals ($5.49) include salad with chicken and mac & cheese. The quiet, upstairs dining room is usually open.

Counter
American
Med. noise
11:00 am-
1 hour
before closing

Cosmic Ray's Starlight Cafe [E-3]   L $16, D $16, S $6   DD PQ   6 5 6

Ray runs the biggest cafeteria at the Magic Kingdom. There's an excellent choice of chicken ($8.19-$9.69), sandwiches ($9.19-$9.39), burgers ($7.59-$9.19), and salad ($7.79), but not all food items are available from all stations. Kids can get peanut butter and jelly, turkey sandwich, and chicken nuggets ($5.49 each). Toppings bar. Kosher menu, too. We think the ½ chicken and BBQ rib combo ($14.19)—see photo—is the best Dining Plan counter-service deal around.

Loving the big portions
© MediaMarx, Inc.

Counter
American
Very noisy
Med. waits
10:00 am-
closing

Planning · Getting There · Staying in Style · Touring · Feasting · Making Magic · Index · Notes & More

Magic Kingdom Eateries
(continued)

Jennifer Dave Readers

The Crystal Palace [C-4]   B $29 L $31, D $46   DD PT   6 6 8

Little more than a stone's throw away from Cinderella Castle (but please, don't throw stones), this replica of a Victorian glass conservatory serves character meals all day long. Breakfast is $28.75 ($15.97/kids 3-9), lunch is $30.88 ($17.03/kids), and dinner is $43.66 ($21.29/kids), tax included. Winnie the Pooh is your host at this popular buffet. The dinner menu changes weekly, but usually offers carved meats, roasted vegetables, shrimp, and a wide variety of salads. There's even a separate kids' buffet and an ice cream sundae "bar." Potted and hanging plants and wrought-iron tables and chairs add to the lovely garden setting. See pages 262-263 for details on the character meal.

Buffet
American
Very noisy
Reservations suggested
Call 180 days
~8-10:30 am,
11:30-3:00 pm,
4 pm-closing

Gaston's Tavern [E-1]   L $15, D $15   DD PQ   – – –

No one eats like Gaston, no one drinks like Gaston, and his decorating ... wow! Roasted pork shank ($7.99), veggies ($3.69) and hummus ($4.39) are the savories. Sweets include chocolate croissant, cinnamon roll, and fruit cup ($2.99-$3.99). LeFou's Brew is an apple juice slushie in a souvenir cup ($9.99) or paper cup ($4.49).

Counter
French
Long waits

Liberty Tree Tavern [C-3]   L $37, D $40   DD PT   6 6 7

One if by land, two if by monorail! Disney's elegant, Colonial-styled inn serves a la carte lunches and all-you-can-eat dinners (note that character dining is no longer offered here). At lunch, choose from an assortment of enticing soups and appetizers ($5.49-$10.99), sandwiches ($12.99), salads ($5.49-$14.49), vegetarian pot pie ($12.99), turkey ($14.99), and New England Pot Roast ($17.99). Kids' meals are $8.59 (turkey, meaty macaroni, pizza, mac and cheese), and includes drink and dessert. The fixed-price dinner offers turkey, carved beef, smoked pork loin, and all the trimmings for $31.99 ($14.99/kids). Seating is at tables and chairs, and the dining rooms are well-themed.

Table
American
Noisy
Reservations suggested
Call 180 days
Short waits
11:30 am-3 pm,
4pm-closing

Main Street Bakery [D-5]   B $12, L $12, S $5   DD PQ   5 6 6

Closing in January 2013 to re-open in summer 2013 with Starbucks coffees alongside its cookies, brownies and cupcakes ($1.49-$6.09). The popular ice cream sandwich cookies will no longer be served here, but you will find them at the Plaza Ice Cream Parlor. Enjoy your treats in the cute dining area with granite-topped tables and counters, or take it outside to the tables near the Plaza Restaurant.

Counter
American
Med. noise
Med. waits
Open all day

Pecos Bill Tall Tale Inn & Cafe [A-4]   L $15, D $15, S $5   DD PQ   7 6 6

Just the place to rustle up a bowl of chili ($3.49), BBQ pork sandwich ($9.39), or cheeseburger ($8.69-$9.69)—they even have a well-stocked fixins' bar. Chicken wraps and salads ($7.79-$9.39) please the health-conscious. Sit on the covered porch to watch the parade. Themed rooms provide delightful indoor seating. Self-service ordering kiosks are in operation here! Tortuga Tavern is next door.

Counter
American
Very noisy
10 am-1 hour before closing

Pinocchio Village Haus [D-1]   L $15, D $15, S $5   DD PQ   6 6 5

Pinocchio's has a popular Italian menu that is nothing to "lie" about. Individual pizzas with side salad ($8.59-$9.69), chicken nuggets ($8.19), Caesar salad with chicken—$7.79 and Mediterranean salad—$8.49 are on the menu. The Swiss-styled stone building fits perfectly with its surroundings. Sit outside at a patio table for Fantasyland sights; some inside tables have a great view of "it's a small world."

Counter
Italian
Noisy
11 am-1 hour before closing

Top Photo Slice: Charming window boxes above Pinocchio Village Haus at the Magic Kingdom (Ⓒ9396) © Cheryl Pendry

Magic Kingdom Eateries

(continued)

Jennifer Dave Readers

The Plaza Restaurant [D-4]	L $33, D $33, S6	🍴DD PT	🏆	7	7	7

This small Main Street standby has an old-fashioned ice cream parlor atmosphere, offering large hot and cold sandwiches, including a Reuben ($10.99), Angus chuck burgers ($13.99), proper malts and shakes ($4.69), banana split ($7.99), and sundaes ($4.99–$5.99). A veggie sandwich ($10.99) and the chicken and strawberry salad ($14.99) are offered as "lighter" fare. Kids' meals are $8.59 with drink. Walk-up guests can expect a short wait before being seated. Tables and half-booths.

Table
American
Reservations suggested
11 am–1 hour before closing

Tomorrowland Terrace [E-4]	L $15, D $15, S $5	🍴DD PQ		5	5	6

Open seasonally with American and Italian fare, including a fried chicken sandwich ($8.99), pasta Alfredo ($8.99), lobster roll ($9.99), citrus shrimp salad ($8.19), and chocolate cake ($3.59). Tables and chairs are in a shaded, open-air (not air-conditioned) terrace that doubles as a shortcut between Main Street and Tomorrowland. Seasonal fireworks dessert parties—see page 282.

Counter
Asian
Med. noise
Short waits
5–9 pm

Tortuga Tavern [A-4]	L $13, D $13, S $6	🍴DD PQ		6	6	7

Open seasonally. Informal meals near Pirates of the Caribbean. The brief menu includes burritos ($5.99), beef nachos ($7.29), and taco salad ($8.19). The kid's meal offers a quesadilla or taco, carrots, grapes, and a drink ($5.49). The indoor and outdoor themed seating area is shared with Pecos Bill's.

Counter
Mexican
Med. noise
11 am–4 pm

Tony's Town Square Restaurant [D-6]	L $39, D $46	🍴DD PT	🏆	8	8	8

Tony's serves Italian cuisine in the heart of Main Street, U.S.A. Familiar dinner entrees include Tony's "special" spaghetti and meatballs from Lady and the Tramp ($16.99) and shrimp scampi pasta ($19.99). Less familiar but perhaps more interesting is a strip steak with port wine sauce ($28.99) and braised lamb shank ($23.99). The lunch menu offers pizzas and sandwiches ($12.99–$15.99), plus more elaborate entrees ($13.99–$16.99) like baked ziti. Tony's lunch menu is a good choice for an economical, early supper. Kids' meals are $8.59 and include choices like pasta primavera and Mickey cheese ravioli.

Table
Italian
Med. noise
Reservations suggested
Call 180 days
12–3:00 pm
5 pm–closing

Selected Magic Kingdom Snack Shops and Carts

Name		Land	Specialties
Plaza Ice Cream Parlor	DD PS	Main Street, U.S.A.	Hand-dipped ice cream
Aloha Isle* 🏆	DD PS	Adventureland	Pineapple Dole Whips (frozen dessert)
Sunshine Tree Terrace* 🏆	DD PS	Adventureland	Citrus Swirl, frozen yogurt
Turkey Leg Cart	DD PS	Adventureland	Smoked turkey legs, drinks
Aunt Polly's Dockside Inn*	DD PS	Frontierland	Ice cream, sundaes, pie (seasonal)
Golden Oak Outpost 🎗	DD PS	Frontierland	Chicken sandwiches, carrot cake
Liberty Square Market*	DD PS	Liberty Square	Fresh fruit, baked potatoes
Sleepy Hollow	DD PS	Liberty Square	funnel cakes, root beer floats, coffee drinks
Friar's Nook	DD PS	Fantasyland	Hot dogs, fries, apples, carrot cake
Storybook Treats	DD PS	Fantasyland	Soft-serve ice cream, shakes
Maurice's Cart 🏆	DD PS	Fantasyland	ice cream, frozen bananas, drinks
Auntie Gravity's 🏆	DD PS	Tomorrowland	Ice cream, smoothies
The Lunching Pad 🏆	DD PS	Tomorrowland	Turkey legs, pretzels, frozen drinks

Note: Some shops and carts may be seasonal. Eateries marked with an asterisk (*) close as early as 3:00–5:00 pm.

Top Photo Slice: The indoor fountain at Tony's Town Square at the Magic Kingdom (ⓘ3212) © Jean Philo

Planning

Getting There

Staying in Style

Touring

Feasting

Making Magic

Index

Notes & More

Epcot Eateries

(park map on page 152)

Jennifer Dave Readers

| | | DD PT | | 7 | 8 | 8 |

Akershus Royal Banquet Hall [B-3]   B $48, L $49, D $59

Enjoy authentic Nordic fare (lunch is $41.53/$28.75 kids ages 3-9, dinner is $55.37/$29.81—includes tax and photo package) in a replica of a rustic Norwegian castle, complete with Disney princesses all day long. Many diners have been happily surprised by food that's both remarkably familiar and somewhat unusual. Cold buffet. Hot specialties are brought to your table. Enjoy meats, cheeses, peel-and-eat shrimp, pasta, pan-seared salmon, Kjottkaker, Swedish meatballs, and a variety of salads. Kids can get chicken breast, cheese ravioli, meatballs, hot dog, or turkey roll-up. Soft drinks and dessert are included. Breakfast ($40.46-$46.85/$24.49-$27.68 kids ages 3-9) offers fruit, pastries, french toast, eggs, bacon, sausage, and hash browns. For character meal details, see pages 262-263.

Table
Norwegian
Med. noise
Reservations recommended
Call 180 days
8:30-10:10 am,
11:40 am-
2:50 pm,
4:20-8:20 pm

| | | DD PT | | 5 | 8 | 8 |

Biergarten [B-1]   L $31, D $44

Willkommen! A Bavarian town square in the midst of Oktoberfest is the setting for a hearty and satisfying German buffet (lunch is $27.68/$14.99 kids; dinner is $39.40/$19.16 kids—tax included). Wurst (sausages) with weinkraut, pork loin, chicken schnitzel, and rosemary roast chicken reign supreme at lunch. A first-rate sauerbraten and beef roulades are added at dinner. Every dish and side dish is several cuts above the typical German eatery. Musicians in lederhosen are on stage to entertain. Can you say "Gemütlichkeit"? (It roughly translates to "good feeling.") A large salad bar may even please some vegetarians, but this isn't the place for a light meal. Desserts and soft drinks are included; beverages are extra. There's Beck's beer on tap and a good German wine list.

Buffet
German
Very noisy
Reservations recommended
Call 180 days
Short waits
Noon-
3:10 pm,
4:00-closing

Dancing during a Biergarten show

© MediaMarx, Inc.

| | | DD P2 | | – | – | – |

Monsieur Paul (was Bistro de Paris) [F-2]   D $79

When this eatery re-opens in December 2012, it will have a new menu, a new name (Monsieur Paul), and a new decor. The revamped restaurant will remain elegant and will continue to serve haute cuisine, but will be less stuffy. Expect a leisurely, quintessentially French meal in mostly quiet and elegant surroundings—a far cry from the bustling restaurant downstairs. The wine list is excellent, but pricey. Ask for a window seat and linger until IllumiNations.

Table
French
Reservations recommended
Short waits
6:00-8:45 pm

| | | DD PQ | | 7 | 7 | 9 |

Boulangerie Patisserie [F-2]   L $14, S $6

Along with the changes to the France pavilion comes a move to bigger digs for this popular bakery. Once it re-opens inside Galerie les Halles shop, you'll have an expanded menu with new offerings such as salads and sandwiches. The ham and cheese croissants ($3.25), a cheese plate ($5.95) and French bread ($2.25) make a nice, light lunch, while croissants ($1.95-$2.85), eclairs ($3.75), chocolate mousse ($3.35), and fruit tarts ($3.85-$4.25) satisfy sweet tooths. The bakery's current space becomes the new Glacier ice cream parlor!

Counter
French
Long waits
~11 am-closing

Epcot Eateries
(continued)

Jennifer Dave Readers

Les Chefs de France [F-2] L $49, D $59 DDPT 👤	**6**	**7**	**8**

Traditional French favorites such as escargot ($12.99), onion soup ($7.99), braised duck aux cerises ($31.99), and grilled beef tenderloin with black pepper sauce ($34.99) carry the imprint of some of France's most famous chefs. The bright, bustling brasserie atmosphere, crowded seating, and overtaxed serving staff can be at odds with the desire for a slow, enjoyable meal. Lunchtime choices such as Crepe Florentine ($14.75), croque monsieur with side salad ($13.95), and Quiche Lorraine ($12.95) will keep things affordable–save the heavier entrees ($17.95–$23) until dinnertime. Prix fixe menus available. Kids' meals are $10–$12. Chairs and half-booths. Special dietary requests are hit or miss here. Remy the rat (from "Ratatouille") makes visits here.	**Table**
	French
	Very noisy
	Reservations strongly recommended
	Call 180 days
	Med. waits
	Noon–3 pm 5 pm-closing

Coral Reef [D-7] L $54, D $56 DDPT 👤	**6**	**7**	**7**

Few restaurants are as breathtakingly beautiful as the Coral Reef–brightly glazed blue mosaic tiles and brushed metal shimmer in the light cast by The Seas with Nemo & Friends aquarium, as fish of all sizes and colors swim by. The inventive seafood menu ($21–$27) covers a variety of international tastes and styles and is generally well-prepared. Meat and veggie lovers will also find foods to enjoy here ($19–$32). If only there was more elbow room, the noise more restrained, and the service more consistent. Tip: Request a tank-side table for the best views. Sweets here are special, especially The Chocolate Wave ($7.99). Kids' meals are $8.99. Enjoy the same view at lunch (entrees $19–$32).	**Table**
	Seafood
	Noisy
	Reservations strongly recommended
	Call 180 days
	Noon–3 pm, 4:30–8:00 pm

Electric Umbrella [C-6] L $15, D $15, S $6 DDPQ 👤	**5**	**4**	**6**

If you're looking for basic burgers ($7.59–$8.09) at Epcot, this is the place. It's also decent for healthier fare, like Greek salad ($6.49) and Caesar salad ($7.19)–you can also swap your fries for an apple. The main seating area is noisy–look for quieter seating upstairs, or dine outside on the terrace. Kids meals are $4.99. Tip: This eatery has an unlimited drink station for refills!	**Counter**
	American
	Med. noise
	Short waits
	~9 am–9 pm

Fountain View Ice Cream /Cafe [D-6] S $8 DDPS	**5**	**6**	**8**

Until it closes in March 2013, you can enjoy hand-scooped Edy's ice cream ($2.69/single scoop and $3.69/double scoop), plus sundaes ($4.19), floats/shakes ($3.99). It will re-open in midsummer 2013 serving Starbucks coffee!	**Counter**
	Coffee
	Hours vary

The Garden Grill Restaurant [F-6] D $44 DDPT	**8**	**7**	**8**

This popular dinner-only character dining experience is tucked away in The Land pavilion. Farmer Mickey, Pluto, Chip, and Dale make the rounds of this rotating restaurant. Watch an ever-changing American landscape while you eat. The grown-ups get breads with maple butter, salad, turkey breast, beef strip loin, fish of the day, smashed potatoes, and greenhouse vegetables. A "homegrown" salad comes with dinner–veggies are from Disney's hydroponic gardens. Vegetarians can make special requests. Kids ages 3–9 get a chicken drumstick, mac & cheese, potato sticks, and veggies. Dessert is a fruit cobbler for adults and "Life's a Bug" cake for kids. Soft drinks included. Price is $37.27/$18.10 ages 3–9. Try for a booth on the lower tier, which is closer to the scenery. See pages 262–263 for character meal details.	**Table**
	American
	Med. noise
	Reservations not always needed
	Call 180 days
	Short waits
	4:00 pm– varies with park hours

Planning · Getting There · Staying in Style · Touring · Feasting · Making Magic · Index · Notes & More

Epcot Eateries
(continued)

Planning
Getting There
Staying in Style
Touring
Feasting
Making Magic
Index
Notes & More

Kringla Bakeri og Kafé [B-3]   L $15, D $15, S $6   DDPQ   5 6 8

This is a must stop for veteran World Showcase visitors. Have a light meal with gourmet sandwiches and soups ($9.99). Or treat yourself to a "kringle" (sweet pretzel–$4.29), schoolbread ($2.69), cloudberry horn (a cream-filled pastry–$3.09), or other desserts ($2.19–$3.99). Kids meals are $5.49. Beer and wine by the glass. Nice outdoor tables. Popular before IllumiNations.

Counter / Norwegian / Med. noise / Long waits / ~11 am-9 pm

La Cantina de San Angel [B-4]   L, $18, D $18, S6   DDPQ   6 6 —

This recently expanded waterside eatery is now offering both indoor and outdoor seating, including viewing areas for IllumiNations. The taco plates are $10.95-$11.95, cheese empanadas are $10.75, nachos are $9.99, and guacamole with chips are $7.50. The ever-popular churritos for dessert are now $3.99. Kids meals $6.99. Their popular margaritas are $9.99-$11.99. Full service offered at dinner (see below).

Counter / Mexican / Med. noise / Med. waits / ~11 am-closing

La Hacienda de San Angel [B-4]   D $53   DDPT   5 8 —

This new table-service restaurant serves dinner only. A mix of the familar and unusual, the flavors are well above typical "Mex." The excellent taco trio starter ($11.25) feeds two, roasted and grilled meats and fish entrees are $22.95-$26.50. Large windows overlook the lagoon and IllumiNations. Kids meals $8.50.

Table / Mexican / Call 180 days / 4 pm-closing

Le Cellier [E-4]   L $54, D $77   DDP2   7 8 7

Oh, Canada! This steakhouse-in-a-stone-cellar is one of World Showcase's gems, and reservations are hard to get. Warm lighting, brocade upholstery, and stained glass make this the coziest cellar around—an upscale steakhouse style with Canadian accents. Lunch has been upgraded to Signature Dining. Starters ($9-$16) include wagyu carpaccio and lobster salad. Entrees ($34-$44) include a bone-in ribeye, mushroom filet mignon, Kurobuta pork, and King salmon. The vegetarian entree ($25) is very tempting. Lunches include an appetizer trio to share ($18), a burger ($15), salmon sliders ($16), chicken Cordon Blue ($22) and steaks, of course ($27-$32). The luscious cheddar cheese soup ($5.50/$7) is a big favorite at any time. Leave room for dessert—chocolate trio with "moose" ($11) anyone?

Table / Canadian / Medium noise / Reservations strongly recommended / Call 180 days / Long waits / 11:30 am-3:00 pm 4:00 pm-closing

A PassPorter reader eyes her Le Cellier "Smores" dessert hungrily

Liberty Inn [C-1]   L $16, D $16, S $7   DDPQ   4 4 5

Hot dogs, hamburgers, and chicken nuggets ($7.79-$9.99) weren't as American as apple pie ($3.59) back in Colonial days, but they are now. A toppings bar adds relish to the basic fare, while a chicken Caesar salad ($7.79) provides an alternative. Kosher items available. Seating indoors and out.

Counter / American / Short waits / ~11 am-closing

Eatery descriptions and ratings are explained on page 230.

Epcot Eateries
(continued)

Lotus Blossom Café [B-3]   L $15, D $15, S $6

Counter
Chinese
Med. noise
Med. waits
~11 am-closing

3 4 5

Chinese food at Epcot leaves a bit to be desired, and what for a while was an interesting menu has been dumbed-down. Start with pot stickers ($4.99) or egg rolls ($3.99). Main course choices are orange chicken, beef noodle soup, beef rice bowl, veggie stir fry, and shrimp fried rice (each $8.49), and sesame chicken salad ($6.99). Desserts are $3.25-$4.65. Kids' meal (sweet and sour chicken) is $6.95. Indoor and covered outdoor seating.

Enjoying a meal at Lotus Blossom Cafe

Restaurant Marrakesh [F-1]   L $49, D $61

Table
Middle Eastern
Noisy
Reservations not always needed
Call 180 days
Short waits
11:30 am–3:45 pm, 4 pm–closing

9 7 8

Enjoy exotic food in an authentic Moroccan setting as modest belly dancers and live musicians lend even more atmosphere. Lamb and chicken are the backbone of the cuisine, either roasted or stewed ($27.99). The flaky pastry-based appetizers ($5.99-$8.99) are a must, especially the chicken bastilla ($8.99). If you've always wanted to try couscous, the Moroccan national dish of stewed meat and/or vegetables over steamed semolina, you'll find it is quite good here ($20.99-$28.99). Order a la carte, or choose from a variety of family-style feasts ($45 per person) at dinnertime. Plan to sample a variety of appetizers and desserts (desserts $5.99-$7.99). Check for bargain-priced specials at lunch. The kids' menu offers "Moroccan" pasta with meatballs, chicken tenders, and kefta (hamburger) with fries ($7.99).

Nine Dragons [B-3]   L $41, D $44

Table
Chinese
Med. noise
Reservations suggested
Call 180 days
Medium waits
12:00 pm–4:30 pm, 4:45 pm–park closing

7 8 6

Nine Dragons has improved the variety and adventure on its menu. Many regions of China are represented by familiar and unusual menu items. Appetizers ($4-$11) include pot stickers, hot and sour soup, and cold spicy beef. Main courses ($13-$26) include fried rice, sweet and sour pork, stir-fried veggies, kung pao chicken, fragrant five-spiced fish, and Chinese chicken salad. The Nine Dragons family dinner set includes soup, entree, and dessert ($23.98/person). Lunch choices and prices are similar, but you could create a dim sum-style meal from the cold and hot appetizers.

The renovated Nine Dragons

A lunch set with a beef soup, choice of entree, and Chinese coleslaw is $18.98/person. Kids' entrees (sweet & sour chicken and/or lo mein with meatballs) are $7.68-$9.98.

Epcot Eateries
(continued)

Getting There
Staying in Style
Touring
Feasting
Making Magic
Index
Notes & More

Jennifer Dave Readers

Rose & Crown Pub and Dining Room [E-3] L $45, D $47 DDPT 7 6 8

They say "heck" is a place where the cooks are English, but the food in this boisterous, crowded pub is quite nice. It's so cozy inside you'd swear you just walked in out of a London fog. Traditional specialties include fish & chips ($15.99), bangers and mash ($15.99), Sunday roast with Yorkshire pudding ($16.99) and veggie shepherd's pie ($14.99). Start your meal (or simply snack) on a cheese plate ($9.99). Pub-style entertainers put in a regular appearance. A quieter meal with a view of IllumiNations may be had on the terrace—request a 7:30 pm (or earlier) reservation, check in early, request an outside table (no guarantee you'll get one, but ask anyway), and have a leisurely dinner. Don't forget a pint of ale, porter, or stout, a side of English "chips" ($2.99). And how about the sticky toffee pudding for dessert ($4.99)? Kids meals $8.59.

Table
English
Very noisy
Reservations strongly recommended
Call 180 days
Long waits
~11:30 am–4:00 pm, 4:30–closing

San Angel Inn [B-4] L $51, D $56 DDPT 7 7 7

Where but Disney can you dine at noon in a romantic, twilit Mexican plaza, while a cool evening breeze caresses your skin, a volcano steams ominously on the horizon and boats float by on the Gran Fiesta Tour (see page 162)? Despite the fine, authentic Mexican food, it's the atmosphere that makes San Angel Inn (pronounced "San Anhel") a favorite. For appetizers, we suggest tostados ($9) or sopa Azteca (tortilla soup, $7). For your entree, try their wonderful Mole Poblano (chicken in unsweetened cocoa sauce, $24), mahi-mahi Veracruzana ($25), or sirloin with chilaquiles ($28). Check the Chef's Selections for tempting items that go beyond simple "Mex." A separate vegetarian menu offers two choices ($13–$18). The kids can choose from quesadillas, tacos, or chicken tenders with Mexican rice ($8.50). La Cava del Tequila lounge is adjacent to this eatery, and offers more than 70 types of authentic tequilas ranging in price from $8 to upwards of $50. You can also get margaritas, tapas, and other appetizers in this 30-seat lounge.

Table
Mexican
Noisy
Reservations strongly recommended
Call 180 days
Med. waits
11:30 am–4:00 pm 4:30–closing

Sommerfest [B-1] L $14, D $14, S $7 DDFQ 5 6 7

Hearty, German fare for light eaters. Sommerfest serves bratwurst ($6.69), frankfurters (with sauerkraut, of course—$6.59), soft pretzels ($4.29), Black Forest cake ($3.59), and apple strudel ($3.59). Wash it down with German wine ($6), schnapps ($7.25), or German beer ($7.50, or $10.75 in a souvenir mug). Covered seating is outdoors, within earshot of the oompah bands.

Counter
German
Noisy
Med. waits
~11 am–closing

Sunshine Seasons [F-6] B $16, L $16, D $16 DDFQ ✿ 6 7 8

Designed to look like an airport food court (to go along with Soarin' nearby), this counter-service eatery features an open kitchen and food stations themed to the seasons. The Soup and Salad station (spring) offers a roasted beet and goat cheese salad ($7.89) and seared tuna noodle salad ($9.99). The Asian Noodles station (summer) has a tofu and veggie noodle bowl ($7.59) and a combination plate with an entree and two sides ($9.99). The Grill station (fall) has a rotisserie chicken ($10.19) and grilled fish ($10.19). And the Sandwich station (winter) offers a Ruben panini ($8.99) and a turkey and cheese sandwich ($8.99). The Bakery station offers various desserts, pastries, cakes, pies, espresso, cappuccino, and ice cream. Kids' meals ($6.99) include a panini, mac and cheese, sweet & sour chicken, or a chicken leg. Seating is inside at tables and chairs.

Counter
Cuisine varies
Noisy
Long waits
~9:00 am–closing

Epcot Eateries

(continued)

Tangierine Cafe [E-1]	L $19, D $19, S $6	DD PQ		7	7	7

	Counter
Tangierine Café offers traditional Middle Eastern sandwiches and combo platters served in a delightfully decorated, open-air café. Choose from shawarma (sliced chicken or lamb), roast chicken or vegetarian platters, and sandwiches and wraps ($8.99-$13.99). Desserts are a deal—for $2.50 you can add baklava to your meal. A coffee and pastry counter is tucked in the back, making this cafe an excellent choice for mid-afternoon espresso and honey-drenched desserts. Kids' meals are $7.99. Indoor and outdoor seating.	Middle Eastern
	Med. noise
	Med. waits
	Noon-closing

Teppan Edo [E-1]	L $53, D $53	DD PT		8	6	8

	Table
The Teppanyaki Dining Room got refreshed decor and a new name a few years ago, but the "teppan" dining concept survives. Guests sit around steel-topped griddle/tables, upon which meat and veggies are cooked by a flamboyant chef. Starters include tempura ($8.50), a bit of sushi ($7.50-$9.50), or novel Yaki-Sushi—	Japanese
	Noisy
	Reservations recommended

Your food is prepared in front of you on the grill

sushi rolls cooked at the table. Entree choices are steak ($27.95-$29.95), chicken ($22.95), or seafood ($25.95-$29.95), alone or in a variety of combos ($26.95-$29.95), all cooked the same way and served with the same veggies and rice. It's tasty, fun, and a good "adventure" for families and timid eaters. Tables seat eight and are often shared by several parties.

Call 180 days | Long waits | 12-3:45 pm, 4:30-closing

Tutto Italia [C-1]	L $63, D $70	DD PT		7	8	7

	Table
"Tutto Italia" means "all Italy," and this eatery's menu surveys the cuisine from south to north. Prices are high, but the quality is easily a match. The mixed antipasto for two ($30) is a delight. Pastas ($23-$29) include fettuccine with	Italian
	Very noisy
	Reservations strongly recommended

pancetta and parmesan cream, lasagna, and seafood risoto. Braised lamb shank, swordfish, rosemary chicken, and polenta with braised meats are hearty entrees ($26-$30). Lunch offers salads ($17-$20), entrees ($24-$28) and panini ($17-$19). Kids meals are $10 and offers pastas or mozzarella sticks. Desserts ($8-$14) include bugie/ chiacchere (their signatured anise and Sambuca-flavored crisp pastry) and cannolis. The new Tutto Gusto wine bar also offers a mouth-watering array of cured meats, cheeses, panini, and tapas-style "small plates" ($8-$22).

Call 180 days | 12-4:15 pm | 4:30-closing

Dave savors the Tutto Italia menu

Epcot Eateries
(continued)

■ **Tokyo Dining** [E-1]	**L $52, D $52**	DD PT	10	8	9

Like Teppan Edo, this restaurant was renovated from a previous incarnation (the former Tempura Kiku and Matsu No Ma eateries) into a larger, more trendy eatery. Tokyo Dining showcases the traditional cuisine of Japan, with an emphasis on sushi. Appetizer choices include edamame ($4.50), miso soup ($3.00), and braised pork ribs ($9.95). Entrees range from tempura ($16.95-$25.95), deep-fried cutlets ($21.95-$28.95), grilled meats ($21.95-$29.95), to bento boxes with a sampling of traditional Japanese delicacies ($25.95-$27.95). Kids meals come in a shinkansen (bullet train) shaped bowl and include your choice of tempura or teriyaki chicken ($10.50-$11.50). Desserts such as green tea pudding ($6.95) and chocolate ginger cake ($6.50) are also good. The sushi bar has a large "mood screen" showing iconic Japanese images—very relaxing on a busy theme park day. The main dining room offers lovely views of the World Showcase Promenade. During IllumiNations, the lights are dimmed and the music is broadcast over the eatery's speakers.

Table
Japanese
Med. noisy
Medium waits
~11 am–closing

■ **Via Napoli** [C-1]	**L $55, D $55**	DD PT	7	-	7

In a pizza mood? This eatery in Italy offers wood-fired pizzas and other Southern Italian favorites. With a design inspired by Naples 45 Ristorante e Pizzeria in NYC, this casual restaurant seats 300 and features three wood-burning ovens named after active volcanos in Italy: Etna, Vesuvius, and Stromboli. Menu items include a variety of appetizers and salads, including minestrone ($8) and calamari ($14). Pizzas are made with imported flour and tomatoes, and water closely resembling that found in Naples—they are available in three sizes (individuals for $16-$18, large 8-slices for $28-$30, and ½ meter 12 slices for $39-$41) and nine varieties. Lasagna ($20) and spaghetti ($21) are also offered, as well as Piatti alla Parmigiana with eggplant ($18), chicken ($24), and veal ($27). Desserts range from tiramisu ($8) to gelato ($7) to Zeppole di Ricotta ($10).

The new Via Napoli

Table
Italian
Reservations recommended
Call 180 days
Long waits
~11 am–closing

■ **Katsura Grill (Yakitori House)** [D-1]	**L $17, D $17, S $7**	DD PQ	6	5	8

Formerly Yakitori House. Of the Japan pavilion's three eateries, we visit here most often for tasty, filling, and economical fare. This classic Japanese quick-meal spot serves skewers of grilled teriyaki chicken, salmon, or beef as a platter or in a combo with shrimp tempura ($8.99-$12.99), satisfying beef curry over rice ($8.49), sushi ($7.99-$9.99) and big, filling bowls of Udon noodle soup ($9.99). Wash it down with hot sake or cold Kirin beer. Dine at tables indoors or out, and take a few minutes to stroll through the nearby bonsai display.

Counter
Japanese
Medium noise
Medium waits
~11 am–closing

■ **Yorkshire County Fish Shop** [E-3]	**L $14, D $14, S $5**	DD PQ	7	8	7

Crowds have been queuing up and strolling away with Harry Ramsden's legendary Fish & Chips ($8.19), and for good reason—it's the real thing! (Dave can't resist it!) An extra side of chips is $2.69. Wash it down with a Bass ale, Guinness, or try a refreshing, hard cider (sweet or dry). Seating at patio tables is often available to the right, or visit the United Kingdom gardens to eat.

Counter
English
Med. noise
Med. waits
~11 am–closing

Eatery descriptions and ratings are explained on page 230.

Epcot Eateries
(continued)

Snacking at Epcot is every bit as diverse and rewarding as feasting in its fine restaurants. The snack carts and shops seem to appear and change regularly, however, so a definitive snack list isn't practical. Instead, we've listed our favorite treats at Epcot and where you can find them—this will give you an idea of the variety of snacks available. If you can't locate one of our favorite munchies, chances are very good you'll find a new tidbit that we haven't yet discovered!

Our Favorite Snacks at Epcot

Treat	Found At
Churros (fried dough rolled in cinnamon sugar) **DD PS**	Mexico (Cantina de San Angel)
Pretzels, Lefse, and School Bread **DD PS**	Norway (Kringla Bakeri og Kafé)
Italian pastries and cappuccino	Italy (along promenade)
Funnel cakes (deep-fried batter with powdered sugar)	The American Adventure
Kaki Gori (shaved ice with sweet flavoring)	Japan (along promenade)
Baklava (flaky pastry with honey, rosewater, and nuts)	Morocco (along promenade)
Wine by the glass	France (along promenade)

Note: Some shops and carts may be seasonal.

International Food and Wine Festival

Eager to sample more international cuisine and exotic tastes? Visit the "World" in autumn, when Epcot hosts the International Food and Wine Festival. Just stroll around the World Showcase Promenade and sample food and drink at more than 25 booths. The generously sized appetizer treats range in price from $2 to $7, while small plastic glasses of wine, beer, champagne, cognac, and port begin at $3 and go up from there. Guests on the Disney Dining Plan may be able to use their snack credits for many of the food items. You can easily make a meal out of the offerings, stopping at booths whenever you discover another appetizing snack. Eating while strolling around isn't always the most relaxing, but there are plenty of benches and quiet nooks at which to munch away. In addition to the treats, you can watch cooking demonstrations by top chefs, participate in beer and wine seminars and tastings, and attend the Eat to the Beat concert series at the America Gardens Theater (no extra charge). With advance reservations, you can join special wine tasting events ($95–$150), a Party for the Senses (a $145 wine-sipping and food-sampling extravaganza), wine schools (day-long education programs for $150), and one-hour Food and Wine Pairings ($65). Sweets lovers will enjoy the 3D Disney's Dessert Discovery event, which includes desserts, cordial samplings, and a VIP viewing of IllumiNations ($55). The 17th annual festival will run from September 27 to November 11, 2013. For more information, call 407-WDW-INFO.

Food booth at the Food and Wine Festival

©12664 © Cheryl Pendry

Top Photo Slice: The frozen sweetness of a Kaki Gori from Japan © MediaMarx, Inc.

Genuine PassPorter Genuine PassPorter Genuine PassPorter Genuine PassPorter Genuine PassPorter Genuine PassPorter Genuine

Disney's Hollywood Studios Eateries
(park map on page 172)

Jennifer Dave Readers

ABC Commissary [C-3]	L $15, D $15, S $6	DDPQ	5 6 5

Carpeted floors, potted palms, and sleek decorating make you feel like a special employee. The International menu features a seafood platter ($9.49), couscous salad ($6.79), Asian salad ($7.19), chcken bleu ($8.99), and burgers ($8.79–$10.99). Kids can get chicken nuggets, a cheeseburger, or a ham and cheese wrap ($5.99). Kosher items available. Shady outdoor seating, too.

Counter / American / Med. noise / Med. waits / Open all day

Backlot Express [C-5]	L $16, D $16, S $7	DDPQ	5 5 7

Rarely crowded and often overlooked, this backstage-themed cafeteria serves up burgers, hot dogs, chicken nuggets, grilled turkey & cheese, and sesame chicken salad ($6.79–$8.99). The children's meal is $5.49 (includes drink). Pleasant indoor and outdoor seating. Perfect spot for watching the parade—stake out a table about a half-hour beforehand. Not always open.

Counter / American / Noisy / Short waits / 11 am-closing

Catalina Eddie's [G-3]	L $14, D $14, S $6	DDPQ	4 5 6

Part of the outdoor Sunset Ranch Market mini food court. Cheese and pepperoni pizza with Caesar salad ($8.99–$9.49), chicken Caesar salad ($7.79), hot Italian deli sandwich ($9.19), carrot and chocolate cakes ($3.79) make up the menu. Outdoor, shaded (and not-so-shaded) seating. Nearby food stands serve fries, fresh fruit, barbecue, burgers, and ice cream.

Counter / American / Med. noise / Short waits / 11 am-closing

Fairfax Fare [G-3]	B $11, L $17, D $17, S	DDPQ	5 4 5

Part of the outdoor Sunset Ranch Market (and formerly Toluca Legs Turkey). Menu includes chicken and ribs ($15.19), barbecued pork sandwich ($8.99), 1/2 slab of ribs ($11.69), and kids' meals of PB&J or mac & cheese ($5.49). Breakfast egg & cheese muffin ($5.99), yogurt ($1.99), and danish ($2.69). Seating is outdoors at covered picnic benches. Other food stands are nearby.

Counter / American / Noisy / Med. waits / 11 am-closing

'50s Prime Time Cafe [E-5]	L $41, D $41	DDPT	8 6 8

Clean your plate in an old kitchenette, while "Mom" serves gussied-up versions of home-cooked meals like meatloaf, pot roast, fried chicken, salmon, grilled pork tenderloin, pasta ($13.49–$20.99), and scrumptious malts, milkshakes, and sundaes ($4.79–$7.49). The lunch menu adds pot pie, sandwiches, and salads ($11.99–$16.99). Vintage TV clips of "I Love Lucy" and "The Honeymooners" play while you eat, and your "brother" and "sister" (your servers) boss you around when your "Mom" isn't watching. This is a unique dining experience if you're willing to play along—not recommended for the overly shy. Veggie burgers on request. The dining areas and adjoining bar/waiting area are a wonderland of '50s-vintage Formica, television sets, and knickknacks. Table and booth seating.

Table / American / Noisy / Reservations strongly recommended / Call 180 days / Long waits / 11 am-4 pm, 4 pm-closing

Eatery descriptions and ratings are explained on page 230.

Tip: The Disney's Hollywood Studios' table-service restaurants <u>may</u> open 30 minutes earlier on days with a morning Extra Magic Hour—check at 407-WDW-DINE.

Planning · Getting There · Staying in Style · Touring · Feasting · Making Magic · Index · Notes & More

Disney's Hollywood Studios Eateries
(continued)

Jennifer · Dave · Readers

Hollywood & Vine [E-5] — B $31, L $36, D $36 — DD PT — 7 7 7

This 1940s-inspired "Cafeteria of the Stars" has star power with a character breakfast and lunch buffet ("Play 'n Dine") with Playhouse Disney friends, including Special Agent Oso and Little Einsteins characters. It's a tasty and economical choice for a pre-Fantasmic! dinner. Stainless steel serving areas, comfy half-booths, retro tables, checkerboard tiles, and a mural of old Hollywood set the scene. The menu changes regularly—choices may include pot roast, salmon, baked chicken, and fish. The kids have their own buffet, and everyone can make sundaes. Breakfast is $26.62–$30.88 ($14.90–$17.03/kids), lunch is $30.88–$35.14 ($17.03–$19.16/kids), and dinner (no characters) is $30.88–$35.14 ($15.90–$18.10/kids). Available with the Fantasmic! dinner package at the same price (see below).

Buffet
American
Noisy
Reservations suggested
Call 180 days
8:00–11:20 am, 11:40–2:25 pm, 4:00 pm–closing

The Hollywood Brown Derby [E-3] — L $69 D $69 — DD P2 — 🍷 — 8 8 8

The famous Brown Derby, complete with "stars," serves enticing starters like potato and leek soup ($10), prawns ($12), and the yummy and original Cobb Salad ($8/$15). Entrees include coriander-dusted grouper ($33), duck two ways ($35), and first-rate roasts and chops ($28-$42). Desserts like the famous grapefruit cake ($7–$9) are quite good, and this is the place for a celebratory bottle of bubbly. Kids' entrees with drink are $6. The Brown Derby is the Studios' most elegant establishment. Off-white walls covered with caricatures of the stars, dark wood trim, crisp, white table linens, and attentive, formal service set the tone. Hollywood "personalities" may jazz up the show. This restaurant offers some special meals—for information on the Fantasmic! Meal Package, see below; for the Dine with an Imagineer experience, see page 267.

Table
American
Med. noise
Reservations strongly recommended
Call 180 days
Long waits
11:30 am–3 pm 3:30 pm–closing

Mama Melrose's Ristorante Italiano [A-4] — L $45, D $45 — DD PT — 🍷 — 6 5 7

Mama's is a brick wall and booth sort of place. A variety of individual wood-fired pizzas ($12.99-$13.99), light pasta specialties, and simple meats grace the menu at Mama's, which changes regularly. Starters include calamari for two ($10.99) and mozzarella with tomatoes ($8.49). Charred strip steak ($29.99), chicken parmigiana ($16.99), wood-grilled tuna ($21.99) or seafood arrabbiata ($22.99) may catch your eye. Sangria, a Bellini cocktail, and desserts like chocolate amarettini cheesecake ($5.49) may catch your attention. Ask about the Fantasmic! Dinner Package, which offers a three-course dinner plus seating at Fantasmic! (see pages 173 and below). Your little "bambini" can get pasta, pizza, grilled fish, or chicken parmigiana for $8.59.

Table
Italian
Med. noise
Reservations suggested
Call 180 days
Short waits
Noon–3 pm, 3:30 pm–closing

Fantasmic! Meal Package — DD PT DD P2

If you're thinking about a table service lunch or dinner at Disney's Hollywood Studios, consider the Fantasmic! Dinner Package. You get a meal at Hollywood Brown Derby, Mama Melrose, or Hollywood and Vine plus seats in the reserved section at the Fantasmic! nighttime show, at the price of the meal alone. To qualify, everyone in your party must order a meal (if you dine at Hollywood & Vine, you must get the fixed-price meal). Credit card deposit required, and there is a $10 cancellation fee if cancelling less than 48 hours beforehand. Call 407-WDW-DINE to make reservations up to 180 days in advance, or ask about it at Lobby Concierge at your Disney hotel or at Guest Relations in the park (see map on page 172 for location). Availability is very limited. Note: Details may change and Fantasmic! is not held every night. Note that no rain checks are issued for your Fantasmic! seating if it is canceled for bad weather.

Top Photo Slice: Dining in "cars" at the Sci-Fi Dine-In Theater (①14907) © Janet Simonsen

Planning · Getting There · Staying in Style · Touring · Feasting · Making Magic · Index · Notes & More

Disney's Hollywood Studios Eateries
(continued)

Jennifer Dave Readers

☐ Rosie's All-American Cafe [G-3]   L $15, D $15, S $7   DD PQ   4 4 6

Part of the outdoor Sunset Ranch Market mini food court on Sunset Blvd., Rosie's is really a hamburger stand offering 1/3 lb. cheddar cheeseburgers ($9.99), veggie burgers ($7.79), chicken nuggets ($8.69), soup ($2.99), and desserts ($3.79). Seating is outdoors at covered picnic benches. Other stands nearby offer pizza, barbecue, ice cream, and fresh fruit.

| Counter |
| American |
| Med. noise |
| Med. waits |
| 11 am–closing |

☐ Sci-Fi Dine-In Theater Restaurant [C-4]   L $44, D $44   DD PT   7 7 6

Build a drive-in theater in a movie soundstage, seat folks in replica vintage cars, serve souped-up drive-in fare, and show old sci-fi movie trailers. Would anyone buy that script? You and the kids will at this fanciful eatery. The menu is fun and portions are huge. Definitely get a shake ($4.69)—you can get "adult" (alcoholic) shakes, too. The kids' menu is classic "drive-in," but the adult menu has upscale choices like butcher steak with red wine glaze ($24.99) and shrimp bow tie pasta ($21.99). At lunch, try the Angus chuck burger ($14.99) or smoked turkey sandwich ($12.99). The desserts are out of this world ($5.99-$7.99). Everyone faces the screen, so chatting is hard. Not all seats are "parked cars"—request one if you want it. Kids' menu is $8.99.

| Table |
| American |
| Noisy |
| Reservations strongly recommended |
| Call 180 days |
| Med. waits |
| 11 am–4 pm |
| 4 pm–closing |

☐ Studio Catering Co. [B-3]   L $16, D $16, S   DD PQ   7 6 6

This eatery offers a melting pot of flavors. Offerings include a buffalo chicken sub ($8.99), turkey club ($9.99), Tuscan deli sub ($8.99), grilled veggie sandwich ($8.99), Greek salad ($6.49), Chicken Caesar Wrap ($8.99), and marble cheesecake ($3.59). Kids can have the choice of chicken nuggets or PB & J ($5.49). Sangria is also offered ($6.95). Tables are outside but sheltered.

| Counter |
| Mediterranean |
| Med. noise |
| Med. waits |
| 11 am–closing |

☐ Toy Story Pizza Planet [B-5]   L $16, D $16, S $6   DD PQ   3 4 6

The name is familiar, but this pizzeria/arcade doesn't look all that much like the pizza palace in Toy Story. Choose from individual pizzas ($8.99-$9.49), meatball sub ($9.19), or a chicken salad ($7.49). There's also a cappuccino cupcake ($3.99) and cookies ($2.19). It's an OK place to eat and rest while your little "Andy" or "Jessie" hits the arcade. Seating upstairs and outside.

| Counter |
| American |
| Very noisy |
| Long waits |
| 11 am–closing |

Disney's Hollywood Studios Snack Shops and Carts

Name	Location	Specialties
Dinosaur Gertie's Ice Cream DD PS	Echo Lake	Soft-serve ice cream
Min & Bill's Dockside Diner DD PS	Echo Lake	Shakes & malts, sausage sub
Peevy's Frozen Concoctions DD PS	Echo Lake	Frozen slushes, bottled drinks
Herbie's Drive-In DD PS	Streets of America	corn dogs, chili dogs
Anaheim Produce DD PS	Sunset Boulevard	Fresh fruit, drinks
Hollywood Scoops DD PS	Sunset Boulevard	Hand-dipped ice cream
Starring Rolls Cafe DD PS	Sunset Boulevard	Baked goods, coffee, sandwiches
Toluca Legs Turkey Co. DD PS	Sunset Boulevard	Turkey legs, beverages

Note: Some shops and carts may be seasonal.

Disney's Animal Kingdom Eateries

(park map on page 186)

Jennifer Dave Readers

Flame Tree Barbecue [E-4]

L $10, D $10, S $7 | DD PQ | 6 6 6

Although we're not sure how barbecue fits in with the Animal Kingdom motif, we can't knock it, because it's good stuff. Pork, chicken, turkey, and beef is smoked right on premises and is available sliced on sandwiches ($8.99) and arrayed on platters ($9.69–$11.99). The condiment stations offer traditional and mustard-based barbecue sauces. A green salad with BBQ chicken in a garlic bread shell ($7.79) is the light alternative. Chicken drumsticks, hot dogs, and PB&J for the kids ($5.49). Shaded outdoor seating in a lovely Asian garden or on decks overlooking the lake and Expedition Everest.

Counter
American/Barbecue
Quiet
No reservations
Med. waits
10 am–5 pm

© MediaMarx, Inc.

Outdoor seating at Flame Tree Barbecue

Pizzafari [B-4]

B $10, L $12, D $12 | DD PQ | 4 4 7

This popular pizzeria centrally located in Disney's Animal Kingdom serves individual cheese and pepperoni pizzas ($8.99–$9.49), chicken Caesar salad ($7.79), and a hot Italian sandwich ($8.99). You can also get a veggie pizza ($9.49). Kids meals are $5.49. Breakfast platters ($8.29), breakfast panini ($5.99), kids French toast ($4.99), and cinnamon rolls ($3.19) are offered in the morning. There's lots of indoor, air-conditioned seating in brightly decorated, uniquely themed dining areas. Look for quieter seating toward the back of the restaurant or outside on the patio. Kosher items available here.

Counter
Italian
Very noisy
Long waits
10:00 am–5:00 pm

© Cheryl Pendry

Pizzafari's colorful exterior

Rainforest Cafe [B-7]

B $16, L $53, D $53 | 5 6 7

Environmentally conscious dining in an artificial rainforest hidden behind a two-story waterfall? It even rains indoors! The Rainforest Cafe puts on quite a show and piles your plate with tasty, inventive foods representing many different cuisines. Hearty breakfasts ($8.99–$13.99), enormous sandwiches ($12.99–$14.99), pastas ($14.49–$20.99), steaks, chicken, and ribs ($18.99–$30.99), seafood ($21.99–$25.99), and mountainous salads ($15.99–$16.99) overflow the menu. Smoothies and specialty alcoholic drinks are popular. Located just outside the gates (no park admission required). This was the first table-service restaurant at Disney's Animal Kingdom. There's a special entrance for folks exiting and re-entering the park. For discounts, see page 229.

Table
American
Very noisy
Call 407-938-9100 for reservations
Long waits
8:30 am–1.5 hours after closing

Planning · Getting There · Staying in Style · Touring · Feasting · Making Magic · Index · Notes & More

Disney's Animal Kingdom Eateries
(continued)

Restaurantosaurus [E-6]   L $17, D $17, S $7   DDPQ   5 5 8

Counter
American
Very noisy
No reservations
Long waits
10:30 am–park closing

DinoLand's only sit-down meal offers choices like a "Dino-Size" $\frac{1}{3}$-lb. burger with fries ($9.19), shrimp po boy ($9.99), chicken nuggets ($8.19), chili salad ($8.69), veggie sub ($9.39), and chocolate mousse or cheesecake in a glass ($3.59). Kids meals are $6.49 for your choice of chicken nuggets or cheeseburger. The indoor, air-conditioned dining areas are fun—it's a weathered, dig site bunker with broken equipment, humorous signs, and educational displays. Note: The fries and nuggets here are no longer McDonald's versions but rather Disney's, and are pretty good.

Tusker House Restaurant [B-2]   B $31, L $33, D $36   DDPT   7 8 8

Table
American
Noisy
Call 180 days 8:00–10:30 am
11 am–varies

This buffet restaurant offers a character breakfast and lunch, plus imaginative food offerings for dinner. You can start your day with "Donald's Safari Breakfast Buffet" with friends like Mickey, Goofy, Daisy, and Donald (of course). Breakfast food includes biscuits and gravy, vegetable frittata, cheese blintzes, scrambled eggs, rotisserie honey-glazed ham, yam casserole, and warm cinnamon rolls for $26.62–$30.88 ($14.90–$17.03/kids). Lunch is $27.68–$31.94 ($15.97–$18.10/kids) and dinner is $30.88–$35.14 ($15.97–$18.10), and both include a wide variety of dishes, including salads, curried rice salad, vegetarian

couscous, salmon filet, carved beef and pork, and curry chicken. A kids' station stocks corn dog nuggets, mac and cheese, chicken drumsticks, and corn (among other items). Desserts are fruit cobbler, warm banana-cinnamon bread pudding, and pastries. Seating is at tables and chairs in several large dining rooms.

A couple of the inventive options at Tusker House

Yak & Yeti (Counter Service) [E-3] L $13, D $13, S $7   DDPQ   6 5 7

Counter
Asian
Noisy
No reservations
Long waits
11:30 am–park closing

This counter next door to the restaurant by the same name (see next page) offers familiar Asian favorites in cute little boxes, such as sweet and sour chicken ($9.99), honey chicken ($9.99), orange beef ($10.99), Asian chicken sandwich ($9.99), and Mandarin chicken salad ($8.99). Sides such as pork egg rolls ($2.49) and chicken fried rice ($3.99) are also available. Kids' meals are $4.99 and include your choice of cheeseburger or chicken bites. Seating is at plentiful tables and chairs, though shade is something of a scarce commodity. You could also take your tray to the riverside seating area behind Drinkwallah (see photo to right).

A Yak and Yeti meal

Eatery descriptions and ratings are explained on page 230.

Disney's Animal Kingdom Eateries
(continued)

Yak & Yeti (*Table Service*) [E-3] L $51, D $51 DD PT 8 8 8	Table
The Asian-themed eatery offers interesting Asian-fusion cuisine. Menu offerings include appetizers such as lettuce cups ($13.99), Thai chili chicken wings ($9.49), and a dim sum basket for two ($13.99). Wonton soup ($4.99) and huge Mandarin chicken salad ($15.99) are also available. Entrees include seared miso salmon ($24.99), duck with Anadapur glaze ($23.99), Shaoxing steak and shrimp ($25.99), and maple tamarind chicken ($19.99). Lo mein noodles are also available ($17.99- $18.99). Desserts include mango pie ($6.99) and fried wontons ($7.99). Kids' entrees are $8.49 and include your choice of mini burger, veggie lo mein, chicken bites, or egg roll, and a drink. The dining rooms on both floors are imaginatively decorated and worth a tour after your meal. The theme is	Asian-American
	Noisy
	Call 180 days
	10:00 am-
	3:45 pm
	4:00 pm-
	closing

evocative of the Western Himalayan foothills in India and Nepal, the dining rooms full of Asian antiques. There's also a shop next door selling Asian-inspired items.

The upper floor of Yak & Yeti offers nice views of Asia

Enjoying lo mein noodles

Disney Animal Kingdom's Snack Shops and Carts

Name	Land	Specialties
Camp Soft Serve DD PS	Camp Minnie-Mickey	Soft-serve ice cream, soda floats
Dawa Bar	Africa	Beer, cocktails
Harambe Fruit Market DD PS	Africa	Fresh fruit, juices, beverages
Kusafiri Coffee Shop & Bakery DD PS	Africa	Pastries, cappuccino & espresso
Tamu Tamu Refreshments DD PS	Africa	Burgers, sandwiches, shakes
Anandapur Ice Cream DD PS	Asia	Soft-serve ice cream. soda floats
Dino Bite Snacks DD PS	DinoLand U.S.A.	Ice cream, sundaes, churros
Dino Diner DD PS	DinoLand U.S.A.	Hot dogs, chips
Trilo-Bites DD PS	DinoLand U.S.A.	Smoked turkey legs, drinks

Note: Some shops and carts may be seasonal.

Downtown Disney Marketplace Eateries

(map on page 206)

Cap'n Jack's Restaurant — L $39, D $39

This casual, nautically themed restaurant hovers over the Lake Buena Vista Lagoon. Tables and chairs line the outer rim of the six-sided main dining room, giving each table glittering views through floor-to-ceiling picture windows. The lights of Downtown perform an enchanting dance on the waters, providing a romantic setting that the lackluster kitchen can't quite match. Appetizers include fresh clams ($8.99), spinach dip ($7.99), and chowder ($5.49), sandwiches at lunch ($12.99–$18.99), and entrees that include crab cakes ($24.99), pasta Alfredo with crab or salmon ($13.99–$19.99), salmon ($19.99), shrimp pasta ($19.99), and roast chicken breast ($18.99). Consider Ghirardelli for dessert and Fulton's for better seafood. Not themed after Pirates of the Caribbean movies.

| 7 | 4 | 6 |

Table
Seafood
Med. noise
Reservations at 407-WDW-DINE
Short waits
11:30 am–10:30 pm

Earl of Sandwich — B $10, L $11, D $11, S

One of the best all around deals on Disney property! This eatery is perfect for a lunch or a light supper in cozy British decor and the menu offers a dozen appetizing hot sandwiches on specialty bread (roast beef & cheddar, ham & brie, and a turkey, bacon, & swiss club—all $5.99 each), Cobb and Chinese chicken salads ($5.99), and refrigerated grab 'n go items—sandwiches ($3.95), tuna, fruit, or chicken salads ($5.99), and yummy tomato soup ($2.99). Hot breakfast sandwiches ($3.99) in the morning, and a kids' menu ($3.99).

| 6 | 6 | 7 |

Counter
Eclectic
Noisy
Medium waits
8:00 am–11:00 pm

Ghirardelli Soda Fountain & Chocolate Shop — S $12

Who can resist the pleasures of San Francisco's famed chocolatier? Sundaes, sundaes, and more sundaes ($8.95–$9.50) tempt dessert fans, or share an eight-scoop Earthquake ($34.95). If that's too much, cones, shakes, malts, and frozen mochas beckon ($6.25–$6.95). Their whipped cream-topped hot chocolate ($3.50) is perfect on cool winter evenings. Sugar- and fat-free ice cream, too.

| 6 | 6 | 8 |

Counter
American
Med. waits
9:30 am–12:00 am

Pollo Campero/Fresh A-Peel/Babycakes — B L $16, D $16, S

A mini-food court replaced Ronald's Fun House (McDonald's) with three establishments offering fresh and healthy cuisine. **Pollo Campero** specializes in chicken, both citrus grilled and fried, with Latin American flair. Combo meals offer a choice of fried chicken, 1/4 citrus grilled chicken, chicken strips with bbq pork, or a chicken sandwich plus one side, for $8.49. Family Feasts feed 3-4, with either 8 pieces of fried chicken, 12 chicken strips, or a whole grilled chicken, plus a large side and corn tortillas, for $21.99. Kids's meals are $5.99. Sides include black beans and rice, beans, sweet plaintains, yuca fries, French fries, chips and salsa, and coleslaw ($2.49–$4.49). Breakfast burritos, sandwiches, and platters feature eggs and chorizo or bacon ($2.49–$3.69). **Fresh A-Peel** offers all-natural beef burgers, veggie burgers and Aidells' hot dogs ($6.99), and a variety of signature salads—chopped vegetable, grilled chicken (in three styles), and skirt steak, in either bowls ($6.99–$7.99) or wraps ($5.99–$6.99). Kid's choices include PB&J, mini-burger, mini hot dog, or mini sausage, for $4.99. Breakfast items are steel-cut oatmeal or French toast ($3.99), and a side of Aidells' chicken sausage is $1.99. **Babycakes NYC** this famous New York-based bakery offers cupcakes, cookies, brownies, loaf cakes, and donuts, free of gluten, diary, eggs, and soy, sweetened with unrefined sugars. Vegan, and Kosher, even! ($1.25 to $3.75 each). Indoor seating.

| 6 | 6 | 7 |

Counter
Latino/Natural/Bakery
Very noisy
Med. waits
11:30 am–11:00 pm

Eatery descriptions and ratings are explained on page 230.

Downtown Disney Marketplace Eateries
(continued)

Jennifer Dave Readers

Rainforest Cafe	L $53, D $53	DD PT	♿	5 6 7

Another Rainforest Cafe? Yes, and it's very similar to the one at Disney's Animal Kingdom (see page 245 for menu items and descriptions). Differences include a smoking volcano atop the restaurant and lunch and dinner only (no breakfast). This is a very popular stop for families. Show up, sign up, and be prepared to wait. Occasional live animal demonstrations help pass the time. If the wait is too long, you can sit at the Juice Bar and order from the regular menu, or browse the Rainforest gift shop. Near the Downtown Disney Marketplace bus stop. Open until midnight on Fridays and Saturdays. For discounts, see page 229.

Table
American
Very noisy
407-827-8500
Very long waits
11:30 am– 11:00 pm

T-Rex	L $57, D $57	DD PT	♿	7 7 7

It's fair to call T-Rex a prehistoric-styled Rainforest Cafe (they're both owned by Landry's Restaurants). Roaring Audio-Animatronics dinos replace trumpeting elephants, and occasional meteor showers substitute for rainstorms. It's a greater, more elaborately-executed spectacle than the nearby Rainforest Café (look for fabulous mineral and fossil specimens). The food is reliably good, with the same approach to flavor (big), serving size (huge) and theming (over the top) as its sister-restaurant—a wide choice of mostly American plus popular international items, with fanciful names. Appetizers ($9.99-$15.99) include bruschetta, nachos, quesadillas, reliably good flatbread pizzas, and a gargantuan and satisfying sampler ($18.99, or $24.99 with ribs). After that, if you have room for entrees, is a long list of oversized entrée salads ($15.99-$17.99), burgers and sandwiches ($12.99-$16.99), pastas ($17.49-$18.99), and meat and fish specialties ($17.99-$31.99). Desserts are $7.99-$14.99. Kids menu is a la carte, with entrees $6.99-$7.99, drinks $1.99, and desserts $2.99.

Table
American
Very noisy
Call 407-827-8500 for reservations
Very long waits
11:30 am– 11:00 pm

Wooly Mammoth beside the glowing Ice Cave
©13809 © Janet Simonsen

Alexander loved his kids meal at T-Rex
© MediaMarx, Inc.

Wolfgang Puck Express	B $14, L $19, D $19, S	DD PQ	♿	6 6 7

Fast food for the trendy, upscale set. Puck's famous wood-fired pizzas ($11-$14), pennette chicken Alfredo ($15), half rotisserie chicken ($16), and oven roasted salmon ($18) are served hot. Salads ($7-$13), and appetizing sandwiches ($10-$13) are available in the refrigerator cabinet. Desserts are $2-$6, and children's items are $7. Drink homemade lemonade, frozen cafe mocha, wines by the bottle and glass, and beer on tap. Dine outside, or take out. See page 252 for Wolfgang Puck Grand Cafe over at the West Side.

Counter
American
Med. noise
Med. waits
9:00 am– 11:00 am, 11 am-10 pm

Planning · Getting There · Staying in Style · Touring · Feasting · Making Magic · Index · Notes & More

Downtown Disney
Pleasure Island & West Side Eateries
(map on page 206)

Jennifer Dave Readers

Bongos Cuban Cafe	L 33, D $45	DD PT		4	6	7

The lively Latin sounds and flavors of Miami's South Beach make Gloria Estefan's Bongos a popular choice for Downtown Disney dining. This is robust, savory fare, with not a chili pepper in sight. Black bean soup ($6), seafood skillet ($40), creole shrimp ($25), skirt steak ($25), ropa vieja ($16), fried plantains ($6), and flan ($5.75) are some of the authentic Cuban choices. The lunch menu offers mainly sandwiches ($8.00–$8.50). Tastes may be too exotic for some diners, and our most recent meal was disappointing. The bar serves classic rum drinks, including the Mojito, a refreshing mix of white rum, mint, and sugar. An outdoor counter serves sandwiches and snacks (avg. meal cost=$16) from 9:30 am–midnight. Lunch served on Friday and Saturday only.

Table
Cuban
Noisy
No reservations
Long waits (allow 20 to 60 min.)
11:00 am–2:00 am

Cookes of Dublin	L $19, D $19, S	DD PQ	6	6	7

This small "chippie" beside Raglan Road offers hand-battered fish & chips ($10.95), scallops ($12.95), chicken ($9.95), Dublin-style meat pies ($11.95) and fried (donut-battered) candy bars ($3.50). Seating is mostly outside and uncovered.

Counter
Irish
3 pm–11 pm

FoodQuest	L $14, D $14, S	DD PQ		5	6	6

FoodQuest serves chicken Caesar salad ($7.79), wraps ($8.99), grilled chicken BLT sandwiches ($8.99), chili dogs ($7.49), burgers ($8.79), and individual pizzas ($6.79–$7.29) to guests at DisneyQuest (you must have DisneyQuest admission to dine here). Desserts and snacks are $2.79–$3.99. Kids' meals are $4.99. Note: FoodQuest is no longer operated by the Cheesecake Factory.

Counter
American
Noisy
11:30 am–10:30 pm

Fulton's Crab House	L $51, D $73	DD P2		6	7	8

A boatload of seafood, served in a replica of a riverboat (sans paddlewheel) just outside Pleasure Island. The fish is flown in fresh every day, and the prices suggest it flew First Class. If you're looking for a fish feast, this is the right place. Preparations are straightforward—grilled, steamed, fried, or raw, with appropriate sauces. Crab lovers can choose from nearly a dozen entrees featuring crab ($26.95–$58.95), Rhode Island lobster ($49), and the finest seasonal fish, shrimp, oysters, and clams ($19.95–$39.95) also appear in many forms. Steaks make a strong showing, too ($44.95). Prices aren't too bad if you avoid crab and lobster. Try the créme brulée. Kids' entrees $6.99–$7.99.

Table
Seafood
Very noisy
Reservations accepted
Med. waits
11:30 am–3:30 pm, 5 pm–11 pm

House of Blues	L $46, D $46	DD PT		8	7	8

The funky House of Blues' menu has changed away from it's Cajun and creole offerings to a more varied menu. The cornbread ($6.99), pulled pork sliders ($9.99), and jambalaya ($16.99) are two beats ahead of any place similar in the "World," and you can get fine burgers ($11.99–$13.99), meatloaf ($16.99), steaks ($27.99–$28.99), ribs ($22.99), salads ($5–$14), and sandwiches ($12.99–$13.99), too. Located near Cirque du Soleil and DisneyQuest, "HOB" looks like a weather-beaten wharfside dive. Inside is an equally aged interior with comfy booths. Live blues bands keep the joint cookin' (and make conversation difficult). Headliners play at the concert hall next door. A Gospel Brunch is held every Sunday (see page 266 for details). Open to 2:00 am on Thu.–Sat.

Table
American
Very noisy
Reservations at 407-WDW-DINE
Call 180 days
Long waits
11:00 am–11:00 pm

Eatery descriptions and ratings are explained on page 230.

Disney's Animal Kingdom Area | Epcot Area | **Downtown Disney Area** | Magic Kingdom Area

Chapter 5: Feasting and Snacking | Topic: Downtown Disney Eateries | 251

Planning

Getting There

Staying in Style

Touring

Feasting

Making Magic

Index

Notes & More

Downtown Disney
Pleasure Island & West Side Eateries

(map on page 206)

Jennifer Dave Readers

☐ **Paradiso 37**	L $52, D $52	DD PT	8	6	7

This waterfront eatery features street foods from the 37 countries of the Americas. Typical menu items include Caribbean crab and fish fritters ($10.99), chorizo and beef skewers for 2 ($17.99), North American corn dogs ($9.99), shrimp ceviche ($9.75), skewered shrimp and jicama orange salad ($7.99), jalapeno burger ($16.99), burritos ($14.99), Colombian whole hen ($20.99), and Argentinian skirt steak ($23.99). Kids meals are $6.99 and include choices such as PB & J sandwich, tacos, cheeseburgers, grilled fish, and chicken fingers. Desserts include the Paradiso 37 "chocolate stack" ($7.99), churros ($5.99), churros and sopapillas ($5.99), and four mini ice cream cones ($7.99). Also offered are signature frozen margaritas, an extensive tequila "tower" with more than 50 types, an international wine bar, and nightly entertainment. Seating is both outdoors and indoors at the colorful, two-level restaurant. We think both the food and atmosphere are unique, and this is a nice change of pace from other eateries at Downtown Disney.

Table
American (North, South, & Central)
Noisy
Reservations recommended
Call 407-934-3700 for reservations
11:00 am–midnight (open until 1:00 am on weekends)

☐ **Portobello**	L $41, D $53	DD PT	5	6	8

Contemporary Italian specialties are served in a bustling setting. Meals are robust and flavorful, and sometimes memorable—we've been disappointed by mediocre meals and excess noise, but we enjoyed others and loved our first. Specialties include an extensive antipasto menu ($12.95-$23.95), grilled meats and fish, including a grilled mahi mahi ($27.95) and flat iron steak ($28.95). Pastas include ravioli gigante ($19.95) and linguini with clams ($23.95). There's a fine, if expensive, wine list. Desserts include sinful chocolates, fresh fruits, and sorbet ($5.95-$7.95). Lunch features pizzas and sandwiches ($9.95-$12.95).

Table
Italian
Very noisy
Reservations accepted
Call 180 days
Med. waits
11:30 am–11 pm

☐ **Raglan Road**	L $49, D $53	DD PT	6	7	7

This large and comfortable Irish pub has a great atmosphere, four bars, live entertainment after 9:00 pm, and a new approach to old Irish comfort foods that make this a worthy stop. Starters of scallops ($15) and "Nom Nom Wings" ($10) are satisfying choices, as are main courses like beef stew ($17) fish and chips ($19), a modernized Shepherd's Pie ($18), and a hearty chicken and mushroom pie ($18). Desserts ($8) missed the mark. Kids' menu ($7-$9) includes burgers, fish & chips, and shepherd's pie.

Table
Irish
Call 180 days
Med. waits
11 am-2:45 pm, 3-11 pm

①2528 © Janet Simonsen

A traditional pub

①7438 © Elizabeth Key

Shepherd's Pie (front) and fish and chips (back)

Downtown Disney
Pleasure Island & West Side Eateries
(continued)

Jennifer
Dave
Readers

Planet Hollywood   L $43, D $43   DDPT   5 5 6

Everyone will be entertained and well-fed inside Planet Hollywood's big, blue globe full of movie and TV memorabilia. Every visitor gets the Hollywood treatment—you have to pass by the bouncers at the bottom of the stairs and walk under a long awning to reach the front door. There's seating on several levels, with views of projection video screens showing TV clips and movie trailers. You don't really come for the food, or do you? The menu can please almost anyone, with entree salads ($13.99-$19.99), sandwiches and burgers ($11.99-$14.99), pastas ($14.99-$19.99), fajitas ($19.99), and grilled and roasted meats ($19.99-$25.99). Kids' meals and desserts are $7.95. Portions are huge, quality is average, and service can be slow. You won't get bored, though.

Table
American
Very noisy
Reservations at 407-WDW-DINE
Call 180 days
Med. waits
11 am-1 am

Wetzel's Pretzels   L $15, S $10   6 5 5

Former Disneyland Jungle Cruise cast member Rick Wetzel has become king of the gourmet soft pretzel. This shop offers a variety of fresh, hand-rolled soft pretzels, "pretzel dogs" (pretzel dough-wrapped weiners), fresh-squeezed lemonade, fruit drinks, and Häagen-Dazs ice cream. A second kiosk can be found at Downtown Disney Marketplace.

Counter
American
Med. noise
11:00 am-11:00 pm

Wolfgang Puck Cafe   L $51, D $51   DDPT   7 6 7

Puck is famous for nearly single-handedly popularizing California cuisine and for putting wood-fired, individual pizzas on the map. Menu favorites include Puck's famous California roll ($13), crab cake ($15), Asian BBQ ribs ($20), steak frites ($29), pumpkin ravioli ($18), those legendary pizzas including BBQ chicken ($15) and smoked salmon ($18), and his Chinois chicken salad ($13). Oh, and the sushi bar is to die for! The decor is trendy, the tables for two are too small, service is spotty, and dinnertime seating requires long waits. If you're in a rush, dine at the bar or outdoors. Conditions are much nicer at lunch. Note: "Grand Cafe" refers to the three restaurants under one roof. Reservations can be made up to 180 days in advance for dining times between 11:30 am-6:00 pm and 9:30 pm-closing.

Table
American
Very noisy
Reservations at 407-WDW-DINE
Very long waits
11:30 am-11:00 pm

Wolfgang Puck Dining Room   D $72   DDP2   8 8 8

Climb the broad staircase inside Wolfgang Puck Grand Cafe and you'll reach the upscale Dining Room, offering refined respite from the crowds below, when not booked for parties. Starters include smoked salmon pizza, duck Napoleon, and roquefort gnocchi ($8.95-$17.95).Entrees include steamed fish Hong Kong style, sushi, "Chinois" rack of lamb , beef short rib goulash, duo of duck (breast and confit), and Wienerschnitzel with potato salad ($28.95-$45.95). Three- and Four-course "Chef Tours" are $49.95 and $52.95, respectively. Call 407-WDW-DINE for reservations and parties. Note: Chef's Table was discontinued .

Table
American
Noisy
Reservations recommended
Call 180 days
Long waits
6-10:00 pm

Wolfgang Puck Express   B $14, L $19, D $19   DDPQ   5 6 8

Fast food for the trendy, upscale set. Puck's famous wood-fired pizzas, rotisseried rosemary garlic chicken, real macaroni and cheese, soups, and pastas are served hot. Enjoy a wide choice of salads and appetizing sandwiches, soft drinks, and alcoholic beverages. Part of Wolfgang Puck Grand Cafe. Dine outside, or take out. See page 249 for Wolfgang Puck Express at Marketplace.

Counter
American
Med. noise
Med. waits
11 am-11pm

Resort Restaurants

Disney's Animal Kingdom Lodge Resort Restaurants

Boma—Flavors of Africa | B $24, D $45 | DD PT | 7 8 9

Savor the many flavors of Africa at a fabulous buffet. Breakfast is $20.23–$24.49 ($11.71–$13.84/kids) and dinner is $35.14–$39.40 ($17.03-$19.16/kids); tax included. At dinner, a dazzling array of unusual soups, stews, salads, veggies, and wood-grilled meats tempt both timid and adventuresome diners (including kids and vegetarians). The wood-burning grill and exhibit kitchen add extra flavor to the marketplace décor. And the dessert station is fabulous—be sure to try the Zebra Domes. Breakfast is equally wonderful but more down-to-earth. Diners are consistently amazed by the wide variety of pleasing new tastes, and even plain meat-and-potatoes lovers are delighted. Book ahead and arrive early, as even the line to check in can be long.

| Buffet |
| African |
| Very noisy |
| Reservations strongly suggested |
| Call 180 days |
| Long waits |
| 7:30 am-11 am, 5:00-10:00 pm |

Jiko—The Cooking Place | D $74 | DD P2 | 9 9 9

African flavorings meet Californian and Asian influences with grace and style at Jiko. Savory appetizers include grilled wild boar tenderloin, crispy beef bobotie roll, and flat breads from wood-burning ovens ($9–$16). Entrees include Nigerian prawns ($35), seared Lake Victoria perch ($39), seared Barbarie duck breast ($39), beef short ribs ($37), and Peri Peri chicken ($30). Jiko boasts a AAA Four Diamond rating, among other honors. Fish and vegetarian items take the limelight, and you'll also find a strong Afro-Mediterranean influence. For dessert, try the flourless chocolate torte with chocolate ganache ($9). Phenomenal South African wines. Kids have their own menu with appetizers ($3–$4) and entrees ($6–$12). Dress code is "business casual" (see page 228).

| Table |
| African |
| Noisy |
| Reservations strongly suggested |
| Call 180 days |
| 5:30 pm-10:00 pm |

Sanaa | L $39, D $46 | DD PT | 7 9 8

Sanaa opened in 2009 at Animal Kingdom Lodge's newly-opened Kidani Village building with a menu that is almost entirely Indian, including samosa appetizers ($7.99), six curries (choose two-$18.99), tandoor-cooked chicken, lamb, or shrimp ($17.99-$20.99), and a good line-up of Indian breads ($8.99 for a sampler that serves two or more) as well as salad and appetizer samplers ($6.99 and $14.99). In addition to seven Indian-style entrees, there is a satisfying African spiced chicken ($17.99), sustainable fish with shrimp and scallops (market), a New York Strip steak ($29.99), and the vegetarian sampler ($14.99). Among the few "misses," avoid the five grain pilaf, which doesn't fit well with traditional Indian cuisine—stick to the basmati rice. The dining room is very attractive, offering great views and a quieter, more intimate version of the rustic style seen at Boma. The wine service here is a big deal, but beer ($6.75 for imports) or a mango lassi smoothie ($4.69) would be more traditional. Lunch offers a similar menu at somewhat lower prices. Kid's meals are $8.59. Desserts ($5.49-$6.99) are never a big deal at Indian eateries, but there are a dozen specialty hot teas ($6.29).

| Table |
| African |
| Med. noise |
| Med. waits |
| Call 180 days |
| 11:00 am-10:00 pm |

PassPorter friends together on opening night at Sanaa

Top Photo Slice: Pretty lights hanging over tables at Boma (①10899) © Gina Pesca

Resort Restaurants

BoardWalk Resort Restaurants

See page 261 for Beach Club eateries.

☐ Big River Grille & Brewing Works L $45, D $47   DDPT ♀   3 4 4

No, you won't see Brewmaster Mickey, but this brewpub chain is a popular family dining spot at the BoardWalk (ESPN Club seems to siphon off the rowdier drinking crowd). Choices range from chicken quesadilla ($9.99) to a grilled chicken cashew salad ($12.99), barbecue pork sandwich ($9.50, lunch only), burgers ($10.99–$13.99), or meatloaf ($14.99). Steaks and ribs are also plentiful ($22.99–$25.99). The decor and seating are simple—we suggest you dine outdoors on the boardwalk in good weather. Our most recent visit was disappointing, with lackluster service, mediocre food, and a dirty floor. They do take reservations 24 hours in advance as well as reservations on the same day at 407-560-0253.

Table
American
Noisy
Reservations accepted within 24 hrs.
Med. waits
11:30 am–11:00 pm

☐ ESPN Club   L $40, D $40   DDPT   4 4 7

100 TVs pipe the big games into every nook and cranny of this very popular (and loud) sports bar. You can even go on camera for a live sports trivia quiz. The lineup is familiar—red wings ($11.49), nachos ($9.99), burgers and sandwiches ($10.49–$14.49), or try some rocky road cake ($5.99), plus beer and mixed drinks. Sit at booths or on stools. Open until 2:00 am on weekends. This eatery is very busy during any sport playoff as well as Sunday afternoons. No reservations.

Table
American
Very noisy
Med. waits
11:30 am–1:00 am

ESPN Club on the BoardWalk

☐ Flying Fish Cafe   D $76   DDP2 ♀   8 8 8

This is a Disney dining hot spot and one of our favorites, serving uniquely prepared, fresh seafood in a trendy-but-fun atmosphere. The menu changes to suit the season and the catch. Appetizers are special. Dave was blown away by their plump steamed mussels ($18). The "Chef's Thunder" portion of the menu offers daily specialties, such as surf and turf brioche and herb-crusted flounder ($37), while the main menu may offer a remarkable red snapper in a crispy, sliced-potato wrapper ($36) or ginger yellowfin tuna ($36). There's strip steak, pork, and pasta for the fish-shy ($28–$42) and not-to-be-missed desserts. The crowds here are loud—ask for a quieter table in the back. Open to 10:30 on Fri. and Sat. Dress code is "business casual" (see page 228).

Table
Seafood
Very noisy
Reservations strongly recommended
Call 180 days
Med. waits
5:30 pm–10 pm

☐ Kouzzina by Cat Cora   B $17, D $57   DDPT ♀   7 7 7

Celebrity chef Cat Cora teamed up with Disney to create a Mediterranean-style menu that pays tribute to the chef's Greek roots. Favorites include the appetizer sampler for two ($18), Kouzzina Trio; a sampler of pastitsio, lamb burger, and chicken with orzo ($22), and a lovely Fisherman's Stew ($26). Breakfast brings turkey-sweet potato hash ($12.50), veggie flatbread ($12), and omelets ($12.50). Jennifer loved the food (and the sangria was to die for!), but felt the service left a lot to be desired. Dave, on different visits, was pleased by both food and service.

Table
Mediterranean
Reservations recommended
Call 180 days
Expect long waits

Eatery descriptions and ratings are explained on page 230.

Resort Restaurants

Caribbean Beach Resort Restaurant

Jennifer   Dave   Readers

☐ **Shutters**	D $45	DD PT	6	6	6

Serving American cuisine inspired by the flavors of the Caribbean, this 120-seat, casual family restaurant has a breezy, island atmosphere. Menu items include a chorizo-black bean soup ($5.49), shrimp fritters ($7.99), penne pasta with chicken, shrimp or vegetarian ($15.99–$17.99), mango-ginger marinated roast chicken ($17.99), and Caribbean pork ribs ($20.99). For dessert, go with the key lime tart ($5.49). Kids meals (pizza, mac & cheese, fish) are $8.59.	**Table** Caribbean/American Reservations suggested 5:30–10 pm

Contemporary Resort Restaurants

☐ **California Grill**	D $89	DD P2	🎗	8	8	8

Beginning January 6, 2013, California Grill is closed for major refurbishment—when it reopens in summer 2013, it will feature an updated menu and new decor. Watch for more news at passporter.com. High atop the Contemporary, overlooking the Magic Kingdom, the California Grill pours fine wines, serves yummy California cuisine, and keeps getting better! The noise can be deafening, but the fireworks bursting over Cinderella Castle are spectacular. The menu changes weekly, but count on inventive dishes. When available, the peaceful Wine Room has the same menu, and you may see Epcot's IllumiNations. Sushi bar seating, too. Dress code is "business casual" (see page 228). Note: Diners check in on the second floor of the Contemporary and are escorted up to the 15th floor when their table is ready. A credit card is required to book.	**Table** American Very noisy Reservations strongly recommended Call 180 days Long waits 5:30 pm–10:00 pm

Big windows, great views

Ⓒ12431 © Cheryl Pendry

☐ **Chef Mickey's**	B $36, D $49	DD PT	🎗	6	6	8

Chef Mickey's fills the Contemporary's cavernous lobby with all sorts of Goofy antics (not to mention Mickey, Minnie, and friends). Mickey's offers separate adult and kid's dinner buffets ($40.46/$20.23 kids 3–9) and a sundae bar. Breakfast buffet ($35.14/$19.16) includes omelettes and pancakes cooked to order. Dinner items change, but on our last visit, we had flavorful roast beef, tasty pork loin, and cod with a curry crust, all of a quality and presentation befitting a deluxe resort. See pages 262–263 for character meal details.	**Buffet** American Very noisy Reservations suggested 7–11:30 am, 5:00–9:30 pm

☐ **The Wave**	B $26, L $46, D $54	DD PT	🎗	7	8	7

In keeping with the Contemporary resort's theme, this eatery focuses on serving locally-grown foods that are organic and sustainable in a "wave of American cuisine." Breakfast choices include smoked salmon ($9.99) and a ham & cheese omelet ($11.49). The lunch menu offers items like Asian chicken salad ($15.49), Reuben sandwich ($13.49) and vegetable stew ($17.99). Dinner brings avocado and citrus salad ($7.99), lamb shank ($25.99), and roast chicken ($17.99). Desserts are $7.99 each and include cheesecake, mousse, and carrot cake. Kid's meals are $8.99.	**Table** American Reservations suggested Call 180 days 7:30–11 am, Noon–2:00 pm, 5:30–10:00 pm

Top Photo Slice: A wave on the ceiling at The Wave in the Contemporary Resort (Ⓒ12440) © Cheryl Pendry

Planning | Getting There | Staying in Style | Touring | Feasting | Making Magic | Index | Notes & More

Resort Restaurants

Coronado Springs Resort Restaurant

Maya Grill	B $21, D $54	DD PT		5 6 5

Maya Grill has re-invented its menu yet again, returning to its Mexican roots. The restaurant is almost too elegant for a moderate resort, with grand, soaring architecture evoking a Mayan temple in warm yellows and accents of deep blue, shimmering gold, and rich woods. Breakfast is a la carte and offers standards like eggs Benedict ($10.99), plus steak and huevos rancheros ($14.99) The dinner menu includes a mixed grill for two with chimichurri steak, chicken al pastor, chorizo, and roasted vegetables ($51), sirloin or shrimp tacos ($25), classic mahi-mahi Veracruzana ($25), chicken a las Rajas ($23), and pan seared tequillla-glazed salmon ($27). Kids' menu available, with entrees running $8.25–$8.95.	**Table**
	American
	Med. noise
	Reservations suggested
	Call 180 days
	Short waits
	7–11 am, 5–10 pm

Fort Wilderness Resort Restaurant

Trail's End Restaurant	B $20, L $36, D $29	DD		7 6 6

One of the best dining deals on Disney property. While the vittles at Trail's End won't win awards for elegance, the food is plentiful, fresh, and tasty. Breakfast buffets ($19.16/$11.71 kids 3-9, tax. incl.) are hearty and heavy on home-style classics—eggs, French toast, Mickey waffles, hash, donuts, biscuits and gravy, cereals, yogurt, and fruit. Lunch is now a la carte, with chili, fried chicken and waffles, sauteed catfish, spicy grilled shrimp, burgers, and fried green tomatoes ($11.49-$15.99). The dinner buffet is gentle on the wallet at $26.62/$14.90, and you still get a tasty soup, salad bar, peel-and-eat shrimp, chicken, ribs, carved meat, fish, good veggies, pizza, and a daily regional specialty. Soup & Salad bar is $11.50.	**Table/Buffet**
	American
	Med. noise
	Reservations accepted
	Short waits
	7:30–11:30 am, 11:30–2:00 pm, 4:30–9:30 pm

Grand Floridian Resort Restaurants

Cítricos	D $78	DD P2		9 8 9

A grand restaurant at the Grand Floridian, Cítricos blends the fresh flavors of Florida and the Mediterranean with simplicity and elegance. Warm colors, tall windows, and well-spaced tables make this a very comfortable place. The menu changes frequently. Sauteed shrimp ($14) and tapas plate ($14) are appealing appetizers. A wonderful braised veal shank is available as an entree ($46), along with pan-seared red snapper ($38), Berkshire pork two ways ($33) and seared tofu ($23). The wine pairings ($29.50) are a fine idea, and the desserts ($8-$10) are gorgeous! May be closed Mondays and Tuesdays on some dates. Kids' menu entrees $6-$13. Dress code is "business casual" (see page 228).	**Table**
	Floridian
	Med. noise
	Reservations suggested
	Call 180 days
	Short waits
	5:30–9:30 pm

Garden View Lounge	S $39			8 7 5

If you've ever yearned for afternoon tea, this is the place for it. The quiet, genteel Victorian setting is perfect for tea sandwiches, scones, and pastries ($3.50–$14.50), with individual teas ($6.50), or do it right with an all-inclusive tea "offering," with or without champagne ($23–$38). Mr.s Potts Tea, for the young ones, is $12. A good variety of teas is served. Site of "My Disney Girl's Tea Party" (see page 274).	**Lounge**
	English
	Call 180 days
	2–6 pm

Eatery descriptions and ratings are explained on page 230.

Resort Restaurants

Grand Floridian Resort Restaurants (continued)

Jennifer / Dave / Readers

Grand Floridian Cafe — B $24, L $40, D $48 — DD PT — 5 6 6

This "informal" cafe features an American menu with all the extra flourishes found in finer restaurants. Hearty breakfasts range from a frittata to lobster eggs Benedict ($9.99-$17.99). Lunch brings entree salads ($14.49-$18.49), shrimp and pasta ($16.99), and sandwiches include a Reuben and a burger with lobster, asparagus, and hollandaise ($10.99-$18.99). Dinner offers steaks, grilled fish, and pasta ($17.99-$28.99), and that over-the-top burger ($18.99). Kids' complete meals are $6.09 at breakfast and $8.59 at lunch and dinner, with pizza, grilled chicken or salmon. Steak is a $2 up-charge.

| Table |
| American |
| Very noisy |
| 7-11 am, 11:45 am-2 pm, 5-9 pm |

Narcoossee's — D $89 — DD P2 — 8 8 8

Narcoossee's open kitchen serves an ever-changing menu of grilled seafoods with savory accompaniments. Perched on the edge of Seven Seas Lagoon, the restaurant has a sedate and casual dockside atmosphere, with lots of bare wood and windows affording views of the Magic Kingdom fireworks and the Electrical Water Pageant. The huge appetizer of steamed mussels with pastis was heavenly ($16). Specials like tilefish with lobster fritters ($36), plus crispy whole snapper ($35) and steamed Maine lobster ($58) are tempting choices, and carnivores can have filet mignon ($45) or chicken breast ($29). Desserts ($8-$15) include a gelato sampler, Key Lime créme brulee, and a cheese plate. Kids' entrees are ($7-$12). Dress code is "business casual" (see page 228).

| Table |
| Seafood |
| Noisy |
| Reservations recommended |
| Call 180 days |
| Short waits |
| 6-10 pm (lounge open 5-10 pm) |

1900 Park Fare — B $26, D $45 — DD PT — 7 7 7

Daily character meals in a jolly Victorian setting, complete with an orchestrion ("player" organ). The upscale buffet breakfast is $22.36-$26.62 ($12.77-$14.90/kids) and features Mary Poppins, Alice in Wonderland, and the Mad Hatter. Waits can be long, but characters may be on hand to keep you occupied. Dinner is $38.33-$42.59 ($19.16-$21.29/kids) with Cinderella and friends hosting. This is one of Disney's finer buffets (keep your eyes open for the strawberry soup—it's scrumptious). The Wonderland Tea Party is held here for kids on Mondays-Fridays. See pages 262-263 and 274 for details.

| Buffet |
| American |
| Very noisy |
| Reservations recommended |
| Call 180 days |
| 8:00-11:30 am 4:30-8:30 pm |

Victoria & Albert's — D $160 — 10 10 9

You have to dress up for Walt Disney World's five-star dining experience—jackets are required and a tux or gown isn't entirely out of place. The continental, five-course, prix fixe menu ($125, plus big up-charges for Kobe beef, caviar, and the like) is redesigned daily, a harpist fills the air with music, and ladies receive roses at meal's end. For an extra-special evening, reserve the "Chef's Table," an alcove in the kitchen where you observe and interact with the chef and staff, or the intimate Queen Victoria's Room—both serve a 10-12 course meal ($200/person, reserve six months in advance). Wine pairing ($60 in the main dining room, $95 for the Chef's Table and Queen Victoria's Room) perfectly match your meal. Is it all worth it? Without a doubt! Your dinner is elegantly prepared, and each course brings new delights. We held our wedding dinner here. Need we say more? State special dietary needs in advance. Must be at least 10 years old. Call 407-824-1089 to confirm 24 hours in advance.

| Table |
| French |
| Quiet |
| Reservations required—call 407-824-1089 |
| Call 180 days |
| Short waits |
| 5:45 pm & 9:00 pm |

Planning | Getting There | Staying in Style | Touring | Feasting | Making Magic | Index | Notes & More

Resort Restaurants

Old Key West Resort Restaurant

| Olivia's Cafe | B $29, L $45, D $45 | DD PT | 6 | 6 | 5 |

	Table
Olivia's Cafe serves an enticing array of Southern- and Caribbean-tinged specialties in a homey, small-island atmosphere. Breakfast includes the classics and a lineup of healthy items ($9.99–$15.99). Lunchtime brings conch chowder ($6.99), salads ($5.99–$7.99), and po boy and roast beef sandwiches ($11.49–$15.49). At dinner, the crab cake ($10.49), prime rib ($27.99), shrimp and grits ($20.99), and pork chop glazed with chipotle bbq sauce ($21.99) will make you smile, and don't pass up the Key Lime tart ($5.49) or individual apple pies ($5.49). Reservations are not always necessary here.	Floridian
	Med. noise
	Short waits
	Call 180 days
	7:30–10:30 am, 11:30 am–5 pm, 5–10 pm

Polynesian Resort Restaurants   See page 261 for the Polynesian Luau

| Kona Cafe | B $23, L $42, D $51 | DD PT | 8 | 7 | 8 |

	Table
A stylish spot for coffee and full meals. Its Asian/eclectic menu brings welcome sophistication to the Polynesian Resort. Breakfast favorites include banana-stuffed "Tonga Toast" ($10.99) and tropical Lilikoi juice blend ($3.99). Lunch offers tempting appetizers ($6.99–$10.99), a huge teriyaki beef salad ($16.99), a satisfying Asian noodle bowl ($13.99), and a traditional Polynesian plate lunch ($14.99). Dinners offer steaks, chops, chicken, and seafood with an Asian flair ($16.99–$28.99), including teriyaki-glazed strip steak ($28.99). Fabulous coffee bar (mornings only) and desserts ($5.49–$6.99), too!	International
	Noisy
	Reservations recommended
	Call 180 days
	7:30–11:30 am, Noon–3:00 pm, 5–10 pm

| 'Ohana | B $26, D $41 | DD PT | 8 | 7 | 7 |

	Table
Aloha, cousins! The Polynesian Resort welcomes you warmly to 'Ohana, a great, fun spot for families and groups. This is an all-you-care-to-eat feast for $25.14–$29.40 ($17.03–$19/16/kids). Appetizers (salad, fried dumplings, and wings) and veggies are served family-style, then the cast members circulate with long skewers of grilled steak, shrimp, chicken, and pork. Kids can do coconut races and hula hoop contests, and entertainers sing Hawaiian melodies. You may even see the Magic Kingdom fireworks! Soft drinks and bread pudding dessert included. The tropical drinks in unusual containers are extra. 'Ohana also hosts a character breakfast for $22.36–$26.62 ($12.77–$14.90/kids) with Lilo and Stitch: "'Ohana means family-style dining, which means no one gets leftovers!" See pages 262–263.	Polynesian
	Very noisy
	Reservations strongly recommended
	Call 180 days
	Long waits
	7:30–11 am, 5–10 pm

Port Orleans Riverside Resort Restaurant

| Boatwright's Dining Hall | D $47 | DD PT | 7 | 5 | 7 |

	Table
Cajun cooking from down the bayou fits the bill perfectly. In keeping with the restaurant's theme, a wooden boat hangs overhead and boat-builders' tools hang on the rustic walls. This is a place for hearty, Southern-style dinners, with appetizers like crawfish bites ($10.49) and chicken andouille gumbo ($6.49). Main courses include jambalaya ($17.99), blackened fish filet ($21.99), voodoo chicken ($17.99), and pork chop with amber ale bbq sauce and cheesy grits ($21.99). Desserts ($5.49–$6.49) include bread pudding and pecan pie. Kids' meals are $8.59.	American
	Call 180 days
	Short waits
	5:00–10:00 pm

Eatery descriptions and ratings are explained on page 230.

Resort Restaurants

Saratoga Springs Resort Restaurant

Turf Club Bar and Grill	D $48	DD PT	6 6 6

Jennifer Dave Readers

This table-service eatery offers wholesome American fare. Menu items include crab cakes ($10.49) and fried calamari ($9.99) for starters. Entrees include spiced salmon salad ($16.49/$19.99), Angus chuck cheeseburger ($12.99), prime rib ($25.99), lamb chops ($22.99), pasta with shrimp ($16.99), and grilled salmon ($19.99). Desserts are $4.49-$6.49. Kids' meals are $8.59 (cheeseburger, grilled chicken, or mac & cheese). Note this eatery now serves dinner only (no lunch).

Table
American
Call 180 days
Short waits
5:00-9:00 pm

Delicious crab cakes
①3868 © Michelle Clark

Swan and Dolphin Resort Restaurants

bluezoo [Dolphin]	D $84	6 7 7

Star chef Todd English presents upscale, inventively prepared seafood at this visually striking establishment. The scallop appetizer with braised short rib ($14) was a savory adventure, the "Dancing Fish" (market) disappointing, king salmon ($33) a winner, and other choices ($25-$60) were satisfying. $79 chef's tasting menu. Separate, lighter menu at the crowded cafe/bar. Not kid-friendly.

Table
Seafood
Noisy
Call 180 days
5 pm-11 pm

Fresh Mediterranean Market [Dolphin]	B $22, L $49	8 7 8

This cheery and appealing eatery offers a wide variety of cooked-to-order items at a breakfast buffet ($17.95/$10.95). The very attentive chefs ply you with all sorts of temptations, both Mediterranean-style and American, all prepared with a light, "fresh" hand. Grilled and rotisseried meats, pastas, cold salads, veggies, and lots of desserts, too! Lunch is available seasonally and is a la carte off a menu.

Buffet
Mediterranean
Med. noise
Call 180 days
6 am-2 pm

Garden Grove [Swan]	B $24, L $39, D $47	5 6 8

This out-of-the-way spot offers a weekday breakfast buffet ($16.99/$10.99 kids 3-9), a Japanese breakfast ($22), a la carte selections, and a character breakfast on weekends from 8:00 to 11:00 am ($20.99/$12.99). Lunch offers salads, sandwiches, and light entrees ($13-$16). In the evenings the eatery transforms into a character dining experience (see pages 262-263). Dinner offers a buffet ($28.99/$12.99 kids 3-9) with rotating seafood, Mediterranean, and bbq themes. Reserve at 407-934-1609.

Table
American
Noisy
Call 180 days
6:30-11:30 am,
11:30 am-2 pm,
5:30-10 pm

Kimonos [Swan]	D $56, S	6 7 6

In search of excellent late-night sushi, drinks, and karaoke? Try the Swan! Now all a la carte. Feast on sushi (2-pc. orders, $5-$8), rolls ($5.50-$15.99) and hot items ($4.95-$17.95) while you get up the nerve to sing (if you dare). Very noisy. Reservations accepted for parties of 6+ (call 407-934-1609).

Table
Japanese
Noisy
5:30 pm-12 am

Top Photo Slice: Bubble baubles overhead at bluezoo (①7991) © Cheryl Pendry

Genuine PassPorter Genuine PassPorter Genuine PassPorter Genuine PassPorter Genuine PassPorter Genuine PassPorter Genuin

Planning | Getting There | Staying in Style | Touring | Feasting | Making Magic | Index | Notes & More

Resort Restaurants

Swan and Dolphin Resorts Restaurants *(continued)*

Il Mulino New York Trattoria [Swan] D $71

Jennifer 8 | Dave 8 | Readers 7

This traditional Italian eatery offers an extensive (if pricey) menu which features dishes from the Abruzzi region of Italy, including arancini (rice balls) ($8), carpaccio ($14), pizzas ($16–$18), risotto con funghi ($26), gnocchi bolognese ($24), ribeye steak ($39), saltimbocca ($33), and seared red snapper ($31). Desserts are heavenly, especially the torta di cioccolati (flourless chocolate cake–$8). At meal's end, adults are served complimentary glasses of limoncello, a sweet digestif.

Il Mulino's Dining Room
© MediaMarx, Inc.

Table
Italian
Very noisy
Reservations suggested– 407-WDW-DINE
5 pm–11 pm

Shula's Steak House [Dolphin]   D $92

8 | 8 | 9

This is the most upscale steakhouse on Disney property. Beautifully grilled, flavorful beef is the focus (if you finish the 48-oz. porterhouse, they'll engrave your name on a plaque!) but perfectly succulent fish ($27.95) gets the utmost respect. Grilled meats cost from $23.95 to $85. If you need to ask the "market price" of the 4-lb. lobster, you can't afford it! With dark wood paneling, Sinatra on the speakers, gilt-framed football photos, and formal, attentive service, you may prefer to wear a jacket or dress. Veggies are $7.95–$12.95 (split an order, and get the potato pancake, too) but the "garnish" of peppers, watercress, and mushrooms on every plate may be enough. The wine list is expansive and expensive. And order the chocolate soufflé for two ($14)!

Table
Steakhouse
Med. noise
Reservations suggested; call 407-WDW-DINE
Call 180 days
Short waits
5 pm–11 pm

Wilderness Lodge Resort Restaurants

Artist Point   D $76

DD P2   10 | 9 | 8

This visually stunning restaurant serves flavorful contemporary fare from the Pacific Northwest and is among our favorites. The dining room is a soaring, log-beamed space graced by large murals of Western landscapes and furnished with comfortable, Mission-style tables and chairs. The menu changes seasonally. For starters, try Dungeness crab salad ($15), steamed mussels ($14), or smoky portobello soup ($9). The old-standby cedar plank Copper River salmon ($48) is always rewarding, or try the grilled beef tenderloin ($43), buffalo strip loin ($43) or seafood and vegetarian entrees ($28–$34) like the Asian-style prawn and crab hotpot. For dessert, the hot berry cobbler is a must ($10). The wine list is excellent—try a wine pairing. Dress code is "business casual" (see page 228).

Table
American
Med. noise
Reservations suggested
Call 180 days
Short waits
5:30 pm– 10:00 pm

Whispering Canyon Cafe   B $23, L $42, D $64

DD PT   8 | 6 | 8

If you hanker for house-made barbecue in a Wild West setting, sashay over to Whispering Canyon, long-famous for its family-style, all-you-can-eat meals (breakfast $16.50/$8.50 and dinner $33). At dinner, choose three of five for your platter: ribs, chicken, carved steak, fish, and sausage (a veggie entree can be requested). Sides and desserts are included, appetizers and drinks are extra. Lunch is now a la carte, with sandwiches and entrees ranging from $12.50-$17. There are activities for the kids, and the servers make sure all have fun. Just don't ask for ketchup. Trust us! Hours: 7:30–11:00 am, Noon–3:00 pm, and 5:00–10:00 pm.

Table
Barbecue
Very noisy
Reservations a must
Call 180 days
Long waits
7:30 am-10 pm

Eatery descriptions and ratings are explained on page 230.

Resort Restaurants

Yacht and Beach Club Resorts Restaurants

Jennifer Dave Readers

Cape May Cafe [Beach Club]   B $31, D $45   DDPT   7 7 8

Seafood lovers line up for this dinner buffet, which is within walking distance of Epcot. For $38.33-$42.59 ($18.10-$20.23/kids), you get an endless supply of chowder, steamed hard shell clams, mussels, baked fish, flank steak, ribs, corn on the cob, and all the trimmings will make any seafood lover happy as a clam. There's plenty for the fish-shy, a kids' buffet (mac & cheese, mini hot dogs, fish nuggets, and chicken strips), a dessert bar, and they bring taffy with the check. The character breakfast buffet is $26.62-$30.88 ($13.84-$17.03/kids) and prized for its relaxed atmosphere (see pages 262-263). Chairs and booths.

Buffet
Seafood
Noisy
Reservations recommended
Call 180 days
7:30-11 am, 5:30-9:30 pm

Captain's Grille [Yacht Club]   B $21, L $37, D $49   DDPT   4 5 8

Formerly the Yacht Club Galley, this casual hotel café offers pleasant surroundings at breakfast, lunch, and dinner. Traditional favorites and a healthy helping of meat and seafood dishes are the specialty here. Breakfast offers a buffet ($15.99/$8.99 kids 3-9) and a la carte selections ($4.49-$14.49). Lunch brings salads ($5.49-$17.49), burgers ($12.49-$14.99), and a lobster roll ($17.99). Dinner offers steaks, chops, and snow crab ($15.99-$29.99).

Table
American
Short waits
7:00-11 am, 11:30 am-2 pm, 6:00-10:00 pm

Yachtsman Steakhouse [Yacht Club]   D $79   DDP2   7 7 9

Until Shula's opened, Yachtsman Steakhouse was the best steakhouse at Disney and it still comes close. Hardwood-grilled steaks are the main attraction at dinner, but vegetarians haven't been neglected. Appetizers include lobster bisque ($9), Maine diver scallops ($14), and salads ($9-$16). Plain and sauced meats ($34-$44) including a popular peppercorn-glazed strip steak ($42), porterhouse ($44), filet mignon ($40), rib-eye ($43), and rack of lamb ($34) fill the menu. Excellent wine and beer list. Kids entrees are $7-$12. Dress code is "business casual" (see page 228).

Table
Steakhouse
Med. noise
Reservations strongly suggested
Call 180 days
5:30-9:45 pm

Beaches and Cream   B $15, L $34, D $34, S   DDPT   8 6 8

This small, seaside-style ice cream parlor is always jammed. Sure, you can get classic luncheonette items like burgers ($8.99-$13.99), roast beef subs ($12.49), veggie burgers ($7.99), and hot dogs ($7.99), plus shakes and malts ($4.99), but you know everyone is here for the ice cream. Why not cut to the chase and go for an ice cream soda, float, ice cream, frozen yogurt, or sundae ($3.19-$7.99)? Or get the Kitchen Sink ($23.99), a huge sundae with every topping. Sit at tables, booths, or at the counter. The average meal costs above are for a "light" meal (no appetizers are available). No reservations. Take-out for ice cream is also available.

Table
American
Very noisy
No reservations
Long waits
11:00 am-11:00 pm

ESPN's Wide World of Sports

ESPN's Wide World of Sports Grill   3 4 6

It's not all hot dogs at the Wide World of Sports complex. Menu offerings include cold sandwiches ($9.19-$9.49) like the roast beef and blue cheese, hot sandwiches ($8.49-$9.59) like the bbq pulled pork, soups ($2.99-$3.49) such as clam chowder, salads ($7.39-$8.99) including Cobb (not Ty), and desserts ($1.19-$3.79). Naturally, wings are available, both Buffalo and bbq ($9.79)!

Counter
American
Reservations not accepted
Hours vary

Planning | Getting There | Staying in Style | Touring | Feasting | Making Magic | Index | Notes & More

Character Dining

Disney offers many opportunities to dine with characters, both those in full guise (like Mickey Mouse) and "face characters" in costume (like Cinderella). While they don't actually sit with you throughout your meal, they do roam around the restaurant and visit your table for interludes. Character meals are more expensive than comparable meals (ranging from $22 to $72 for adults and $13 to $43 for kids ages 3–9), but the chance to meet the characters in an unhurried atmosphere makes it worthwhile. Even if characters aren't at the top of your menu, character dinners are a good deal—the cost of these buffets and family-style meals is usually less than a la carte meals when you factor all costs. Character meals are *extremely* popular—make reservations as far in advance as possible at 407-WDW-DINE. Bring your camera and an autograph book!

Be aware that there's a mad rush for reservations for meals at Chef Mickey's, Akershus, Crystal Palace, and Cinderella's Royal Table. Folks start phoning and logging in at 7:00 am Eastern time, exactly 180 days prior to their desired date, and tables are often gone in a matter of minutes. If you get a table at Cinderella's, expect to pay for the meal in full by credit card at the time of reservation—this payment is refunded if you cancel up to 48 hours in advance. If you miss out on these popular character meals, don't despair. Try again once you get to Disney. Cancellations are possible, so it never hurts to ask for a table, even as you're walking through Cinderella Castle. If you are set on dining with a princess, try the character dinner at 1900 Park Fare.

✔ Some character breakfasts start prior to park opening. All Disney resorts offer special Disney bus transportation to the early character breakfasts.

✔ For the best character experience, dine off-hours. While Mickey may only give you a quick hello during busy mealtimes, you might end up with a close, personal relationship when tables are empty.

✔ Don't be shy, grown-ups! Even if you aren't dining with kids, the characters visit your table. If you'd rather sit things out, they will simply give you a nod or handshake.

✔ The "head" characters don't speak, but that doesn't mean you have to keep quiet around them. Talk to them and they'll pantomime and play along!

✔ Most character meals take just one table-service credit on the Disney Dining Plan.

© MediaMarx, Inc.

Alexander holds hands with a furry friend at the Crystal Palace character meal. (His friend asked to remain anonymous because he's so bashful.)

Character Dining Location Chart

The chart below shows all the character meals at the time of writing. The location of each meal is given in parentheses, along with the meal served (B=breakfast or brunch, L=lunch, D=dinner, All=all three meals), the type (buffet=buffet-style, family=family-style, plate=buffet items brought to you on a plate, menu=from the menu), and the prominent characters (note that a specific character's appearance is not guaranteed).

Restaurant	Meal	Type	Characters
Akershus Royal Banquet Hall DD/PT	All	Family	Snow White, Belle, Jasmine
Dine in a castle with princesses Belle, Ariel, Jasmine, and Snow White. (Page 234)			
Cape May Cafe (Beach Club) DD/PT	B	Buffet	Goofy, Donald, Pluto
Casual, beach party atmosphere and good, standard breakfast foods. (Page 261)			
Chef Mickey's (Contemporary) DD/PT	B/D	Buffet	Mickey, Minnie, Goofy, Pluto
Bustling, popular destination. Superior food. Try to dine at off-hours. (Page 255)			
Cinderella's Royal Table (MK) DD/P2	All	Plate	Cinderella, Fairy Godmother
Gorgeous setting, hottest reservation at WDW. Original "princess" meal. (Page 232)			
Crystal Palace (MK) DD/PT	All	Buffet	Pooh, Tigger, Eeyore, Piglet
A favorite spot for satisfying meals in bright and airy surroundings. (Page 231)			
Donald's Safari (AK) DD/PT	B/L	Buffet	Donald, Mickey, Goofy
Inventive cuisine and classic favorites in a market atmosphere. (Page 246)			
The Garden Grill (Epcot) DD/PT	D	Plate	Mickey, Chip, Dale, Pluto
Tasty dining in an unusual setting. Good spur-of-the-moment choice. (Page 235)			
Garden Grove (Swan)	B/D[1]	Buffet/Menu	Timon or Goofy
A la carte menu makes this an expensive character dinner. (Page 259)			
Hollywood & Vine (Studios) DD/PT	B/L	Buffet	JoJo, Little Einsteins, Manny
Play 'n Dine character meal appeals to the Playhouse Disney set. (Page 243)			
My Disney Girl's Tea Party (GF)	Tea[2]	Snack	Princess Aurora
A special tea and brunch, plus a My Disney Girl doll. (Pages 257 and 274)			
1900 Park Fare (Grand Floridian) DD/PT	B/D	Buffet	Mary Poppins (B) Cinderella (D)
First-rate food, comfy Victorian surroundings, and lots of character. (Page 257)			
'Ohana (Polynesian) DD/PT	B	Family	Lilo, Stitch, Mickey, Pluto
Aloha, Cousins! A relaxed atmosphere (no more Minnie, alas!). (Page 258)			
Wonderland Tea Party (GF)	Tea[3]	Snack	Alice in Wonderland
"Tea," stories, and cupcakes with Alice at 1900 Park Fare. (Page 257)			

[1] Character breakfasts are weekends at 8:00–11:00 am; dinners are held 6:00–10:00 pm every night (Timon and Rafiki on Mon. and Fri., and Goofy and Pluto at all other times).

[2] My Disney Girl's Princess Tea Party has limited availability—see page 274 for details.

[3] Wonderland Tea Parties are held Monday through Friday, 1:30–2:30 pm.

Note: The Liberty Tree Tavern character dinner ended in 2009.
PassPorter's Character Yearbook is a detailed guide to character meet-and-greets. See page 314.

Top Photo Slice: Looking down at Chef Mickey's at the Contemporary Resort (①6628) © Cheryl Pendry

Planning | Getting There | Staying in Style | Touring | Feasting | Making Magic | Index | Notes & More

Planning

Getting There

Staying in Style

Touring

Feasting

Making Magic

Index

Notes & More

Hoop-Dee-Doo Musical Revue

DD P2

The Hoop-Dee-Doo Musical Revue is a **hilarious hoedown** in an Old West-style dance hall at the Fort Wilderness Resort. The song-and-dance vaudeville act relies heavily on slapstick humor, hokey gags, corny puns, and lots of audience participation. The Wild West performers interact with the audience, and guests celebrating birthdays and anniversaries may be singled out for special attention.

The **all-you-care-to-eat meal** includes salad, barbecue ribs, fried chicken, corn, baked beans, and bread, with strawberry shortcake for dessert (kids can request mac and cheese and hot dogs instead). Complimentary beverages include soda, beer (Bud Light Draft), wine (house red, white, and rose), and sangria. Cocktails and bottled beer extra.

We've been lucky to get this stage-side table at the Hoop-Dee-Doo twice!

Prices vary by seat category—cheapest seats are in category 3 (left or right side of the balcony) at $58.99/adults and $29.99/kids 3–9 (includes tax and tip). Category 2 seats are $62.99/adults and $30.99/kids 3–9 and are located in the back of the main floor or in the center of the balcony. Category 1 premium seats are $67.99/adults and $34.99/kids 3–9, located front and/or center on the main floor. Guests who need wheelchair access may only be seated in category 1. Disney Dining Plan credits are accepted here—two credits per person) for category 1 (8:30 show only) and categories 2 and 3 (all shows). Shows are at 4:00 pm, 6:15 pm and 8:30 pm nightly (the 8:30 pm show is the easiest to get in). A photo is taken before the show, and you can purchase photo packages from a cast member who circulates during dinner.

This show is **very popular**—reserve up to 180 days in advance at 407-WDW-DINE. The earlier you reserve, the better your table (within your category, of course). Full payment is required with reservation, refundable up to 48 hours in advance. Hoop-Dee-Doo Musical Revue is located in Pioneer Hall at the Fort Wilderness Resort. See travel directions below.

Mickey's Backyard Barbecue
DD P2

This old-fashioned, open-air barbecue features good ol' Disney characters (Minnie, Mickey, Goofy, Chip, and Dale), live country music, carnival games, and line dancing. Vittles include chicken, hot dogs, ribs, salads, corn, cole slaw, beans, vegetables, rolls, and (of course!) watermelon—all served buffet-style at picnic tables under a huge pavilion. Includes all-you-can-drink soft drinks and beer. Typically held on Thursdays and Saturdays at 6:30 (ends at 8:00 pm) from March through December. Cost: $54.99/adults and $31.99/kids 3–9 (prices include all taxes and gratuities). Call 407-WDW-DINE to inquire about availability and make reservations up to 180 days in advance. Full payment is required with your reservations, refundable up to 48 hours in advance, unless you're on a dining plan.

Getting to the Fort Wilderness Dinner Shows

To get to either Hoop-Dee-Doo or Backyard Barbecue, take the boat to Fort Wilderness from the Magic Kingdom, Contemporary, or Wilderness Lodge. Special buses run to and from some resorts, or take any Fort Wilderness-bound theme park bus. Driving (parking is free) is an option, too. The Hoop-Dee-Doo is in Pioneer Hall; Backyard Barbecue is next door to Pioneer Hall (around back). Allow 60 to 90 minutes for travel.

Spirit of Aloha Dinner (Luau)

DD P2

Aloha! The Spirit of Aloha Dinner is an **exotic, South Pacific-style celebration** of color, style, history, music, and dance. Everything you expect from a luau is here—women in "grass" skirts, men in face paint, fire dancers, traditional music, plus a little bit of Elvis—showcasing the cultures and traditions of Polynesia and connecting them all to the modern Hawaii seen in Lilo and Stitch. The show is held together by Auntie Wini, the heart of a group of young islanders who have learned to love traditional values including 'ohana (family). The show is held nightly in Luau Cove, an outdoor stage surrounded by a torch-lit garden. Upon arrival, guests are presented with a complimentary lei and entertained in the garden before dinner. While you wait for the show, you can buy drinks and souvenirs and have a family photo taken. Guests are seated at long, wooden tables that fan out from the stage, all under shelter in the event of rain.

The **all-you-care-to-eat meal**, served family-style for your party, includes salad, fresh pineapple, roasted chicken, BBQ ribs, rice, and sautéed vegetables, with a special "volcano dessert" (shown in photo below—the name is the most exciting part). Included with your meal is your choice of unlimited soda, coffee, iced tea, milk, beer (Bud and Bud Light Draft), and wine (house red, white, and blush). Specialty drinks are extra. The show begins after dinner with Hawaiian music and plenty of South Seas dancing by both men and women. Kids are quite welcome at the Luau—young ones will be invited on stage for a special dance number. Photos taken before the show are circulated during dinner by a cast member.

Prices vary by seat category—cheapest seats are in category 3 (extreme far left or right of the stage on the lower level, or on the upper level) at $58.99/adults and $29.99/kids 3-9 (prices include taxes and gratuities). Category 2 seats are $62.99/adults and $30.99/kids 3-9 and are located on the left or right side of the stage, or on the upper level tables in the center-rear. Category 1 premium seats are $67.99/adults and $34.99/kids 3-9, located front and/or center on the lower level. Disney Dining Plan credits are accepted here (two credits per person) for categories 2 and 3 only. Shows are held at 5:15 pm and 8:00 pm, Tuesdays through Saturdays. We prefer the later seating as the darkness adds to the mystique and romance of the show. Ask about discounts for the late show. In the cooler months, the late show may be canceled.

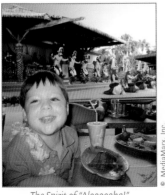

© MediaMarx, Inc.

The Spirit of "Alooooha!"

Make your reservations as early as possible (up to 180 days in advance)—they book up early. Full payment is required with your reservation, refundable up to 48 hours prior to the show.

Getting to the Polynesian Dinner Show

To get to the Polynesian dinner show, either drive directly to the Polynesian Resort or take the monorail from the Magic Kingdom or Epcot. From other parks and resorts, bus to the Magic Kingdom and take the monorail (daytime) or bus to Downtown Disney and transfer to a Polynesian bus. Once inside the resort, follow signs to Luau Cove. Allow plenty of time for travel, especially if coming from another resort.

Planning | Getting There | Staying in Style | Touring | Feasting | Making Magic | Index | Notes & More

Special Dinner Shows

Holidays

Holidays are always special at the Walt Disney World Resort. The parks and resorts overflow with special entertainment and decorations that vary from season to season and year to year (see pages 289 for details). The Christmas and New Year's season is especially magical, with all kinds of celebrations throughout the property. One big Christmas favorite is the Candlelight Processional at World Showcase in Epcot, which is available free to Epcot guests (show only) or as an Epcot lunch or dinner package offering special seating for the show (call 407-WDW-DINE).

House of Blues

House of Blues has a concert hall separate from its restaurant (page 250) that features performances by top musicians. On Sundays at 10:30 am and 1:00 pm, they serve an all-you-care-to-eat Gospel Brunch with soul food and glorious gospel music—price is $34.25/adults and $18.00/kids 3–9. Reservations can be made up to a month in advance at the House of Blues box office (or call 407-934-2583). Tickets for evening performances are available through the box office or Ticketmaster, and range from $13 to $60. The House of Blues is located at Downtown Disney West Side.

Restaurants With Entertainment

Several Disney restaurants offer performances or entertainment during meals. At the Magic Kingdom, a piano player may tickle the ivories at Casey's Corner. At Epcot, Biergarten has traditional German music and dancing, Restaurant Marrakesh features belly dancing and Moroccan musicians, and Rose & Crown plays host to pub performers. At Disney's Hollywood Studios, '50s Prime Time Cafe has TVs and cast members who act like "sisters" and "brothers," and the Sci-Fi Dine-In Theater Restaurant shows old movie trailers. Both 'Ohana (Polynesian Resort) and Whispering Canyon Cafe (Wilderness Lodge Resort) offer fun activities for the kids (big and little). And Raglan Road at Downtown Disney hosts Irish music, dancing, and storytelling.

Moroccan dancer and musicians at Restaurant Marrakesh

Special Dining Opportunities

On Mother's Day during Epcot's International Flower & Garden Festival (March 6–May 19, 2013), you can experience the **Food Among the Flowers Brunch**. This is an elaborate meal offering dozens of inventive and tantalizing choices—some may even include edible flower blossoms. Then, during the Epcot's International Food & Wine Festival (anticipated dates are September 27–November 11, 2013), there are special **wine tasting dinners** and other special meals (see page 288 for more about the Festival). Finally, during the **Christmas season**, when all the familiar eateries are overflowing, there is often a **holiday buffet** at a special location. For all these meals, call 407-WDW-DINE for information and reservations, but walk-up diners are often welcome at the holiday buffet.

Holiday dinners at the resorts and selected theme park restaurants usually go unheralded, but you can be fairly certain that many resorts will have something happening on Easter Sunday, Mother's Day, Thanksgiving Day, Christmas week, and New Year's Eve. Start by phoning your Disney resort. If you strike out at your resort, call around to the various deluxe resorts (holiday meals aren't always listed with 407-WDW-DINE). Magic Kingdom and Epcot full-service restaurants are also good candidates. Call 407-WDW-DINE to ask about special meals at the theme parks.

Dine with a Disney Imagineer offers a close-up peek at the people who create Disney's entertainment, attractions, parks, and resorts. These special meals are available select weekdays at 11:30 am at Hollywood Brown Derby or 5:30 pm at the Flying Fish Cafe, and feature intimate conversations with an Imagineer. Guests are served a special four-course meal while they learn about "their" Imagineer's work. Each guest receives a souvenir that may be autographed. Available for groups of 2–10 guests, and groups may be combined. Lunch is $60.99/adults ($34.99/kids 3–9), though it's not really a kids' event (and Disney suggests that it would be most appreciated by those 14 and older). Reserve up to 180 days in advance at 407-WDW-DINE—note that prepayment is required and you must cancel at least 48 hours in advance to get your money back.

Tomorrowland Terrace Fireworks Dessert Party provides a delicious way to view the Magic Kingdom's fireworks, from a reserved standing area. An elaborate buffet of dessert items and non-alcoholic beverages is served, starting about an hour before the fireworks, on select nights. Seasonal prices, $29.99-$35.99/adults, $14.99-$17.99/kids 3-9. Reserve up to 180 days in advance at 407-WDW-DINE. Prepayment is required.

Looking for the **Fantasmic! Meal Package**? See page 243.

Planning · Getting There · Staying in Style · Touring · Feasting · Making Magic · Index · Notes & More

Electronic, interactive worksheet available— see page 316

Meal Worksheet

The first step in planning your meals is determining your needs. Start by checkmarking the meals you'll need in the worksheet below. Next, write down where you would like to eat your meals—be specific ("cereal in room" or "Brown Derby at Studios"). If you're using the Dining Plan (see pages 223–225), indicate the number of snacks **S**, quick-service **Q**, and table-service **T** credits to be used per meal. Circle the meals that require reservations, then use the worksheet on the next page to make the arrangements.

Meal	Location				Meal	Location			
Day One–Date:		S	Q	T	**Day Six–Date:**		S	Q	T
☐ Breakfast					☐ Breakfast				
☐ Lunch					☐ Lunch				
☐ Dinner					☐ Dinner				
☐ Other					☐ Other				
Day Two–Date:		S	Q	T	**Day Seven–Date:**		S	Q	T
☐ Breakfast					☐ Breakfast				
☐ Lunch					☐ Lunch				
☐ Dinner					☐ Dinner				
☐ Other					☐ Other				
Day Three–Date:		S	Q	T	**Day Eight–Date:**		S	Q	T
☐ Breakfast					☐ Breakfast				
☐ Lunch					☐ Lunch				
☐ Dinner					☐ Dinner				
☐ Other					☐ Other				
Day Four–Date:		S	Q	T	**Day Nine–Date:**		S	Q	T
☐ Breakfast					☐ Breakfast				
☐ Lunch					☐ Lunch				
☐ Dinner					☐ Dinner				
☐ Other					☐ Other				
Day Five–Date:		S	Q	T	**Day Ten–Date:**		S	Q	T
☐ Breakfast					☐ Breakfast				
☐ Lunch					☐ Lunch				
☐ Dinner					☐ Dinner				
☐ Other					☐ Other				

(Dining Plan Credits: S Q T)

Planning · Getting There · Staying in Style · Touring · Feasting · Making Magic · Index · Notes & More

Advance Reservations Worksheet

Electronic, interactive worksheet available— see page 316

Once you've determined what meals you plan to eat in table-service restaurants, note them in the chart below, along with your preferred dining time. Next, call 407-WDW-DINE or go online at DisneyWorld.com to make advance reservations (have a credit card handy for certain reservations). Note the actual meal time and confirmation number below. When dining arrangements are finalized, transfer the information to your PassPockets.

			Before calling, fill in everything	
Our Resort: **Our Arrival Date:**			← *to the left of this line.*	
Date	**Restaurant Name**	**Preferred Time**	**Actual Time**	**Confirmation Number**

Planning | Getting There | Staying in Style | Touring | Feasting | Making Magic | Index | Notes & More

A Recipe for Fun

Make the most of your dining experience at Walt Disney World with these tips and tricks from fellow vacationers like you:

" If you want a reservation at some of the **more popular restaurants** (Cinderella's Royal Table, Chef Mickey's, or Le Cellier), try to book them for later in your trip. Due to the 180+10 booking policy for those staying on-site, you are more likely to be able to score those coveted reservations later in your trip. "
— Contributed by Melissa Sorrells Galley, a winner in our Reader Tip Contest

" If you enjoy the feeling of **having your meals pre-paid** but don't think you get your money's worth by purchasing the Dining Plan, put the cost of the dining plan on to a gift card. Use that gift card to pay for your meals during the duration of your trip. At the end of your trip you may just find you have enough money left over for a shopping spree in Downtown Disney or to book a Bounceback offer at your resort. "
— Contributed by Jen Johnson, a winner in our Reader Tip Contest

" We love to have some nice meals on our trip. But, with a family of six it can get very expensive. So we have started having our **big fun meal at lunch time**. It does still cost more than we would like to, but it is worth it. After having a big meal, some of us are hungry again later in the day. Others are okay with some healthy snacking to tide us over till morning. We do bring some snacks with us to the parks. It really comes in handy with the kids standing in line. I am usually still full from the late lunch. It really keeps the cost of food down while still giving us the 'magic' of Disney dining. "
— Contributed by Lisa Wilson, a winner in our Reader Tip Contest

" Instead of carrying a card or piece of paper with my dining reservations information, I **put all the information on my phone** which I carry with me all the time. I have the information whenever I need it and don't have to worry about forgetting to take the information with me each day. "
— Contributed by Holli Goetz, a winner in our Reader Tip Contest

Magical Memory

" We went with another family for nine days in Orlando and stayed 15 minutes from Disney at a condo. We decided to plan our meals as a way to save money and eat more balanced meals, taking advantage of the kitchen facilities. We had one character breakfast planned, but ate all the rest of the morning meals at the condo. Once we learned we could take food into the park with us, we packed sandwiches and snacks for our days in the parks as well as some other side trips we took. We also invested in hydration backpacks, filled them with ice and water every morning, and froze two bottles of water per person. The water kept the sandwiches and fruit cold until we were ready to eat, and provided us something to drink. We also planned suppers in the condo for all but two nights. At the end we totaled up our expenses and, setting our character breakfast aside, we spent less than $50 on food in our six days in the parks, under $100 in other restaurants, and about $200 on groceries for four adults and two 9-year-olds. We thought we did well! "

...as told by Disney vacationer Sharon Allen

Top Photo: A birthday cupcake presented at Chef Mickey's (①8064) © Cheryl Pendry

Making More Magic

You're bold. You're daring. You're a Disney vacationer. Now, here's your passport to an even more magical Walt Disney World Resort vacation!

Once you've tasted the Walt Disney World Resort, you'll hunger for more. Most visits can only *nibble* at the many wonders the "World" holds. There

FIND the hidden attractions at Disney

is much, much more that can be done to make your vacation magical. We've been to Disney more than most and yet there are *still* things we haven't done, and we add new discoveries to the wish list after every trip. It can all be a bit overwhelming, not to mention habit-forming.

To help you undertake your own magical explorations of the Walt Disney World Resort, we present a collection of useful information about some of its lesser-known aspects and attractions. This is our "everything else" chapter. To begin, we give you a backstage pass to the guided tours, special classes, and educational programs Disney offers—from peeks behind the scenes to dives under the seas. From there, we lead you on a treasure hunt for

LEARN how to get special treatment at Disney!

fun tucked away inside the parks—both real "treasure hunts" and hunts for items you'll treasure. We've even added a mini worksheet for those of you who love to shop! Next we share our special tricks for feeling and looking like a VIP on your trip—a little extra-special attention can go a long way! Then we give you the lowdown on childcare programs. Your kids may find these more fun than the theme parks themselves—no kidding! Special occasions and events aren't forgotten either, with ideas, tips, and details on celebrating birthdays, engagements, weddings, honeymoons, anniversaries, holidays, and more. Before we say goodbye, we'll leave you with information for explorations beyond Orlando at other Disney vacation spots—from exotic ports of call to home lands.

PEEK behind the magic with tours and classes

CELEBRATE the holidays and special occasions

So get out that pixie dust and don your sorcerer's hat—we're making magic, Disney-style!

Top Photo Slice: PassPorter reader dancing with a cast member on Main Street, U.S.A. (①13219) © Dawn Erickson

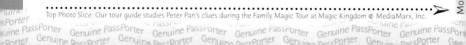

Backstage Passes

Disney does such a good job of hiding the figurative ropes and pulleys that you'll be disappointed if you hope to catch a glimpse of what makes Disney really work. To meet the growing demands of interminably curious guests, Disney offers tours and programs that satisfy the need to "peek."

Guided Tours

Unless otherwise noted, advance reservations may be (and should be) made up to 180 days in advance at 407-939-8687, or through your resort's Lobby Concierge desk. Some discounts are available to Annual Passholders, Disney Visa cardholders, AAA, or Disney Vacation Club members. Tours are only open to guests 16 and older unless otherwise noted. Many tours require substantial walking and most are wheelchair accessible. In general, no photos of backstage areas are allowed on the tours. Cancel 48 hours in advance to avoid penalties. Tours that require regular park admission are noted with the ticket ( ) icon. Important: Bring photo ID with you for tour check-in.*

Keep Moving Forward (Segway) [Epcot]

This three-hour tour offers a unique opportunity to ride a Segway (a self-balancing, two-wheeled "vehicle"). Learn to ride for the first hour, then practice riding around World Showcase. 100–250 lbs. weight restriction; pregnant and special needs guests may not participate. Offered daily at 7:45, 8:30, 9:00, and 9:30 am. (A one-hour tour, Simply Segway Experience, is also available on most days—see next page.)

$99
Ages 16 & up
On-stage only

Backstage Magic [Magic Kingdom, Disney's Hollywood Studios, and Epcot]

This seven-hour tour of three major parks explores how Disney's magic is created and maintained. Go beneath the Magic Kingdom to explore the underground "utilidors," enjoy a special lunch at Whispering Canyon Cafe, and see the computer systems at Epcot. Tours depart Monday–Friday at 8:45 am. Price includes lunch. Park admission is not required. Reserve well in advance.

$229
Ages 16 & up
Backstage peek at three theme parks

Backstage Safari Tour [Disney's Animal Kingdom]

A three-hour, behind-the-scenes peek at Disney's Animal Kingdom park to see how they care for our four-legged friends. No photography is allowed in backstage areas. Tours depart at 8:15 am and 1:00 pm on Mondays, Wednesdays, Thursdays, and Fridays. Park admission is required (not included in price).

$72
Ages 16 & up
Backstage peek

Family Magic Tour [Magic Kingdom]

This fun, 2½-hour tour offers guests an interactive adventure through the Magic Kingdom in search of a Disney character (such as Peter Pan). The tour is open to all and is held daily at 10:00 am. This is a popular tour and reservations are strongly recommended. Park admission required.

$34
All ages
On-stage only

Keys to the Kingdom [Magic Kingdom]

This 4½-hour guided tour of Magic Kingdom gives an overview of the park's highlights, history, and backstage areas, plus lunch at Columbia Harbour House. The route varies, but usually visits up to three attractions and two backstage areas (even a peek in the "utilidors"). Offered daily at 8:30, 9:00, and 9:30 am. Guests without reservations can inquire at City Hall, but the tour is very popular and we recommend you book it well in advance. Park admission is required.

$74
Ages 16 & up
Backstage peek (including the utilidors)

More at ① aiuided-tours (tip: enter this keyword at http://www.passporter.com/i for more information!)

Top Photo Slice: Our tour guide studies Peter Pan's clues during the Family Magic Tour at Magic Kingdom © MediaMarx, Inc.

Looking for Epcot Seas Aqua Tour, Dolphins in Depth, or Divequest? See page 275.

☐ The Magic Behind Our Steam Trains [Magic Kingdom]

Railroad fans get an inside look at the Walt Disney World Railroad in the Magic Kingdom. Join the opening crew, view the roundhouse, and explore Walt's passion for steam trains. The three-hour tour is held Monday–Tuesday and Thursday–Saturday at 7:30 am. Park admission is required.	**$49**
	Ages 10 & up
	Backstage peek

☐ Walt Disney: Marceline to Magic Kingdom Tour [Magic Kingdom]

New! Embark on a "walking timeline" to discover how the events in Walt's life shaped his vision for Walt Disney World. Available on Mondays, Wednesdays, and Fridays at 8:15 am. Park admission required.	**$30**
	Ages 12 & up
	Backstage peek

☐ Simply Segway Experience [Epcot]

Want to try a Segway without committing to three hours with the Keep Moving Forward tour? This is the one-hour "Segway Lite" tour where you get instruction, but only ride the two-wheeled vehicles indoors. Daily at 11:30 am. Park admission required. Age and weight restrictions same as the Keep Moving Forward tour.	**$35**
	Ages 16 & up
	On-stage only (no backstage)

☐ Undiscovered Future World [Epcot]

This 4 1/2-hour walking tour of the pavilions in Future World goes backstage. Tour highlights include a visit to a VIP lounge, a walk-through of the Cast Services building, an opportunity to meet an International Ambassador, and a peek at where the IllumiNations barges are stored. Guests may receive a limited edition trading pin, discounts on lunch and purchases in the China pavilion, and/or special seating for IllumiNations that evening. Tours are offered on Mondays, Wednesdays, and Fridays at 8:45 am. Park admission is required.	**$55**
	Ages 16 & up
	Backstage peek (including Epcot marina)

☐ VIP Tours

Custom-designed six- to eight-hour tours may be booked by individuals or groups of up to ten people. Tours must include a meal. Cost is $175–$315+ per hour per tour guide (six-hour minimum) and does not include park admission. VIP Tours may be booked from 72 hours to three months in advance. Blackout dates apply; call 407-560-4033 for availability and reservations.	**$275–$315**
	All ages
	On-stage only (no backstage)

☐ Wild By Design [Disney's Animal Kingdom]

This three-hour walking tour takes you around Disney's Animal Kingdom to learn about the represented cultures, historic artifacts, and storytelling. Guests wear headphones to hear the tour guide better. Tours leave at 8:30 am on Thursdays and Fridays. Price includes a light continental breakfast. Park admission required.	**$60**
	Ages 14 & up
	On-stage only

☐ Wild Africa Trek [Disney's Animal Kingdom]

A special three-hour adventure at the Harambe Wildlife Reserve riding in open-air vehicles, walking over a rope bridge, and dining at a private safari camp. Must be between 45 and 310 lbs, and at least 48 inches tall.	**$189**
	Ages 8 & up
	Backstage peeks

☐ Wilderness Back Trail Adventure Segway Tour [Fort Wilderness]

Take a ride on the Segway X2 off-road vehicles during this two-hour tour of Disney's Fort Wilderness Resort & Campground. The tour is offered on Tuesdays, Wednesdays, Thursdays, Fridays, and Saturdays at 8:30 am and 11:30 am. Minimum weight requirement of 100 lb./maximum weight of 250 lb.	**$90**
	Ages 16 & up
	On-stage only

In the holiday spirit? Two special tours are available during the holiday season—Yuletide Fantasy visits the parks and hotels ($84/person) and Disney's Holiday D-Lights Tour takes a closer look at the castle lights, Osborne Spectacle of Lights, and the Candlelight Processional ($199/person).

More at ① simply-segway | wild-by-design | wild-africa-trek | nature-inspired-design-segway-tour | wild-africa-trek

Sidebar tabs: Planning | Getting There | Staying in Style | Touring | Feasting | Making Magic | Index | Notes & More

Childrens Tours, Parties, and Activities

Fun stuff for kids! You can reserve fee-based activities by calling 407-WDW-DINE up to 90 days in advance; free activities take no reservations.

Albatross Treasure Cruise [Yacht Club Resort]

Follow the clues on this cruise around Crescent Lake, visit "exotic" ports of call, and listen to a reading of "The Legend of the Albatross." Cruise includes lunch (PB&J sandwich, cookie, and juice) and a split of the "buried treasure."	**$36.21**
	Ages 4–12
	9:30–11:30 am

Disney's Pirate Adventure [Grand Floridian Resort]

Ahoy, mateys! Cast off from the Grand Floridian marina on a cruise around the Seven Seas Lagoon in search of treasure. Little buccaneers get a bandana to wrap around their heads, hear a reading of "The Legend of Gasparilla," learn pirate songs, and receive a bag of "loot" (treats). Lunch is included.	**$36.21**
	Ages 4–12
	9:30–11:30 am
	M, W, Th, Sa

Wonderland Tea Party [Grand Floridian Resort]

Take tea with Alice in Wonderland! Kids make and eat cupcakes, participate in projects, and meet Alice, the Mad Hatter, and friends. Held in the 1900 Park Fare restaurant in the Grand Floridian Resort on Monday–Friday.	**$43.00**
	Ages 4–12
	2:00–3:00 pm

My Disney Girl's Perfectly Princess Tea Party [Grand Floridian Resort]

Pure pampering for your little princess. This five-part party is held in the Grand Floridian's Garden View Lounge and may have a visit from Princess Aurora. Includes tea, brunch, dessert, a My DisneyGirl doll, and the participation of one adult. Siblings or friends can attend for $165 each and extra adults are $85 each. Many girls come dressed as their favorite princess, though this is not required, of course.	**$281.25**
	Ages 3–11
	10:30–noon Su, M, W, Th, F

Bayou Pirate Adventure Cruise [Port Orleans Riverside]

Cruise along the Sassagoula River and hunt for Pirate Jean Lafitte's treasure. Includes a light snack and juice, and a share of the "treasure." Held on Sundays, Tuesdays, and Thursdays. Formerly the Sassagoula River Adventure.	**$36.21**
	Ages 4–12
	9:30–11:30 am

Islands of the Caribbean Pirate Adventure [Caribbean Beach Resort]

Discover the story of Old Port Royale as you sail about Barefoot Bay in a boat resembling an old battle relic. Kids wear pirate bandanas, search for treasure, rustle up grub (snacks, juice), and divide the loot. Held on Tuesdays, Fridays, and Sundays.	**$36.21**
	Ages 4–12
	9:30–11:30 am

Boma Kids' Activities [Disney's Animal Kingdom Lodge]

Daily activities for kids—such as cookie decorating—are available in the restaurant (Boma) and lobby of Disney's Animal Kingdom Lodge. Ask for the daily schedule of events at the hotel's front desk or at Boma.		**Free**
		Ages 3–12
		Times vary

Making crayon rubbings of the African symbols on the floor of the Animal Kingdom Lodge lobby

07491 © Tammy Wright

Classes and Educational Programs

Behind the Seeds: A Special Guided Greenhouse Tour—This one-hour walking tour delves deeper into the innovative greenhouses seen in the Living With the Land exhibit at Epcot. Cost is $18/adult and $14/child age 3–9 (no minimum age), 13 people max. per tour. Park admission to Epcot is required. Sign up at the counter outside Soarin' (in The Land) or call 407-WDW-TOUR. Tours leave every 45 minutes between 11:15 am and 4:30 pm.

Dolphins in Depth—This unique three-hour program highlights the dolphin research at The Seas with Nemo & Friends in Epcot. Guests play an active part in the research as they learn about dolphin behavior. Guests must be 13 or older, and 13- to 17-year-olds must be with a participating adult. Offered on Tuesdays–Saturdays beginning at 9:45 am. Cost is $194/person and includes a photo, soda, and souvenir T-shirt. Dolphin interaction is not guaranteed. Park admission to Epcot is not required to participate in this program.

Epcot Divequest—Open Water SCUBA-certified divers ages 10 and older can dive the 6-million-gallon pool at The Seas with Nemo & Friends (guests 10–12 must be with a participating adult). The 3-hour program includes a presentation on marine research and conservation. Divers suit up and are guided in small groups for a 40-minute dive. The cost includes use of gear, refreshments, a certificate, a dive log stamp, and a shirt. Proof of certification must be shown and divers have to sign medical and legal waivers. Dives are Tuesdays–Saturdays at 4:30 and 5:40 pm. Cost is $175/person. Park admission to Epcot is not required. Advance reservations are required.

Epcot Seas Aqua Tour—A $2\frac{1}{2}$-hour SNUBA-assisted snorkel that takes place in The Seas with Nemo & Friends. You do not need to be SCUBA certified; equipment and instructions are provided. Actual snorkel time is 30 minutes. Offered Tuesdays–Saturdays at 12:30 pm for guests ages 8 and up (8- to 12-year-olds must be with an adult). Cost is $140 and includes use of gear, a backpack, and a group photo. Park admission not required.

Typhoon Lagoon Learn-to-Surf Program—The Learn-to-Surf program at Typhoon Lagoon water park teaches guests surfing basics. Learn on dry land for the first half-hour, then try your new skills on the big waves in the park's huge wave pool for the remaining two hours. The $2\frac{1}{2}$-hour class is currently offered on Mondays, Tuesdays, Thursdays, and Fridays at 5:45 am, though starting time varies with park operating hours (class is held before the park opens). Class is open to resort guests ages 8 and up who are strong swimmers. Cost is $150/person, and park admission is not required. Call 407-WDW-PLAY for reservations. See pages 197–200 for details on Typhoon Lagoon. (You can book special "private surf parties" at Typhoon Lagoon—call 407-WDW-SURF for details.)

Recreation and Water Sports

A variety of options are available at moderate and deluxe resort hotels, water parks, and the Downtown Disney marina. While not all activities are offered in all locations, you can expect to find biking (regular and surrey), fishing, canoeing, boating, sailing, parasailing, waterskiing, wakeboarding, tubing, surfing, horseback riding, and carriage rides somewhere in the World. Call 407-WDW-PLAY or your resort to get details. Sammy Duvall's Watersports Centre at the Contemporary offers personal watercraft excursions, waterskiing, parasailing, and wakeboarding (included in some packages)—call 407-939-0754 or visit http://www.sammyduvall.com. Also see page 216.

More at ① dive-quest

Planning · Getting There · Staying in Style · Touring · Feasting · Making Magic · Index · Notes & More

Planning

Getting There

Staying in Style

Touring

Feasting

Making Magic

Index

Notes & More

Treasure Hunts

There is hidden treasure at the Walt Disney World Resort. While it may not consist of golden doubloons, it is every bit as priceless. There are countless sets of often-hidden and always-valuable Disneyesque items for you to find during your vacation. Sometimes these items are purposefully hidden; other times they are out in plain view for all to see but few to notice. Hunting for your favorite item can add a new dimension to your vacation! If you enjoy treasure hunting, look for a new edition of *PassPorter's Treasure Hunts at Walt Disney World* book (see page 314). Here are our favorite things to collect:

Disney Characters and Autographs

Live Disney characters abound, and kids of all ages delight in spotting them. You can discover where some characters are "hiding" by checking with Guest Relations at each major park. If you want to "bag your catch," take photographs—and try to get yourself or your family in the picture! Keep in mind that characters are popular and crowds will form. If you know when your characters will appear, show up early to greet them. (Tip: Ask a Disney cast member about character appearances for the day.) You can also collect autographs from characters who are able to sign their name. Special autograph books are available at most shops, or you can bring your own. Or use the PassPorter's autograph space on pages 306–307. Try to bring a wide-barreled pen or marker so the character can hold it easily. You can also have the characters sign hats or shirts (which must be Disney or non-commercial), but shirts cannot be worn while they are being signed and you need something to slip under the fabric to provide a writing surface. We have an entire 266-page e-book called *PassPorter's Disney Character Yearbook*, which is all about finding, meeting, photographing, and getting character autographs, and includes a full page dedicated to each character you can meet at Walt Disney World—for details, see http://www.passporter.com/disney-character-yearbook.asp.

Pressed Pennies and Quarters

One of the least expensive souvenirs at the Walt Disney World Resort is pressed coins. Souvenir Pressed Coin machines, found throughout the "World," press different Disney designs onto pennies or quarters. Cost is 51 cents for a pressed penny and $1.25 for a pressed quarter. Designs differ from machine to machine, making a complete collection a worthy achievement. Bring rolls of shiny pennies and quarters along with you—the hunt for a money-changing machine isn't as much fun. While there are good lists of pressed coin machine locations on the Internet (try http://www.presscoins.com), finding them is half the fun! **Tip**: Buy a keepsake book at Disney's gift shops to store your coins.

14685 © Lissette Brito

A pressed coin machine in Tomorrowland at the Magic Kingdom

Free Stuff

Disney may seem to be a mecca to capitalism, but there are still free things for the taking, and they make great souvenirs! Some may even become collector's items one day. You can collect guidemaps, brochures, napkins, paper cups and plates, containers, bags, menus, and more.

More at ① unexpected-treasures

Hidden Mickeys

Believe it or not, Disney intentionally hides "Mickeys" all over the place! The internationally recognized Mickey Mouse head (one big circle and two smaller circles for the ears) has been discovered hidden in murals, fences, shows—you name it, you can probably find a Mickey hidden somewhere in it! Disney fans maintain lists of these Hidden Mickeys—try http://www.hiddenmickeys.org and http://www.hiddenmickeysguide.com. You will also enjoy the "Hidden Mickeys" field guide by Steven M. Barrett, available in bookstores. We made a list of our favorite Hidden Mickeys for a rainy day activity—how many hiding places can you find? Write your answers below.

#	Location	Hint	Hiding Place
1.	General	Isn't it good to know Disney cares for the environment?	
2.	General	Ka-ching! Look at what you get when the cash register rings!	
3.	General	Bubble, bubble, toil, and trouble, look to laundry for three bubbles.	
4.	Magic Kingdom	Clippity clop, clippity clop! I pull a trolley past the Main St. shops.	
5.	Magic Kingdom	Look to your feet for the holes in the street.	
6.	Magic Kingdom	A Mickey up a sleeve—no joke— check the Grim Reaper's cloak.	
7.	Epcot	Test the Track, can you cope? Find the Mickey in the rope.	
8.	Epcot	As you stand in Maelstrom's line, find him in the hands of time.	
9.	Epcot	Now turn your glance to the gardens of France.	
10.	Disney's Hollywood Studios	Look for a tower and we'll bet if you say "terror" you're all wet.	
11.	Disney's Hollywood Studios	All around the park I run, my thin black bars protect the fun.	
12.	Disney's Hollywood Studios	On your tour of the backlot put the refrigerator on the spot!	
13.	Disney's Animal Kingdom	Amid the trees near Simba's fest hangs a house that holds a nest.	
14.	Disney's Animal Kingdom	Near Pangani you'll pass some fruit. Don't squish Mickey under your boot!	
15.	Disney's Animal Kingdom	There is a froggie near Pizzafari. Now that's the end of this safari!	

Hidden Mickey hiding places are found on page 291.

More at ① hidden-mickeys

Planning / Getting There / Staying in Style / Touring / Feasting / Making Magic / Index / Notes & More

Taking Photos

Click! Whirrr! Zzzzzzzap! Clack! Whatever sound a still camera or camcorder makes, you can be sure you'll hear it at Walt Disney World. Disney characters wrap little ones in warm hugs, Kodak Picture Spots swim before beleaguered eyes, and everyone scrambles to **capture the legendary magic** on film, tape, and digital memory card. Many vacationers bring a camera or a camcorder to record their trip. Here are our tips for great vacation photos:

You've finally got your family lined up in front of Cinderella Castle for the biggest photo of your trip of a lifetime. "OK everyone, stand right there!" And you back up. And you zoom in. And back up some more. And zoom all the way in. But now that you can see everyone's faces, you can't see enough of the castle. So you back up until the entire castle is in view. Now you're 20 feet away from your family, and when you get your prints you need a microscope to see those happy faces. The trick is to **get closer to the people and the backdrop**, not farther away. Zoom the lens out to maximum wide angle, and walk in until the castle fills the viewfinder as desired. Now have everyone stand close to the camera, so they're all heads and shoulders (or at least waist up). That's right, get in their faces! When you frame things right your family will now loom as large as the World around them.

Here are some ideas for **fun photograph collections**: Disney puns and visual gags that often go unnoticed (try "holding up" Spaceship Earth in your photos); your favorite spot at different times of the day; all of the "Kodak Picture Spot" signs; and pictures through the eyes of your children (give them their own camera). How about a photo of each family member next to their favorite attraction? If you take these same photos on return trips, you can make a "growth chart" over time.

Another idea is to hold a family **photo scavenger hunt** for fun things and places around Walt Disney World.

You'll find many ideas for fun and magical photographs in our **photo supplement** at the back of this guidebook and in the large PassPorter Photo Archive online at http://www.passporter.com/photos.

A photo "growth chart" at Epcot's Test Track (Alexander at 0, 1, & 2, and 4, riding for the first time!)

More at ① great-photos | fireworks-photos | digital-camera-tips

Disney's PhotoPass

Disney's parks have been awash in official photographers since Disney's PhotoPass hit the scene. PhotoPass has added new convenience to having professional photos taken in the parks, and its popularity has multiplied the ways vacationers can enjoy (and purchase) those photos when they return home.

When you have your first photo taken by an official Disney's PhotoPass photographer, you are given a **free PhotoPass card**—it looks just like a credit card. There is no cost for the photographer to take your photo and code it to your PhotoPass card, and generally the photographers know the best spots, angles, and lighting for great pictures, so there's no reason not to give this a try. At the next photo op, hand your PhotoPass card to the photographer and he/she will slide it through a card reader. Later, whether at a photo shop in the park or at the PhotoPass web site (http://www.disneyphotopass.com), all your photos will be together in one place. You can order prints or purchase a CD with some or all of the shots from your vacation. You may continue using the same card on every visit, or combine the photos from several cards into a single online account. The best thing, as far as we're concerned, is that you don't have to wait in long lines at the park's photo shop to get your pictures. Just be sure to login and view new photos online within 30 days of when your first picture was taken—you'll then have 30 days from that login date to make modifications to your pictures (such as adding borders, cropping, etc.) and to order a PhotoPass CD.

You'll find PhotoPass photographers nearly everywhere—at the most popular locations, at many character meet-and-greets, and just roaming the park. While park guests used to have (maybe) one "official" shot taken each day, some now seek out the PhotoPass photographers throughout the day. If you purchase the photo package offered at your character meal, those photos will be sent to PhotoPass, too. Even some official ride photos can be added to PhotoPass (only Test Track, Space Mountain, and Tower of Terror have this as of press time). Private PhotoPass Portrait Sessions can be arranged at some Disney resorts, and PhotoPass portraits are part of Bibbidi Bobbidi Boutique packages. You can also upload your own photos to the PhotoPass site. They can be combined with PhotoPass shots in your online albums for family and friends to view, professionally printed (4"x6" prints are $0.19 each), and added to PhotoPass merchandise. Not satisfied with your own shots and/or shots featuring your family? PhotoPass has a gallery of photos you can use in your online PhotoPass album and/or have printed on PhotoPass merchandise.

PhotoPass photos can be downloaded in JPG format for $14.95 each. For downloads of 10 or more images, a PhotoCD containing all PhotoPass images is a better deal at $149.95 (check for a pre-purchase discount). PhotoPass+ ($199.95, $149 at least 14 days in advance at http://www.disneyphotopass.com/specialoffers/wdwppp.htm) adds photos from select character meals and rides to your portfolio (and CD), plus a special PhotoPass+ card and lanyard. A PhotoCD containing only your uploaded photos is $19.95, and a pre-made CD with over 300 generic Disney photos is $39.95. The PhotoPass web site lets you crop, and add Disney-themed borders and character autographs to the photos, too. And those edited versions will be included on your PhotoCD. Disney's Photo Book lets you customize an 11" x 8.75", hard cover souvenir book, starting at $79.95. Select up to four photos per page, choose background styles, layout, and add captioning/text, add a CD version for $14.95 more.

Tip: PhotoPass photographers will also usually take a photo with your own camera, as well as their own. Just ask!

More at ⓘ photopass

Planning
Getting There
Staying in Style
Touring
Feasting
Making Magic
Index
Notes & More

Top Photo Slice: A PhotoPass photographer taking photos in front of Cinderella Castle © MediaMarx, Inc.

Shopping for Souvenirs

If you enjoy taking home souvenirs but you're tired of the usual T-shirts or postcards, consider beginning a new collection. Chances are that if you can collect it, Disney has it somewhere on its property.

We list our favorite shops at each of the four major parks back in chapter 4 (look for the charts right after each fold-out map). What do we like to collect? Here are favorites: enamel trading pins (see page 283 for details), patches (you can sew them onto your packs), mugs, figurines, hats, clothing, stuffed animals, and Disney beanie babies. Love shopping? Use the worksheet below to help you organize the items you want to purchase for yourself and others at Walt Disney World! This is a great spot to make a note of those souvenirs you promised to bring back for friends and family, too!

Hats at the World of Disney store

Ⓓ15313 © Lindsay Jones

Who	What	Size/Color	$$	✔

More at ① shopping-savings

Planning | Getting There | Staying in Style | Touring | Feasting | Making Magic | Index | Notes & More

In Search Of...

Quite often we're on the lookout for specific items, whether they be souvenirs or necessities. To help hunt down your treasures, here is a partial list of places to find some of the more commonly sought items:

Alcohol—You can buy a mixed drink, wine, or beer at any of the resorts or parks—even the Magic Kingdom now serves beer and wine at the Be Our Guest restaurant. You can also purchase bottled alcohol at most resort general stores and at Downtown Disney.

Baby Needs—The baby care centers in the four major parks sell common baby items, such as diapers, wipes, and formula. Your resort's gift shop stocks these items as well.

Groceries—Snacks are available at most of the resort stores, and a small selection of groceries is available at resorts with in-room cooking facilities. For more serious marketing, visit the Winn-Dixie half a mile north of the Crossroads Shopping Center. You may also want to try GardenGrocer.com (http://www.gardengrocer.com) for deliveries!

Gum—Gum is not sold on Disney property nor at the airport to avoid messes.

Lost Items—Lost and Found centers are located everywhere you go—generally near the front of the park or complex. Jennifer dropped a favorite scarf at Downtown Disney and within 15 minutes she had recovered it at Lost and Found (much to her relief). You can also call Lost and Found at 407-824-4245. Lost and found items are generally kept at each park only until closing. After that, they are usually transferred to Central Lost and Found at the Transportation and Ticket Center (inside the Kennel). Remember to label everything!

Medicine—Order prescription and over-the-counter drugs through Turner Drugs at 407-828-8125 from 8:00 am to 8:00 pm. Deliveries (for a fee) are available between 9:00 am and 9:00 pm. (Insurance paperwork is available so you may file claims upon your return.) Tip: Check with your insurance company to see which pharmacies will accept your insurance. Over-the-counter medicine and bandages are kept under the counter at many Disney shops—ask a cast member. Aspirin and bandages are also available at no charge at the first-aid stations staffed by licensed medical personnel in each park and resort front desks.

Missing or Lost Persons—Should you become separated, immediately alert a cast member or go to Guest Relations. Teach kids how to recognize cast members by their white nametags. A message system is available at Guest Relations to help coordinate things, even if you aren't lost (yet). It's a good idea to choose a meeting place each day in the event you are separated from your family or friends. You may also find it helpful to give each member of your party a two-way radio or cell phone to stay in touch with one another. We also suggest you take a digital photo of kids each morning—this will help you if a child is lost. Consider using "Who's Shoes ID" tags (http://www.whosshoesid.com), too!

Money—ATMs (cash machines) are located in all the parks and resorts. See our park maps or Disney's guidemaps for locations. The Walt Disney World Resort accepts American Express, MasterCard, Visa, Discover, JCB, Diner's Club, traveler's checks, cash, Disney Dollars and Gift Cards, and the Disney Dream Reward Dollars card (see page 10 for details on the Disney Rewards Visa card). Personal checks may be used to buy tickets or settle resort bills; checks can be cashed at the resort where you are staying for $50/day with photo I.D.

Rain Gear—If you didn't bring an umbrella or poncho along, Disney will sell you one at virtually any shop. You may need to ask, but chances are they'll have something. Tip: If your poncho rips, bring it back to any shop and they'll replace it. Disney sells clear ponchos to make it easier to spot your companions in the rain.

More at ⓘ babies-at-disney

Planning | Getting There | Staying in Style | Touring | Feasting | Making Magic | Index | Notes & More

Top Photo Slice: Victoria searches Minnie's refrigerator (ⓘ1784) © Laura Dawson

Genuine PassPorter Genuine PassPorter Genuine PassPorter Genuine PassPorter Genuine PassPorter Genuine PassPorter Genuine PassPorter

VIP Tips

Wake-Up Call

If you're staying at a Disney resort, start your day with a call from Mickey. Just use the phone system to arrange a wake-up call, and when the phone rings, Mickey, Stitch, or one of their friends welcomes you to the new day! When the phone rings with your wake-up call, press the speakerphone button so everyone in the room can hear it! Tip: Make your wake-up call for an off-time, such as 7:03, to help ensure you get Mickey.

Box Seats

Magic Kingdom Dessert Party—
The Tomorrowland Terrace hosts the Tomorrowland Terrace Fireworks Dessert Party on select nights. The party begins an hour before Wishes (check the schedule for times) and includes a self-service dessert buffet on the patio of the Tomorrowland Terrace. The dessert party is $26.99–$35.99/adults and $14.99/kids ages 3-9. Call 407-WDW-DINE to inquire about availability (reservations are hard to obtain). Pre-payment is required.

①17320 © Monica Gauvin

Treats at the Magic Kingdom Dessert Party

Contemporary Resort—Enjoy a meal in the California Grill during the Magic Kingdom fireworks (the music that normally accompanies the fireworks is broadcast in the restaurant). While the California Grill observation deck is open only to diners, there's another viewing area on the north end of the Grand Concourse (4th floor).

Fireworks Cruises—Do you have something to celebrate? Rent a pontoon boat or the Grand 1 Yacht to view the fireworks at Epcot or the Magic Kingdom. Cruises are booked per boat rather than per passenger, and all include a pilot. Call 407-WDW-PLAY for rates and reservations. You can book up to 180 days in advance, and we recommend you call at 7:00 am Eastern Time exactly 180 days in advance, as these cruises are extremely popular. Note: These are sometimes called "specialty" cruises by Disney, as they can't promise that the fireworks won't be cancelled.

Note: The option to ride in the monorail's front cab has been discontinued; no word on when or if it will return. Additionally, Disney no longer sells photos for the Leave a Legacy monument in front of Spaceship Earth.

More at ① fireworks-cruises

Pins and Passports

Trading Pins

Colorful, enameled commemorative pins are a favorite Disney collectible, available at nearly every shop for $6.95 and up. Disney designs thousands of these colorful, cloisonné pins, which commemorate the theme parks, resorts, attractions, characters, and events. Over the years, Disney stepped up pin trading activity by introducing Pin Trading Stations at the parks and the Disney's Pin Traders shop at Downtown Disney, where you can buy and swap pins. Bring (or buy) your own Disney pins, and trade pins with other guests and with cast members wearing special pin-trading lanyards around their neck or boards at their waist. Look for "Scoop Sanderson," a special Main Street, U.S.A. cast member who offers pin trading classes and tips. Note that cast members wearing green lanyards trade only with children. Buy a Disney pin lanyard, or display your pins in a scrapbook, or on a vest or hat. Tip: If pin collecting is your thing, keep an eye on Disney's Official Pin Trading page at http://www.disneypins.com, where news on pin releases and special events are announced.

Name Badges

Show everyone how special you are with an oval Disney name badge, personalized with your first name. The badges make great conversation starters—you may even get more personal attention from cast members while wearing one. In years past, you could purchase badges in the parks and at Downtown Disney for $6, though readers report having problems locating them recently. Another option is our own PassPorter Badge, which our readers requested to help them spot fellow fans in the parks. PassPorter Badges are $4 and also come with free personalization. You can order PassPorter Badges at http://www.passporter.com/badge.asp.

Park Passports

The Epcot Passport is a great way to tour the World Showcase. Once you have a passport, you can get it "stamped" at each pavilion or land by a cast member. The passports—which kids love—can be purchased at shops and carts for about $10 and include an "I'm a World Showcase Traveler" pin and a set of stickers. A similar passport is available at Disney's Animal Kingdom.

Vinylmation Figures

A new collectible are these vinyl, designer toys—most are just 3" tall. They usually have a common shape (such as Mickey Mouse) but come in different designs—and typically you don't know what you get until you open the box! You can trade Vinylmation with others, or even trade one back in to Disney for one in a clear case or a mystery box. Prices range from $9.95 for a 3" tall figure. Learn more at http://www.disneystore.com/vinylmation.

Planning · Getting There · Staying in Style · Touring · Feasting · Making Magic · Index · Notes & More

Childcare Programs

"We're going to Walt Disney World. Why in the 'World' would we need childcare?" The Walt Disney World Resort is an adult playground, too! The "World" offers an exciting nightlife and leaves lots of room for romance. All you need is a sitter. Not surprisingly, Disney delivers with a variety of childcare options and a few programs that may seem like childcare to you (but don't tell the kids). The two main options are childcare programs at the resorts and private, in-room baby-sitting.

Many of Disney's deluxe resorts offer childcare programs. These childcare programs are a good bit like daycare, but unlike daycare, their "day" usually starts at 4:00 pm or 4:30 pm and runs until midnight. They offer a variety of structured activities and usually include a full meal. All programs accept children from 3 to 12 years of age, and all children must be potty-trained. Rates are $12/hour, and there is a two-hour minimum stay. Programs usually also have an overtime rate—the kids won't be evicted if your coach turns into a pumpkin on the way back from Cinderella Castle. Parents are given pagers, too. Some programs are available only to Disney resort guests, and some only for guests staying or dining in the particular resort. Make your status clear when you phone so there are no disappointments. No matter which program you contact, we recommend you call well in advance and ask plenty of questions. Reservations can be made with the club itself or at 407-WDW-DINE. Each resort offers different services and rules, and all are subject to change. Cancel at least 24 hours in advance to avoid a $20/kid fee. **Allie's Kid Tip:** "It's cool to stay at the kids' clubs so you can do what you like to do and grown-ups can do what they want to do."

Childcare Near Epcot and Disney's Hollywood Studios

☐ **Sandcastle Club** [Beach Club]	407-934-3750
Large club with plenty of Legos, games, computers, and video games (free) to play with. Meals are served at 6:00, 7:00, or 8:00 pm. This club is available only to Disney resort guests. **Allie's Kid Tip:** "There are fun games to play."	**$12/hour** 4:30 pm–Midnight

☐ **Camp Dolphin** [Swan and Dolphin]	407-934-4000 ext. 4241
Kids have fun with arts and crafts, video games, and movies. Price includes a meal at 7:00 pm–kids are usually taken to the Picabu eatery in the resort. Note that participation is not limited to Swan and Dolphin guests.	**$12/hour** 5:30 pm–Midnight

Childcare Near Disney's Animal Kingdom

☐ **Simba's Cubhouse** [Disney's Animal Kingdom Lodge]	407-938-4785
The club with a view of the savanna and animals. Plenty of movies and games. Price includes a meal (serving time varies). **Allie's Kid Tip:** "This is my first choice! I liked the people and the decorations. And I loved watching the animals."	**$12/hour** 4:30 pm–Midnight

Top Photo Slice: Play things in the Neverland Club at the Polynesian Resort © MediaMarx, Inc.

Childcare Programs

Childcare Near the Magic Kingdom

■ Mouseketeer Club [Grand Floridian]	407-824-2985	
A medium-sized club with movies, games, and crafts. Price includes a meal if child is checked in by 6:30 pm (meal is at 7:30 pm). Two-hour minimum stay. This club is available only to Grand Floridian resort and restaurant guests.	$12/hour	4:30 pm–Midnight

■ Cub's Den [Wilderness Lodge]	407-824-1083	
A smallish club with structured activities, movies, arts and crafts, and games. Price includes a meal (choice of hot dog, hamburger, cheeseburger, chicken strips, mac & cheese, or PB&J, plus ice cream) served between 6:30–8:00 pm.	$12/hour	4:30 pm–Midnight

■ Never Land Club [Polynesian]	407-824-2000	
This is the largest, most creatively themed club! Price includes a meal (buffet of kid-friendly items) served 6:00–8:00 pm. The club has its own movie theatre and game arcade, and you enter through the Darling nursery window, just like in the movie (see photo)! Open house daily from noon to 4:00 pm for Polynesian resort guests. **Allie's KidTip:** "I like the people here, and the toy stairs are fun to sit on and watch movies. The TV here is big!" **Alexander's KidTip:** "I pretended to be a pirate in Neverland!"	$12/hour	4:00 pm–Midnight

Alexander goes to Neverland

Other Childcare Options

Kids Nite Out offers Disney-sanctioned, private in-room babysitting, 24 hours a day, seven days a week. Rates are $16/hour for one child, $18.50/hour for two children, $21/hour for three children, an $23.50/hour for four children. Note that a $10 fee for transportation is automatically applied for each session, and a $2/hour surcharge is applied to caregiving that begins after 9:00 pm. There is a four-hour minimum. Two other independent childcare agencies, **Fairy Godmothers** and **All About Kids**, offer similar services. The professional sitters will take kids to the theme parks if you make arrangements in advance (ask at time of reservation) and watch infants and children with some special needs. The sitters show up equipped to keep the kids occupied with games and activities. They are well-trained, bonded, and insured. Rates vary, depending on the age and number of kids under care. For reservations, contact Kids Nite Out at 800-696-8105 or 407-828-0920 or visit http://www.kidsniteout.com. Fairy Godmothers is at 407-275-7326. All About Kids is at 407-812-9300.

More at ① toddlers-at-disney

Top Photo Slice: Having fun in "the club" © MediaMarx, Inc.

Special Occasions

It seems natural to celebrate a special occasion at Disney. It's designed for fun and comes predecorated! So whether you plan a trip around a special day or want to celebrate one that falls during your vacation, you can do it at Disney! Here are our tips and tricks for a magical celebration:

Birthdays—What better place to celebrate a birthday than at Disney? If you're at a Disney resort, press "0" on your room phone and ask for the special "birthday message." Be sure to request a free "Happy Birthday!" button at the Guest Relations desk at the theme parks or at your hotel's concierge. If you want to celebrate in style, all sorts of birthday parties and cruises can be arranged in advance—you can even "invite" Disney characters (though they're very expensive). For kids ages 4–12, you can arrange a birthday party at the BoardWalk or the Yacht & Beach Club—call 407-WDW-PLAY. For parties in other restaurants, call 407-WDW-DINE. Birthday cruises (407-WDW-PLAY) are also available. One year, Jennifer surprised her mom Carolyn with a special birthday event, planned in part by Gifts of a Lifetime (see sidebar on next page). Families that celebrate Quinceañera, a daughter's 15th birthday, are invited to contact Disney's event planning department to plan their party at 321-939-4555.

Engagements—Disney is a magical place to propose. For $300, you can propose at Cinderella's Royal Table—price includes a meal, glass slipper, photo, and special dessert!

Weddings—From intimate to traditional to themed, Disney's Fairy Tale Weddings have something for virtually every budget. Learn more at http://www.disneyweddings.com or call 407-828-3400. Vow renewals are also available. You can also get free "Just Married" buttons to wear—ask about them at Guest Relations in any of the four major parks and resort front desks. You may wish to purchase and wear the bridal Mickey ears (white veil and black top hat) for $15 each. Learn much more in our full-length guidebook, *PassPorter's Disney Weddings & Honeymoons* by Carrie Hayward—it's available immediately as an e-book or in a handy print edition. It includes hard-to-obtain information, prices, photos, and delightful details on planning a special wedding or honeymoon! Learn more at http://www.passporter.com/weddings.asp.

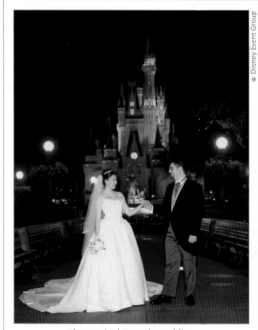

The magical Dattalo wedding

Honeymoons—Walt Disney World is the #1 honeymoon destination in the world, believe it or not. Not only are romantic spots found around virtually every corner, but Disney goes out of its way to make newlyweds welcome. Lodging packages, romantic rooms, candlelit dinners, and adult-oriented entertainment abound. Even if you do nothing more than mention that it is your honeymoon to cast members, you may be in for a special treat. For details, call Disney at 407-934-7639.

Anniversaries—Like birthdays, anniversaries are always in style at the Walt Disney World Resort. You can get free "Happy Anniversary" buttons to wear—ask about them at Guest Relations in any of the four major parks. You can plan a special night out at a romantic restaurant or shape an entire vacation

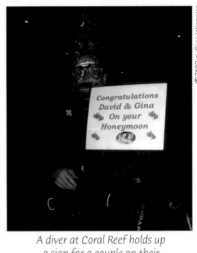

A diver at Coral Reef holds up a sign for a couple on their honeymoon

around your special day. Be sure to mention your anniversary when making advance dining reservations (especially at Cinderella's Royal Table)—you may be pleasantly surprised. If you're staying at a resort, mention your anniversary at check-in, too.

Group Events—With all the conventions it hosts each year, Disney is a pro at group parties and functions. We've planned several ourselves and found plenty of options and many helpful cast members. You can have a private party virtually anywhere in the "World," for small or large groups. For parties in any of the resorts, call 407-828-3074. If you're interested in having a private party at one of the parks, call Group Sales at 407-828-3200. We can't say it'll be cheap, but you can plan one within a reasonable budget if you're careful. Of course, you can go all-out, too—companies rent entire theme parks. Planet Hollywood at Downtown Disney hosts private functions, too. In fact, PassPorter readers like to plan gatherins of like-minded individuals. If you'd like to learn about our next gathering, visit http://www.passporterboards.com/forums/backyard-gatherings-meets-group-trips.

☝ Special Services for Special Occasions

It's a challenge to organize a special occasion long-distance. An innovative company, **Presentations: Gifts of a Lifetime**, helps you shop for that perfect gift, arrange a magical event, and even put on the whole show! To learn more, visit their web site at http://www.giftsofalifetime.com or call 407-909-0593.

You can also have the **Walt Disney World Florist** (http://www.disneyflorist.com, 407-827-3505) prepare a fruit or snack basket and deliver it to a guest room.

Need a little help remembering that special occasion? Another unique service, **MouseMemories**, can create custom memory albums from your own photos. If you prefer to create your own memory albums, they offer scrapbooking supplies. To learn more, visit http://www.mousememories.com.

More at ① romance-at-disney | vow-renewals | gatherings

Special Events at Disney

Disney really knows how to celebrate. Nearly every holiday seems to have at least one event, and Easter, Halloween, Christmas, and New Year's Eve spark extended festivities. Disney also is a master at battling periods of slow attendance with specially themed events throughout the year. Call Disney's main information line at 407-824-4321 or visit their web site at http://www.disneyworld.com for more information.

Sports

January brings the sell-out **Walt Disney World Marathon Weekend** (Jan. 10-13, 2013), which includes the Family Fun Run and the Kids' Festival (open to all ages), as well as Goofy's Race and a Half Challenge (Jan. 12-13)—call 407-939-7810 for information and sign-up. There's also the **Tinker Bell Half-Marathon** on January 18-20 2013. The **Atlanta Braves** baseball spring training is in February and March. The **Princess Half-Marathon** is held February 20-24, 2013, with a focus on women's fitness. The Expedition Everest Challenge is May 4, 2013. There's also a **Disney Spring Training** event from February 21-April 21, 2013, featuring team training for baseball, golf, lacrosse, softball, and track & field. Many more sport opportunities are available at ESPN Wide World of Sports Complex—for more details, visit http://www.disneyworldsports.com and http://www.rundisney.com.

Festivals and Fun

The **Epcot International Flower & Garden Festival** (March 6-May 19, 2013) fills the park with exhibits, seminars, tours, demonstrations, the Food Among the Flowers Brunch (see page 267), and special entertainment at the America Gardens Theatre. On selected dates in May and June, Disney's Hollywood Studios has **Star Wars Weekends** with celebrity appearances and special events. The Friday and Saturday after Labor Day bring the popular **Nights of Joy** to Disney's Hollywood Studios to celebrate contemporary Christian music ($49.95/day/person in advance; see http://www.nightofjoy.com). The 16th Annual **Epcot International Food & Wine Festival**, which will be held September 27-November 11, 2013, turns the World Showcase into an even greater gourmet delight (see page 241). Note that a new party may pop up to replace the Mickey's Pirate & Princess Party at the Magic Kingdom, which has been discontinued. Also note that the **ABC Super Soap Weekend** held its last event at Walt Disney World in 2009 and the last **Grad Night** was held in 2011.

Other Parties, Holidays, and Observances

All parks participate in February's **Black Heritage Celebration**. May 28-June 3, 2013 are the **Unofficial Gay Days events** (visit http://www.gaydays.com). No word yet on whether **Destination D**, a D23 event, will return to Walt Disney World again, but it wouldn't surprise us if it did! There are smaller D23 events at Walt Disney World, however, such as D23's Magic and Merriment holiday events that took place on December 7-8 and 9-10, 2012.

Check out PassPorter's Festivals and Celebrations at Walt Disney World for 78 pages of details on all the **wonderful and magical festivals**, celebrations, parties, and holidays at Walt Disney World. Details at http://www.passporter.com/wdw/festivals-celebrations.asp.

Holidays at Disney

Easter *(March 31, 2013)*
Spring crowds reach a peak during Easter week. Easter egg hunts and candy scrambles may be held at some of the resorts for their guests. Check with your resort for details. Some restaurants offer Easter meals, such as Chef Mickey's (see page 255), 'Ohana (see page 258), Whispering Canyon Cafe (see page 260), and Mickey's Backyard BBQ (see page 264).

Independence Day *(July 4, 2013)*
The Magic Kingdom traditionally puts on a spectacular fireworks show, as does Disney's Hollywood Studios. Epcot's IllumiNations is enhanced with Fourth of July fun, too!

Halloween *(October 31, 2013)*
Mickey's Not So Scary Halloween Party brings kid-friendly spookiness to the Magic Kingdom for 20+ nights (7:00 pm–midnight) in September and October (usually Tuesdays, Fridays, and Sundays, plus Halloween night). Enjoy Mickey's Boo to You Halloween Parade, a kids' costume parade, trick-or-treating around the park, Halloween-themed fireworks, storytellers, fortune tellers, and access to most rides. We recommend you make time for the Liberty Belle Riverboat, which offers Halloween cruises with storytellers and live entertainment—it was the highlight of our night! Advance tickets at press time were at $59.59–$74.50/adult, $54.26–$69.17/child (price includes tax). Call 407-934-7639 well in advance as tickets sell out, especially for Halloween night—expect tickets to go on sale on May 1, 2013.

Thanksgiving *(November 28, 2013)*
Crowds take a bump up for this All-American holiday. Disney's holiday decorations are already up, and a number of the full-service restaurants at the parks and almost all of the Disney resorts host special holiday dinners, with and without Disney characters.

Christmas *(December 25, 2013)*
Christmas is a very special time, with delightful decorations, holiday entertainment, and countless ways to enjoy the season. Decorations go up by mid-November, so there's more than a month of merriment. Try to come during the first two weeks of December when the crowds are a little thinner, rates are a little lower, the party is in full swing, and the "World" is decked with holiday cheer. **Mickey's Very Merry Christmas Party** is a big favorite. Packed full of special shows and special fun, the Magic Kingdom is open for five extra hours for about 18 nights in November and December. Snow falls on Main Street, fireworks and music fill the air, and the big rides are open. And let's not forget the castle lighting ceremony, holiday-themed entertainment, strolling carolers, and complimentary cookies and hot cocoa. Advance tickets at press time are $62.78–$69.17/adult, $57.46–$67.04/child, prices include tax—expect tickets to go on sale May 1, 2013. At Epcot, the **Candlelight Processional** runs two to three times nightly. A celebrity narrator, chorus, and orchestra present the Christmas tale. No extra admission required, but a special dinner package offers reserved seating (call 407-WDW-DINE). Be sure to **view the resort decorations** (try the Yuletide Tour—see page 273) and enjoy merriment at **Downtown Disney**. The **Osborne Family Spectacle of Dancing Lights** sparkles throughout the Streets of America Set at Disney's Hollywood Studios—see page 179.

New Year's Eve *(December 31, 2013)*
The Magic Kingdom, Epcot, Disney's Hollywood Studios, and Atlantic Dance at the BoardWalk all host big New Year's celebrations. The theme parks overflow during the Christmas–New Year's week, and reservations at resorts are extremely hard to get. Disney does not charge anything more than regular admission to the parks on New Year's Eve.

Top Photo Slice: Iced turrets on Cinderella Castle at the Magic Kingdom (①10632) © JustLorri

More at ⊕ holidays-at-disney

Planning | Getting There | Staying in Style | Touring | Feasting | Making Magic | Index | Notes & More

Beyond Walt Disney World

We're pretty infatuated with Disney, but there is life beyond Walt Disney World. At least that's what we hear. We don't venture far beyond the gates, preferring to spend more time immersed in Disney's magic rather than battle traffic to get to another park. We do know that families hope to visit other theme parks during their visit to central Florida, so here is a list of Florida parks and attractions. For more information, check out *PassPorter's Orlando and Beyond: Everything but the Mouse* guidebook by Cheryl Pendry (coming in 2013).

Name	Number	Web Site
Busch Gardens	813-987-5082	http://www.buschgardens.com
Discovery Cove	407-370-1428	http://www.discoverycove.com
Gatorland	800-393-JAWS	http://www.gatorland.com
LEGOLAND Florida (see page 315)	877-350-5346	http://florida.legoland.com
Kennedy Space Center	321-452-2121	http://kennedyspacecenter.com
Medieval Times	407-396-1518	http://medievaltimes.com
Sea World	407-363-2613	http://seaworld.com
Universal Studios/Islands of Adv.	407-363-8000	http://www.usf.com
Wet 'n' Wild	407-351-1800	http://www.wetnwild.com

Beyond Orlando

Like any other forward-thinking organization, The Walt Disney Company has expanded into other locales. Here are a few of them:

Disney Cruise Line—"Take the magic of Disney and just add water!" The Disney Cruise Line set sail in 1998 with the same enthusiasm and energy you find at the Walt Disney World Resort. See pages 106–107, and pick up a copy of our popular guidebook, *PassPorter's Disney Cruise Line and Its Ports of Call* (available in bookstores or order at http://www.passporter.com/dcl—more details about the guidebook on page 312).

The AquaDuck water coaster on the Disney Dream ship

Adventures by Disney—Adventures by Disney is making the world a Disney "park." These deluxe escorted tours feature separate activities for adults and kids as well as all together, and visit a growing list of fabulous destinations in the US and abroad. http://www.adventuresbydisney.com

Disney's Vero Beach Resort—Vero Beach, Florida, is Disney's first oceanside resort, a two-hour drive from Disney World. Call 561-234-2000 for more information, or visit http://www.disneyvacationclub.com and click Resorts. Also learn about our in-depth e-book on the Disney Vacation Club at http://www.passporter.com/dvc.

Disney's Hilton Head Island Resort—For southern grace and charm, experience the South Carolina Low Country lifestyle at Disney's Hilton Head Island Resort. Hilton Head is a golfer's nirvana, boasting 12 nearby golf courses. The tennis and beaches are also big draws. It's an ideal spot for small group retreats. For more information, call 843-341-4100.

More at ① busch-gardens | kennedy-space-center | universal-orlando | disney-cruising | hilton-head

Top Photo Slice: Universal Studios globe with Islands of Adventure in the background (①1899) © Brad K.

Disney Parks Around the World

Disneyland Resort

Disneyland Resort (California)—The original "Magic Kingdom," near Los Angeles. Disneyland was the model for the Magic Kingdom in Florida and still keeps a step or two ahead of its offspring, since Disney's Imagineers live close by. The official Disneyland hotels are right next door if you want to make a week out of it. Disneyland's "other" park, Disney California Adventure, recently completed a huge expansion and re-design, to rave reviews. We cover the entire Disneyland Resort and other area attractions, such as Universal Studios, Knott's Berry Farm, LEGOLAND, Hollywood, San Diego Zoo, and SeaWorld in our award-winning guidebook: *PassPorter's Disneyland Resort and Southern California Attractions*. For more details and to order a copy, visit http://www.passporter.com/dl (see page 313).

Disneyland Paris

Disneyland Paris Resort (France)—The first (and only) Disney resort in Europe, the park has a similar layout to Disneyland, with the major change being a substitution of Discoveryland for Tomorrowland. A second park, the Walt Disney Studios, features several popular attractions from Disney's Hollywood Studios in Florida—and one of its original attractions (Lights, Motors, Action!) made its way to Florida, too. Visit http://www.disneylandparis.com. A third theme park, new eco-tourism resort hotel, and a housing development is expected to be built here, as well! We visited and stayed at the Disneyland Hotel—immediately adjacent to the park—and adored it. Look for PassPorter's complete guidebook to Disneyland Paris (see page 315).

Tokyo Disney Resort (Japan)—Disney, Japan-style! Tokyo Disney Resort is located in Urayasu, just outside Tokyo. It is similar to Disneyland in California, incorporating the quintessential "American" things. When Jennifer visited, she found it squeaky clean and definitely Disney, with just a touch of Japanese peeking through. In 2001, the Tokyo DisneySea theme park opened immediately adjacent to Tokyo Disneyland. The aquatically themed park has seven lands and three resort hotels, including the new Tokyo Disneyland Hotel. Visit http://www.tokyodisneyresort.co.jp and click English.

Hong Kong Disneyland—Opened in September 2005, this theme park overlooks the water of Penny's Bay, Lantau. For details, visit http://www.hongkongdisneyland.com.

Hawaii—Aulani, a new Disney resort and spa, is located at the Ko Olina Resort and Marina west of Honolulu on the island of Oahu. The 21-acre facility offers a total of 800 hotel rooms and Disney Vacation Club villas, and opened on August 29, 2011. For more details, visit http://www.aulani.com.

Hidden Mickey Hiding Places (from list on page 277)

1) In the Disney Recycles logo on bags, napkins, etc.; 2) On cash register receipts; 3) The "Soap Stop" vending machines in the resort laundry rooms; 4) Main Street vehicle horse harnesses; 5) In the center of manhole covers; 6) In the sleeve of a cloak on a Grim Reaper ghost in the Haunted Mansion; 7) In coiled ropes on Test Track (visible in the ride photo); 8) Drilling platform worker's watch; 9) Hedges trimmed into circles; 10) Eiffel water tower; 11) The ironwork fence around Disney's Hollywood Studios; 12) The yellow refrigerator on the Backlot Tour; 13) Birdhouse near Festival of the Lion King; 14) On the sidewalk near the Harambe Fruit Market; and 15) On the frog statue outside of the women's restroom near Pizzafari.

More at ① disneyland | disneyland-paris | tokyo-disneyland | tokyo-disneysea

Your Own Walt Disney World

Make Walt Disney World your personal playground with these tips:

> When we go to Walt Disney World, I like to **send a postcard** to each one of our children from their favorite Disney character. When we get home from our Disney vacation, the magic lives on when they get a special message from a character that they love so much.
> — Contributed by Nicole Zoncki, a winner in our Reader Tip Contest

> Pressed Pennies are some of the **cheapest souvenirs** at Walt Disney World. To keep coins handy, buy and consume a tube (or multiple tubes!) of mini M&M's, then save the tubes! Now stack sets of two quarters and a penny in order in the tube. Carry the tubes with you and you'll always be ready with the exact needed coinage.
> — Contributed by Debbie Anderson, a winner in our Reader Tip Contest

> If you ever want to celebrate a special occasion, the **Cake Hotline** at Walt Disney World (407-827-2253) is excellent at making whatever themed cake you want. What makes it more special is that they will deliver your cake to any (Disney) resort.
> — Contributed by Jennifer Gallion, a winner in our Reader Tip Contest

Magical Memory

> Soon after my daughter Stefanie was born, my husband Luke and I began to affectionately call her 'Monkey.' But quite a few years ago, she informed us she was not a monkey. Instead she said, 'I'm a giraffe. Baa!' (Baa is the sound giraffes make, just like sheep.) She knew giraffes were my favorite animals, and I think maybe that's why she wanted to be a giraffe. In fact, she gave me a giraffe for Christmas and then asked me what I was going to name it. I told her almost immediately Stefanie. That made us both very happy! Forward now to this summer when Morgan, Luke, and I were on the Wild Africa Trek at Animal Kingdom. While on the trek, we stopped to observe the elephants, including a new baby boy elephant only a few months old. Someone asked about how he got his name. The guide told us that when mom is pregnant that cast members can submit possible names according to criteria that the keepers have established. For instance, elephants get African names. He also, just as a side note, mentioned that animals that are acquired from other zoos keep their original names, which explains why they have one named 'Stefanie.' Luke, Morgan, my friend Ann, and I all exchanged glances. Of all the names he could have mentioned, he had said Stefanie. But I wasn't composed enough to ask him which animal. I posted this story on PassPorter a few days back. One of my friends there Laurie is a huge fan of Disney's Animal Kingdom (an even bigger fan than me) and she has become friends with several of the keepers and vets. She told me she was going to check with some of them to find out which animal it was. Here's what she said, 'Cam, I have the answer for you on what kind of animal Stefanie at Animal Kingdom is.... I hope you're sitting down. She's a 4-year-old Masai Giraffe!!! And more... She was received at Animal Kingdom at the end of April. If that isn't a message from your angel I don't know what is. I burst into tears when I got this news and am crying now, but so happy. You can visit Stefanie Giraffe every time you ride the safari.' Notice she arrived at Animal Kingdom right at the time Stefanie died. Wow!"
> ...as told by Disney vacationer and PassPorter Guide Cam Matthews

[This edition of PassPorter's Walt Disney World is dedicated to Stefanie, a devoted PassPorter fan and Disney lover. May she forever live in our hearts. — Jennifer & Dave]

Index

We feel that a comprehensive index is very important to a successful travel guide. Too many times we've tried to look something up in other books only to find there was no entry at all, forcing us to flip through pages and waste valuable time. When you're on the phone with a reservation agent and looking for that little detail, time is of the essence.

You'll find the PassPorter index is complete and detailed. Whenever we reference more than one page for a given topic, the major topic is in **bold** and map references are in *italics* to help you home in on exactly what you need. For those times you want to find everything there is to be had, we include all the minor references. We have plenty of cross-references, too, just in case you don't look it up under the name we use.

P.S. This isn't the end of the book. More nifty features begin on page 306!

Planning
Getting There
Staying in Style
Touring
Feasting
Making Magic
Index
Notes & More

Planning

Getting There

Staying in Style

Touring

Feasting

Making Magic

Index

Notes & More

Planning
Getting There
Staying in Style
Touring
Feasting
Making Magic
Index
Notes & More

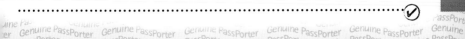

Web Site Index

Planning

Getting There

Staying in Style

Touring

Feasting

Making Magic

Index

Notes & More

Autographs

Kids and kids-at-heart love to get autographs from Disney characters! These two pages beg to be filled with signatures, paw prints, and doodles from your favorite characters. We've even provided places to write the actual name of the character (they can be hard to read—they are autographs, after all), plus the location where you discovered the character and the date of your find. Even if you bring or purchase an autograph book, use these pages when you fill it up or just plain forget it. (Been there, done that!) Be sure to see page 276 for tips and tricks on how to get character autographs, too!

Character: Location: Date:

Character: Location: Date:

Character: Location: Date:

Autographs Anonymous

We know. We understand. Bouncing tigers and giant mice can be intimidating. After several months of research and development, we came up with the following system that can help both the interminably shy and the overstimulated. Just write your name in the blank below, take a deep breath, and hold out your book. Now, wasn't that easy?

Hi, my name is _____. May I have your autograph?

(write your name here)

Character:
Location: *Date:*

Character:
Location: *Date:*

Character: *Location:*   *Date:*

Character: *Location:*   *Date:*

Planning

Getting There

Staying in Style

Touring

Feasting

Making Magic

Index

Notes & More

Planning

Getting There

Staying in Style

Touring

Feasting

Making Magic

Index

Notes & More

Register Your PassPorter

We are <u>very</u> interested to learn how your vacation went and what you think of the PassPorter, how it worked (or didn't work) for you, and your opinion on how we could improve it! We encourage you to register your copy of PassPorter with us—in return for your feedback, we'll send you **two valuable coupons** good for discounts on PassPorters and PassHolder pouches when purchased directly from us. You can register your copy of PassPorter at http://www.passporter.com/register.asp, or you can send us a postcard or letter to P.O. Box 3880, Ann Arbor, Michigan 48106.

Report a Correction or Change

Keeping up with the changes at Walt Disney World is virtually impossible without your help. When you notice something is different than what is printed in PassPorter, or you just come across something you'd like to see us cover, please let us know! You can report your news, updates, changes, and corrections at http://www.passporter.com/report.asp.

Contribute to the Next Edition of PassPorter

You can become an important part of the 2014 edition of *PassPorter's Walt Disney World*! The easiest way is to rate the resorts, rides, and/or restaurants. Your ratings and comments become part of our reader ratings throughout the book and help future readers make travel decisions. Want to get more involved? Send us a vacation tip, magical memory, or photograph—if we use it in a future edition of PassPorter, we'll credit you by name in the guidebook and send you a free copy of the edition! Do all this and more at http://www.passporter.com/customs.

Get Your Questions Answered

We love to hear from you! Alas, due to the thousands of e-mails and hundreds of phone calls we receive each week, we cannot offer personalized advice to all our readers. But there's a great way to get your questions answered: Ask your fellow readers! Visit our message boards at http://www.passporterboards.com/forums, join for free, and post your question. In most cases, fellow readers and Disney fans will offer their ideas and experiences! Our message boards also function as an ultimate list of frequently asked questions. Just browsing through to see the answers to other readers' questions will reap untold benefit! This is also a great way to make friends and have fun while planning your vacation. But be careful—our message boards can be addictive!

PassPorter Online

A wonderful way to get the most from your PassPorter is to visit our active web site at http://www.passporter.com. We serve up valuable PassPorter updates, plus useful Walt Disney World information and advice we couldn't jam into our book. You can swap tales (that's t-a-l-e-s, Mickey!) with fellow Disney fans, play contests and games, find links to other sites, get plenty of details, and ask us questions. You can also order PassPorters and shop for PassPorter accessories! The latest information on new PassPorters to other destinations is also available on our site. To get our page-by-page PassPorter updates, visit http://www.passporter.com/customs/bookupdates.htm.

PassPorter Web Links	Address (URL)
Main Page: PassPorter Online	http://www.passporter.com
Walt Disney World Forum	http://www.passporter.com/wdw
PassPorter Message Boards	http://www.passporterboards.com
PassPorter Photo Archive	http://www.passporter.com/photos
PassPorter Article Collection	http://www.passporter.com/articles
Book Updates	http://www.passporter.com/customs/bookupdates.htm
Contribute to PassPorter	http://www.passporter.com/contribute.asp
Register Your PassPorter	http://www.passporter.com/register.asp
PassPorter Deluxe Edition Information	http://www.passporter.com/wdw/deluxe.htm

PassPorter Articles and Photos

Still hungry for more information to make your Walt Disney World trip the best it can be? You'll **find all the things we couldn't fit** into our guidebook in our extensive photo and article collections, available online at the PassPorter.com web site. At press time, we offer more than 800 articles (which amounts to about 3500+ pages of information) and more than 37,000 images ... all neatly organized and searchable!

The **PassPorter Article Collection** (view at http://www.passporter.com/articles) contains full-length, feature articles on a variety of topics related to Disney and travel. Each article can be downloaded as a fully-formatted Adobe PDF, printed, and placed in your PassPorter for additional reference. You can search or browse the collection to find articles that interest you. Tip: Use the special keywords we've listed in the lower right margin of many pages in this guidebook and then type the keyword at http://www.passporter.com/i to zip right to a related article! Most of our articles come with photos, links to the related forum in our message boards, and reader comments! If you enjoy our articles, be sure you're subscribed to the free PassPorter News, in which most of our articles originally appear each week! Subscribe at http://www.passporter.com/news.htm.

The huge **PassPorter Photo Archive** is a great way to get a closer look at Walt Disney World before you ever arrive. Photos are contributed by authors and readers, giving you a wide range of perspectives. Our archive offers several features, including searching, commenting, rating, slide shows, and even fun e-postcards. PassPorter's Club members (see page 316) can also zoom in on each photo up to 25 times in size to see all the delightful detail. We encourage all of our readers to contribute to the archive—your photo may be selected as a PhotoPick of the week or even chosen to appear in an

upcoming PassPorter guidebook! Tip: Use the special numbers we've listed with most photos in this guidebook and then type the number at http://www.passporter.com/i to zip right to the photo for a better look!

PassPorter Goodies

PassPorter was born out of the necessity for more planning, organization, and a way to preserve the memories of a great vacation! Along the way we've found other things that either help us use the PassPorter better, appreciate our vacation more, or just make our journey a little more comfortable. Others have asked us about them, so we thought we'd share them with you. Order online at http://www.passporterstore.com/store, call us toll-free at 877-929-3273, or use the order form below.

✂ -

PassPorter® PassHolder is a small, lightweight nylon pouch that holds passes, ID cards, passports, money, and pens. Wear it around your neck for hands-free touring, and for easy access at the airport. The front features a clear compartment, a zippered pocket, and a velcro pocket; the back has a small pocket (perfect size for FASTPASS) and two pen slots. Adjustable cord. Royal blue. $4\,^7/_8$" x $6\,^1/_2$"

Quantity:
____ x $8.95

PassPorter® Badge personalized with your name! Go around the "World" in style with our lemon yellow oval pin. Price includes personalization with your name, shipping, and handling. Please indicate badge name(s) with your order.

I'm Going Around the "World" with **PassPorter** *Jennifer* *Meet me at www.passporter.com*

Quantity:
___ x $4.00

Name(s): _____

Please ship my PassPorter Goodies to:

Name ....

Address..

City, State, Zip ....

Daytime Phone...

Payment: ❏ check (to "MediaMarx") ❏ charge card
❏ MasterCard ❏ Visa ❏ American Express ❏ Discover

Card number ....Exp. Date. ....

Signature ....

Sub-Total:

Tax*:

Shipping**:

Total:

* Please include sales tax if you live in Michigan.
**Shipping costs are:
$5 for totals up to $9
$6 for totals up to $19
$7 for totals up to $29
$8 for totals up to $39
Delivery takes 1-2 weeks.

Send your order form to P.O. Box 3880, Ann Arbor, MI 48106, call us toll-free at 877-WAYFARER (877-929-3273), or order online http://www.passporterstore.com/store.

➤

Planning · Getting There · Staying in Style · Touring · Feasting · Making Magic · Index · Notes & More

More PassPorters

You've asked for more PassPorters—we've listened! We have eight PassPorter print books and fourteen e-books (and growing), all designed to make your Disney vacation the best it can be. And if you've wished for a PassPorter with all the flexibility and features of a daily planner, check out our Deluxe Editions (described below). To learn more about the new editions and release dates, visit us at http://www.passporter.com.

PassPorter's Walt Disney World Deluxe Edition

Design first-class vacations with this loose-leaf ring binder edition. The Deluxe Edition features the same great content as *PassPorter's Walt Disney World* spiral guide. Special features of the Deluxe Edition include ten interior storage slots in the binder to hold guidemaps, ID cards, and a pen (we even include a pen). The Deluxe PassPorter binder makes it really easy to add, remove, and rearrange pages ... you can even download, print, and add in updates, feature articles, and supplemental pages from our web site, and refills are available for purchase. Learn more at http://www.passporter.com/wdw/deluxe.htm. The Deluxe Edition is available through bookstores by special order—just give your favorite bookstore the ISBN is 978-1-58771-111-4 (2013 Deluxe Edition).

PassPorter's Disney Cruise Line and its Ports of Call

Updated annually! Get your cruise plans in shipshape with our updated, award-winning field guide ... includes details on all new ports and the new ships to come! Authors Jennifer and Dave Marx cover the Disney Cruise Line in incredible detail, including deck plans, stateroom floor plans, original photos, menus, entertainment guides, port/shore excursion details, and plenty of worksheets to help you budget, plan, and record your information. We also include reader tips, photos, and magial memories! In its tenth edition in 2012, this is the original and most comprehensive guidebook devoted to the Disney Cruise Line! Our 10th edition covers the new ships and ports of call that the Disney ships visit. Learn more and order your copy at http://www.passporter.com/dcl or get a copy at your favorite bookstore. ISBN for the 10th edition paperback, no PassPockets is 978-1-58771-115-2. Also available in a Deluxe Edition with organizer PassPockets (ISBN: 978-1-58771-116-9).

> **Did you know?** If you purchase these guidebooks directly from PassPorter, you also get the online edition free! This offer is only available to those who order directly through PassPorter; we regret we're unable to offer it to those who purchase it from a bookstore.

Even More PassPorters in Paperback

Planning

PassPorter's Disney 500
This popular book has more than 500 time-tested Walt Disney World tips—all categorized and coded! We chose the best of our reader-submitted tips over a six-year period for this book and each has been edited by author Jennifer Marx. For more details, visit http://www.passporter.com/wdw/disney500.asp. ISBN-13: 978-1-58771-090-2

PassPorter's Free-Book
It's hard to believe anything is free at Walt Disney World, but there are actually a number of things you can get or do for little to no cost. This book documents more than 150 free or cheap things to do before and during your vacation. Visit http://www.passporter.com/wdw/free-book.asp. ISBN-13: 978-1-58771-102-2

PassPorter's Disney Vacation Club Guide
A 170-page in-depth guide to all aspects of the Disney Vacation Club, from deciding whether to join to deciding where and when to use your points. Included are numerous photos and tips on maximizing your experience. If you've ever wondered what the club is all about or wanted to learn more, this is the perfect introduction. Get more details at http://www.passporter.com/disney-vacation-club.asp. ISBN-13: 978-1-58771-087-2

PassPorter's Disney Weddings & Honeymoons
This is both a guidebook and a bridal organizer tailored to the unique requirements of planning a wedding, vow renewal, or commitment ceremony at Walt Disney World or on the Disney Cruise Line. It takes you through the entire process, outline your options, offer valuable tips, organize your information, and help you plan down to the last detail! Details at http://www.passporter.com/weddings.asp. ISBN-13: 978-1-58771-088-9

PassPorter's Walt Disney World for British Holidaymakers
New in print! Brits, you can get super in-depth information for your Walt Disney World vacation from fellow Brit and PassPorter feature columnist Cheryl Pendry. More than 250 pages long and filled with amazing detail on Walt Disney World and Orlando-area attractions. Learn more at http://www.passporter.com/wdw/brits.asp. ISBN-13: 978-1-58771-094-0

PassPorter's Disney Speed Planner
Coming soon to print! Author Justine Fellows offers a fast, easy method for planning practically perfect vacations—great for busy people or those who don't have lots of time to plan. Follow this simple, ten-step plan to help you get your vacation planned in short order so you can get on with your life. For more details, visit http://www.passporter.com/wdw/speedplanner.asp. ISBN: 978-1-58771-089-6

PassPorter's Cruise Clues: First Class Tips for Disney Cruise Trips
Coming soon to print! Get the best tips for the Disney Cruise Line—all categorized and coded—as well as cruise line comparisons, a teen perspective, and ultimate packing lists! This popular e-book is packed with 250 cruiser-tested tips. For more details, visit http://www.passporter.com/dcl/cruiseclues.asp. ISBN-13: 978-1-58771-096-4

Getting There

Staying in Style

Touring

Feasting

Making Magic

Index

Notes & More

PassPorter E-Books

Looking for more in-depth coverage on specific topics? Look no further than PassPorter E-Books! Our e-books are inexpensive (from $5.95–$9.95) and available immediately as a download (Adobe PDF format). And unlike most e-books, ours are fully formatted just like a regular PassPorter print book. A PassPorter e-book will even fit into a Deluxe PassPorter Binder. We offer fourteen e-books at press time, and have plans for many, many more!

PassPorter's Disney 500: *Fast Tips for Walt Disney World Trips*
Our most popular e-book has more than 500 time-tested Walt Disney World tips—all categorized and coded! We chose the best of our reader-submitted tips over a six-year period for this e-book and each has been edited by author Jennifer Marx. For more details, a list of tips, and a sample page, visit http://www.passporter.com/wdw/disney500.asp.

PassPorter's Cruise Clues: *First-Class Tips for Disney Cruise Trips*
Get the best tips for the Disney Cruise Line—all categorized and coded—as well as cruise line comparisons, a teen perspective, and ultimate packing lists! This popular e-book is packed with 250 cruiser-tested tips—all edited by award-winning author Jennifer Marx. For more details, visit http://www.passporter.com/dcl/cruiseclues.asp.

PassPorter's Disney Character Yearbook
A 268-page compendium of all the live Disney characters you can find at Walt Disney World, Disneyland, and on the Disney Cruise Line. Also includes tips on finding, meeting, photographing, and getting autographs, plus a customizable autograph book to print! For more details, visit http://www.passporter.com/disney-character-yearbook.asp.

PassPorter's Disney Speed Planner: *The Easy Ten-Step Program*
A fast, easy method for planning practically perfect vacations—great for busy people or those who don't have lots of time to plan. Follow this simple, ten-step plan to help you get your vacation planned in short order so you can get on with your life. For more details, visit http://www.passporter.com/wdw/speedplanner.asp.

PassPorter's Free-Book
A Guide to Free and Low-Cost Activities at Walt Disney World
It's hard to believe anything is free at Walt Disney World, but there are actually a number of things you can get or do for little to no cost. This e-book documents more than 150 free or cheap things to do before you go and after you arrive. Visit http://www.passporter.com/wdw/free-book.asp.

PassPorter's Sidekick for the Walt Disney World Guidebook
This is a customizable companion to our general Walt Disney World guidebook—you can personalize worksheets, journals, luggage tags, and charts, plus click links to all the URLs in the guidebook! Details at http://www.passporter.com/wdw/sidekick.asp.

PassPorter's Festivals and Celebrations
at Walt Disney World
Get in on all the fun in this updated 78-page overview of all the wonderful and magical festivals, celebrations, parties, and holidays at Walt Disney World. Included are beautiful color photos and tips. Read more and see a sample page at http://www.passporter.com/wdw/festivals-celebrations.asp.

PassPorter's Answer Book
Get answers to the most popular topics asked about Walt Disney World, Disneyland, Disney Cruise Line, and general travel. You've asked it, we've answered it! The e-book's questions and answers are sorted geographically and topically. Details at http://www.passporter.com/answer-book.asp.

PassPorter's Disney Weddings & Honeymoons
This is both a guidebook and a bridal organizer tailored to the unique requirements of planning a wedding, vow renewal, or commitment ceremony at Disney World or on the Disney Cruise. It will take you through the entire process, outline your options, help you plan your event down to the last detail! Details at http://www.passporter.com/weddings.asp.

PassPorter's Disney Vacation Club Guide
A 170-page in-depth guide to all aspects of the Disney Vacation Club, from deciding whether to join to deciding where and when to use your points. Included are beautiful color photos and tips on maximizing your experience. If you've ever wondered what the club is all about or wanted to learn more, this is the perfect introduction. Get more details at http://www.passporter.com/disney-vacation-club.asp.

PassPorter's Walt Disney World for Brit Holidaymakers
Brits, you can get super in-depth information for your Walt Disney World vacation from fellow Brit and PassPorter feature columnist Cheryl Pendry. This e-book is more than 250 pages long and filled with amazing detail on both Walt Disney World as well as other Orlando-area attractions. Learn more at http://www.passporter.com/wdw/brits.asp.

PassPorter's Disneyland Paris
This comprehensive, 204-page book covers every aspect of visiting Disneyland Paris, including traveling to France from the United States and the United Kingdom. We provide all the information you need to get the most out of your stay! Read more and see a sample page at http://www.passporter.com/disneyland-paris.asp.

And coming soon ...

PassPorter's Orlando and Beyond: Everything But the Mouse!
This is the Disney fan's guide to Central Florida's numerous other theme parks, covering Universal Studios, Islands of Adventure, Wet 'n Wild, SeaWorld, Aquatica, Discovery Cove, LEGOLAND, Kennedy Space Center and Busch Gardens with the same helpful format and attention to detail found in *PassPorter's Walt Disney World*. Whether you're traveling to Orlando for the first time and want to see it all or returning for the umpteenth time and want to see something new, this book is for you!

Learn more and order at: http://www.passporterstore.com/store/ebooks.aspx

Planning

Getting There

Staying in Style

Touring

Feasting

Making Magic

Index

Notes & More

Do you want more help planning your Walt Disney World vacation? Join the PassPorter's Club and get all these benefits:

✔ "All-you-can-read" access to EVERY e-book we publish (see current list on the previous page). PassPorter's Club passholders also get early access to these e-books before the general public. New e-books are added on a regular basis, too.

✔ New! Anyone who commits to an annual pass in the PassPorter's Club also receives free access to all our Online Editions, including the one for this book!

✔ Interactive, customizable "e-worksheets" to help make your trip planning easier, faster, and smoother. These are the electronic, interactive worksheets we've been mentioning throughout this book. The worksheets are in PDF format and can be printed for a truly personalized approach! We have more than 50 worksheets, with more on the way. You can see a sample e-worksheet to the right.

✔ Access to super-sized "e-photos" in the PassPorter Photo Archives—photos can be zoomed in up to 25 times larger than standard web photos. You can use these e-photos to see detail as if you're actually standing there—or use them for desktop wallpaper, scrapbooking, whatever!

✔ Our best discount on print guidebooks ... 35% off!

There's more features, too! For a full list of features and current e-books, e-worksheets, and e-photos, visit http://www.passporter.com/club. You can also take a peek inside the Club's Gallery at http://www.passporterboards.com/forums/passporters-club-gallery. The Gallery is open to everyone—it contains two FREE interactive e-worksheets to try out!

Price: A PassPorter's Club pass is currently $5.95/month, or the cost of just one e-book!

How to Get Your Pass to the PassPorter's Club

Step 1. Get a free community account. Register simply and quickly at http://www.passporterboards.com/forums/register.php.

Step 2. Log in at http://www.passporterboards.com/forums/login.php using the Member Name and password you created in step 1.

Step 3. Get your pass. Select the type of pass you'd like and follow the directions to activate it immediately. We currently offer monthly and annual passes. (Annual passes save 25% and get extra perks!)

Questions? Assistance? We're here to help! Please send e-mail to club@passporter.com.

Electronic, interactive worksheet available— see page 316

My Important Numbers

Enter your important numbers in the boxes below. Once you obtain your park passes, write down the number on the back in the appropriate places below—you will need this number if your passes are ever lost. Consider using a personal code to conceal sensitive information.

Personal Information:

Driver's License number(s):
Passport number(s):
Frequent Flyer number(s):
Insurance number(s):
Park pass number(s):

Financial Information:

Voucher number(s):
Gift card number(s):
Traveler check number(s):
Other number(s):

Planning

Getting There

Staying in Style

Touring

Feasting

Making Magic

Index

Notes & More

Electronic, interactive worksheet available— see page 316

Vacation At-A-Glance

Create an overview of your itinerary in the chart below for easy reference. You can then make copies of it and give one to everyone in your traveling party, as well as to friends and family members who stay behind. Get a FREE electronic version of this worksheet at http://www.passporter.com/club.

Name(s):	
Departing on: Time: #:	
Arriving at:	
Staying at: Phone:	

Date:	Date:
Park/Activity:	Park/Activity:
Breakfast:	Breakfast:
Lunch:	Lunch:
Dinner:	Dinner:
Other:	Other:
Date:	Date:
Park/Activity:	Park/Activity:
Breakfast:	Breakfast:
Lunch:	Lunch:
Dinner:	Dinner:
Other:	Other:
Date:	Date:
Park/Activity:	Park/Activity:
Breakfast:	Breakfast:
Lunch:	Lunch:
Dinner:	Dinner:
Other:	Other:
Date:	Date:
Park/Activity:	Park/Activity:
Breakfast:	Breakfast:
Lunch:	Lunch:
Dinner:	Dinner:
Other:	Other:
Date:	Date:
Park/Activity:	Park/Activity:
Breakfast:	Breakfast:
Lunch:	Lunch:
Dinner:	Dinner:
Other:	Other:

Departing on: Time: #:
Returning at:

Planning | Getting There | Staying in Style | Touring | Feasting | Making Magic | Index | Notes & More

Reader Photo 38082
Mindy Stanton

Disney
Dreaming

**Celebrating the magic of Disney through
photographs by PassPorter authors and readers**

A photo supplement

If you can dream it ...

Reader Photo 22636.
Alicia Bruce

Reader Photo 36934.
Charity Boughner

Walt Disney World is for dreamers.
Sometimes, it's a dream of a lifetime, born in front of a television in a childhood long ago, nurtured on VHS, DVD, and heartstring-tugging TV commercials—a dream that may not come to life until the dreamers have little dreamers of their own. Dreams of Tinker Bell, flitting through the night over a shimmering castle; a hug from Mickey, Minnie, Tigger, or the Goof; a childhood waiting to be revisited; a hope for magic at an age when "reality" overwhelms us daily.

For other dreamers, it's a return to a **golden childhood** that magically remains untarnished, with new marvels joining the old. Whole new worlds may have appeared, waiting to be explored. Old friends remain, waiting patiently for memories to be passed from parent to child.

Other dreamers just can't stay away, returning to their **laughing place** year after year, sharing the magic with family and friends. Their minds swirl with memories of castles, warm evening breezes, twinkling lights, kindness from strangers, familiar wonders shared with awestruck crowds, or perhaps a few moments when the crowds disappear into the mist and it's just two of you, dancing in front of an outdoor stage to a nameless rock band playing "Hotel California," finding a deeper love than you thought possible.

It's brides dreaming of horse-drawn coaches and liveried footmen, and a trio of siblings at the youngest's Golden anniversary, finding there are still new wonders to mingle with the memories. It's dreams of a **better, brighter world**, with less care, and more delight.

321

Reader Photo 37696: Marc Lorenzo

Reader Photo 22863: Rebecca Smith

PassPorter is a book about dreaming it and doing it—it's about charting a course, plotting a feast, maximizing the precious days and nights, and recording some of those moments for a cold night in Minnesota, or a bit of magic after a long, stressful day. It's learning where and how the magic and memories can find you (because the harder you chase the magic, the faster that pixie will fly from your grasp). It's about a place where tens of thousands of people labor daily to bring these dreams to life, and hundreds of millions have managed to explore fantasy, history, nature, humanity, childhood, the wide world, and the dreams of an extraordinary man, **Walt Disney**, and the people he continues to inspire.

Your authors have had a share in all these dreams and doings; shared with our closest family, and with strangers who are connected to us only by the pages of our books and an address on the Internet. What **began as a dream** of enhancing the magic for others and charting an independent course for ourselves was launched in print more than 13 years ago, on May 3, 1999. Over the years, PassPorter has become so much more—a community of readers sharing a common love, making new friends, nurturing each other's dreams and achievements, and exchanging knowledge, experience, and magic.

Join us as we **explore the magic** that is Walt Disney World, as seen through our eyes and the eyes of the PassPorter reader community. It is our dream that these images help you imagine yourself there.

... then you can do it!

Make believe

Reader Photo 21256:
Danielle Fortin

The fireworks will just blow you away!

Reader Photo 21659:
Rae Mills

Reader Photo 22275:
Brent Key

A Disney Do! Goofin' in Liberty Square

Reader Photo 21803:
Charity Boughner

Reader Photo 21620:
Megan Caceres

Dining in the Castle

Magic Kingdom

is a world of wonder for all ages. It is the place most of us think of when we picture Walt Disney World, and it is the embodiment of all things magical. Enter these gates and you look through the eyes of a child, where magic is real again and something extraordinary awaits you around every corner. Let your imagination soar!

Reader Photo 36758:
Alicia Bruce

Going down Splash Mountain

Find your inner child

Magical Mexican Marketplace

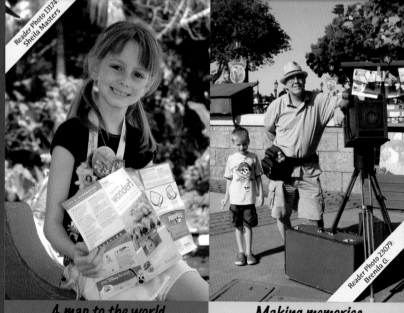

A map to the world *Making memories*

Reader Photo 37749:
Megan Caceres

Trying on the perfect hat in France

Epcot

is broad vistas, bold architectural statements, and a lagoon that unites a world. Go rocketing through space, glide peacefully over California, walk from Mexico to Norway, to China, and beyond.

Reader Photo 2257:
Carolyn Brooke

Gargoyles in France

Reader Photo 37682:
Mayra Lopez

Reader Photo 21027:
Debra Ortiz

Havin' a ball!

Wish upon a star

Reader Photo 36701:
Denise Hand

MONAHANS

Reader Photo 22210:
Regina Thomas

Getting in the Act!

Singin' in the rain

Disney's Hollywood Studios,

where the star-struck and soundstage-struck gather to explore their dreams, the dream-maker's dreams, and the method behind the magic. The bold line up to be terrorized, star tourists rocket to Endor, stuntmen tumble, and wannabes hope to become Idols.

Reader Photo 22426:
Marianne Goode

HOLLYWOOD
STUDIOS

Plants and stars

Minnie Mouse
Thanks Everyone
XOXO
5/1/89

Hugs and Kisses from Star Minnie

BUZZ
LIGHTYE
SPACE

Jedi Training

Props!

Be more playful

Talk to animals

Reader Photo 2927: Cheryl Pendry

Tigger, is that you?

Reader Photo: Hope Rupp

Jammin' in the jungle

Reader Photo 22930: Andrea Popovits

Get up close and personal

Reader Photo 23094: Tricia Davids

Morning at the dig site

Disney's Animal Kingdom

allows you to explore the high Himalayas, dry African savannahs, and lush Asian rainforests. Encounter every creature from ant to elephant, dino to Yeti, and from Simba to Nemo. Fantasy may take a back seat to True Life Adventure, but whimsy and wonder are always close at hand.

Reader Photo 21281: Debbie Ernest

Yellin' for the Yeti!

Author Photo: MediaMarx, Inc.

Spot little ones

Reader Photo 22269: Keith Stanton

ANANDAPUR

Special delivery of fun

Be inspired by nature

Daydream

Reader Photo 22925:
Joseph Marchewka

Sun-drenched Italy

Days of dazzling Florida sunshine, bright colors, broad vistas, glorious flowers and gardens at every turn, fanciful parades, enchanting faces, and unexpected encounters. Days at Walt Disney World can indeed be a living, waking dream. Sit on a bench, feel the warm breeze, and take a few minutes to let the quieter joys come to you.

Reader Photo 37645:
Joseph Marchewka

Face painting at the Magic Kingdom

Reader Photo 31702:
Tom Panzella

Rainbow over the Magic Kingdom

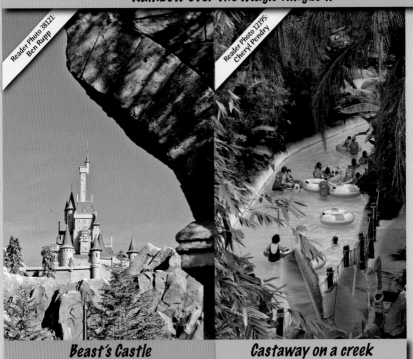

Reader Photo 38121:
Ben Rupp

Reader Photo 12195:
Cheryl Pendry

Beast's Castle

Castaway on a creek

Sunshine comin' your way!

Enchanted evenings

Reader Photo 37233:
Ben Rupp

Lighting up the night at the Magic Kingdom

Reader Photo 23084:
Francis T. Tewey

Expedition Everest on an enchanted evening

Nights with fairy lights filling long, enchanted hours. Fear finds only those who seek it in haunted mansions and pirates' caves, while the rest of us revel in a midsummer night's dream. Everyone stays up way past bedtime for a bit of music, explosions, fireworks-filled awe, and the "extra magic," and we all wait for a "kiss goodnight."

Reader Photo 37713: Jennifer Arnold

Haunted Mansion in Fog

Reader Photo 23015: Amy Rupp

Reflections of Earth

Dream with your eyes open

Feast on dreams

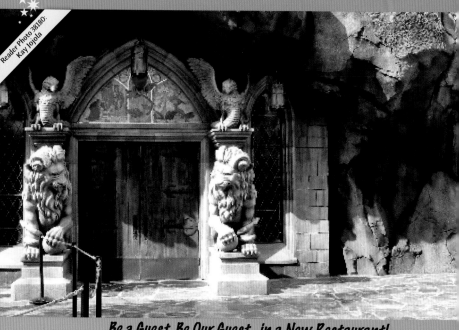

Be a Guest, Be Our Guest, in a New Restaurant!

One child, two treats

Celebrating a wedding at 1900 Pa

Dining at the Walt Disney World Resort is truly fundamental, experimental, sentimental, and elemental. A world of flavors waits, from the simplest snack to five-star delights. Many find the feast as important as the fantasy, and reserve tables for dinners six months hence. A festival of food and wine packs the parks at the slowest time of year. Others savor simple chicken nuggets from a Mickey plate, a frozen treat that delights the taste buds on those hot Florida days, or a delectable dessert at tea time.

Kaki Gori on a Hot Day

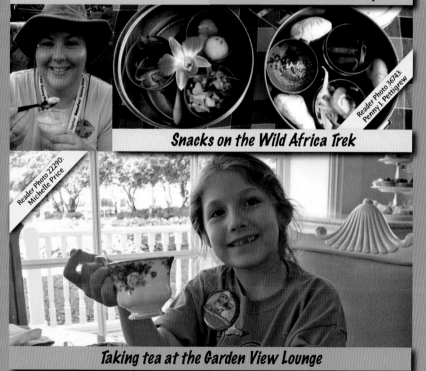

Snacks on the Wild Africa Trek

Taking tea at the Garden View Lounge

Try something new

Sound asleep at Pop Century Resort

Delight upon seeing the savanna

Port Orleans Royal Room

Claiming the perfect hammock at the Caribbean Beach Resort

Lodging

Lodging here is luxury, fantasy, nostalgia, and comfort. The savannah, South Seas, back woods, and seashore. New Orleans, New England, Southwest, and Northwest; keys, bayous, and boardwalks. Fantasies for the frugal. Elegant indulgence. A welcoming home for vacation club members, playful pools, and satisfying meals. Soft pillows, clean linens, and a towel sculpture greet you after a magical day in the parks.

Fun at the Animal Kingdom Lodge Pool

Stay in style

Make some magic

Ready for the Luau

Going to see Nemo ... for the fifth time!

Picked as Grand Marshals for the Parade

Magic can be found anywhere in "The World," and there are countless ways that it can happen. Get a personal escort into your favorite park. See your movie friends come alive before your eyes. Dress up to the nines for a romantic dinner. Take in a pick-up game of duck duck goose. Make your own magic!

Just Engaged!

He proposed at Walt Disney World!

Notice the little things

Be together

Reader Photo 13191:
Angie Lambert

Families, including Walt Disney's own, inspired the theme park dream. Is there any doubt he succeeded? The joy he has given millions of families from around the world is incalculable. Loving moments, life-long memories, and uninhibited parent-and-child play await all those who take the time to be together here.

Jumpin' for Joy on Main Street

Reader Photo 36238:
Catie Hiltz

We Go Together!

Reader Photo 37219:
Ben Rupp

Family Totem Pole

Reader Photo 14954: Carrie Owens

The best place to rest

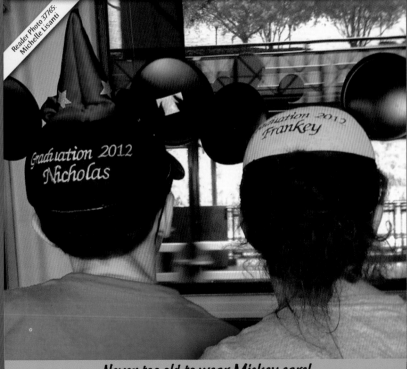

Reader Photo 37765: Michelle Lisanti

Never too old to wear Mickey ears!

Families are like fudge
... mostly sweet with a few nuts

Friendships

We meet through PassPorter ...   ... and even get engaged!

Touring the backlot

Sharing a drink   Sharing a meal

Coming together for PassPorter's 10th birthday on May 3, 2009

PassPorter Moms

Friends to share the good times. Reach beyond family to friends from back home, and even friends you meet online. Passion for all things Disney has spawned thousands of web sites, forums, podcasts, blogs, chats, and even marriages. Friendships are cemented here, as members of online communities "meet" to enjoy rides, share meals, do good works, and explore "The World."

It takes a village

Spread your wings

Reader Photo 21970.
Brent Key

LIFE VEST

Invited to sit in the cockpit after landing in Orlando

Reader Photo 37230.
Ben Rupp

Having fun and driving us crazy

Author Photo 873.
MediaMarx, Inc.

"A Friendship" Can Take You Places

Reader Photo 27593: Rebecca Smith

A Monorail Odyssey

Author Photo: MediaMarx, Inc.

Ride Home After a Long Day

Journeys of a thousand miles often end in Orlando. For some, it may be their first flight, or longest drive. Even after you've reached this sprawling place, it's an adventure to get from here to there. There's the astounding network of highways and byways, a fleet of boats shuttling between park and resort, buses headed everywhere, and the legendary monorail gliding quietly overhead.

Reader Photo 13923: Bonnie McCarty

Gold monorail pulls in to the station

Go on an adventure

Discoveries

Disneyland Paris

Bow of the Disney Magic

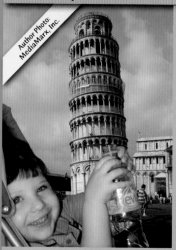
Pisa, Italy

Beyond this "World" lies much more to explore. There's nothing like a visit to "The World" to spark wanderlust, and Disney is happy to oblige. Cruise the seas and visit far-flung ports of call with Disney Cruise Line. Visit theme parks in California, Japan, France, and China, and the wondrous places nearby. Tour with Adventures by Disney, or maybe head east or west down the road to either of Florida's coasts—Gulf, or Space.

Tokyo and Big Thunder Mountain Railroad

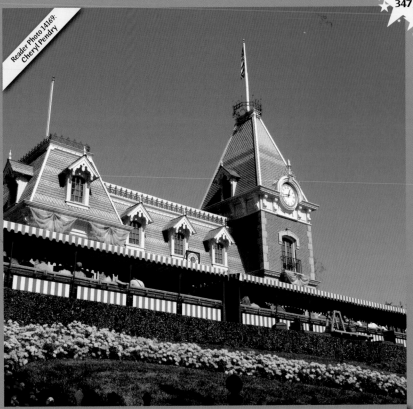

Reader Photo 14169:
Cheryl Pendry

Disneyland Railroad Station in California

Reader Photo 6093:
Cheryl Pendry

Sleeping Beauty Castle at Hong Kong Disneyland

Explore your world

PassPorter's 10th Birthday Party in The Seas VIP Salon at Epcot

We had a dream. We followed it and it led us
to develop, write, and publish PassPorter more than ten years ago.
Little did we know how it would grow and blossom! To celebrate this
"decade of dreams," we invited our family, friends, and PassPorter
readers to party with us onboard the Disney Magic, at Walt Disney
World and Disneyland, and even on Broadway in New York City!
Thank you to our core team and hundreds of thousands of readers
who have supported PassPorter over the last ten years. Here's to
another magical decade with you!

Storming the castle!

A surprise gift from our Guides

First Visit to American Idol

PassPorter Quest Winners

Celebrating onboard the Disney Magic

An evening on Broadway

All Gussied Up

I found treasure!

Bon Voyage Deck Party

Thanks for believing in me, Mom!

What's your dream?

Thank You ...

To our fabulous readers who contributed photos to the PassPorter Photo Archive and allowed us to reprint them for this supplement: Jennifer Arnold, Charity Boughner, Carolyn Brooke, Alicia Bruce, Megan Caceres, Tricia Davids, Heather DiFulvio, Sean Dunham, Debbie Ernest, Danielle Fortin, Marianne Goode, Brenda G., Denise Hand, Catie Hiltz, Kay Jojola, Brent Key, Elizabeth Key, Angie Lambert, David Latoundji, Michelle Lisanti, Mayra Lopez, Marc Lorenzo, Joseph Marchewka, Sheila Masters, Cam Matthews, Bonnie McCarty, Lisa Miller, Rae Mills, Bill Myers, Amanda Nash, Debra Ortiz, Carrie Owens, Melissa Lynn Page, Tom Panzella, Cheryl Pendry, Penny J. Pettigrew, Andrea Popovits, Melissa Potter, Michelle Price, Amy Rupp, Ben Rupp, Hope Rupp, Rebecca Smith, Keith Stanton, Mindy Stanton, Francis T. Tewey, Regina Thomas, Kurt Ulrich, and Shannon Wellnitz

And a special thank-you to the many readers who appear in the photographs—your smiling faces spread magic to us all!

You can view thousands of more photographs—both from your authors and fellow readers—online in the PassPorter Photo Archive at http://www.passporter.com/photos

Reader Photo 37694:
Marc Lorenzo

Let the Memories Begin!

Customize Your PassPorter

Use these labels to personalize your PassPockets for your trip. The color rectangles at the right can be folded over the edge of pages to create your own tabs or flags!

Our Cruise

Our Honeymoon

Our Wedding

Our Anniversary

Our Reunion

Our Gathering

My Birthday

Our Special Day

Our Journey

Our Eleventh Day

Our Twelvth Day

Our Thirteenth Day

Our Fourteenth Day

Our Return

PLANS PLANS

TRAVELS TRAVELS

ROOMS ROOMS

PLAY PLAY

FOOD FOOD

PLACES PLACES

MAGIC MAGIC

Create
Your
Own
Labels
&
← Tabs →

*Keep everything you need for your
journey together here in one place, such as maps,
tickets, coupons, reservation numbers... even passports!*

Our Journey

Departing at _____   Arriving at _____

Airline/Train/Bus Company _____

Flight/Route Number(s) _____

Flight Reservation Number(s) _____   Seat(s) _____

Cruise Reservation Number _____   Stateroom _____

Auto/Trip Insurance _____

Rental Car/Shuttle/Limo Company _____

Type _____   Reservation Number _____

Details _____

Returning at _____   Arriving home at _____

Flight/Route Number(s) _____   Seat(s) _____

Note(s) _____

_____

⬇ *Store small items in here like baggage claim tickets and receipts* ⬇

Things to Do

☐ _____   ☐ _____

☐ _____   ☐ _____

☐ _____   ☐ _____

☐ _____   ☐ _____

Notes

_____

_____

_____

_____

_____

OUR JOURNEY: Travel Information, Itineraries, Maps, Tickets

Memories of Our Journey

The weather was... _____ ... when we left

and... _____ ... when we arrived

The best thing about our journey was... _____

_____

The worst thing about our journey was... _____

_____

The funniest thing about our journey was... _____

_____

During our journey we tried... _____

and the result was... _____

The most magical moment during our journey was... _____

_____

📷 Photos and Snapshots

☐ Photos taken today (card/roll # ____)

Shot #   Description

_____   _____

_____   _____

_____   _____

_____   _____

_____   _____

_____   _____

🍳 Meals and Snacks

Breakfast: _____

$ _____

Lunch: _____

$ _____

Dinner: _____

$ _____

Snacks: _____

$ _____

💰 Budget and Expenses

Target travel budget: $ _____

Fares: $ _____

          $ _____

Fuel: $ _____

Tips: $ _____

Meals: $ _____

          $ _____

Other: $ _____

          $ _____

Total: $ _____

✒ Notes for Next Time

_____

_____

_____

_____

_____

_____

_____

_____

_____

_____

_____

_____

*Use your notes here to remind yourself
to inquire about special requests at check-in,
such as room preferences, discounts, and amenities.*

Our Room(s)

Hotel/Motel/Ship: _____ Phone: _____

Arriving: _____ Departing: _____

Room Type: _____ Location: _____

Special Requests: _____

Reservation Number: _____

Room Number: _____ Floor/Building: _____

Additional Stay: _____ Phone: _____

Arriving: _____ Departing: _____

Room Type: _____ Location: _____

Special Requests: _____

Reservation Number: _____

Room Number: _____ Floor/Building: _____

↓ *Store small items in here like card keys, receipts, and luggage tags* ↓

Things to Do

- ☐ _____   ☐ _____
- ☐ _____   ☐ _____
- ☐ _____   ☐ _____
- ☐ _____   ☐ _____

Notes

_____

_____

_____

_____

_____

Memories of Our Rooms

The first impression of our room(s) was... _____

The best thing was... _____

_____

The worst thing was... _____

_____

The amenities were... _____

_____

We tried... _____

and the result was... _____

_____

The most magical moment was... _____

_____

_____

📷 Photos and Snapshots

▢ Photos taken here (card/roll # ____)

Shot #   Description

_____   _____

_____   _____

_____   _____

_____   _____

_____   _____

🎞 Rooms and Views

Our room was... _____

_____

_____

The view was... _____

_____

_____

Best feature: _____

Worst feature: _____

🎥 Budget and Expenses

Target room budget: $ _____

Room(s): $ _____

             $ _____

Options: $ _____

             $ _____

Tips: $ _____

             $ _____

Other: $ _____

             $ _____

Total: $ _____

✒ Notes for Next Time

_____

_____

_____

_____

_____

_____

_____

_____

_____

_____

_____

_____

_____

_____

*Take it easy on your first day so
you don't wear yourself out early in the trip.
Your entire vacation is ahead of you—relax and enjoy it!*

Our First Day

Confirmation Numbers

____ : ____	Wake up:	
____ : ____	Early Morning:	
____ : ____	Breakfast:	
____ : ____	Morning:	
____ : ____		
____ : ____	Lunch:	
____ : ____	Afternoon:	
____ : ____		
____ : ____	Dinner:	
____ : ____	Evening:	
____ : ____		
____ : ____	Before bed:	

Special plans for today: _____

_____

⬇ *Store small items in here like ticket stubs and receipts for meals and purchases* ⬇

Things to Do, Places to Go, Attractions to Visit

- ☐ _____ ☐ _____
- ☐ _____ ☐ _____
- ☐ _____ ☐ _____
- ☐ _____ ☐ _____

Notes

_____

_____

_____

_____

Day: _____ **Date:** _____

OUR FIRST DAY: Itinerary · Information · Tickets · Guides · Maps

Memories of Our First Day

The weather today was... _____

The best thing today was... _____

_____

The worst thing today was... _____

_____

The funniest thing today was... _____

_____

Today we tried... _____

and the result was... _____

_____

The most magical moment today was... _____

_____

📷 Photos and Snapshots

📷 Photos taken today (card/roll # ____)

Shot #	Description
_____	_____
_____	_____
_____	_____
_____	_____
_____	_____
_____	_____

🍳 Meals and Snacks

Breakfast: _____
_____ $ ____

Lunch: _____
_____ $ ____

Dinner: _____
_____ $ ____

Snacks: _____
_____ $ ____

🎞 Budget and Expenses

First day budget: $ ____

Admission: $ ____
Meals: $ ____
             $ ____
             $ ____
Shopping: $ ____
             $ ____
Other: $ ____
             $ ____

Total: $ ____

✒ Notes for Next Time

_____

_____

_____

_____

_____

_____

_____

_____

_____

_____

_____

_____

_____

*Remember to drink plenty of fluids,
eat substantial meals, use sunblock, wear a hat,
and take frequent breaks as necessary during your day.*

Our Second Day

Confirmation Numbers

___ : ___ Wake up:

___ : ___ Early Morning:

___ : ___ Breakfast:

___ : ___ Morning:

___ : ___

___ : ___ Lunch:

___ : ___ Afternoon:

___ : ___

___ : ___ Dinner:

___ : ___ Evening:

___ : ___

___ : ___ Before bed:

Special plans for today:

⬇ *Store small items in here like ticket stubs and receipts for meals and purchases* ⬇

Things to Do, Places to Go, Attractions to Visit

☐ _____   ☐ _____
☐ _____   ☐ _____
☐ _____   ☐ _____
☐ _____   ☐ _____

Notes

_____
_____
_____
_____

Day: **Date:**

Memories of Our Second Day

The weather today was... _____

The best thing today was... _____

_____

The worst thing today was... _____

_____

The funniest thing today was... _____

_____

Today we tried... _____

and the result was... _____

_____

The most magical moment today was... _____

_____

📷 Photos and Snapshots

🖵 Photos taken today (card/roll # ____)

Shot #   Description

_____   _____

_____   _____

_____   _____

_____   _____

_____   _____

🎂 Meals and Snacks

Breakfast: _____

_____ $ _____

Lunch: _____

_____ $ _____

Dinner: _____

_____ $ _____

Snacks: _____

_____ $ _____

🏛 Budget and Expenses

Second day budget: $ _____

Admission: $ _____

Meals: $ _____

              $ _____

              $ _____

Shopping: $ _____

              $ _____

Other: $ _____

              $ _____

Total: $ _____

✎ Notes for Next Time

_____

_____

_____

_____

_____

_____

_____

_____

_____

_____

_____

_____

_____

*When you skip activities for lack of
time or energy, flip ahead in your PassPorter and
jot them down for another day so you don't forget to return!*

Our Third Day

_____ :	Wake up: _____
_____ :	Early Morning: _____
_____ :	Breakfast: _____
_____ :	Morning: _____
_____ :	_____
_____ :	Lunch: _____
_____ :	Afternoon: _____
_____ :	_____
_____ :	Dinner: _____
_____ :	Evening: _____
_____ :	_____
_____ :	Before bed: _____

Special plans for today: _____
_____

↓ *Store small items in here like ticket stubs and receipts for meals and purchases* ↓

Things to Do, Places to Go, Attractions to Visit

☐ _____   ☐ _____
☐ _____   ☐ _____
☐ _____   ☐ _____
☐ _____   ☐ _____

Notes

_____
_____
_____
_____

Day: _____   **Date:** _____

Memories of Our Third Day

The weather today was... _____

The best thing today was... _____

_____

The worst thing today was... _____

_____

The funniest thing today was... _____

_____

Today we tried... _____

and the result was... _____

_____

The most magical moment today was... _____

_____

📷 Photos and Snapshots

🗌 Photos taken today (card/roll # ____)

Shot #	Description
_____	_____
_____	_____
_____	_____
_____	_____
_____	_____

🍳 Meals and Snacks

Breakfast: _____
_____ $_____

Lunch: _____
_____ $_____

Dinner: _____
_____ $_____

Snacks: _____
_____ $_____

📷 Budget and Expenses

Third day budget: $_____

Admission: $_____

Meals: $_____

$_____

$_____

Shopping: $_____

$_____

Other: $_____

$_____

Total: $_____

✒ Notes for Next Time

_____

_____

_____

_____

_____

_____

_____

_____

_____

_____

_____

_____

_____

*When you find a souvenir you want,
get it right away—there is no guarantee you'll
be able to find that same treasure later in your trip.*

Our Fourth Day

: _____	Wake up:
: _____	Early Morning:
: _____	Breakfast:
: _____	Morning:
: _____	
: _____	Lunch:
: _____	Afternoon:
: _____	
: _____	Dinner:
: _____	Evening:
: _____	
: _____	Before bed:

Special plans for today: _____

⬇ *Store small items in here like ticket stubs and receipts for meals and purchases* ⬇

Things to Do, Places to Go, Attractions to Visit

☐ _____ ☐ _____
☐ _____ ☐ _____
☐ _____ ☐ _____
☐ _____ ☐ _____

Notes

_____
_____
_____
_____

Day: _____ **Date:** _____

Memories of Our Fourth Day

The weather today was... _____

The best thing today was... _____
_____

The worst thing today was... _____
_____

The funniest thing today was... _____
_____

Today we tried... _____
and the result was... _____
_____

The most magical moment today was... _____
_____
_____

📷 Photos and Snapshots

📷 Photos taken today (card/roll # ____)

Shot #	Description
_____	_____
_____	_____
_____	_____
_____	_____
_____	_____

🎞 Budget and Expenses

Fourth day budget: $ _____

Admission: $ _____
Meals: $ _____
             $ _____
             $ _____
Shopping: $ _____
             $ _____
Other: $ _____
             $ _____
Total: $ _____

☕ Meals and Snacks

Breakfast: _____ $ _____

Lunch: _____ $ _____

Dinner: _____ $ _____

Snacks: _____ $ _____

✒ Notes for Next Time

_____
_____
_____
_____
_____
_____
_____
_____
_____
_____
_____
_____
_____

*Take stock of what you wanted to do
and what you've actually done while you still
have time, then make the time to fulfill your dreams!*

Our Fifth Day

_____ :   Wake up: _____

_____ :   Early Morning: _____

_____ :   Breakfast: _____

_____ :   Morning: _____

_____ :   _____

_____ :   Lunch: _____

_____ :   Afternoon: _____

_____ :   _____

_____ :   Dinner: _____

_____ :   Evening: _____

_____ :   _____

_____ :   Before bed: _____

Special plans for today: _____

_____

⬇ *Store small items in here like ticket stubs and receipts for meals and purchases* ⬇

Things to Do, Places to Go, Attractions to Visit

☐ _____   ☐ _____

☐ _____   ☐ _____

☐ _____   ☐ _____

☐ _____   ☐ _____

Notes

_____

_____

_____

_____

Day: **Date:**

Memories of Our Fifth Day

The weather today was... _____

The best thing today was... _____
_____

The worst thing today was... _____
_____

The funniest thing today was... _____
_____

Today we tried... _____
and the result was... _____
_____

The most magical moment today was... _____
_____

📷 Photos and Snapshots

🗔 Photos taken today (card/roll # ____)

Shot #   Description
_____   _____
_____   _____
_____   _____
_____   _____
_____   _____

🍳 Meals and Snacks

Breakfast: _____
_____ $____

Lunch: _____
_____ $____

Dinner: _____
_____ $____

Snacks: _____
_____ $____

📸 Budget and Expenses

Fifth day budget: $____

Admission: $____
Meals: $____
             $____
             $____
Shopping: $____
             $____
Other: $____
             $____
Total: $____

✒ Notes for Next Time
_____
_____
_____
_____
_____
_____
_____
_____
_____
_____
_____

Break out of the typical tourist mold and customize your vacation with one of the tips in your PassPorter. Don't forget the sunglasses!

Our Sixth Day

_____ : _____	Wake up: _____
_____ : _____	Early Morning: _____
_____ : _____	Breakfast: _____
_____ : _____	Morning: _____
_____ : _____	_____
_____ : _____	Lunch: _____
_____ : _____	Afternoon: _____
_____ : _____	_____
_____ : _____	Dinner: _____
_____ : _____	Evening: _____
_____ : _____	_____
_____ : _____	Before bed: _____

Special plans for today: _____

⬇ *Store small items in here like ticket stubs and receipts for meals and purchases* ⬇

Things to Do, Places to Go, Attractions to Visit

❑ _____   ❑ _____
❑ _____   ❑ _____
❑ _____   ❑ _____
❑ _____   ❑ _____

Notes

_____
_____
_____
_____

Day: _____ **Date:** _____

Memories of Our Sixth Day

The weather today was... _____

The best thing today was... _____
_____

The worst thing today was... _____
_____

The funniest thing today was... _____
_____

Today we tried... _____

and the result was... _____
_____

The most magical moment today was... _____
_____
_____

📷 Photos and Snapshots

📷 Photos taken today (card/roll # ____)

Shot #   Description

_____   _____

_____   _____

_____   _____

_____   _____

_____   _____

📹 Budget and Expenses

Sixth day budget: $ _____

Admission: $ _____
Meals: $ _____
                     $ _____
                     $ _____
Shopping: $ _____
                     $ _____
Other: $ _____
                     $ _____

Total: $ _____

🍰 Meals and Snacks

Breakfast: _____
_____ | $ _____

Lunch: _____
_____ | $ _____

Dinner: _____
_____ | $ _____

Snacks: _____
_____ | $ _____

✒ Notes for Next Time

_____
_____
_____
_____
_____
_____
_____
_____
_____
_____
_____
_____
_____
_____

Address your postcards and store them in your PassPorter for safe keeping until you can mail them. This also helps you remember to send them!

Our Seventh Day

Confirmation Numbers

___ : ___	Wake up: _____
___ : ___	Early Morning: _____
___ : ___	Breakfast: _____
___ : ___	Morning: _____
___ : ___	_____
___ : ___	Lunch: _____
___ : ___	Afternoon: _____
___ : ___	_____
___ : ___	Dinner: _____
___ : ___	Evening: _____
___ : ___	_____
___ : ___	Before bed: _____

Special plans for today: _____

⬇ *Store small items in here like ticket stubs and receipts for meals and purchases* ⬇

Things to Do, Places to Go, Attractions to Visit

❑ _____   ❑ _____
❑ _____   ❑ _____
❑ _____   ❑ _____
❑ _____   ❑ _____

Notes

_____
_____
_____
_____

Day: **Date:**

Memories of Our Seventh Day

The weather today was... _____

The best thing today was... _____
_____

The worst thing today was... _____
_____

The funniest thing today was... _____
_____

Today we tried... _____

and the result was... _____
_____

The most magical moment today was... _____
_____
_____

📷 Photos and Snapshots

☐ Photos taken today (card/roll # ____)

Shot #	Description
_____	_____
_____	_____
_____	_____
_____	_____
_____	_____
_____	_____

🎥 Budget and Expenses

Seventh day budget: $ _____

Admission: $ _____
Meals: $ _____
$ _____
$ _____
Shopping: $ _____
$ _____
Other: $ _____
$ _____
Total: $ _____

🍳 Meals and Snacks

Breakfast: _____
$ _____

Lunch: _____
$ _____

Dinner: _____
$ _____

Snacks: _____
$ _____

✒ Notes for Next Time

_____
_____
_____
_____
_____
_____
_____
_____
_____
_____
_____

*Running out of steam? Try taking
a day to relax away from the excitement.
Take a dip in the pool, or just hang out in your room.*

Our Eighth Day

Confirmation Numbers

:	Wake up:
:	Early Morning:
:	Breakfast:
:	Morning:
:	
:	Lunch:
:	Afternoon:
:	
:	Dinner:
:	Evening:
:	
:	Before bed:

Special plans for today:

⬇ *Store small items in here like ticket stubs and receipts for meals and purchases* ⬇

Things to Do, Places to Go, Attractions to Visit

- ❏ _____
- ❏ _____
- ❏ _____
- ❏ _____

- ❏ _____
- ❏ _____
- ❏ _____
- ❏ _____

Notes

_____

_____

_____

_____

Day: **Date:**

Memories of Our Eighth Day

The weather today was... _____

The best thing today was... _____
_____

The worst thing today was... _____
_____

The funniest thing today was... _____
_____

Today we tried... _____
and the result was... _____
_____

The most magical moment today was... _____
_____

📷 Photos and Snapshots

📷 Photos taken today (card/roll # ____)

Shot #   Description

_____   _____

_____   _____

_____   _____

_____   _____

_____   _____

🍴 Meals and Snacks

Breakfast: _____
_____ $ _____

Lunch: _____
_____ $ _____

Dinner: _____
_____ $ _____

Snacks: _____
_____ $ _____

💰 Budget and Expenses

Eighth day budget: $ _____

Admission: $ _____
Meals: $ _____
             $ _____
             $ _____
Shopping: $ _____
             $ _____
Other: $ _____
             $ _____
Total: $ _____

✏ Notes for Next Time

_____
_____
_____
_____
_____
_____
_____
_____
_____
_____
_____
_____
_____

On the next to last day of your trip,
confirm your return travel arrangements and
pack whatever you can for a less stressful departure.

Our Ninth Day

Confirmation Numbers

:	Wake up:
:	Early Morning:
:	Breakfast:
:	Morning:
:	
:	Lunch:
:	Afternoon:
:	
:	Dinner:
:	Evening:
:	
:	Before bed:

Special plans for today:

⬇ *Store small items in here like ticket stubs and receipts for meals and purchases* ⬇

Things to Do, Places to Go, Attractions to Visit

❏ _____   ❏ _____
❏ _____   ❏ _____
❏ _____   ❏ _____
❏ _____   ❏ _____

Notes

_____
_____
_____
_____

Day: **Date:**

Memories of Our Ninth Day

The weather today was... _____

The best thing today was... _____
_____

The worst thing today was... _____
_____

The funniest thing today was... _____
_____

Today we tried... _____
and the result was... _____
_____

The most magical moment today was... _____
_____
_____

📷 Photos and Snapshots

☐ Photos taken today (card/roll # ____)

Shot #	Description
_____	_____
_____	_____
_____	_____
_____	_____
_____	_____
_____	_____

🎞 Meals and Snacks

Breakfast: _____
_____ $ _____

Lunch: _____
_____ $ _____

Dinner: _____
_____ $ _____

Snacks: _____
_____ $ _____

🎥 Budget and Expenses

Ninth day budget: $ _____

Admission: $ _____
Meals: $ _____
$ _____
$ _____
Shopping: $ _____
$ _____
Other: $ _____
$ _____

Total: $ _____

✎ Notes for Next Time

_____
_____
_____
_____
_____
_____
_____
_____
_____
_____
_____
_____
_____
_____
_____

*Your visit may be ending soon, but
the memories you've made can last a lifetime.
Record them in your PassPorter now before you forget.*

Our Tenth Day

_____ : _____	Wake up: _____
_____ : _____	Early Morning: _____
_____ : _____	Breakfast: _____
_____ : _____	Morning: _____
_____ : _____	_____
_____ : _____	Lunch: _____
_____ : _____	Afternoon: _____
_____ : _____	_____
_____ : _____	Dinner: _____
_____ : _____	Evening: _____
_____ : _____	_____
_____ : _____	Before bed: _____

Special plans for today: _____

↓ *Store small items in here like ticket stubs and receipts for meals and purchases* ↓

Things to Do, Places to Go, Attractions to Visit

☐ _____   ☐ _____
☐ _____   ☐ _____
☐ _____   ☐ _____
☐ _____   ☐ _____

Notes

_____
_____
_____
_____
_____

Day: _____   **Date:** _____

Memories of Our Tenth Day

The weather today was... _____

The best thing today was... _____

The worst thing today was... _____

The funniest thing today was... _____

Today we tried... _____

and the result was... _____

The most magical moment today was... _____

📷 Photos and Snapshots

📷 Photos taken today (card/roll # ____)

Shot #	Description
_____	_____
_____	_____
_____	_____
_____	_____
_____	_____

📹 Budget and Expenses

Tenth day budget: $ _____

Admission: $ _____
Meals: $ _____
 $ _____
 $ _____
Shopping: $ _____
 $ _____
Other: $ _____
 $ _____

Total: $ _____

☕ Meals and Snacks

Breakfast: _____ $ _____

Lunch: _____ $ _____

Dinner: _____ $ _____

Snacks: _____ $ _____

✎ Notes for Next Time

_____
_____
_____
_____
_____
_____
_____
_____
_____
_____
_____
_____

Design your own PassPocket!
Use it for extra days, special events, projects, or
remove it and bring it along on days you don't carry your book.

Confirmation Numbers

_____

Write your day, event, or subject above.

_____

_____

_____

_____

_____

_____

_____

_____

_____

_____

_____

_____

⬇ *Store small items in here like ticket stubs and receipts for meals and purchases* ⬇

☐ _____   ☐ _____
☐ _____   ☐ _____
☐ _____   ☐ _____
☐ _____   ☐ _____

Notes

_____

_____

_____

_____

Day: **Date:**

Write your subject above.

Your memories will last longer if you record them while they are fresh in your mind. What made you laugh? Smile? Cry? Write it down here!

Our Magic Memories

Our most memorable day was... _____

because... _____
_____
_____

Our most memorable place was... _____

because... _____

Our most memorable attraction was... _____

because... _____

Our most memorable activity was... _____

because... _____

↓ *Store small items in here that you want to save as souvenirs and mementos* ↓

Our most memorable meal was... _____

because... _____

Our most magic moment of all was... _____

because... _____

Special memories of our vacation: _____
_____
_____
_____

Our Trip Report

Use this page to write about your vacation for your family and friends, or even for the benefit of others at school, work, or on the Internet. A trip report is also a good activity for school-age children, especially if they missed school during their adventure. If you run out of room on this page, just continue it on paper and tuck the sheets in this PassPocket for safekeeping.

When did you go? _____

Who did you go with? What are their ages? _____
_____

Was this your first trip? _____ If not, how many trips have you had? _____

Where did you sleep? _____
_____

What attractions did you visit? _____
_____
_____
_____
_____

What special things did you do? _____
_____
_____
_____
_____

What would you do again? Why? _____
_____
_____
_____

What would you never do again? Why not? _____
_____
_____

What tips do you have for your fellow vacationers? _____
_____
_____
_____
_____
_____
_____
_____
_____

Would you like to share your trip report with other PassPorter readers? Visit us on the web at http://www.passporter.com. You can also make a copy of this page and mail it to us—our address is P.O. Box 3880, Ann Arbor, MI, 48106. Please include your full name, address, and phone number so we may contact you if necessary.